To Marshall,
with respect and
appreciation.
Franco Uccelli
LASA 9/26/92

BRAZIL IN REFERENCE BOOKS, 1965-1989

An Annotated Bibliography

ANN HARTNESS

The Scarecrow Press, Inc.
Metuchen, N.J., & London
1991

British Library Cataloguing-in-Publication data available

Library of Congress Cataloging-in-Publication Data

Hartness-Kane, Ann.
Brazil in reference books, 1965-1989 : an annotated bibliography / by Ann Hartness.
p. cm.
Includes indexes.
ISBN 0-8108-2400-0 (alk. paper)
1. Brazil--Bibliography. 2. Reference books--Brazil. I. Title.
Z1671.H39 1991
[F2508]
016.981--dc20 90-28356

Manufactured in the United States of America
Printed on acid-free paper

For Jonathan, Stephen, and Andrew,

who are always there ...

CONTENTS

INTRODUCTION

Brazil--its long history, its vast and varied geography, and its rich and complex culture--is the subject of this bibliography. The need for reference materials to provide bibliographic data, define terms, locate places, identify individuals, and supply statistics associated with this complicated subject is obvious, and this work, a bibliography of reference sources published 1965-1989, is an effort to meet that need.

It is designed for use by those interested in the humanities, the fine arts, or the social sciences, and coverage of subjects in those areas is extensive, although not exhaustive. Other areas (for example, education, natural history, and agriculture) are also included, but with greatly restricted coverage. They cite only basic works considered to be potentially helpful to primary users of this bibliography. For example, the glossary ABC do café, which defines terms associated with coffee culture and trade and is found in the chapter "AGRICULTURE," could be useful to those interested in economics, history, literature, folklore, and other fields, as well as to the agriculture specialist.

Coverage is limited to books, pamphlets, serials such as yearbooks or regularly issued bibliographies, and in a few cases, chapters of books. Single chapters are cited when no other material on a topic was located, when the quality of a chapter was exceptionally good, or when it complemented other works. The only journal articles cited are those which comprise the entire content of a journal issue. Virtually all of the publications included in the bibliography were examined by the author; the few exceptions are noted as they occur.

Several types of publishers are represented: commercial houses, university presses, organizations, government agencies, and even individuals. A special effort was made to identify publications issued by government agencies at the state and national levels since they are frequent sources of excellent but poorly publicized reference sources.*

Although publications issued from 1965 through 1989 form the chronological parameters of this bibliography, it also includes some 1990 imprints which were identified before the book went to press. Although it cites a significant number of works published in 1989, some may be omitted because they were unavailable for review by early 1990 when work was completed. Facsimile editions of works originally published prior to 1965 are cited if publication of the facsimile falls within the stated time frame, as are multi-volume works with some volumes published before 1965 and others published after.

Arrangement is by broad subject areas, with further subdivisions by format, geographic unit, or narrower subjects when necessary. Since many works could be placed in more than one subject category, users of the bibliography should consult the Subject Index for additional titles related to their area of interest. The Author Index further facilitates the use of this work.

Recognition and thanks for helping to make this work possible are due to several institutions and individuals. Much of my research was conducted at the Nettie Lee Benson Latin American Collection, The University of Texas at Austin. Special thanks go to Laura Gutiérrez-Witt, its Head Librarian, who gave me encouragement and support, and to Penelope Frere, Public Services Assistant, who provided valuable information and assistance during a time that I was away from the Benson Collection for an extended leave.

The Library of Congress Office, Rio de Janeiro, was a frequent source of information over a period of several years, including the months in which the work was completed, when I was its Acting Field Director. Carmen Meurer Muricy, its Chief Librarian for Programs, was a valuable source of information about new publications and an informant about the fate of old ones.

I conducted research in a number of Brazilian libraries, and the staffs of the following were especially helpful: the Biblioteca Nacional and the library of the Fundação Getúlio Vargas in Rio de Janeiro; the Biblioteca Mário de Andrade; and the libraries of the Centro Cultural São Paulo and the Museu Lasar Segall in São Paulo. The Institute of Latin American Studies at The University of Texas at Austin supported research for this book through summer research grants from the Mellon Foundation, and thanks are due to two of its directors, Dr. William Glade and Dr. Richard N. Adams.

---

*A detailed discussion of the role of governments in publishing reference materials can be found in my article, "Governments as Publishers of Reference Materials: Mexico and Brazil, 1970-1980," Latin American Research Review, vol. 17 (2) 1982, pp. 142-155.

Last, but not least, Dr. Laurence Hallewell, Ibero-American Bibliographer, University of Minnesota, expert on the subject of publishing in Brazil, and colleague in the field of Latin American librarianship, gave me useful advice and encouragement.

Information about reference works published 1965-1989, as well as those published after those dates, would be welcomed by the author if sent in care of the publisher.

Ann Hartness
Rio de Janeiro
March 1990

BIBLIOGRAPHIES

GENERAL BIBLIOGRAPHIES

1 Accessions List, Brazil and Uruguay, vol. 15, no. 1-, Jan./Feb. 1989-. Rio de Janeiro: Library of Congress Office, Rio de Janeiro, 1989-. A bimonthly bibliographic record of Brazilian and Uruguayan monographs, serials, and other library materials acquired by the U.S. Library of Congress Office, Rio de Janeiro. An annual author and title index appears in the last issue of each year. Volumes 1-14, 1975-1988, issued under the title, Accessions List, Brazil.

2 Accessions List, Brazil and Uruguay: Cumulative List of Serials. 1989-. Rio de Janeiro: Library of Congress Office, Rio de Janeiro, 1990?-. An annual bibliographic record of Brazilian and Uruguayan serials acquired by the U.S. Library of Congress Office, Rio de Janeiro. Incorporates new serials, and changes and deletions recorded in the issues of Accessions List, Brazil and Uruguay. Continues Accessions List, Brazil: Cumulative List of Serials, which was published annually 1983-1988. An edition covering 1975-1980 was published in 1981, and one for 1981-1982 appeared in 1983.

3 Araújo, Zilda Galhardo de. Guia de bibliografia especializada. Rio de Janeiro: Associação Brasileira de Bibliotecários, 1969. 207 p. A guide to Brazilian and foreign reference works on all subjects. Especially useful for identifying older but basic Brazilian reference materials.

4 Baltar Célia de Queiroz. Livros norte-americanos traduzidos para o português e disponíveis no mercado brasileiro: bibliografia compilada até fevereiro de 1987. Brasília: Serviço de Divulgação e Relações Culturais dos Estados Unidos da América, 1987 or 1988. 294 p. This catalog of U.S. imprints translated into Portuguese lists 9849 titles arranged by subject with an author/publisher index.

5 Basseches, Bruno. A Bibliography of Brazilian Bibliographies. Uma bibliografia das bibliografias brasileiras. Detroit: Blaine Ethridge Books, 1978. 185 p. An unannotated bibliography of 2488 Brazilian bibliographies related to the humanities and the social sciences. Includes bibliographies appearing in books, periodicals, newspapers, conference proceedings, and other publications. Although not exhaustive--the author states that many items published outside of Brazil are omitted--this is a useful work.

6 Bercht, Domitila Maria. Lazer e turismo: bibliografia. São Paulo: Gráfico Tiradentes, 1982. 237 p. This unannotated bibliography cites 1091 books and periodical articles in Portuguese about recreation and tourism.

7 Bibliografia brasileira. Rio de Janeiro: Biblioteca Nacional, vol. 1, no. 1/2- (Jan./June 1983), 1984-. This publication serves as the Brazilian national bibliography, since it is based on the legal deposit of publications at the Biblioteca Nacional. Also includes works by Brazilian authors published abroad. It replaces the Boletim bibliográfico da Biblioteca Nacional, and begins its coverage with entries for 6050 publications registered in the first half of 1983. Also available on magnetic tape and in microfiche. Volumes examined: 1, 1983; 2, 1984; 3, 1985; 4, 1986; 5, 1987; 6, no. 1, 1988.

8 Bibliografia brasileira de transportes, Rio de Janeiro: Grupo de Estudos para Integração da Política de Transportes, 1969/ 1972-. An unannotated bibliography of publications related to the technical, social, and economic aspects of transportation in Brazil.

9 Bibliografia brasileira mensal. Rio de Janeiro: Instituto Nacional do Livro, vol. 1-5, nov. 1967-dic. 1972. This monthly publication served as the Brazilian national bibliography from November, 1967 through 1972. Publication was suspended in 1973 when the Boletim bibliográfico da Biblioteca Nacional resumed publication.

10 Biblioteca Bastos Tigre. Catálogo da imprensa alternativa e episódica do Brasil. Catálogos, 1. Rio de Janeiro: Associação Brasileira de Imprensa, Biblioteca Bastos Tigre, 1979. 55 leaves. A directory of periodicals published by the alternative press. Publications with political content predominate, but many others are included, ranging from the Folha da Formiga issued by favela dwellers in Rio de Janeiro, to literary journals. Information provided is not uniform, but data which may be included are place of publication, publisher, address, director, beginning date, frequency, and number of copies printed.

11 Biblioteca Municipal Mário de Andrade. Catálogo de obras raras da Biblioteca Municipal Mário de Andrade. São Paulo: Secretaria

de Educação e Cultura, Departamento de Cultura, 1969. 537 p. Bibliographic descriptions of 4681 rare books, published from the fifteenth through twentieth centuries, in the public library of São Paulo, with those from the eighteenth and nineteenth centuries predominating.

12 Boletim bibliográfico da Biblioteca Nacional. Rio de Janeiro: 1951-1967; 1973-1982. This Brazilian national bibliography, based on the legal deposit of publications in the Biblioteca Nacional, was suspended 1968-1972 and the Bibliografia brasiliera mensal served its function. In 1973 publication resumed and continued through 1982 when it was replaced by the Bibliografia brasileira.

13 Brasilien-Bibliothek der Robert Bosch GmbH. Katalog. Stuttgart: Deutsch Verlags-Anstalt, 1986-. A well-illustrated descriptive catalog of the library of rare Brasiliana owned by a German auto-parts firm. Vol. 1: Abgeschoissen zum Jahrsend 1983 (1986; 516 p.); Vol. 2: Nachlass des Prinzen Maximilian zu Wied-Neuwied (1988; 217 p.)

14 Brazil. Arquivo Nacional. Biblioteca. Catálogo de jornais brasileiros, 1808-1889. Série instrumentos de trabalho no. 12. Rio de Janeiro: 1979. 36 p. Transcribes catalog cards for Brazilian newspapers, 1808-1889, in the library of the Arquivo Nacional. Includes newspapers from all over Brazil.

15 Brazil. Biblioteca Nacional. Periódicos brasileiros em microformas: catálogo coletivo, 1984. Rio de Janeiro: 1985. 503 p. A list of 2700 current and retrospective Brazilian serials, with their places and dates of publication, along with information on libraries in Brazil and elsewhere which have all or part of them in microform. Includes several types of serials such as newspapers, periodicals focusing on specific topics such as the abolition of slavery, and the annual reports of government agencies. Besides its primary purpose, this is a useful source of bibliographical data about the serials cited, especially for their dates of publication. An "edição preliminar," Jornais brasileiros em microfilme, listing 102 titles, was published in 1976, and two earlier editions of the current title were issued: 1979, 1981.

16 ________. ________. I Repertório bibliográfico nacional de obras dos séculos XV e XVI. Coleção Roldolfo Garcia, 23. Rio de Janeiro: 1989. 77 p. A catalog of fifteenth-and sixteenth-century books available in seventeen Brazilian libraries.

17 ________. ________. Publicações da Biblioteca Nacional: catálogo 1873-1977. 2. ed. Rio de Janeiro: 1978. 120 p. A catalog of the 558 publications issued by this important Brazilian cultural institution over a period of 104 years. It is useful

not only for the bibliographic data that it contains, but also for its reflection of the Brazilian intellectual and cultural scene for the period covered. In this regard, one of its most interesting sections covers catalogs of exhibits mounted at the BN, because they mirrored the interests of the times and commemorated events deemed important. Updates an earlier edition published in 1975.

18 Brazil. Exército. Centro de Documentação. *Relação das publicações do Exército: atualizada até 31 Dez. 87.* Brasília: Ministério do Exército, Secretaria-Geral do Exército, Centro de Documentação do Exército, 1988. 168 p. An unannotated list of Army publications by subject, which is updated periodically. An earlier edition examined was *Relação das publicações do Exército: atualizada até Dez. 1982* (Brasília: 1983. 164 p.)

19 Brazil. Ministério da Educação e Cultura. Serviço de Documentação. *Catálogo das publicações do Serviço de Documentação 1947-1965.* Rio de Janeiro: 1965. 156 p. A catalog of almost 600 titles, many on cultural topics, published by this government agency. Many entries have extensive annotations describing the content of the work cited.

20 Bryant, Solena V. *Brazil.* World Bibliographical Series, vol. 57. Santa Barbara, CA: ABC-Clio, 1985. 244 p. An annotated bibliography with more than 800 entries emphasizing books for the English-language reader, and concentrating on materials published in the 1970s and early 1980s. Covers all subject areas although the major focus is on the social sciences, humanities, and fine arts.

21 Camargo, Ana Maria de Almeida. *Hemeroteca Júlio Mesquita, Instituto Histórico e Geográfico de São Paulo.* 9 vols. São Paulo: 1975. A bibliography of the periodicals in this important serials collection. Vol. 1: *Catálogo alfabético*; Vol. 2: *Catálogo geográfico*, and Vols. 3-9: *Catálogo cronológico*, cover the actual holdings of the collection. The author's doctoral dissertation, *A imprensa como objeto de trabalho: catálogo de Hemeroteca Júlio de Mesquita do Instituto Histórico e Geográfico de São Paulo* (Universidade de Sao Paulo: 1905. 150 p.), includes a good bibliography on Brazilian periodicals and their publishing history.

22 Camargo, Maria de Lourdes Sampaio Cintra de. *Guia de obras de referência brasileiras.* Edição preliminar. São Paulo: Associação Paulista de Bibliotecários, Biblioteca Central da Universidade de São Paulo, 1967. 69 p. A tentative list of 530 Brazilian reference works on all subjects, located in São Paulo libraries.

23 Canstatt, Oscar. Repertório crítico da literatura teuto-brasileira. Rio de Janeiro: Editora Presença, 1967. 294 p. A fact-filled, chronological survey of German writings about Brazil from colonial days to 1902 divided into ten-year periods, and published originally under the title, Kritisches Repertorium der Deutsch-Brasilianischen literatur (Berlin: 1902). Also included is Suplemento ao Repertório crítico da bibliografia alemã-brasileira (Berlin: 1906) arranged in the same chronological format. Unfortunately, this work is not indexed.

24 Cardillo, Ana Eugênia Gallo Cassini. Bibliografia sobre ouro no Brasil, 1840-1983. Brasília: Ministério das Minas e Energia, Departamento Nacional da Produção Mineral, 1983. 50 p. An unannotated bibliography of 1911 entries of materials related to all aspects of gold in Brazil during the period covered. Includes both Brazilian and foreign publications, but the vast majority were published in Brazil.

25 Carvalho, Isabel Maria de Castro Ferreira. Fontes de informação em... guia de bibliografia especializada: manual para estudantes. Cantaduva, SP: 1979. 85 p. An annotated bibliography of reference books arranged by subject, universal in scope, which includes many Brazilian publications.

26 Catálogo coletivo de publicações periódicas em ciências sociais e humanidades. 2 vols. Rio de Janeiro: Instituto Brasileiro de Informação em Ciência e Tecnologia, 1978. A union list of 14,404 periodicals in the social sciences and humanities reflecting the holdings of more than 900 Brazilian libraries. This list, in computer print-out format, is part of a program begun in 1966 by the then Instituto Brasileiro de Bibliografia e Documentação to develop an automated national union list of serials.

27 Catálogo da Exposição de História do Brasil. Ed. facsimilar. 3 vols. Coleção Temas brasileiras, vol. 10. Brasilia: Editora Universidade de Brasília, 1981. This catalog of books on Brazil in any language published between 1500 and 1881 is the facsimile edition of a catalog based on an exhibition held at the Biblioteca Nacional in Dec. 1881. The introduction to this edition is by the well-known historian José Honório Rodrigues.

28 Catálogo do Banco de Teses. Brasília: Ministério da Educação e Cultura; Conselho Nacional de Desenvolvimento Científico e Tecnológico, vol. 1-, 1976-. A record of theses produced at public and private Brazilian universities in all academic disciplines at the master's, doctoral, livre-docência, and post-graduate levels, arranged by broad subject areas. Includes abstracts. Volumes examined: 1, 1976; 2, 1977; 3, 1978; 4, 1979; 5, 1982.

29 Catálogo de imprensa alternativa. Rio de Janeiro: Secretaria Municipal de Cultura, Centro de Imprensa Alternativa e Cultura Popular; RIOARTE, 1986. 106 p. This catalog claims to be the most complete list of alternative periodicals yet published in Brazil. It provides bibliographic information, physical description, and notes about contents.

30 Centro de Documentação do Pensamento Brasileiro. Catálogo do acervo. Salvador: 1985. 443 p. An unannotated bibliography of almost 3000 titles in the fields of philosophy, political thought, sociology, and anthropology, arranged by broad subjects, with author and title indexes.

31 Centro de Pastoral Vergueiro. Setor de Documentação e Pesquisa. Informe bibliográfico: mulher. São Paulo: 1988. 20 p. A partially annotated bibliography of articles and books related to women, including such topics as women and the constitutional convention, women and work, International Women's Day. Many items cited are from the alternative press.

32 Centro Informação Mulher. Catálogo, 1985. São Paulo: 1985. 192 p.

33 ______. Catálogo, 1985: índice de autores. São Paulo: 1986. 49 p. An unannotated bibliography of 2599 books, periodicals, and periodical articles on women, arranged by subject. The bibliography, which is international in scope, is based on the holdings of the CIM library, and includes many publications about women in Brazil. The index of authors was separately published.

34 Conniff, Michael, and Fred Gillette Sturm. Brazilian Studies: A Guide to the Humanities Literature. The Brazilian Curriculum Guide Specialized Bibliography. Albuquerque: Latin American Institute, 1985 or 1986. 97 p. "This guide is intended to introduce the reader to Brazilian studies, with an emphasis on history and philosophy. It spans the entire history of Brazil, emphasizing particular themes and continuities." Annotated bibliographies for each section.

35 Cooperation in Documentation and Communication. Bibliographical Notes for Understanding the Brazilian Model: Political Repression & Economic Expansion. Common Catalogue no. 2. Washington: CoDoC, 1974. 72 p. A listing of documents available from seven documentation centers in Europe, Latin America, and the United States.

36 Evans, Peter; Alida Rubini Liedke; and Enno D. Liedke. The Political Economy of Contemporary Brazil: A Study Guide. The Brazilian Curriculum Guide Specialized Bibliography. Albuquerque: Latin American Institute, University of New

Mexico, 1985 or 1986. 21 p. Cites about seventy sources related to contemporary economics and politics. In addition to general overviews, the specific topics covered are authoritarianism, democracy, industrialization, economic growth, social welfare, urban living conditions, labor, urban social movements, rural social structures and the development of agriculture.

37 Fundação Carlos Chagas. Mulher brasileira: bibliografia anotada. 2 vols. São Paulo: Editora Brasiliense, 1979. A bibliography with extensive descriptive annotations covering monographs, periodical articles, conference proceedings, and other publications related to women in Brazil. Includes Brazilian and foreign publications. Vol. 1: História, família, grupos étnicos. Vol. 2: Trabalho, direito, educação, arte e meios de comunicação.

38 _______. A saúde da mulher no Brasil: bibliografia anotada. Textos FCC no. 3/89. São Paulo: 1989. 178 p. A bibliography of almost 500 monographs and journal articles published in Brazil related to the health of women in both its medical and social aspects.

39 Fundação Getúlio Vargas. Instituto de Documentação. Biblioteca. Guia de publicações da FGV, 1944-1974. Rio de Janeiro: 1974. 536 p. An unannotated bibliography of the publications of this important Brazilian research institution. Emphasis is on the social sciences broadly defined.

40 Fundação Instituto Brasileiro de Geografia e Estatística. Bibliografia das bibliografias existentes na Biblioteca Central do IBGE. Rio de Janeiro: 1984. 93 p. An unannotated bibliography of 454 entries citing bibliographies related to many aspects of the social sciences.

41 _______. Publicações editadas pelo IBGE. 2 vols. Rio de Janeiro: 1984-1985. Vol. 1: Periódicos; Vol. 2: Monografias. A bibliography of ninety serials and 1301 monographs issued by the IBGE since its beginning in 1936. Cites a variety of statistical publications, and many on the technical and descriptive aspects of geography. Since the IBGE is the most important Brazilian publisher of this kind of information, this is an indispensable tool. Thorough indexes make it easy to use. Revises and updates the Catálogo de publicações periódicas do IBGE (no. 67).

42 Garraux, Anatole Louis. Bibliographie brésilienne: catalogue des ouvrages français & latins relatifs au Brésil 1500-1898. 1898. Reprint. Amsterdam: B. R. Grüner, 1971. 400 p. Basic bibliographic data in alphabetical order by author, with a subject index. Many detailed descriptive notes.

43 Gillett, Theresa. Catalog of Luso-Brazilian Material in the University of New Mexico Libraries. Metuchen, NJ: Scarecrow Press, 1970. 961 p. An unannotated subject catalog of some ten thousand items published in Brazil, Portugal, and the Portuguese dependencies; material about these places published elsewhere; and material in the Portuguese language or translated from it, regardless of place of publication. About half of the items cited relate to Brazil.

44 Graham, Richard, and Valiela, Virginia. Brazil in the London 'Times' 1850-1905: A Guide. SALALM Bibliography 1. Carbondale, IL: 1969. 101 p. A subject index to articles about Brazil appearing The (London) Times during the last half of the nineteenth century and at the turn of the century.

45 Habitat: bibliografia/Bibliography/bibliographie. 2 vols. Camaçeari: Centro de Pesquisas e Desenvolvimento, Setor de Documentação e Informação e Projeto Tecnologias do Habitat, 1978. An unannotated bibliography related to our physical environment, citing publications on such topics as human settlements, demography, planning, urbanization, land use, urban legislation, housing, urban renewal, architecture, construction, and energy and related technologies. Although not limited to publications about Brazil, it includes many such works. Part 1 (893 p.) is the bibliography, and Part 2 (described in Part 1 as an author and title index) was said to be in preparation, but was not located.

46 Hahner, June. Women in Brazil: Problems and Perspectives. The Brazilian Curriculum Guide Specialized Bibliography. Albuquerque: Latin American Institute, University of New Mexico, 1985 or 1986. 24 p. A selected annotated bibliography comprises more than half of this guide. It is preceded by an essay tracing the development of women's studies for Brazil, and summarizing the roles played by women in Brazilian society.

47 Harmon, Ronald M., and Chamberlain, Bobby J. Brazil: A Working Bibliography in Literature, Linguistics, Humanities, and the Social Sciences. Tempe: Arizona State University, 1975. 101 p. An unannotated bibliography emphasizing basic works about Brazil, especially those published since the mid-1960's which are readily available to readers in the United States. Also includes older works which are classics.

48 Hispanic and Luso-Brazilian Council. Canning House Library. Canning House Library, Luso-Brazilian Council, London: Author Catalogue A-Z and Subject Catalogue A-Z. 4 vols. Boston: G. K. Hall, 1967. Cites about 6000 publications from the nineteenth and twentieth centuries, covering Brazilian and Portuguese cultures. A two-volume supplement, published in 1973, updates the original catalog.

49 Horch, Rosemarie Erika. Catalogo dos folhetos da Coleção Barbosa Machado. Anais da Biblioteca Nacional, vol. 92, 1972, tomo 1-. Rio de Janeiro: Biblioteca Nacional, 1974-. A catalog of the seventeenth- and eighteenth-century Portuguese imprints from the library of the Portuguese bibliographer Diogo Barbosa Machado, which was donated to the Real Biblioteca de Ajuda (the royal library, Portugal) came to Brazil with the Court in 1808, and eventually formed the nucleus of the Biblioteca Nacional. It records many titles related to Brazil. Volumes examined: t.1, Até 1639; t.2, 1640-1660; t.3, 1661-1699; t.4, 1700-1715; t.5, 1716-1739; t.6, 1740-1752; t.7, 1753-1770. These seven volumes were published between 1974 and 1982.

50 ISSN: publicações periódicas brasileiras. Brasília: Conselho Nacional de Desenvolvimento Científico e Tecnológico, Instituto Brasileiro de Informação em Ciêneia e Tecnologia, 1983. 409 p. Lists 2303 Brazilian periodicals by subject, title, and ISSN number.

51 Indice de ciências sociais. Rio de Janeiro: Instituto Universitário de Pesquisas de Rio de Janeiro--IUPERJ, 1979-. Summarizes the content of academic articles appearing in Brazilian journals related to sociology and political science from 1930 to the present. The most recent issue examined (June 1985) covered twenty-two journals, and it provided a list of the issues analyzed.

52 Instituto Brasileiro de Bibliografia e Documentação. Periódicos brasileiros de cultura. Rio de Janeiro: 1968. 280 p. A list of 2048 Brazilian periodicals in all fields which were being published in 1960 or later. Information for each one includes title, subtitle, place of publication, publisher, frequency, beginning date if known, where indexed, and address. Includes a useful list of periodicals known to have ceased publication.

53 Instituto Brasileiro de Informação em Ciência e Tecnologia. Guia de publicações seriadas brasileiras. Brasília: 1987. 672 p. This publication continues the effort begun by Periódicos brasileiros de cultura (1956), and continued by Periódicos brasileiros de ciência e tecnologia (1977), and ISSN: publicações periódicas brasileiras (1983; see no. 50) to provide and maintain a permanent record of current Brazilian serials. Although the emphasis is on science and technology, some serials in the humanities, social sciences, and fine arts are included. The 1577 titles are arranged by broad subject categories, with additional access by indexes of narrower subject headings and titles. Also includes a list of publishers and their addresses, and a list by ISSN.

54 Instituto Euvaldo Lodi. Automação. 2 vols. Série bibliografias. Rio de Janeiro, 1985. An unannotated bibliography focusing on the economic, social, and political aspects of automation. Universal in scope, but emphasizes Brazil.

55 Instituto Nacional de Alimentação e Nutrição. Catálogo de publicações técnicas. Brasília: 1985. 173 p. Many of the publications listed in this unannotated bibliography about food and nutrition are about social, economic, and political aspects of the subject. The catalog, which is arranged in alphabetical order by author, has no index.

56 Instituto Nacional do Livro. Catálogo do Instituto Nacional do Livro. Brasília. Summarizes and describes books published with the support of the INL, often as co-editions with commercial publishers. Since the works are usually new editions of out-of-print titles or of Brazilian classics, and the description of their content is very thorough, this catalog will be helpful to a variety of users. It can be approached either through its main listing in alphabetical order by author, or by its subject index. The edition examined was for 1979/1980, which in addition to the content described above, includes a listing of the works described in an earlier edition, Catálogo do Instituto Nacional do Livro, 1974/1978. The introduction refers to a still earlier, Catálogo de co-edições do INL, 1971/1974.

57 ________. Instituto Nacional do Livro, 1937-1987: 50 anos de publicações. Brasília: 1987. 219 p. Lists 2272 titles issued by the INL. Includes a brief history of the Institute and a list of its series, as well as series of other publishers with whom it has co-published titles.

58 Knopp, Anthony. Brazil Books. New York: Center for Inter-American Relations, 1973. 20 p. An annotated bibliography "designed to provide a broad survey of literature on modern Brazil" for the nonspecialist. Includes "books written in or translated into English dealing with contemporary Brazil," including fiction, nonfiction, and books for children and young people. Although it is somewhat out of date, this bibliography still provides a good basic list for reading about Brazil.

59 Levine, Robert M. Brazilian Reality Through the Lens of Popular Culture. The Brazilian Curriculum Guide Specialized Bibliography. Albuquerque: Latin American Institute, University of New Mexico, 1985 or 1986. 19 p. An essay providing an overview of the major elements in Brazilian popular culture is followed by a selective bibliography covering Afro-Brazilian life, indigenous culture, mores and popular behavior, cinema, music, photography, and sports.

60 _______. Brazil Since 1930: An Annotated Bibliography for Social Historians. New York: Garland, 1980. 336 p. The 1845 citations to books, articles, unpublished papers, theses, and government documents are "concerned with Brazil since 1930 in the broadest sense, not only with its political evolution but with its society and culture as well." The state, economics, rural and urban Brazil, society, culture, and education are some of the topics treated.

61 Moraes, Rubens Borba de. Bibliographia brasiliana: Rare Books About Brazil Published from 1504 to 1900 and Works by Brazilian Authors of the Colonial Period. Revised and enlarged ed. 2 vols. Los Angeles: UCLA Latin American Center Publications; Rio de Janeiro: Livraria Kosmos Editora, 1983. This work, prepared by a major Brazilian bibliographer and book collector, is an expanded revision of the first edition, which was published in 1958. It also incorporates entries from his Bibliografia brasileira do período colonial (1969; below). In addition to the detailed bibliographic data appropriate for the description of rare books, each entry is annotated, and the work includes many reproductions of title pages. A detailed index provides enhanced access to this work.

62 _______. Bibliografia brasileira do período colonial: catálogo comentado das obras dos autores nascidos no Brasil e publicadas antes de 1808. São Paulo: Instituto de Estudos Brasileiros, 1969. 437 p. An exhaustive, annotated bibliography of books published before 1808 by authors born in Brazil. Includes many title page facsimiles.

63 Musso Ambrosi, Luís Alberto. Bibliografia uruguaya sobre Brasil. 2. ed. Montevideo: Instituto de Cultura Uruguayo-Brasileño, 1973. 166 p. An annotated bibliography of books, pamphlets and periodicals, published in Uruguay, which are about Brazil or are by Brazilian authors. An appendix cites works by Uruguayan authors about Brazil published in other countries, or works by Uruguayan authors published in Brazil. This bibliography documents an important aspect of cultural relations between these neighboring countries: the exchange of ideas through publishing. The second edition updates the first (1967).

64 Newberry Library. Catalogue of the Greenlee Collection, The Newberry Library, Chicago. 2 vols. Boston: G. K. Hall, 1970. The catalog of a collection specializing in the history and cultural achievements of Portugal at home and abroad, with emphasis on the early nineteenth century. Publications related to Brazil are an important part of the collection.

65 Oficina de livros: novidades catalogadas na fonte vol. 1-, Dec. 1973/Apr. 1974-. São Paulo: Centro de Catalogação na

Fonte, Câmara Brasileira do Livro, 1975-. Reproduces catalog cards prepared by the Centro de Catalogação na Fonte, showing what is being processed for the year in question. Subject, author, and title indexes. The edition examined (Vol. 11, 1984) provided card copy for 1351 books, plus 486 textbooks at the elementary and secondary levels. Published irregularly until 1978; annual since 1979.

66 Oliveira Lima Library. Catalog of the Oliveira Lima Library, The Catholic University of America, Washington, D.C. 2 vols. Boston: G. K. Hall, 1970. This catalog of a library specializing in Brazilian and Portuguese history, literature, and culture includes rare books as well as more ordinary materials.

67 Paiva, Maria Helena Gomes de, and Ana Maria Raeder Ramos. Catálogo de publicações periódicas do IBGE. Rio de Janeiro: Fundação Instituto Brasileiro de Geografia e Estatística, 1982. 99 p. A catalog of the serial publications of this important agency covering both current publications and those suspended or no longer published. Very useful for identifying them and for tracing their detailed and sometimes tortuous bibliographic history. For updated information see no. 41.

68 Passos, Alexandre. Um século de imprensa universitária (1831-1931). Rio de Janeiro: Editora Pongetti, 1971. 101 p. A bibliography of periodicals and newspapers published by institutions of higher education during the century covered. Publications are cited under the name of the institution, and there is a title index.

69 Phillips, Philip Lee. A List of Books, Magazine Articles, and Maps Relating to Brazil, 1800-1900. Facsimile ed. Washington: Government Printing Office, 1901. Ann Arbor, MI: University Microfilms, 1970. 145 p. An unannotated bibliography of nineteenth-century publications about Brazil.

70 Prober, Kurt. Imprensa maçônica brasileira. Paquetá: 1982. 84 p. Lists Masonic serial publications, giving bibliographic information under titles, with an index by city.

71 Processo de modernização do Brasil, 1850-1930: economia e sociedade, uma bibliografia. Rio de Janeiro: Fundação Casa de Rui Barbosa, Biblioteca CREFSUL, 1985. 364 p. A well-annotated bibliography covering a wide range of topics associated with the social, economic and political modernization of Brazilian society: reference works, collections of documents, biographies, correspondence and memoirs, reports, travelers' accounts, and studies related to economics, finance, and social aspects of life in Brazil.

72 Ramos, Vitor. A edição de língua portuguêsa em França (1800-

1850): repertório geral dos títulos publicados e ensaio crítico. Paris: Fundação Gulbenkian; Centro Cultural Português, 1972. 193 p. Besides providing bibliography related to Brazil and Portugal, this work sheds light on some aspects of the cultural relations of France with those two nations in the first half of the nineteenth century. Many of the 563 entries, which include bibliographic data and some annotations, deal with Brazil.

73 Rio de Janeiro (City). Superintêndencia de Documentação. Divisão de Biblioteca. Catálogo da Biblioteca. Rio de Janeiro: 1982. 136 p. Lists some 1150 titles in a library specializing in administration, law, library science, documentation, and archives.

74 Rocha, Juracy Feitosa. Periódicos e seriados brasileiros. Brasília: Instituto Brasileiro de Informação em Ciência e Tecnologia--IBICT, 1988-. Volume 1, Guias e repertórios gerais e especializados is an annotated bibliography of bibliographies, catalogs, and guides to Brazilian periodicals and other serials, and of works about serials. A projected second volume, to be entitled Indices individuais e por assuntos, will deal with retrieval of information from specific periodicals through indexes, data bases, and other means.

75 Rosso, Hespéria Zuma de. Bibliografia das bibliografias existentes na biblioteca do IBGE. 2. ed. revista e aumentada. Série obras de referência da Biblioteca do IBGE, 6. Rio de Janeiro: Fundação Instituto Brasileiro de Geografia e Estatística, Centro de Documentação e Disseminação de Informações, Gerência de Documentação e Biblioteca, 1987. 129 p. An unannotated bibliography of 595 entries citing bibliographies in book form and in periodicals in the library of the IBGE, related directly or indirectly to geography and statistics. Arranged by broad subject, with indexes by author, subject, and periodicals cited.

76 ________, and Severino Bezerra Cabral Filho. Obras raras da biblioteca do IBGE. Série obras de referência da biblioteca do IBGE, 11. Rio de Janeiro: IBGE, Gerência de Documentação e Biblioteca, 1988. 144 p. An annotated bibliography of 246 rare works found in the library of the Fundação Instituto Brasileiro de Geografia e Estatística. Many of them are related to the fields of geography or statistics. Title and subject indexes, as well as an index by date of publication.

77 Sodré, Nelson Werneck. O que se deve ler para conhecer o Brasil. 5th ed. Rio de Janeiro: Civilização Brasileira, 1976. 377 p. A partially annotated, basic bibliography of Brazilian history and culture. Although this edition was updated to some

degree, the vast majority of citations are for books published before 1960. The bibliography is divided into chronological or subject chapters and each one begins with an introductory essay.

78 Sumários correntes brasileiros: ciências sociais e humanas. Brasília: Conselho Nacional de Desenvolvimento Científico e Tecnológico; Instituto Brasileiro de Informação em Ciência e Tecnologia--IBICT. A monthly publication which reproduces tables of contents of Brazilian journals in the social sciences and humanities. Issue examined--vol. 1, no. 2 (Feb. 1986) included coverage for thirty-four journals.

79 United States. Library of Congress. Catalog of Brazilian Acquisitions of the Library of Congress, 1964-1974, compiled by William V. Jackson. Boston: G. K. Hall, 1977. 751 p. A catalog of "all publications relating to Brazil, or with Brazilian imprints, acquired and cataloged by the Library of Congress from mid-1964 through 1974." The catalog, containing about 15,000 entries, is especially strong in history, the social sciences, and literature, although it covers all subjects.

80 _______. _________. Hispanic Division. Human Rights in Latin America, 1964-1980: A Selective, Annotated Bibliography. Washington: 1983. 257p. An annotated bibliography about human rights in Latin America in the recent past. About 120 of its 1827 entries deal specifically with Brazil or were written by Brazilians.

81 Universidade de São Paulo. Escola de Comunicações e Artes. Biblioteca. Catálogo de teses. São Paulo: 1985. 60 p. Cites 347 master's theses and doctoral dissertations received by the library of the School of Communications and Arts through 1984, covering a wide variety of topics in the fields of communications, the arts, library science, and others. There are no abstracts. Indexed by subject and advisor.

82 University of Wisconsin--Madison. Land Tenure Center. Library. Agrarian Reform in Brazil: A Bibliography. 2 vols. Training and Methods Series, no. 18-19. Madison: 1972. An unannotated bibliography of books, periodical articles, conference proceedings, and other publications, arranged by subject. Volume 2 is concerned with regional development. A Supplement, issued in 1977, updates this publication.

83 Valladares, Licia. Petit guide de le recherche urbaine au Brésil. Série especial, 1. Rio de Janeiro: Instituto Universitário de Pesquisas do Rio de Janeiro--IUPERJ, 1988. 109 p. A forty-page bibliographic essay on general characteristics, and current and emerging themes in urban research related to Brazil is followed by a bibliography of works cited in the

text and an inventory of institutions engaged in teaching and research in the field of urban studies.

BIBLIOGRAPHY--REGIONS

North

84 Amazônia: bibliografia. 2 vols. Rio de Janeiro: Instituto Brasileiro de Bibliografia e Documentação; Instituto Nacional de Pesquisas da Amazônia, 1963-1972. Volume 1 (7688 entries) and Volume 2 (5708 entries) cite references to publications on all subjects related to the Amazon Basin. The unannotated bibliographical citations are for books and periodical articles published in Brazil and abroad, spanning a time frame from 1601 to 1970.

85 Carajás: informações documentais. Belém: Museu Paraense Emilio Goeldi, 1982-. An annotated bibliography of materials related to the region of Grande Carajás, that is, large portions of Maranhão and Pará. Includes items covering economic, political, and social aspects as well as scientific and technical publications. Volumes examined: 1 (1982), 2 (1983).

86 Cunha, Valdea, and Eloisa Costa. Catálogo de obras raras sobre a Amazônia, 1800-1899. Belém: Banco da Amazônia, Centro de Documentação e Biblioteca, 1977. 66 p. An annotated bibliography of nineteenth century books about the Amazon Basin, with subject and title indexes.

87 Domínguez, Camilo. Bibliografia de la Amazônia colombiana y areas fronterizas amazónicas. Bogotá: DAINCO--Corporación Araracuara; COLCIENCIAS, 1985. 226 p. An unannotated, well-indexed bibliography of 4092 publications. Includes many Brazilian books and journal articles dealing with all aspects of the frontier area.

88 Pesquisas amazônicas. Belém: Rede de Bibliotecas da Amazônia --REBAM, 1976-. Identifies and abstracts studies related to Amazônia done at member institutions of REBAM. The first issue included studies in the fields of anthropology, sociology, economics, religion, and others in the humanities and social sciences, as well as many scientific and technical studies.

89 Superintendência do Desenvolvimento da Amazônia. Departamento de Recursos Humanos. Inventário e avaliação da produção técnico-científica sobre migração na Amazônia legal. Belém: 1989. 273 p. A partially annotated bibliography with 1863 entries focusing on the social, political, and economic aspects

of migration in the region. Includes books, periodicals, government publications, unpublished materials, and other items published in Brazil and elsewhere. Author and subject indexes. Provides a list of researchers on Amazônia and their addresses.

90 Universidade Federal do Pará. Biblioteca Central e Documentação. Coleção Amazônia: catálogo. Belém: 1972. 111 p. An unannotated subject bibliography of materials relating to all aspects of the Amazon region. Includes many hard-to-identify local imprints and older works, although contemporary works are also well represented.

Northeast

91 Bibliografia brasileira do semi-árido. Campina Grande: Universidade Federal da Paraíba, Centro de Informação do Semi-Arido, vol. 1-, 1982-. Cites many publications of potential interest to social scientists on such topics as the economic aspects of semi-arid agriculture, development policies and programs, and rural sociology, as well as those on more technical aspects of semi-arid regions. Basic bibliographic information with no annotations.

92 Brazil. Biblioteca Nacional. Nordeste brasileiro: catálogo da exposição. Rio de Janeiro: Biblioteca Nacional, Divisão de Publicações e Divulgação, 1970. 86 p. An unannotated bibliography of 548 entries citing publications and manuscripts about the Northeast, arranged by subject. Since it is an exhibition catalog it is not comprehensive in coverage, but it lists a variety of works published from the colonial period through the twentieth century, on the history, geography, economy, folklore, and arts of the region.

93 O campo do Nordeste: bibliografia analítica, seletiva e retrospectiva. n.p.: International Development Research Centre (IDRC); Centro Josué de Castro; Rede Nacional de Informações do Nordeste (RECANE), n.d. 203 p. An annotated bibliography of books, periodicals, theses, proceedings of meetings, and other publications related to social aspects of agriculture and agrarian problems. Author, title, and subject indexes.

94 Catálogo coletivo de periódicos/NE. 2 vols. Brasília: Coordenação de Aperfeiçoamento de Pessoal de Nível Superior, Instituto Brasileiro de Informação em Ciência e Tecnologia, 1979. A union catalog of serials in 200 libraries of the Northeast, including many titles published in that region.

95 Loureiro, Gildete de Azevedo. Seca: documentos disponíveis em bibliotecas do RN. Natal: Fundação Norte-Rio-Grandense

de Pesquisa e Cultura, 1982-. An unannotated bibliography of 5130 entries citing books, periodical articles, and government publications on a variety of subjects related to the periodic droughts of the Northeast. Cites materials about social, economic, and political aspects of the Northeast in general, and Rio Grande do Norte specifically, as well as those on topics such as water resources development. Volumes examined: 1, 2

96 Superintendência do Desenvolvimento do Nordeste. Coordenação de Informática. Catálogo das publicações da SUDENE, 1970-1980, Maria Antonieta Oliveira de Barros Leal, ed. Recife: 1983. 132 p. Supplies basic bibliographic data (no annotations) for 1251 items. Cites articles published in SUDENE periodicals, as well as monographs, annual reports, etc. Includes a few items published before 1970, although most of these are covered in an earlier SUDENE bibliography, Bibliografia sôbre SUDENE e o Nordeste (no. 97)

97 ______. Divisão de Documentação. Biblioteca. Bibliografia sobre a SUDENE e o Nordeste. Recife: 1969. 386 p. A bibliography of 1475 unannotated entries--books, pamphlets, periodical articles, laws, interviews, speeches, and reports covering the period 1959, when SUDENE was organized, to 1969.

BIBLIOGRAPHY--STATES

Acre

98 Biava, Marina de Lourdes. Bibliografia do Acre. Brasília: Empresa Brasileira de Pesquisa Agropecuária, Unidade de Execução de Pesquisa de Ambito Estadual de Rio Branco, Departamento de Informação e Documentação, 1981. 521 p. An unannotated bibliography of 1637 items about the state and former territory of Acre. The books, periodical articles government publications, and newspaper articles were published between the end of the nineteenth century and mid-1981. Although one major focus of the bibliography is agriculture--a major component of the state's economy--it also covers many topics of interest to social scientists: public administration, archeology, political science, economics, education, statistics, history, geography, transportation, communications, and law. An important contribution to information about this state.

Bahia

99 Bahia. Secretaria do Planejamento, Ciência e Tecnologia. Centro

de Estatística e Informações. Planejamento na Bahia: bibliografia. Salvador: 1987. 322 p. An annotated bibliography of planning documents produced in Bahia by twenty-four agencies and organizations since 1955. Arranged by producing agency with a detailed subject index.

100 Bahia. Secretaria do Planejamento, Ciência e Tecnologia. Fundação Centro de Pesquisas e Estudos. Municípios baianos: bibliografia. Salvador: 1980. 191 p. An unannotated bibliography of 864 references to works about Bahian municípios encompassing the areas of municipal administration, history, geography, tourism, economics, and agriculture. Many of the publications cited are state government documents, but books and journal articles are also well represented.

101 Bahia. Secretaria do Planejamento, Ciência e Tecnologia. Fundação de Pesquisas. Bibliografia baiana. 3 vols. Salvador: 1977?-1979. An unannotated bibliography of the state of Bahia with 7788 entries. Includes many publications of government agencies, commercial institutions, and organizations, in addition to those by individual authors. Cites past and contemporary works.

102 _______. _______. _______. Estudos econômico-sociais sobre a Bahia: informes bibliográficos--artigos de periódicos Série bibliografias, 2. Salvador: Secretaria do Planejamento, Ciência e Tecnologia, Fundação de Pesquisas, 1977. 72 p. An unannotated bibliography of 700 periodical articles which appeared in fifty-six indexed journals published from the early twentieth century through the early 1970s. Indexes of authors and subjects.

103 Universidade Federal da Bahia. Pró-Reitoria de Pesquisa e Pós-Graduação. Produção científica, literária e artística da UFBA, 1980. Salvador: 1980. 383 p. Cites 522 items arranged by division of the university in which they were produced. Includes bibliographic data and description of content.

Ceará

104 Souza, Maria da Conceição. Estudos bibliográficos cearenses. Fortaleza: Imprensa Universitária da Universidade Federal do Ceará, 1973-. A partially annotated bibliography of the state of Ceará, arranged by subject. Volume 1 is devoted to books and pamphlets. The introduction states that Volume 2 covers serial publications, although this volume was not located.

Distrito Federal

105 Brazil. Congresso. Câmara dos Deputados. Centro de Documentação e Informação. Brasília: Bibliografias, 3. Brasília: 1972. 1078 p. An unannotated bibliography with 6242 citations to publications about Brasília, published in Brazil and elsewhere. Covers the concept of the new capital and preliminary studies, construction, the move to Brasília, public opinion, legislation, administration, satellite cities, cultural, social, economic, and political aspects, prominent visitors, and the University of Brasília. Indispensable for a serious study of this topic.

106 Imprensa alternativa e cultural, 1970-1984: catálogo de títulos. Brasília: Arquivo Público do Distrito--ARPDF [e] Companhia de Desenvolvimento do Planalto Central--CODEPLAN, 1989. 55 p. Brief information about the content, frequency, numbers published, editors/directors, art/layout/photography, publishers/printers, and printing process used for twenty-eight alternative or cultural periodicals published in Brasília during the time period indicated.

107 Universidade de Brasília: produção científica e artística. Brasília: Fundação Universidade de Brasília, Centro de Apoio à Pesquisa e Pós-Graduação. Lists works published, those presented at meetings, theses defended, artistic production, and other types of academic production. Author index. Edition examined: 1987

Espírito Santo

108 Espírito Santo: informações bibliográficas. Série documentos capixabas, vol. 4. Vitória: Secretaria de Estado do Planejamento; Fundação Jones dos Santos Neves, 1979. 157 p. An unannotated survey of sources for the study of historical and contemporary Espírito Santo in archives and libraries in the state, in other states and in Portugal. Cites both manuscripts and published sources. Those in Portugal focus on the colonial period, while those in Brazil cover the nineteenth and twentieth centuries through the late 1970's.

109 Universidade Federal do Espírito Santo. Biblioteca Central. Bibliografia comentada de obras capixabas. Vitória: Universidade Federal de Espírito Santo; Banco do Estado do Espírito Santo; Aracruz Celulose, 1987. 172 p. An annotated bibliography of 350 books related to the history, geography, literature, and other aspects of Espírito Santo, or by authors from that state. Arranged alphabetically by author with a subject index.

Goiás

110 Catálogo bibliográfico de Goiás. Goiânia: Estante do Escritor Goiâno, 1966. 108 p. An unannotated bibliography of books by goiânos or by those closely associated with the state.

Maranhão

111 Grupo de Entre-Ajuda dos Bibliotecários Oficiais do Estado do Maranhão. Documentos maranhenses. São Luís: Associação Profissional dos Bibliotecários do Estado do Maranhão, 1974. 74 leaves. An unannotated bibliography of 161 official publications related to socio-economic aspects of the state, with time coverage from the late 1960's through 1974.

Mato Grosso

112 Motta, Antônio Carlos; João Batista Tavares da Silva; and Miraci de Arruda Câmara Pontual. Região mato-grossense: resumos informativos. Brasília: Empresa Brasileira de Pesquisa Agropecuária, Departamento de Informação e Documentação, 1980-. Volume 1, which was the only one located, cites 542 publications covering a wide range of topics dealing with Mato Grosso. It provides bibliographic data, abstracts, and author, subject, and place indexes.

Minas Gerais

113 Universidade Federal de Minas Gerais. Produção científica UFMG. Belo Horizonte: 1980-. Cites and summarizes articles published by people associated with UFMG in the fields of architecture, economics, education, library science, literature, and the social sciences, as well as in science and technology. Editions examined: 1980, 1981.

Pará

114 Instituto do Desenvolvimento Econômico-Social do Pará. Memória técnica do IDESP: bibliografia. Belém: 1985. 98 p. An unannotated bibliography of 753 periodicals, periodical articles, proceedings of meetings, reports, and other publications related to social and economic aspects of Pará. Most of them were prepared or published by IDESP.

115 ______. Resumos bibliográficos: a questão fundiária paraense e termos afins. Belém: 1987. 106 p. Summarizes the contents of 288 books, periodical articles, and theses related to land,

land use, agrarian reform, and related topics in Pará and the Amazon region. Arranged chronologically, with author and title indexes.

116 Universidade Federal do Pará. Pró-Reitoria de Pesquisa e Pós-Graduação. Biblioteca Central. Catálogo de teses e dissertações de docentes da UFPA. Belém: 1987. 300 p. Lists 677 theses and dissertations accepted by the university from its beginning, as well as those submitted to the independent faculties of law, medicine, and dentistry, which preceded it, and those of the Núcleo de Altos Estudos Amazônicos. Arranged by academic department, with author/advisor and subject indexes.

117 Universidade Federal do Pará. Pró-Reitoria de Pesquisa e Pós-Graduação. Departamento de Pesquisa. Pesquisas em execução na Universidade Federal do Pará. Belém: 1986. 99 p. A list of research projects under way in all academic fields including title, department, coordinator and collaborators, time period, financing, and objective.

Paraíba

118 Almeida, Horácio de. Contribuição para uma bibliografia paraibana. Rio de Janeiro: 1972. 195 p. An unannotated bibliography of 2310 items published in Paraíba or about it. Its four sections cover books and pamphlets, official publications, periodicals, and literatura de cordel. The latter section lists 550 titles, some published as early as the 1930's.

119 Brito, Edna Maria Torreão. Catálogo da produção científica do Centro de Ciências Sociais Aplicadas. João Pessôa: Universidade Federal da Paraíba, Centro de Ciências Sociais Aplicadas, 1984. 185 p. Cites 363 dissertations and theses written by professors and graduate students of the Center.

120 Pereira, Marília Mesquita Guedes, and Norma Maria Fernandes Nogueira. Catálogo de teses defendidas na UFPb, 1970/1979. João Pessoa: Universidade Federal da Paraíba, Biblioteca Central, 1980. 318 p. This first catalog of theses defended at the university is arranged by academic discipline. Entries provide bibliographic data, name of supervisor, area of concentration, date of defense, and abstracts in Portuguese and English. Author, title, and subject indexes.

Paraná

121 Documentação paranaense: catálogo bibliográfico. 2 vols. Curiti Biblioteca Pública do Paraná, Divisão de Documentação

Paranaense e Secretaria da Cultura e do Esporte, 1980-1983. An unannotated list of works by Paraná authors, works about Paraná, and books published in the state, 1965-1982. Based on the collection of the Public Library of Paraná, the legal depository for such works.

122 Universidade Federal do Paraná. Pró-Reitoria de e Pesquisa. Coordenação de Pesquisa. Pesquisa na Universidade Federal do Paraná. Curitiba: Editora da Universidade Federal do Paraná: 1985. 192 p. Describes research projects completed and in progress at the university. Covers all disciplines including those in the social sciences, humanities, and fine arts.

123 Universidade Federal do Paraná. Pró-Reitoria de Pós-Graduação. Resumos de teses e dissertações de pós-graduação da Universidade Federal do Paraná. Curitiba: 1981. 548 p. Cites theses and dissertations presented at the university arranged by academic discipline. In addition to bibliographic data, each entry provides the name of the supervisor, the objective of the work, and a summary and conclusions. Indexed by author, supervisor, and title.

Pernambuco

124 Pernambuco. Arquivo Público Estadual. Catálogo das publicações da Imprensa Oficial do Estado, 1926-1966. Recife: Arquivo Público Estadual, 1966. 36 p. This publication, in honor of the fortieth anniversary of the founding of the state's official press, provides bibliographic data for the books and periodicals that it issued during its first forty years.

125 ______. ______. Catálogo de obras raras. Recife: 1982. 57 p. An unannotated bibliography of 445 rare books in the archive. Many of them are about Pernambuco, although many other subjects are also included.

126 Pernambuco, Arquivo Público Estadual Jordão Emerenciano. Levantamento bibliográfico de publicações de interesse para Pernambuco existentes na Biblioteca do Arquivo Público Estadual Jordão Emerenciano em julho de 1983. Recife: 1984. 84 p. An unannotated bibliography of 1197 citations in alphabetical order by author, with a good subject index.

127 Pernambuco. Conselho de Desenvolvimento. Pernambuco: uma bibliografia básica sobre desenvolvimento. Recife: 1973. 63 p. An unannotated bibliography of 237 items bearing upon a variety of subjects related to the development of Pernambuco. Many of the publications cited are those of government agencies, banks, and development corporations.

128 Universidade Federal de Pernambuco. Catálogo de publicações da Imprensa Universitária. Recife: 1955-1965-. This catalog of university press publications cites many works about Pernambuco and the Northeast. Issues examined: 1955-1965, 1966, 1967, 1968, 1969-1970.

Piauí

129 Catálogo de dissertações e teses de Universidade Federal do Piauí. Teresina: Universidade Federal do Piauí, Pró-Reitoria de Pesquisa e Pós-Graduação, Coordenaria de Informação em Ciência e Tecnologia, 1979-. Bibliographic data for, and summaries of theses and dissertations of professors and staff of the university in all fields, including many specifically related to Piauí. Volumes examined: 1, 1979; 2, 1984; 3, 1985; 4, 1987; 5, 1988.

130 Domingos Neto, Manuel. Indicações bibliográficas sobre o Estado do Piauí: selecionadas e comentadas. Teresina: Fundação Centro de Pesquisas Econômicas e Sociais do Piauí, 1978. 50 leaves. A well-annotated subject bibliography of ninety-three basic works on Piauí covering history, the economy, society, culture, natural history, and diagnostic studies. Includes books, periodical articles, theses, and government publications.

131 Gomes, José Airton Gonçalves. Bibliografia piauiense. Teresina: Fundação Centro de Pesquisas Econômicas e Sociais do Piauí, 1978. 120 p. An unannotated subject bibliography of 1042 items about Piauí or by piauienses available in libraries in Teresina.

132 Produção intelectual da Universidade Federal do Piauí. Teresina: Universidade Federal do Piauí, Pró-Reitoria de Pesquisa e Pós-Graduação, Coordenaria de Informação em Ciência e Tecnologia. Cites publications by the university faculty in all academic disciplines. Volume examined: 2, 1986-1987.

133 Santos, Lúcia Maria Gurjão, and Carmen Cortez Costa. Catálogo de publicações do Sistema Estadual de Planejamento, 1956-1985. Teresina: Fundação Centro de Pesquisas Econômicas e Sociais do Piauí, 1985. 80 p. An unannotated bibliography of 655 titles focusing on economic and social topics associated with Piauí, including related statistics.

Rio de Janeiro

134 Brazil. Biblioteca Nacional. Catálogo de jornais e revistas do Rio de Janeiro (1808-1889) existentes na Biblioteca Nacional.

Anais da Biblioteca Nacional, vol. 85. Rio de Janeiro: Biblioteca Nacional, Divisão de Publicações e Divulgação, 1965. 208 p. A list of nineteenth century newspapers and journals published in Rio de Janeiro, which gives bibliographic data including names of persons such as editors associated with them. The list, in alphabetical order by title, is followed by a chronological list of the same publications and an index of personal names.

135 Fundação Universidade do Rio de Janeiro. Pró-Reitoria Acadêmia. Catálogo da produção técnico-científica e artística, 1985. Rio de Janeiro: 1987. 258 p. Records the publications, papers presented, performances (such as recitals), and other scholarly activities of members of the university community. Arranged by type of publication/activity, with abstracts when appropriate. Indexed by author and subject.

136 Instituto Universitário de Pesquisas do Rio de Janeiro. Catálogo de teses, 1971-1986. Rio de Janeiro: IUPERJ, 1987? 73 p. Bibliographic data and abstracts for about 100 theses in sociology and political science produced by IUPERJ students over a fifteen-year period. Entries include bibliographic information about published books based on the theses.

137 Ipanema, Marcello de, and Cybelle de Ipanema. Catálogo de periódicos de Niterói. Rio de Janeiro: Instituto de Comunicação Ipanema, 1988. 195 p. Cites 597 serials published in Niteroí, 1828-1988, in chronological order of beginning date. Information provided varies from title to title. Indexed by date, title, publisher, and personal name (see also no. 1374).

138 Memória fluminense. Rio de Janeiro: Instituto Estadual do Livro, Divisão de Bibliotecas, Centro de Bibliografia e Documentação, no. 1-, 1977-. Number 1 of this series is a bibliography focusing on materials related to the state and city of Rio de Janeiro found in two special collections located in the Biblioteca Estadual de Niterói and the Biblioteca Estadual do Rio de Janeiro.

139 Universidade Federal do Rio de Janeiro. Theses and Dissertations Abstracts. Rio de Janeiro: 1981? 453 p. Abstracts in English for 643 dissertations and theses in all subject areas submitted to the university in 1980.

140 Universidade Federal Fluminense. Núcleo de Documentação . Catálogo de teses de dissertações da UFF, 1970/1976. Niterói: 1977. 207 p. Cites 333 theses for the mestrado and livre docência in all subjects defended between 1970 and 1976, with bibliographic information and annotations. Arranged by broad subjects and then departments, with author and subject indexes providing additional access.

Rio Grande do Norte

141 Fundação José Augusto. Catálogo das publicacões da Fundação José Augusto, 1965-1984: exposição bibliográfica promovida pele Biblioteca Pública Câmara Cascudo. Natal: 1984. 69 p. A chronological list of the publications of this important cultural institution of Rio Grande do Norte, which includes many titles on regional topics and by local literary figures.

142 Onofre, Manuel. Estudos norte-riograndenses. Natal: Fundação José Augusto, 1978. 154 p. This bibliography is devoted to the history, geography, municípios, ethnography, folklore, sociology, literature, journalism, and biography of Rio Grande do Norte. The annotations, extensive in some cases, are highly subjective.

Rio Grande do Sul

143 Barreto, Abeillard. Bibliografia sul riograndense: a contribuição portuguesa e estrangeira para o conhecimento e a integração do Rio Grande do Sul. 2 vols. Rio de Janeiro: Conselho Federal de Cultura, 1973-1976. A scholarly bibliography of works by foreigners related to Rio Grande do Sul, encompassing scientific writers (such as botanists), cartographers, other specialists, and general travelers.

144 Rio Grande do Sul. Biblioteca Pública do Estado. Catálogo do Setor de Documentação do Rio Grande do Sul. Porto Alegre: 1977. 192 p. An annotated bibliography of 1116 works about Rio Grande do Sul.

145 Superintendência do Desenvolvimento da Região Sul. Listagem bibliográfica dos documentos constantes no acervo da Divisão de Documentação, Rio Grande do Sul. Porto Alegre: SUDESUL, 1976. 139 p. An unannotated bibliography of 626 citations of works on all subjects related to Rio Grande do Sul. The collection emphasizes the social sciences, agriculture, and industry, as might be expected in the library of a development agency. Publications issued between 1960 and 1975 predominate.

146 Universidade Federal do Rio Grande do Sul. Biblioteca Central. Catálogo de teses e dissertações: 1898-1987. 2 vols. Porto Alegre: Universidade Federal do Rio Grande do Sul, Pró-Reitoria de Pesquisa e Pós-Graduação, Biblioteca Central, 1988. A record of theses and dissertations submitted to the University and the faculdades which preceded its founding over a period of one hundred years.

147 Villas Bôas, Pedro. Panorama bibliográfico do regionalismo.

Coleção cadernos gaúchos, no. 4. Porto Alegre: Fundação Instituto Gaúcho de Tradição e Folclore, 1978. 48 p. Brief bibliographical information and biographies of past and present writers of Rio Grande do Sul.

Santa Catarina

148 Fundação Catarinense de Cultura. Catálogo de jornais catarinenses, 1850-1980. Florianópolis: Fundação Catarinense de Cultura, Programa de Apoio e Estímulo à Pesquisa, Informação, e Documentação, 1980. 120 p. A catalog of Santa Catarina newspapers in the collection of the Biblioteca Pública do Estado. Data provided include the title, place, and beginning date of publication, and dates of issues owned by the library.

São Paulo

149 Catálogo de teses e dissertações defendidas na PUC/SP. São Paulo: Editora da PUC-SP [Pontifícia Universidade Católica de São Paulo] vol. 1-. 1986-. Volumes 1-7, issued in 1986, which were those examined, provide bibliographic data and summaries of theses defended through 1985, arranged by academic program, with indexes of authors, advisors, and titles. They state that beginning with 1986, annual volumes will be published.

150 Pontifícia Universidade Católica de São Paulo. Vice-Reitoria Acadêmica. Produção científica, 1987. São Paulo: EDUC, 1988. 209 p. Lists publications of the faculty, presentations at academic events, research in progress, and theses and dissertations accepted. Arranged by department, with no indexes.

151 São Paulo (State). Imprensa Oficial do Estado. 90 anos de produção gráfica, 1891-1981. São Paulo: 1983. 295 p. A bibliography of the publications of this important state press in chronological order since its beginning.

152 São Paulo (State). Secretaria de Economia e Planejamento. Departamento de Estatística. Imprensa periódica no Estado de São Paulo, jornais, revistas, boletins: cadastro, por município, em 31/01/1973. São Paulo: 1973. 85 p. A município-by-município list of newspapers and periodicals published in the state of São Paulo: title, periodicity, subject, and publisher.

153 Universidade de São Paulo. Biblioteca Central. Catálogo de dissertações e teses da Universidade de São Paulo recebidas

pela Biblioteca Central: 1978-1979. São Paulo: USP, Coordenadoria de Atividades Culturais, 1980. 120 p. Cites 1193 theses and dissertations on all subjects, providing bibliographical data but no abstracts.

154 Universidade de São Paulo. Sistema Integrado de Bibliotecas. Produção técnico-científica e artítistica do corpo docente e pesquisadores da USP, 1985. 2 vols. São Paulo: 1986.

155 _______. Suplemento, 1986. 3 vols. in 4. São Paulo: 1987?

156 _______. Suplemento, 1987. São Paulo: 1988? This publication, covering all academic disciplines, is expected to be produced annually.

157 Universidade Estadual de Campinas. Teses defendidas nos cursos de pós-graduação. Campinas: Setor de Publicações, Coordenação dos Cursos de Pos-Graduação, Universidade Estadual de Campinas, 1979-. Lists theses defended in all subject areas. Volumes examined: 1: Desde o início até junho de 1979; 2: De julho de 1979 a dezembro de 1980; 4: Ano de 1982.

BIBLIOGRAPHY--CITIES

158 Brasil, Maria Irene. Bibliografia sobre o bairro de Botafogo. Rio de Janeiro: Fundação Casa de Rui Barbosa, 1989. 59 p. An unannotated bibliography of 824 entries citing periodical articles and books on an important Rio de Janeiro neighborhood. Provides basic bibliographic data and cites library in which work was consulted. Includes a subject index.

159 Frota, Guilherme de Andréa. O Rio de Janeiro na imprensa periódica. Rio de Janeiro: 1966. 302 p. Cites 4833 periodical articles about many aspects of the city of Rio de Janeiro, with brief annotations when the subject of an article is not evident from the title.

160 Horch, Rosemarie E. Albuns do Rio de Janeiro existentes no IEB. Revista do Instituto de Estudos Brasileiros, no. 5. São Paulo: Instituto dos Estudos Brasileiros, 1968. 31 p. Detailed descriptions of eighteen albums of prints illustrating nineteenth- and twentieth-century Rio de Janeiro. In addition to complete bibliographic data, each entry has a brief annotation, and a list of the prints that the album contains.

161 Rio de Janeiro (City). Secretaria Municipal de Cultura. Divisão de Documentação e Biblioteca. Bibliografia carioca. Rio de

Janeiro: 1987. 80 p. An unannotated list of 458 books in the "popular libraries" (formerly regional libraries) and the library of the Arquivo Geral da Cidade do Rio de Janeiro on the history, life, and customs of the city.

GENERAL SOURCES

General sources include encyclopedias, dictionaries, handbooks, and other works encompassing several aspects of life in Brazil, its regions, and its states. Most works on specific topics, such as geography or literature are found in the appropriate sections of this bibliography. However, a few specialized items have been included here if they do not readily fit into other categories. Throughout this bibliography, the only cities for which reference works have been cited are Rio de Janeiro, São Paulo, and Brasília.

ENCYCLOPEDIAS

This section includes both universal encyclopedias and those specific to Brazil. However, even the universal encyclopedias cited include more entries on Brazilian topics than the typical encyclopedia published elsewhere.

162 Colorama: enciclopédia universal ilustrada. 13 vols. São Paulo: Britannica do Brasil, 1973. A universal encyclopedia with many illustrations, which contribute to its eye-appeal and contemporary appearance.

163 Enciclopédia Abril. 13 vols. São Paulo: Abril, 1971. A universal encyclopedia covering a wide range of basic topics, with two volumes devoted to biography.

164 Enciclopédia Barsa. 16 vols. Rio de Janeiro: Encyclopaedia Britannica Editôres, 1967. A universal encyclopedia which emphasizes Brazilian places, people, and topics. Vol. 14 includes an atlas.

165 Enciclopédia brasileira Mérito. 20 vols. São Paulo: Mérito, 1967. An encyclopedia focusing on Brazil, including its

history, geography, biography, and regionalisms, as well as other topics.

166 Enciclopédia Delta universal. 15 vols. Rio de Janeiro: Delta, 1980. A universal encyclopedia intended for secondary school students, but its clear language and explanations make it useful for a wider audience. Many illustrations, maps, and diagrams enhance the text.

167 Enciclopédia Mirador internacional. 20 vols. São Paulo: Britannica do Brasil, 1976. A universal, popular encyclopedia with many illustrations, maps, statistical tables, and charts elucidating its content. Updated with yearbooks.

168 Grande enciclopédia Delta Larousse. 15 vols. Rio de Janeiro: Delta, 1977. Extensive articles on basic topics, accompanied by illustrations and maps. The approach is popular, with unsigned articles and no bibliographic citations. Updated by yearbooks.

169 Pequena enciclopédia Melhoramentos. São Paulo: Melhoramentos, 1978. 1094 p. A one-volume encyclopedia, universal in scope. Good coverage of Brazilian cities and organizations.

170 Pequeno dicionário enciclopédico Koogan Larousse. Rio de Janeiro: Larousse do Brasil, 1980, 1644 p. A universal, one-volume encyclopedia with 71,000 entries and many illustrations and maps. Covers many topics specific to Brazil.

DICTIONARIES OF ACRONYMS

171 Banco Nacional de Habitação. Glossário de siglas. 6. ed. n.p.: Secretaria dos Orgãos Colegiados, 1981. 151 p. A compilation identifying all acronyms and abbreviations found in documents generated by BNH or registered by it. Since the bank deals with a broad cross-section of institutions, this is a useful work for identifying acronyms of government agencies, associations, commercial institutions, public enterprises, and entities in the areas of housing, mortgage and development banking, sanitation, and related fields. The glossary has been updated and issued in a new edition about every two years.

172 Empresa Brasileira de Pesquisa Agropecuária. Departamento de Informação e Documentação. Siglas agropecuárias brasileiras. Brasília: 1977. 308 p. Identifies 1591 acronyms associated with all aspects of agriculture including economics and land reform.

173 Instituto Brasileiro de Bibliografia e Documentação. Siglas brasileiras. 2. ed. Rio de Janeiro: 1975. 577 p. Identifies 17,000 acronyms in use in all areas of activity. Includes address and telephone number of each entity identified, and has an index of names corresponding to the acronyms. First edition published in 1970.

174 Instituto Brasileiro de Informação em Ciência e Tecnologia. Siglas de entidades brasileiras. Versão preliminar. Rio de Janeiro: 1979. 789 p. The most recent directory of Brazilian acronyms published by this official agency. It identifies the acronyms for 5436 entities and is complementary to Siglas brasileiras (no. 173) providing the same type of information.

175 Miléa, Antonino Paolo and Marc Dorell. Dicionário de siglas e abreviaturas nacionais e internacionais. São Paulo: Nova Epoca Editorial, 198-? 443 p. Identifies acronyms used in Brazil and elsewhere in their language of origin. Earlier editions under the title, Dicionário de siglas y abreviaturas, published 1958, 1965, and 1976.

OTHER SOURCES

176 Almanaque Abril. São Paulo: Editora Abril. A general almanac, universal in scope, but emphasizing factual information about Brazil. Issued annually. Editions examined: 1986, 1987, 1988, 1989.

177 Almanaque dos esportes. 1.-, 1975-. Rio de Janeiro: Rio Gráfica e Editora. Current and retrospective information about eight sports played in Brazil and elsewhere. Much more space is devoted to futebol (soccer) than to any other sport.

178 Almeida, J. B. Pereira de. Enciclopédia de jogos. Rio de Janeiro: 1975. 288 p. Card games--Brazilian and those of foreign origin--which are popular in Brazil. Gives instructions for playing each game and information on its origin.

179 Andrade, Margarette Sheehan de. Brazilian Cookery: Traditional and Modern. Rutland, VT: Tuttle, 1965. 349 p. An excellent cookbook in English, with measurements and ingredients adapted for easy use by Americans.

180 Anuário das artes: teatro, música erudita, literatura, cinema, dança, música popular, artes visuais, televisão, circo. São Paulo: Associação Paulista de Críticos de Arte; Secretaria da Cultura, Ciência e Tecnologia do Estado de São Paulo, 1972-1977. A compilation of comments of critics of the arts.

Illustrated with photographs of scenes from performances, and other artistic activities or products. Editions examined: 1972, 1973/1974, 1977; not published 1975 and 1976.

181 Atlas das potencialidades brasileiras: Brasil grande e forte. São Paulo: Melhoramentos, 1974. 158 p. A handsomely illustrated economic and social atlas of Brazil, which depicts many aspects of life: education, transportation, communications, agriculture, industry, health, sanitation, jurisdictions of development agencies, and other topics.

182 Avila, Fernando Bastos de. Pequeno dicionário de moral e civismo. 3. ed. Fundação Nacional de Material Escolar, 1982. 630 p. The introduction describes this work, intended primarily for students and teachers, as a "...fonte de informação elaborada com propósito de ressaltar os valôres humanos que constituem a essência da organização política, social e econômica brasiliera." Defines and discusses a wide variety of terms and concepts within the Brazilian context. Very useful for the study of official values. First edition published in 1967; second edition issued in 1972; third edition first published in 1978 by the Campanha Nacional do Ensino.

183 Brasil Come Along: A Complete Handbook for Your Trips. São Paulo: Quatro Rodas, 1974. 194 p. A well-written English language guidebook covering major tourist attractions, accomodations, restaurants, transportation, and other topics. Maps of the centers, entrances to and exits from the state capitals are a useful feature.

184 Brasil dia-a-dia: o retrato dos últimos 50 anos. São Paulo: Editora Abril, 1988. 258 p. A chronology of major events recorded in Brazilian newspapers. Emphasis is on the fifteen-year period, 1973-1987, although the years 1930-1972 are covered more briefly. Arranged by broad subject areas from politics to sports. Includes obituaries, accidents, and topics specific to Brazil for the period covered, such as censorship.

185 Brasil: histórias, costumes e lendas. 2 vols. São Paulo: Editora Três, 1987. A well-illustrated reference work intended for a general audience covering the highlights of the folklore, folk art, popular festivals, legends, and traditional dress of each state, as well as general chapters on some of the same topics. No bibliography.

186 Brasil: Tourist Calendar. Calendrier touristique. Calendário turístico. Rio de Janeiro: Embratur. An annual chronological list of events of interest to tourists: expositions, conventions, competitions, and festivals are types of events covered. There is a geographical index. Consulting this

calendar in conjunction with the Calendário cultural do Brasil (no. 192) gives a good idea of what is going on in Brazil in a given year. Text in English, French and Spanish. Also published in Portuguese and English under the title Brasil: calendário turístico. Issues examined 1979, 1980.

187 Brazil. Brasília: Grupo de Trabalho para a Elaboração do Livro Brasil, 1976. 637 p. A handbook in English containing a wealth of information on Brazilian history, administrative and political organization, geographical and climatic characteristics, demography, culture, social and economic conditions, sports, and tourism, with accompanying illustrations and statistics. Issued also in Spanish (3. ed., 1972); French (1984); and Portuguese (nova ed.; 1979).

188 Brazil: A Country Study. 4th ed. Area Handbooks Series. Washington, D.C.: U.S. Govt. Printing Office, 1983. 410 p. Describes contemporary Brazil in terms of its history, social and economic conditions, politics, and military situation. Includes a useful bibliography with many of the sources cited in English. This work was prepared under the Country Studies Area Handbook Program for the Department of the Army by the Foreign Area Studies Program, The American University. Earlier editions published under the title, Area Handbook for Brazil in 1964, 1971, and 1975.

189 Brazil. Exercito. Centro de Documentação. Normas para a preservação das tradições das organizações militares do Exército Brasileiro. Brasília: Ministério do Exército, Secretaria-Geral do Exército, Centro de Documentação do Exército, 1987. 440 p. Organization charts and "family trees" provide graphic outlines of the history and development of Brazilian army units from their beginnings to the present.

190 Brugalli, Alvino Melquides. Meu Brasil brasileiro: símbolos nacionais e históricos. Caxias do Sul: EDUCS, 1986. 152 p. Provides texts of laws referring to national symbols and those of the state of Rio Grande do Sul. Illustrates current and historic flags of Brazil as well as the current flags of each state in color. Includes information on flag etiquette, and provides the music and words of the national anthem and other patriotic songs.

191 Cadastro das pesquisas culturais. Brasília: Ministério da Educação e Cultura, Secretaria de Informática, Serviço de Estatística de Educação e Cultura. vol. 1-, 1983-. A list of cultural agencies and organizations, their addresses and telephone numbers. Vol. 1: Radiodifusão, imprensa periódica, empresas editoras de livros e folhetos. Vol. 2: Cinemas, teatros e cine-teatros, museus, associações culturais.

192 Calendário cultural do Brasil. Rio de Janeiro: Conselho Federal de Cultura, 1976-. An annual chronological list of festivals, holidays, and cultural events throughout Brazil. Includes colored photographs.

193 Carvalho, André. Dicionário de datas. Belo Horizonte: Editôra Comunicação, 1982. 147 p. A universal dictionary of significant dates in chronological order, with emphasis on Brazil. Includes historical background on many dates at both national and state levels.

194 Catálogo nacional das instituições que atuam na área do meio ambiente. 1980-. Brasília: Secretaria Especial do Meio Ambiente, Secretaria Adjunta de Planejamento. An annual publication listing agencies concerned with the historic and cultural patrimony, public health, energy, conservation of natural resources, and urban planning and development, as well as those dealing with more technical aspects of the environment, such as pollution control. Provides their addresses and describes their responsibilities. The 1980 edition was entitled, Cadastro nacional das instituições que atuam na área do meio ambiente.

195 Centro de Integração Empresa Escola. Dicionário das profissões: estudos ocupacionais referentes a profissões e cursos de formação em 2. e 3. graus (nível médio e superior). 4 vols. 21. ed. São Paulo: 1978. Detailed information on 136 legally recognized professions requiring secondary or university education, ranging from "administração bancária" to "zootécnia." Provides information on the history of each profession, types of positions available, required personal characteristics and education, remuneration, job market, means of entering a profession, and bibliography. Although this work is intended for young people and their parents, it is very useful for others seeking information on professions as they are constituted in Brazil.

196 Conselho Nacional dos Direitos da Mulher. Grupos, instituições, associações de mulheres. Brasília: Conselho Nacional dos Direitos da Mulher--CNDM, 1989. 203 p. A directory of Brazilian women's organizations providing name, address, telephone number, date founded, areas of interest, objectives/activities, and type of clientele for each one. An appendix lists publications of the groups.

197 Dicionário de ciências sociais. Rio de Janeiro: Editora da Fundação Getúlio Vargas, 1986. 1422 p. The 1457 entries in this dictionary cover basic ideas and concepts in the social sciences. Although it is basically a translation of A Dictionary of the Social Sciences (1964) and Diccionario de ciências sociales (2 vols., 1975-1976), this edition includes

276 entries specific to Brazil and more than 125 complementary notes prepared for Brazilian users. Examples of the former type of entry are "correção monetária" and "tenentismo."

198 Dicionário de estudos sociais ilustrado. 4 vols. São Paulo: Melhoramentos, 1973. Vol. 1-2: Geografia do Brasil. Vol. 3-4: Moral e civismo. História do Brasil. This dictionary, which includes people, organizations, terms, and concepts, defines the subjects covered very broadly. Many illustrations.

199 Embarcações típicas do Brasil. Typical Boats of Brazil. n.p.: Indústrias Reunidas Caneco, 1985. 134 p. Identifies small sailing vessels, canoes, and other boats typical of the regions of Brazil through line drawings, color photographs, and text. Includes a glossary of boating terms and of tools associated with boats. Very useful for the non-specialist seeking information about boats mentioned in literary works and elsewhere.

200 English, Adrian. Armed Forces of Latin America: Their Histories, Development, Present Strength and Military Potential. London: Jane's Publishing Company, 1984. 490 p. A country-by-country survey of the armed forces in Latin America, including forty pages (91-131) devoted to Brazil. In addition to the topics mentioned in the title, it also includes data on each country's defense expenditures as a percentage of the GNP, and on U.S. military aid to Latin American countries. Glossary of military terms in English, Spanish, and Portuguese.

201 Ferrarini, Sebastião. Armas, brasões, e símbolos nacionais. 2. ed. Curitiba: Editora Curitiba, 1983. 128 p. Colored illustrations and text depict and describe the Brazilian flag and its historic Portuguese and Brazilian antecedents, beginning with the flag of the Ordem Militar de Cristo which accompanied Cabral on his voyage to the New World. Includes the history, lyrics and scores of the national anthem and other patriotic songs. The first edition was published in 1979.

202 Fodor's Brazil, 1988. New York: Fodor's Travel Publications, 1987. 214 p. A guide-book for the traveler providing general background information and specific information for places a tourist is likely to visit.

203 Fontanele, Airton Silveira. Futebol: seleção das seleções. Fortaleza: Banco do Nordeste do Brasil, 1986. 264 p. A history of Brazilian soccer in text, photographs, and lists. Excellent for quick reference.

204 Freitas, Mário César de. Os 120 assuntos que todo brasileiro

precisa conhecer: um manual de cidadania. 7. ed. ampliada. Rio de Janeiro: Editora Universo, 1979. 331 p. A handbook for the citizen on many aspects of individual and corporate privileges and responsibilities, covering topics such as voter registration, social security, birth certificates, and military service. Although this edition is described as enlarged, it actually has fewer pages than the second edition of 1972. It is, however, revised. For example, it covers the divorce law passed in 1977. Provides a useful look at the laws and practices which govern the lives of Brazilian citizens.

205 Fundação Instituto Brasileiro de Geografia e Estatística. Regiões de influência das cidades. Rio de Janeiro: IBGE, 1987. 212 p. An update of Divisão do Brasil em regiões funcionais urbanas (Rio de Janeiro: 1972), which describes urban areas in Brazil through maps and through tables listing the regional metropolis and its subordinate municípios. This work does not provide statistical data.

206 Fundação Nacional de Arte. Núcleo de Estudos e Pesquisas. Levantamento das fontes de apoio financeiro à área cultural: nível federal. Rio de Janeiro: 1983. 101 p. A directory of sources of support by the federal government for cultural projects.

207 Gontijo, Silvana. 80 anos de moda no Brasil. Rio de Janeiro: Nova Fronteira, 1987. 131 p. A visual history of women's fashion in Brazil covering the period 1900-1979 through photographs, reproductions of advertisements, and sketches, with explanatory and descriptive notes. In addition to dresses and sportswear, this work covers accessories, lingerie, beachwear, makeup, and hairstyles. Supplementary material includes a section devoted to "Os Grandes Nomes" (biographical data about major designers and brief histories of well-known fashion houses), a glossary of terms associated with fashion, and a bibliography. A separate color chart illustrates the colors in vogue during each decade.

208 Guia Brasil. São Paulo: Editora Abril, 1966-. An annual guide to travel in Brazil with the introduction in Portuguese, English, and Spanish. Includes information on large and small cities: population, economic activity, transportation, hospitals and major tourist attractions. Rates the quality of hotels and restaurants. Provides maps of many city centers. Its title has varied over the years that it has been published: 1966-1978: Guia quatro rodas do Brasil; 1979-1982: Guia quatro rodas Brasil: 1982-1984: Guia do Brasil.

209 Guia de eventos culturais: calendário, espaço, instituições. Brasília: minC--Ministério da Cultura, 1988. Lists events all over Brazil in chronological order in the following fields

of activity: drama, art, cinema and photography, books and libraries, music, and cultural promotions such as craft fairs. Edition examined: 1988.

210 Instituto Brasileiro de Informação em Ciência e Tecnologia. Fontes de informação em meio ambiente no Brasil. Brasília: 1983. 147 p. A guide to government agencies, universities, and organizations working in fields related to the environment, as well as a bibliography of periodicals and reference works on the subject. Although many of these sources provide technical information on such matters as sanitation and pollution, others deal with urban and regional planning, policy aspects of public health, public awareness, legislation, and administration.

211 Landim, Leilah. Sem fins lucrativos: as organizações não-governamentais no Brasil. Rio de Janeiro: Instituto de Estudos da Religião--ISER, 1988. 167 p. A directory of "ONGs"--non-profit, non-governmental organizations, divided into three sections: "SMPs" (organizações a serviço do movimento popular), women's organizations, and ecological organizations. An introductory essay on non-profits by Rubem César Fernandes precedes the directory. Indexed by state and by acronym.

212 Levine, Robert. Brazil: Field Research Guide in the Social Sciences. New York: Columbia University, Institute of Latin American Studies, 1966. 298 p. Although some of the material in this handbook is outdated, much of the information in it is still useful.

213 Luz, Milton Fortuna. Os símbolos nacionais. Ed. comemorativa do 165. ano da Indepêndencia e 98. da República. Brasília: Secretaria de Imprensa e Divulgação da Presidência da República, 1986. 96 p. Symbolism, history, and color illustrations of Brazilian flags, coats of arms, and other patriotic symbols from colonial days to the present. Includes text of the 1971 law (no. 5700) , covering the flag, the national anthem, the national seal, and related topics.

214 Macedo, Sérgio D. T. O livro de ouro dos estados. Rio de Janeiro: Edições de Ouro, 197-? 129 p. Brief information on each state, including the origin of its name and an outline map locating major cities and geographical features.

215 Nagel's Encyclopedia-Guide: Brazil. 5th ed. Geneva: Nagel, 1979. 479 p. A general introduction to many aspects of Brazil is followed by descriptions and specific information for each state and major city with the traveler in mind. Includes useful maps of city centers, and fold-out maps of Rio de Janeiro and São Paulo showing the general plan of each.

216 Ogleari, Braz, and Ieda de Barros Carvalho. Dicionário básico de dados do Brasil. 2 vols. Curitiba: Excelsior Empresa Editorial, 1972. Data about places, people, and many aspects of Brazilian life. Intended for students, but very useful for general purposes.

217 Paioli, Caetano Carlos. Brasil olímpico. São Paulo: Impresa Estadual de São Paulo, 198-? 373 p. Lists Brazilian participants in the Olympic Games, 1920-1983, and identifies its representatives to the International Olympic Committee and other officials.

218 Rêde Ferroviária Nacional. Síntese ferroviária brasileira. n.p.: 1981. 58 p. Information on contemporary railway transportation through statistics, maps, charts, and photographs.

GENERAL SOURCES--REGIONS

Center-West

The Center-West region (Centro-Oeste) is comprised of Mato Grosso, Mato Grosso do Sul, Goiás, Tocantins, and the Distrito Federal.

219 The Brazilian Center-West. 9 vols. Brasília: Superintendência do Desenvolvimento da Região Centro-Oeste, 1981. Vol. 1: Brazilian Center-West; Vol. 2: Social Aspects; Vol. 3: Economic Aspects; Vol. 4: Agricultural and Agro-industrial Potential; Vol. 5: Energy Potential; Vol. 6: Mineral Potential; Vol. 7: Tourism Potential; Vol. 8: Institutional Apparatus; Vol. 9: Credit Financing, and Fiscal Incentives; Vol. 10: Foreign Investments. Also issued in Portuguese under the title, Centro-Oeste brasileiro.

220 Centro-Oeste, a nova fronteira: um painel de informações. n.p.: Superintendência de Desenvolvimento da Região Centro-Oeste, 1982? 106 p. Summarizes basic data on the area comprised of Rondônia, Mato Grosso, Mato Grosso do Sul, Goiás and the Distrito Federal, with the purpose of stimulating investment in the region. Statistics, text, and maps provide information on many aspects of the region: climate, terrain, urbanization, transportation, energy, minerals, agriculture, existing development projects, and development policy. Useful for a good overview of this relatively little-known region.

North

The North region (Norte) is comprised of Acre, Amapá, Amazonas, Pará, Rondônia, and Roraima.

221 Guia instituições, especialistas e pesquisadores da Amazônia. Belém: Rede de Bibliotecas da Amazônia--REBAM. A guide to institutions--universities, libraries, and others--involved in research on Amazônia, and to individual researchers working in all subjects related to the area. Gives fairly detailed information in outline form. Volume examined: 2, no. 1, 1977.

222 Roque, Carlos. Grande enciclopédia da Amazônia. 6 vols. Belém: AMEL--Amazônia Editôra Ltda., 1967-1968. An encyclopedia covering all aspects of the huge geographic area comprising the Amazon Basin: places, plants, animals, people, indigenous tribes, geographical features, and many other subjects. Illustrated with line drawings and photographs. A bibliography concludes the sixth volume.

Northeast

The states of Alagoas, Bahia, Ceará, Maranhão, Paraíba, Pernambuco, Piauí, Rio Grande do Norte, and Sergipe comprise the Northeast region (Nordeste).

223 Bezerra, José Fernandes. Retalhos do meu sertão. Rio: 1978? 103 p. The vaqueiros of the sertão of the Northeast are the subject of this work. The first part provides information about daily life and gives the texts of some of their songs and poetry. The second part, entitled "Biografias e linhagems: fazendeiros, vaqueiros e derrubadores" supplies biographical data about past and contemporary figures of the sertão, and includes some portraits. Although this work is uneven in quality, its usefulness in the absence of other sources is undisputed.

GENERAL SOURCES--STATES

Acre

224 Tocantins, Leandro. Estado do Acre: geografia, história e sociedade. Rio de Janeiro: Philobilion; Rio Branco: Assessoria da Comunicação Social do Estado do Acre, 1984. 114 p. Short narrative chapters on various aspects of past and contemporary Acre are supplemented by a glossary of regionalisms, a chronological list of governors, and a bibliography.

Amazonas

225 Diagnóstico industrial dos centros sub-regionais do desenvolvimento

do Estado do Amazonas. 8 vols. Manaus: Centro de Assistência Gerencial à Pequena e Média Empresa do Estado do Amazonas--CEAG-AM, 1979. Basic data and statistics about demography, the infrastructure, and economic and social conditions in the areas designated as development sub-regions: Vol. 1: *Itacoatiara*; Vol. 2: *Paratins*; Vol. 3: *Tefé*; Vol. 4: *Benjamin Constant*; Vol. 5: *Labrea*; Vol. 6: *Eurunepé*; Vol. 7: *Borba*; Vol. 8: *Barcelos*.

226 Salles, Waldemar Batista de. *O Amazonas: o meio físico e suas riquezas naturais*. São Paulo: L. Oren Editora, 1973. 222 p. Basic information about geography, primary resources, agriculture, fishing, navigation, minerals, the infrastructure, and other topics. Illustrated with photographs of poor quality.

Bahia

227 Bahia. Secretaria de Indústria e Comércio. *Bahia: A Socio-Economic Profile*. Salvador: 1982. 103 p. A guide in English intended for potential investors, which outlines information on the state's economy, investment opportunities, credit and financial support, and technical and local support. Although it is aimed at a specific audience, the data presented is useful for a variety of other purposes.

228 Escola de Administração Fazendária do Estado da Bahia. *Cadastro municipal da Bahia*. Salvador: 1979. unpaged. Summarizes data on each município of the state in tabular format: area, population, demographic density, geographic coordinates, distance from capital, names of chief officials, election statistics, level of education, health services, agricultural production, communications, sanitation, and public finance are some of the topics covered.

229 _______. *Catálogo de informações sócio-econômicas dos municípios*. Salvador: 1984. 356 p. Data on demographic, physical, economic, social, cultural, and financial aspects of Bahian municípios in tabular format.

230 Fundação Cultural do Estado da Bahia. *A política cultural do Estado no quadriênio 1979-82: o desempenho da Fundação Cultural da Bahia neste contexto*. Salvador: 1983. 251 p. A record of cultural activities sponsored by the Fundação, which includes a year-by-year list of events in art, libraries, publishing (including a bibliography of works published by the agency), cinema, photography, dance, music, theatre, and miscellaneous events. Also provides an organization chart of the Fundação and its budget, as well as the names and addresses of cultural agencies associated with it. This is a useful work because of the significance of the Fundação

in promoting cultural life; it serves as an incomplete but important record of cultural activity of the period.

Ceará

231 Anuário do Estado do Ceará. Fortaleza: Stylus-Consultoria de Investimento, Publicidade e Planejamento. Current information on each município of the state, state government, health, education, the economy, cultural and religious activity, the infrastructure, and other aspects of life in the state. Includes portraits of officials and other leaders. Issues examined: 1971-1972.

232 Girão, Raimundo, and Antônio Martins. O Ceará. 3. ed. Fortaleza: Editora Instituto do Ceará, 1966. 547 p. Articles on many aspects of life in Ceará in an encyclopedic format. Provides basic information on each município, including brief biographical data on prominent citizens past and present. Other articles focus on topics such as education, religion, history and medicine.

233 Girão, Raimundo. Os municípios cearenses e seus distritos. Fortaleza: Superintendência do Desenvolvimento do Estado do Ceará--SUDEC, 1983. 384 p. Information provided for each município includes its area in square kilometers, altitude, geographic coordinates, latitude, longitude, districts, meaning of name, history (including former names), prominent natives, description of its physical setting, and limited bibliography.

234 Superintendência do Desenvolvimento do Estado do Ceará. Estudo geo-sócio-econômico do Estado do Ceará. 2 vols. Fortaleza: 1971-1972. A comprehensive survey of Ceará, providing detailed information on many aspects through text, statistical tables, charts, maps, graphs, and other means. Vol. 1: Recursos naturais; Vol. 2: Aspectos sócio-econômicos.

Espírito Santo

235 Anuário do Espírito Santo, 1973/1974-. Vitória: Precisa Publicidade e Assessoria Limitada. Up-to-date information on Espírito Santo with articles on each of its municípios, coverage of state government agencies, major industries, commercial enterprises, and cultural activities. Includes portraits of government officials, business leaders, and others. Issue examined: 1973/1974.

236 Espírito Santo. Secretaria da Industria e do Comércio. Informações infraestruturais. Vitória: 1981. 53 p. Text and statistics

provide data "sobre a realidade econômica e social do Espírito Santo" (Apresentação). The sectors of activity covered are those determined by the government to have development priority: the Centro Industrial de Grande Vitória, transportation, ports, communications, electric energy, water supply, housing, higher education, technical education, and the financial system. See also no. 238.

237 _______. _______. Manual de informações para empresários interessados em investir no Espírito Santo. Vitória: 1975. 48 leaves. An overview of the state with information on population, economic activity, support services, raw materials, the labor force, and similar subjects. A series of maps locates important geographic features and the physical infrastructure: airports, railroads, electrical generation plants.

238 ______. ______. Informações infraestruturais do Espírito Santo. Vitória: 1985. 53 p. A summary in statistics and text of the geography, population, social and economic conditions, infrastructure, and financial aspects of Espírito Santo. Updates information provided in earlier publications such as that found in no. 236.

239 Valle, Eurípedes Queiróz do. O Estado do Espírito Santo e os espírito-santenses: dados, fatos, e curiosidades (os 10 mais.... 3.ed. Vitória: Apex Gráfica e Editôra, 1971. 350 p. Brief data on many aspects of the state: geography, history, literature, biography, and others, citing "the ten most..." in each category. First edition published in 1959 under the title, Pequeno dicionário informativo do Estado do Espírito Santo.

Goiás

240 Goiás. Secretaria da Indústria e Comércio. Guia do investidor: informações básicas. Goiânia: 1978. 191 p. Basic data about the state of Goiás--its geography, economic activity, communications, transportation, energy, tax legislation, public finance, and incentives for business and industry.

241 _______. _______. Levantamento histórico e econômico dos municípios goianos. 3. ed. n.p.: 1973. 423 p. Brief historical data on the origins of each micro-region and the municípios comprising it, and information on present-day communications and transportation. Includes contemporary statistics.

242 Lisita, Ciro. Dicionário enciclopédico de Goiás. Goiânia: Editôra Universidade Católica de Goiás, 1984. 376 p. 3068 entries

including 258 providing biographical data, and others on places, local vocabulary, organizations, etc. Longer articles provide an overview of the state and cover topics such as the press, sports, and other aspects of life there. Many illustrations.

Maranhão

243 Perfil do Maranhão, 1979. São Luís: Prelo Comunicação, 1980. 343 p. A good overview of many aspects of life in the state. Subjects covered include physical setting, history, the economy, state government, municípios, social conditions, natural resources, culture, religion, tourism, demography, literature, higher education, business, and statistics. Provides biographical data about politicians, writers, artists, and others.

Mato Grosso

244 Rondón, Lucídio. Recursos econômicos de Mato Grosso: terras, águas, potenciais e usinas hidrelétricas, revestimentos vegetativos, faunas--aquática e terrestre, indústria, agricultura, pecuária, exportação, população, vias de transportes. São Paulo: 1972. 236 p. Summarizes the varied resources of economic value to be found in Mato Grosso, and in doing so gives a good overview of many facets of the state.

Mato Grosso do Sul

245 Fundação Brasileira de Geografia e Estatística. Mato Grosso do Sul. Rio de Janeiro: 1979. 163 p. The geography, demography, and economic activity of the state is presented in text, statistical tables, color photographs, and maps.

Minas Gerais

246 Barbosa, Waldemar de Almeida. Dicionário da terra e da gente de Minas. Belo Horizonte: Arquivo Público Mineiro, 1985. 208 p. A dictionary of terms associated with Minas Gerais. Excludes biography. Cites sources of information.

247 Minas Gerais. Secretaria de Estado do Governo. Coordenaria de Cultura. Guia de entidades culturais. 3. ed. Belo Horizonte, 1982. 139 p. Names and addresses of cultural groups and organizations arranged by type of activity: artisanry, art, libraries, cinema, dance, music, drama, and others.

248 Minas Gerais. Superintendência de Estatística e Informações. Minas Gerais: municípios e localidades. Belo Horizonte: 1977. unpaged. Basic information in tabular format about 6299 places in the state. Each place is categorized (povoado, lugarejo, cidade, etc.), its district and município is identified, and the number of dwellings and commercial and industrial establishments is given. Population and area of each município are listed in a separate section.

249 Pinto, Wellington Almeida. Minas: dicionário estatístico, geográfico e histórico de Minas Gerais. Belo Horizonte: Edita-Grupo Editorial e Jornalístico, 1983. 144 p. A dictionary of Minas Gerais emphasizing geographic and statistical information, thereby complementing to some degree the work by Waldemar de Almeida Barbosa, Dicionário histórico geográfico de Minas Gerais, (no. 246), which is chiefly historical. It concentrates on the state's municípios, providing current statistical and descriptive data. The officials of each one are listed in a separate section.

Pará

250 Loureiro, João de Jesus Paes, and Violeta Refkalefsky Loureiro. Inventário cultural e turístico do Baixo Tocantins. 2. ed. Belém: Instituto do Desenvolvimento Econômico-Social do Pará; Secretaria de Estado da Cultura; Fundação Cultural Tancredo Neves; Companhia Paraense de Turismo, 1987. 87 p.

251 Loureiro, Violeta Refkalefsky, João de Jesus Paes Loureiro; and Camilo Martins Viana. Inventário cultural e turístico do Salgado. 2. ed. Belém: Instituto do Desenvolvimento Econômico-Social do Pará; Secretaria de Estado da Cultura; Fundação Cultural Tancredo Neves; Companhia Paraense de Turismo, 1987. 77 p.

252 Nascimento, Aldenor Gonçalves do; João de Jesus Paes Loureiro; and Violeta Refkalefsky Loureiro. Inventário cultural e turístico da Bragantina. Belém: Instituto do Desenvolvimento Econômico; Secretaria de Estado da Cultura; Fundação Cultural Tancredo Neves; Companhia Paraense de Turismo, 1987. 57 p. Surveys of folklore and cultural events in the municípios of three areas of the state of Pará, including description, calendars of events, photographs of poor quality, and other material. These reedições were originally published in 1981, 1979, and 1982 respectively, and according to the introductions they contain updated information.

Pernambuco

253 Enciclopédia dos municípios. Recife: Fundação de Desenvolvimento

Municipal do Interior de Pernambuco, Secretaria de Planejamento, 1982-. A multi-volume work, planned to provide detailed data about 155 municípios of the interior of the state in text, photographs, and statistics. Information includes history, location, population, natural resources, infrastructure, transportation, communications, economic activities, education, health services, and housing for each one. Twenty-seven municípios (from Afogados da Ingazeira to Buíque) are covered in the first volume (239 p.)

254 Sette, Débora. O guia do guia pernambucano: geografia, história, arquitetura, artesanato, folclore, roteiros. Recife: Editora Raiz, 1987. 216 p. This work, prepared by an experienced tourist guide, provides information about Pernambuco in the areas described in the title.

255 Silva, Leonardo Dantas. Pequeno calendário histórico cultural de Pernambuco. Recife: Secretaria de Educação e Cultura, 1977. 56 p. A month-by-month list of historical occasions and cultural events in Pernambuco. Includes events observed on a regular basis, such as civic and religious holidays, and annual exhibitions.

Piauí

256 Piauí: caminhos da industrialização. Teresina: Governo do Estado do Piauí, Secretaria de Indústria e Comércio, 1988. unpaged. A profile of the state in Portuguese and English with information on its physical, economic, and social aspects, and the infrastructure for the support of industry. Includes statistical tables, maps, and many illustrations.

257 Piauí: visão sumária. 3. ed. Teresina: Governo do Estado do Piauí, Fundação Secretaria de Planejamento, Fundação Centro de Pesquisas Econômicas e Sociais do Piauí--CEPRO, 1982. 53 p. An overview of the state in terms of its geography, population, communications, transportation, energy, health resources, and economic activity. Illustrated with color maps and photographs. A 1974 edition was published by the Fundação Centro Regional de Produtividade do Piauí.

Rio de Janeiro

258 Nosso estado, nosso governo: Estado do Rio de Janeiro, 1979-1983. Rio de Janeiro: Secretaria de Planejamento e Coordenação Geral, 1983. 176 p. A survey prepared at the end of the administration of Governor Chagas Freitas, comprised of two parts. The first provides a social and economic profile of the state through statistics and text; the second summarizes

the activities of government agencies, emphasizing economic development and social services during the period covered.

259 Pérfil sócio-econômico do Estado do Rio de Janeiro. Rio de Janeiro: LIGHT--Serviços de Eletricidade S.A., 1985. 234 p. Text, statistics, and maps provide a detailed socio-economic profile of the state.

Rio Grande do Sul

260 Aspectos sócio-econômicos dos municípios do Rio Grande do Sul. Alegre: Governo do Estado do Rio Grande do Sul, Secretaria da Indústria e Comércio. Covers the socio-economic and financial characteristics and the infrastructure of the 244 municípios of Rio Grande do Sul in a tabular format. Appendix provides statistical data for the state as a whole. Editions examined: 1984/1985; 1986/1987.

261 Fagundes, Antonio Augusto. Indumentária gaúcha. 3. ed. Porto Alegre: Martins Livreiro, 1986. 80 p. Illustrates traditional costumes of the state.

262 Stedile Zattera, Vera. Traje típico gaúcho. Traditional Dress of the Gaucho. Porto Alegre: VSZ-Arte e Cultura; Caxias do Sul: Universidade de Caxias do Sul, 1989. 132 p. Excellent color and black and white illustrations depict typical regional dress over time beginning with the Indians and the colonial period and ending with contemporary dress. The text is bilingual (Portuguese and English). Includes a bibliography.

Rondônia

263 Rondônia (Territory). Secretaria da Educação e Cultura. Calendário cultural: 1981/1985. São Paulo: Imprensa Oficial do Estado de São Paulo, 1981. 133 p. A calendar of events related to a variety of activities.

264 Rondônia. Secretaria de Planejamento. Divisão de Apoio Técnico e Articulação com os Municípios. Levantamento básico dos municípios e distritos de Rondônia. n.p.: 1980. 193 leaves. Covers geo-political, economic, social, and other aspects of each município in the Federal Territory of Rondônia in text and statistics. Includes a useful map of political/administrative divisions.

São Paulo

265 Armorial paulista. São Paulo: Secretaria de Estado da Cultura,

1982. unpaged. Color illustrations, descriptions, and references to the laws establishing the coats of arms of the state of São Paulo and of its municípios.

266 Federici, Hilton. Símbolos paulistas: estudo histórico-heráldico. São Paulo: Conselho Estadual de Artes e Ciências Humanas, 1981. 101 p. Illustrations and history of flags, coats of arms and other symbols of the state, along with citations to laws associated with them.

267 Os melhores de São Paulo, 1956-1982. São Paulo: Imprensa Oficial do Estado, 1983. unpaged. Lists awards made by the Associação Paulista de Críticos de Artes over a twenty-seven year period in theatre, art music, art, literature, children's literature, children's theatre, popular music, radio, dance, cinema, and television. Important as a reflection of the view of excellence in the arts in a major cultural center.

GENERAL SOURCES--CITIES

Rio de Janeiro

268 Campos, Alexandre. Dicionário de curiosidades do Rio de Janeiro. São Paulo: Comércio e Importação de Livros, 1965. 304 p. A dictionary of people, places, and terms associated with the city, illustrated with photographs and line drawings of poor quality.

269 Brazil. Ministério das Relações Exteriores. Mapoteca. Catálogo de plantas e mapas da cidade do Rio de Janeiro. Rio de Janeiro: 1966. 171 p. An annotated catalog of plans and maps of the city of Rio de Janeiro from the sixteenth through the twentieth centuries. Thorough indexing provides access to features of the maps, such as specific fazendas, roads, aqueducts, etc.

270 Informações básicas da Cidade do Rio de Janeiro. Rio de Janeiro: Secretaria Municipal de Planejamento. Statistical tables providing quantitative data about demography, commerce, public health, education, urban services and other aspects of life in Rio de Janeiro. Cites sources for the statistics. Editions examined: 1979, 1981/1982, 1981/1984.

271 Rio antigo: roteiro turístico cultural do centro da cidade. Rio de Janeiro: EMBRATUR-AGGS, 1979. 201 p. Identifies, locates, describes, and gives the history of important points of tourist and cultural interest in the center of the city. Includes a good bibliography.

272 Rio de Janeiro (City). Secretaria Municipal de Planejamento e Coordenação Geral. Bairros do Município do Rio de Janeiro. Rio de Janeiro: 198-? 122 p. Defines the administrative regions of Rio de Janeiro and describes the geographic boundaries of its bairros. Includes an excellent map delineating the area encompassed by each bairro.

273 Silva, J. Romão da. Denominações indígenas na toponímia carioca. Rio de Janeiro: Livraria Editora Brasiliana, 1966. 341 p. Identification and etymology of streets, praças, and other places with Indian names in the city of Rio de Janeiro.

São Paulo

274 Empresa Metropolitana de Planejamento da Grande São Paulo. A Grande São Paulo hoje. São Paulo: 1982. 105 p. Text, statistical tables and attractive color maps outline the history of the metropolitan area including its spatial development and the growth of its economy. A bibliography and index complement the information presented.

AGRICULTURE

Although agriculture might reasonably be expected to fall outside the scope of this bibliography, a few basic publications useful to specialists have been included. Specialized dictionaries and bibliographies covering economic, historic, and social aspects of agriculture as well as its technology are examples. A few works related to agricultural products of great significance in Brazilian history and economic development, such as coffee, are also cited.

BIBLIOGRAPHY

275 Bibliografia brasileira de agricultura. vol. 1-, 1975/1977-. Brasília: Empresa Brasileira de Assistência Técnica e Extensão Rural. This publication, which is projected to be published annually, cites monographs, theses, periodical articles, legislative acts, and maps which are related to agriculture in its technical, economic, and social aspects. In addition to the usual bibliographic information, titles are translated into English. Supersedes the Bibliografia brasileira de ciências agrícolas (no. 276).

276 Bibliografia brasileira de ciências agrícolas. vol. 1-, 1967/1968-. vol. 8, 1974/1975. Rio de Janeiro. Although this is principally a bibliography related to technical aspects of agriculture, it covers social and economic aspects also through such topics as land reform, prices, cooperatives, markets, agricultural economics, and others. Superseded by the Bibliografia brasileira de agricultura (above).

277 Bibliografia cana-de-açúcar. vol. 1-, 1817/1976-. Brasília: BINAGRI; Piracicaba: PLANALSUCAR, 1979-. Includes entries related to economics, rural sociology, agricultural and industrial policy, and other topics related to the social sciences, although it emphasizes technical aspects of sugar culture and production. Volumes examined: 1, 2.

278 Bibliografia do café. Brasília: Sistema Nacional de Informação e Documentação Agrícola, Coordenação de Informação Rural. An unannotated bibliography of Brazilian publications on coffee, covering the years 1860 to the mid-1970's. Although the emphasis is on technical aspects of coffee culture and processing, there are also sections devoted to its history, politics, and economics. At least three volumes have been published: 1 (1975), 2 (1977), and 3 (1984).

279 Biblioteca Nacional de Agricultura. Bibliografia de agroindústria. Levantamentos bibliográficos, 2. Brasília: BINAGRI, 1979. 88 p. An unannotated bibliography, international in scope, of books, pamphlets, reports, and periodical articles on agribusiness. Many of the publications cited deal with Brazil.

280 Carvalho, Eliezita Romcy. Bibliografia de estatística. Brasília: EMBRAPA. Departamento de Informação e Documentação, 1982. 306 p. An unannotated bibliography citing 714 publications on theoretical and applied statistics with emphasis on their application to agriculture. Arranged by broad subjects, with author and detailed subject indexes.

281 Comissão Executiva do Plano da Lavoura Cacaueira. Centro de Pesquisas no Cacau. Catálogo de teses. Ilhéus: 1982. 161 p. An annotated bibliography of theses in this center's library, many related to social, historical, and economic aspects of agriculture in general, and cacau culture more specifically.

282 Pinto, Aloísio de Arruda, and Maria das Graças Moreira Ferreira. Bibliografia das bibliografias agrícolas do Brasil. Série bibliografia especializada, 6. Viçosa: Universidade Federal de Viçosa, Biblioteca Central, 1974. 86 p. An unannotated bibliography of 438 bibliographies related to agriculture, including those appearing in periodicals.

283 Planejamento agrícola no nordeste do Brasil no período 1960-1980. Levantamentos bibliográficos, 4. Brasília: Biblioteca Nacional de Agricultura, 1981. 164 p. This unannotated bibliography of 878 entries related to agricultural planning cites many publications focusing on policy and on the social and economic aspects of agriculture.

CENSUS MATERIALS

VIII recenseamento geral, 1970

284 Fundação Instituto Brasileiro de Geografia e Estatística. Censo agropecuário. 24 vols. VIII recenseamento geral, 1970. Série

regional, vol. 3. Rio de Janeiro: Ministério de Planejamento e Coordenação Geral, IBGE, Diretoria Técnica, Superintendência de Estatísticas Primárias, Departamento de Censos, 1974-. Detailed statistics for agriculture and livestock-raising at the microregion and município levels, based on the census of 1970.

285 _______. Censo agropecuário: Brasil. VIII recenseamento geral, 1970: Série nacional, vol. 3. Rio de Janeiro: Secretaria de Planejamento da Presidência da República, IBGE, Superintendência de Estatísticas Primárias, Departamento de Censos, 1975. 299 p. A summary of agricultural and livestock-raising statistics at the national and state levels, based on the census of 1970.

Censos econômicos de 1975

286 Fundação Instituto Brasileiro de Geografia e Estatística. Censo agropecuária. 24 vols. Censos econômicos de 1975: Série regional, vol. 1. Rio de Janeiro: IBGE, 1979. Detailed statistics for agriculture and livestock-raising at the microregion and município levels, based on the economic census of 1975.

287 _______. Censo agropecuário: Brasil. Censos econômicos de 1975: Série nacional. Rio de Janeiro: IBGE: 1979. 469 p. A summary of agriculture and livestock-raising at the state and national levels, based on the economic census of 1975.

IX recenseamento geral do Brasil--1980

288 Fundação Instituto Brasileiro de Geografia e Estatística. Censo agropecuária. 26 vols. IX recenseamento geral do Brasil--1980: vol. 2, tomo 3. Rio de Janeiro: IBGE, 1983-1984. The first volume summarizes agricultural and livestock-raising statistics for the country as a whole, and on a state-by-state basis, and the other twenty-five volumes supply more detailed statistics for each state by microregion and by município.

Censos econômicos, 1985

289 Fundação Instituto Brasileiro de Geografia e Estatística. Sinopse preliminar do censo agropecuário. Censos econômicos, 1985, vol. 4, no. 1-. Rio de Janeiro: IBGE, 1987-. A preliminary summary of the agricultural and livestock-raising census of 1985 by macroregion. Volumes examined: 1: Região Norte; 5: Região Centro Oeste. 6: Brasil.

OTHER SOURCES

290 Brazil. Ministério da Agricultura. Secretaria de Desenvolvimento Administrativo. Orgãos, entidades e titulares: setor público agrícola. Brasília: 1988. 177 p. A directory of federal and state agencies and other institutions involved in national agricultural policy and production. Information includes name of entity and its chief executive, address, and telephone number. Loose-leaf format, with the provision of revised information planned.

291 Brazil. Sistema Nacional de Planejamento Agrícola. Unidade Central. Areas de concentração de agricultura brasileira. 4 vols. Brasília? 1979? Maps and statistical tables at the município level locate the areas devoted to the cultivation of many agricultural products and record the production of each area. A calendar for each crop marks the appropriate months for soil preparation, planting, cultivation, and harvest. A very useful source for agricultural planners, and those studying land use, agricultural economics, and economic geography.

292 Instituto Brasileiro de Economia. Centro de Estudos Agrícolas. Produção agrícola brasileira: municípios mais importantes. Rio de Janeiro: Fundação Getúlio Vargas, 1986. 188 p. Statistical tables indicating municípios responsible for one percent or more of the Brazilian production of eighteen principal agricultural products, milk, wool, and livestock. Shows the quantity produced and its relation to total Brazilian production.

293 Instituto Brasileiro do Café. Café: legislação brasileira 1952/1977. Rio de Janeiro: 1978. 426 p. "...uma coletânea de atos normativos sobre café, que facilita a pesquisa histórica da política seguida pelo Brasil desde 1952." Arranged in chronological order, this list is intended to be as complete as possible. It includes federal legislation, resolutions and communications of the Instituto Brasileiro do Café, the Banco Central, and other government agencies. Essential to anyone studying the politics of coffee and its implications for other aspects of Brazilian life for the twenty-five year period covered.

294 ______. Departamento Econômico. ABC do café. 2. ed. Rio de Janeiro, 1973. 73 p. A glossary of terms used in coffee culture and in the coffee trade.

295 Lima, José Luís; Iraci del Nero da Costa; and Francisco Vidal Luna. Estatísticas básicas do setor agrícola no Brasil. 2 vols. Série estatísticas básicas da economia brasileira, vol. 2-3. São Paulo: Instituto de Pesquisas Econômicas, 1983-1985. A statistical compilation focusing on agricultural exports

and production for internal consumption. Volume 1 presents statistics in series for eight traditional exports: sugar, cotton, rubber, cacao, coffee, hides, mate, and tobacco from the earliest dates of export through 1980, as well as statistics for three recent exports: oranges, orange juice, and soy bean products. It also includes agricultural exports in the aggregate, 1821-1980 and statistics on agricultural production for the internal market. Volume 2 provides data on the export of peanut oil, jute, meat and poultry, and on the production of many agricultural products, as well as meat and poultry.

296 Morais, Clodomir Santo de. Diccionario de reforma agrária: Latinoamérica. 2. ed. San Jose: Editorial Universitaria Centroamericana, 1983. 533 p. A dictionary defining terms used in Latin American countries, related to agrarian reform in all its aspects. Contains a significant number of Brazilian terms, including many regional ones. Covers agricultural, legal, social and economic aspects as well as terms associated with agricultural implements, rural workers' associations, weights and measures, forms of tenancy, etc. Introduction by Josué de Castro, well-known Brazilian agrarian reform activist.

ARCHITECTURE

BIBLIOGRAPHIES

297 Corona, Eduardo, and Lúcio Gomes Machado. Bibliografia mínima para escolas de arquitetura. São Paulo: Associação Brasileira de Escolas de Arquitetura, 1976. 168 p. A general bibliography of basic works in the field of architecture, which cites many Brazilian publications.

298 De Fiore, Ottaviano C. Architecture and Sculpture in Brazil. The Brazilian Curriculum Guide Specialized Bibliography. Albuquerque: Latin American Institute, University of New Mexico, 198-? 33 leaves. Summarizes the development of architectural styles and sculpture from colonial days to the present and provides a partially annotated bibliography which emphasizes architecture.

299 Indice de arquitetura brasileira 1950-1970. Pesquisa e coordenação Eunice R. Ribeiro Costa e Maria Stella de Castilho. São Paulo: Universidade de São Paulo, Faculdade de Arquitetura e Urbanismo, Biblioteca, 1974. 661 p. Sixteen thousand author and subject citations of articles from fifteen important Brazilian journals in the fields of architecture, construction and engineering, and articles related to the historic and artistic patrimony. The content of an earlier publication, Indice de arquitetura brasileira, 1967-1969, issued by the same publisher in 1970, is incorporated into this work.

300 Indice de arquitetura brasileira, 1971-1980. Pesquisa e coordenação Eunice R. Ribeiro Costa. Brasília: Ministério da Educação e Cultura, Secretaria de Educação Superior, Subsecretaria do Desenvolvimento da Educação Superior e Universidade de São Paulo, Faculdade de Arquitetura e Urbanismo, Biblioteca, 1982. 313 p. Continues to index the journals covered in Indice de arquitetura brasileira 1950-1970 (above) while adding four new titles for a total of nineteen. Uses the same author and subject access as the earlier publication.

DICTIONARIES

301 Avila, Affonso, João Marcos Machado Gontijo, and Reinaldo Guedes Machado. Barroco mineiro: glossário de arquitetura e ornamentação. São Paulo: Fundação João Pinheiro; Fundação Roberto Marinho; Companhia Editora Nacional, 1980. 220 p. A handsome dictionary of terms associated with the baroque architecture and decoration of Minas Gerais, illustrated with many line drawings and photographs. A short, introductory essay, a glossary of weights and measures of the period, and a bibliography complete this useful work.

302 Corona, Eduardo, and Carlos A. C. Lemos. Dicionário da arquitetura brasileira. São Paulo: Edart--São Paulo: Livraria Editora, 1972. 479 p. An illustrated dictionary of terms pertaining to Brazilian architecture, including both historical and contemporary definitions when meanings have changed over time.

OTHER SOURCES

303 Banco Nacional da Habitação. BNH: projetos sociais. Rio de Janeiro: 1979. 239 p. Information, statistics, photographs, and plans for forty housing projects financed by the BNH over a period of thirteen years. The floor plans for single-family dwellings and apartment buildings are useful examples of the layouts of typical Brazilian housing.

304 Barbosa, Antonio. Relíquias da Paraíba: guia aos monumentos históricos e barrocos de João Pessôa e Cabedelo. Rio de Janeiro, Eu e Você, 1985. 117 p. Focuses on churches, forts, educational institutions, and other buildings of the colonial period. Many color photographs. Although the text is intended for tourists, this guide provides useful information about historic buildings of Brazil that are not widely known.

305 Câmara de Souza, Oswaldo. Acervo do patrimônio histórico e artístico do Estado do Rio Grande do Norte. Natal: Fundação José Augusto, 1981. 427 p. Short essays illustrated by photographs of poor quality describe major historic buildings and sites of the state.

306 Carrazzoni, Maria Elisa. Guia dos bens tombados: Brasil. 2. ed. Rio de Janeiro: Expressão e Cultura, 1987. 534 p. A state-by-state guide to 924 historical buildings protected by the Secretaria do Patrimônio Histórico e Artístico Nacional (SPAHN). Provides a history and description of each

building, as well as the name of its owner, the date of "tombamento," its current use, and bibliography related to it. Line drawings depict some of the buildings. Includes a glossary of architectural and construction terms and a general bibliography. First edition published in 1980 under the title, Guia dos bens tombados.

307 Costa, Irio Barbosa da and Helena Maria Mesquita. Tipos de habitação rural no Brasil. Rio de Janeiro: Superintendência de Recursos Naturais e Meio-Ambiente (SUPREN), 1978. 72 p. Photographs, line drawings, and floor plans of rural houses in all areas of Brazil, accompanied by descriptive text and brief notes on the socio-economic factors influencing their design. Bibliography.

308 Fabris, Annateresa. Ecletismo na arquitetura brasileira. São Paulo: Nobel; Edusp, 1987. 296 p. Photographs of buildings and architectural details, text, extensive notes, and bibliography contribute to this survey of eclecticism in Brazilian architecture of the nineteenth and twentieth centuries in Rio de Janeiro, São Paulo, Minas Gerais, Pará, Pernambuco, Ceará, and Rio Grande do Sul, along with a chapter on European eclecticism for background.

309 Ficher, Sylvia, and Marlene Milan Acayaba. Arquitetura moderna brasileira. São Paulo: Projeto, 1982. 124 p. An amply illustrated overview of all types of modern Brazilian architecture from the late 1920's to the present. Covers its origins, its development in major cities, Brasília, and regional trends since 1960. Although the quality of the illustrations is only fair, their variety and quantity make this a useful visual reference source.

309a Fundação do Patrimônio Histórico e Artístico de Pernambuco. Inventário do Patrimônio Cultural do Estado de Pernambuco: Sertão do São Francisco. Recife? 1987. 282 p. A detailed inventory of the architectural patrimony of a microregion of the state, including brief historical notes, physical description, current physical condition, floor plan, bibliography, and a photograph of poor quality of each monument.

310 Fundação João Pinheiro. Assessoria Técnica da Presidência. Atlas dos monumentos históricos e artísticos de Minas Gerais: circuito de Santa Bárbara. Belo Horizonte: 1981?- This unillustrated work describes monuments of historic and architectural interest, placing them in their historical context. Volume examined: 2, Região de Santa Bárbara, part 1 (1981); Volume 1, Sabará, is cited in vol. 2, but was not examined.

311 Fundação Nacional Pró-Memória. Bens móveis e imóveis inscritos nos livros do tombo do Patrimônio Histórico e Artístico Nacional.

Brasília: Subsecretaria do Patrimônio Histórico e Artístico Nacional, 1982. 195 p. A state-by-state list of buildings and places designated as part of the national patrimony, with the dates of designation, and citations for the records in which they are registered.

312 Gaspar, Byron. Fontes e chafarizes de São Paulo. São Paulo: Conselho Estadual de Cultura, 1970. 138 p. Description and history of thirty-eight ornamental fountains and public watering places of São Paulo, with drawings depicting them and a map locating them.

313 Guia dos bens tombados: Bahia. Rio de Janeiro: Expressão e Cultura, 1983. 323 p. A guide to protected historic buildings in the state of Bahia.

314 Habitaçoes indígenas. São Paulo: Livraria Nobel; Editora da Universidade de São Paulo, 1983. 196 p. This collection of essays by various authors is useful for reference because it covers several indigenous groups in short sections, and has excellent illustrations and a good bibliography. In addition to photographs of finished dwellings, there are many sketches illustrating the details of various phases of construction, and drawings and aerial photographs depicting the typical layouts of the villages of different tribes.

315 Maia, Tom, and Thereza Regina Camargo de Maia. Velha Bahia de hoje. Bilingual ed. Rio de Janeiro: Expressão e Cultura, 1985. unpaged. Line drawings of historic buildings in Bahia with descriptive text in Portuguese and English.

316 Maia, Tom; Thereza Regina de Camargo Maia; and Pedro Calmon. Velho Brasil de hoje. Rio de Janeiro: Expressão e Cultura, 1983. 328 p. Line drawings of 150 historic buildings all over the country which reflect its Portuguese heritage. Brief text provides information about each one. Includes a bibliography.

317 Maranhão. Secretaria da Cultura. Departamento do Patrimônio Histórico, Artístico e Paisagístico. Bens tombados no Maranhão: tombamentos estaduais. São Luís: 1987. 82 p. A guide to historic buildings protected by the state government of Maranhão, illustrated with excellent color photographs and line drawings. Includes a glossary and a bibliography.

318 Maurício, Augusto. Igrejas históricas do Rio de Janeiro. Nova ed., atualizada. Rio de Janeiro: Livraria Kosmos/SEEC--Secretaria Estadual de Educação e Cultura, 1978. 286 p. Histories and descriptions of outstanding features of thirty-eight historic churches of Rio de Janeiro. Includes photographs of fair quality. Originally published in 1947 under the title, Templos históricos do Rio de Janeiro.

319. Reis, Nestor Goulart. Guia dos bens tombados: São Paulo. 2. ed. Rio de Janeiro: Expressão e Cultura, 1985. 192 p. A guide to historical buildings under the protection of the Conselho de Defesa do Patrimônio Histórico, Artístico, Arqueológico e Turístico de São Paulo. Information for each building includes a history and description, location, owner, date of "tombamento," current use, and related bibliography. A line drawing of each building enhances the text. First edition issued in 1982.

320 Rodrigues, José Wasth. Documentário arquitetônico relativo à antiga construçao civil no Brasil. São Paulo: Editora da Universidade de São Paulo; Livraria Martins Editora, 1975. 324 p. Descriptions and illustrations of the details of colonial buildings, emphasizing those with secular uses, including residences. Doors, windows, iron grilles and railings, ceramic tiles and many other features are treated in this excellent visual source.

321 Silva, Geraldo Gomes da. Arquitetura do ferro no Brasil. São Paulo: Nobel, 1986. 248 p. A history in text, photographs, and line drawings of iron buildings prefabricated in Europe and imported to Brazil from the mid-nineteenth century on.

322 Souza, Wladimir Alves de. Guia dos bens tombados: Minas Gerais. 2. ed. Rio de Janeiro: Expressão e Cultura, 1985. 446 p. A guide to protected historical buildings in the state of Minas Gerais. First edition: 1984; preface to first edition by Tancredo Neves and to second edition by Aureliano Chaves.

323 Telles, Augusto Carlos da Silva. Atlas dos monumentos históricos e artísticos do Brasil. Rio de Janeiro: FENAME--Fundação Nacional de Material Escolar, DAC--Departamento de Assuntos Culturais, 1975. 347 p. A collection of photographs of historic buildings, many of which are also noted for their architectural features or the decoration of their interiors. The accompanying text summarizes the history of each building, and notes the outstanding features. Occasional sketches elaborate on architectural detail. Although most of this publication is devoted to the sixteenth through nineteenth centuries, one chapter covers contemporary buildings. Includes a glossary of technical terms used in the text, and a bibliography. An excellent source for the history of religious and secular architecture.

ART

PAINTING AND SCULPTURE

Bibliography

324 Handbook of Latin American Art. Manual de arte latinoamericano: A Bibliographic Compilation. 3 vols. Santa Barbara, CA: ABC-Clio Information Services, 1984-1986. This excellent annotated bibliography, covering general references for Latin American art and architecture, as well as the art and architecture of the colonial period and the nineteenth and twentieth centuries, includes many citations for Brazil.

325 Rego, Stella de Sá, and Marguerite Itamar Harrison. Modern Brazilian Painting. The Brazilian Curriculum Guide Specialized Bibliography. Albuquerque: Latin American Institute, University of New Mexico, 198-? 42 leaves. A concise, twenty-page overview of nineteenth and twentieth century painting precedes a good, annotated bibliography of the subject.

326 Universidade de São Paulo. Escola de Comunicações e Artes. Biblioteca. Balanço da modernidade: bibliografia. São Paulo: 1986. 34 p. An unannotated bibliography of modernism in painting and sculpture, international in scope, but focusing on Brazil. Covers books, theses, journal articles, exhibition catalogs, and slides available in the library which published the bibliography.

327 _______. _______. _______. Expressionismo: bibliografia. São Paulo: 1985. 59 p. A bibliography of expressionism as it is manifested in art, cinema, theatre, and music, citing materials in the library responsible for preparing it. Although the bibliography is international in scope, it includes many publications on expressionism in Brazil. Cites recordings, scores, art exhibition catalogs, and slides, in addition to publications. Unannotated.

328 Yolanda, Regina. O livro infantil e juvenil brasileiro: bibliografia de ilustradores. São Paulo: Melhoramentos; Brasília: Instituto Nacional do Livro, 1977. 151 p. A bibliography of the work of illustrators of children's books, past and contemporary. Includes fiction, poetry, drama, and biography. Excludes textbooks. Under each illustrator's name are listed the authors, titles, and publication data of the books illustrated. Black-and-white reproductions of some of the illustrations are interspersed throughout the text.

Other Sources

329 Alves, Marieta. Dicionário de artistas e artífices na Bahia. Salvador: Universidade Federal da Bahia, Centro Editorial e Didático, Núcleo de Publicações, 1976. 210 p. A biographical dictionary of artists and artisans of Bahia from 1549 through the nineteenth century. Entries include the source of the information. Indexed by type of art practiced.

330 Amaral, Araci Abreu. Arte y arquitectura del modernismo brasileño: 1917-1930. Caracas: Biblioteca Ayacucho, 1978. 236 p. A collection of essays and articles, written by well-known artists, architects, and critics in the 1920's and 1930's. Emiliano Di Cavalcanti, Mário de Andrade, Tarsila do Amaral, and Lúcio Costa are some of the authors represented. The articles, on important topics such as the Semana de Arte Moderna, the architectural theories of LeCorbusier, and critical comments on art exhibitions, represent the highlights of the art and architecture scene of this period. Illustrations (some color) enhance the reference value of this work, as does a chronology of modernism. An introductory essay provides an overview of this important era in Brazilian art history.

331 _______. Artes plásticas na Semana de 22: subsídios para uma história das artes no Brasil. 2. ed. São Paulo: Perspective; Editora da Universidade de São Paulo, 1972. 333 p. Information on this important event is presented in a well-indexed narrative, enhanced with numerous illustrations, biographical data on the participants, texts of major speeches, and a good bibliography.

332 Anuário artes plásticas. São Paulo: Departamento de Informação e Documentação Artísticas, Centro de Pesquisa de Arte Brasileira, 1977- . A record of many of the art exhibitions held in São Paulo during the year covered. Quotes extensive excerpts from exhibition catalogs, critical reviews, and other sources. The only edition found was for the year 1977, but the significance of São Paulo as a major cultural center makes even this limited coverage important.

333 Aquino, Flávio de. Aspectos da arte primitiva brasileira. Aspects of Brazilian Primitive Painting. New York: Alpine Fine Arts Collection, 1981. 195 p. About sixty primitive painters from the period of the late 1940's to the present are represented. Excellent color reproductions of examples of their works are complemented by biographical sketches. The text in English and Portuguese surveys Brazilian primitive art. An indispensable source for the study of this subject. Originally published in 1978 (Rio de Janeiro: Spala Editora).

334 L'art au Brésil. Berne: Ministère de Rélations Extérieures du Brésil, 196-? 171 p. Brief summaries of the contemporary state of art, music, cinema and theatre in Brazil are followed by biographical data about major practitioners of these arts. Includes illustrations. The work closes with a list of museums in each state.

335 Arte baiana hoje. n.p.: Raizes, 1983. 112 p. Color reproductions of the works and brief notes about the artistic careers of forty-eight contemporary Bahian artists.

336 Ayala, Walmir. O Brasil por seus artistas. Brazil Through Its Artists. São Paulo: Círculo do Livro; Rio de Janeiro; Editorial Nórdica, 1979? 211 p. Although the purpose of this work is to present a picture of Brazilian life, landscapes, and symbols through the eyes of artists, and it is organized to reflect that purpose, it is also a useful source of biographical information in Portuguese and English about approximately 100 twentieth century artists. An excellent color reproduction representing the work of each artist is accompanied by bilingual text about his life and work. The lack of an index is a flaw that makes its use as a reference source awkward, but it can be easily scanned to determine whether information about a particular artist is included.

337 Bardi, Pietro Maria. Profile of the New Brazilian Art. Rio de Janeiro: Livraria Kosmos Editora, 1970. 160 p. The preface describes this work as a "general survey of the best that Brazil is producing in the arts." Its three sections, comprised mainly of color and black-and-white illustrations, deal with art of the Indians, popular art, and art of many types produced by professional artists. The latter category includes painting, architecture, sculpture, commercial art, clothing, jewelry, furniture design, stage settings and other aspects of art. The "General Index" provides brief biographical notes and often portraits of the artists represented. It is especially useful for those outside the fields of painting and sculpture, who may not be found in other sources. Text in English.

338 Bardi, Pietro Maria, and Jacob Klintowitz. Um século de escultura no Brasil. One Century of Sculpture in Brazil. São Paulo: 1982. 152 p. A visual survey of Brazilian sculpture, 1870 to the early 1980's. In addition to excellent photographs of the pieces of sculpture, the places and dates of the births and deaths of the sculptors are given, when known, and the titles of the pieces, their dates, mediums, and heights are included. The lack of an index of sculptors is an unfortunate omission in this otherwise useful work.

339 Batista, Marta Rossetti, Telê Porto Ancona Lopez, and Yone Soares de Lima. Brasil: I.° tempo modernista--1917/29: documentação. São Paulo: Instituto de Estudos Brasileiros, Universidade de São Paulo, 1972. 459 p. A collection of key documents associated with the beginning of Brazilian modernism in architecture, art, literature, and music. Also includes the catalog of an exhibition on the same topic and a bibliography.

340 Bienal Internacional de São Paulo. Catálogo. São Paulo: Fundação Bienal de São Paulo. The catalog of this major international event held bienially summarizes the works representing each country, and lists each artist exhibiting along with the medium, title, and size of the work. Also provides a list of jury members, the text of the regulations governing the event, a list of prizes, and artists winning prizes at every Bienal from its beginning in 1951 to the present. Includes many black-and-white reproductions. The importance of this catalog as a reference source which reflects trends and the tastes of the Brazilian art establishment should not be overlooked. Published every two years. Editions examined: 15th, 1979; 17th, 1983; 18th, 1985.

341 Brazil. Biblioteca Nacional. A moderna gravura brasileira: catálogo da exposição. Rio de Janeiro: 1974. 20 p. An exhibition catalog listing the works exhibited by forty-three twentieth-century Brazilian printmakers. Gives birth and death dates of the artists, but no other biographical data. Illustrated with a few examples of the prints shown. A glossary defines the different processes used in printmaking.

342 Brazil. Departamento de Assuntos Culturais. Arte gaúcha/74. n.p. 1974? 97 p. The catalog of an exhibition featuring artists of Rio Grande do Sul. Includes reproductions of the works, brief biographical data, portraits, critical notes, and summaries of the careers of twenty-four contemporary artists.

343 Catálogo pernambucano de arte. 1. ed. Recife: Grupo X Promoções e Emprendimentos, 1987. Unpaged. Covers 128 contemporary painters and sculptors of Pernambuco, providing color reproductions of their works and biographical data and addresses. Excellent illustrations.

344 Cavalcanti, Carlos. Dicionário brasileiro de artistas plásticas. 4 vols. Brasília: Ministério da Educação e Cultura, Instituto Nacional do Livro, 1973-1980. A biographical dictionary of contemporary and historical figures in the visual arts, including Brazilian artists, foreign-born artists in Brazil, and major foreign artists represented in the collection of the Museu Nacional de Belas Artes. Painters, sculptors, architects, photographers, cartoonists, silversmiths, goldsmiths and others are among the categories of artists included. Entries include brief biographical information and a summary of artistic accomplishments. Also provides examples of some of the artists' works in 1500 black-and-white reproductions. A valuable source of information about lesser-known contemporary artists working outside of Rio de Janeiro and São Paulo.

345 Campofiorito, Quirino. História da pintura brasileira no século XIX. 5 vols. Rio de Janeiro: Edições Pinakotheke, 1983. Surveys Brazilian art, 1800-1918, through biographical sketches of artists and color and black-and-white reproductions illustrating their works in this set of slim volumes intended for a popular audience. Each volume covers a significant period: Vol. 1: A pintura remanescente da Colônia, 1800-1830; Vol. 2: A Missão Artística Francesa e seus discípulos, 1816-1840; Vol. 3: A pintura posterior à Missão Francesa, 1835-1870; Vol. 4: A proteção do Imperador e os pintores do Segundo Reinado, 1850-1890; Vol. 5: A República e a decadência da disciplina neoclássica 1890-1918.

346 150 anos de pintura no Brasil, 1820/1970. Rio de Janeiro: Colorama, 1989. 490 p. This work, based on examples from the Sérgio Sahione Fadel collection, includes excellent color reproductions, and considerable biographical/artistic information about each artist represented.

347 Cunha, Carlos. A Páscoa das gaivotas: panorama maranhense contemporâneo das artes plásticas. São Luis: Edições Mirante, 1987. 148 p. Biographical sketches, portraits, and exhibitions of about thirty-five contemporary artists of Maranhão: painters, engravers, ceramists, and others.

348 Etzel, Eduardo. O barroco no Brasil: psicologia--remanescentes em São Paulo, Goiás, Mato Grosso, Paraná, Santa Caterina, Rio Grande do Sul. São Paulo: Edições Melhoramentos; Editora da Universidade de São Paulo, 1974. 314 p. Although this is not strictly a reference book in terms of its format, its geographical arrangement, numerous illustrations, and detailed table of contents make it a valuable source of information about the less well-known manifestations of baroque style in Brazil outside of the famous examples of Minas Gerais. Includes details about the history and the decoration of important buildings, principally churches. Introductory chapters

give background on baroque style and its transplantation to Brazil. Concludes with a bibliography.

349 Fekete, Joan. Dicionário universal das artes plásticas. Rio de Janeiro: Companhia Brasileiro de Artes Gráficas, 1979. 377 p. A biographical dictionary, universal in scope, which includes many Brazilian artists.

350 Fernandes, Luiz Felipe. Contemporary Brazilian Artists. Portuguese-English ed. Rio de Janeiro: Edições de Arte, 1984. 62 p. Rather superficial information in English and Portuguese about the artistic careers of twenty-five contemporary artists, illustrated with a reproduction of a representative work of each artist.

351 Figueiredo, Aline. Artes plásticas no Centro-Oeste. Cuiabá: Edições UFMT/Museu de Arte Contemporânea, 1979. 360 p. An illustrated summary of the visual arts in Goiás, Brasília, and Mato Grosso. Includes a biographical dictionary of artists.

352 Guia das artes plásticas de São Paulo: galerias, feiras, entidades culturais, museus, museus do interior, artistas, ateliês. São Paulo: Secretaria da Cultura, Ciência e Tecnologia do Estado de São Paulo, Departamento de Artes e Ciências Humanas, 1978. 126 p. A directory of art galleries, associations, cultural entities promoting art, museums, and currently active artists of the state, which supplies address, telephone number, hours, and artistic medium of each individual or entity. The directory of artists is the most important feature, both in the space that it occupies (94 of 126 pages), and in the information that it supplies, since much of the information would otherwise be very difficult to obtain.

353 Leite, José Roberto Teixeira. Dicionário crítico da pintura no Brasil. Rio de Janeiro: Artlivre, 1988. 553 p. A dictionary of 2000 entries and 700 black and white illustrations covering painters, groups, collectors, events, museums, movements, techniques, styles, schools, and many other categories associated with painting. The length of entries ranges from a few lines to short essays, and they include bibliography.

354 ________. Pintura moderna brasileira. Rio de Janeiro: Editora Record, 1978. 162 p. Color reproductions of the works of fourteen major twentieth-century painters are accompanied by biographical notes and critical commentary. Artists included are Tarsila do Amaral, Lasar Segall, Alberto da Veiga Guignard, Alfredo Volpi, Emiliano Di Cavalcanti, Vicente do Rego Monteiro, Ismael Nery, José Pancetti, Cândido Portinari, Cícero Dias, Djanira da Motta e Silva, Iberê Camargo, Milton Dacosta, and Antônio Bandeira. A name index refers to other important figures, institutions, publications, and movements in the

Brazilian art world. Provides a bibliography of general works and of publications about each artist included.

355 Lemos, Carlos, José Roberto Teixeira Leite, and Pedro Manuel Gismonti. The Art of Brazil. New York: Harper & Row, 1983. 318 p. A richly illustrated survey of Brazilian art and architecture from the early sixteenth century to the present. The text and color plates are supplemented by brief biographies of 137 artists and by a chronology of Brazilian art, as well as an index of names mentioned in the text. This work is a translation of Arte no Brasil (São Paulo: Livros Abril, 1982).

356 Louzada, Júlio. Artes plásticas: seu mercado, seus leilões. São Paulo: J. Louzada, 1984-. Covers Brazilian artists, past and contemporary, including many who are not well-known. Along with information on the monetary value of their works this publication provides information on the artistic development and the exhibitions of each artist, as well as birth and death dates, when known. Volumes examined: 1, 1984; 2, 1987; 3, 1989 (Artes plásticas Brasil)

357 Medeiros, João. Dicionário dos pintores do Brasil. Rio de Janeiro: Irradiação Cultural, 1988. 197 p. A dictionary of past and contemporary artists, providing biographical and artistic data of uneven quality. The many black-and-white illustrations are poor. This dictionary should serve primarily as a supplementary source.

358 Modernidade: art brésilien du 20° siècle. Paris: Ministère des Affaires Etrangères; Association Française d'Action Artistique, 1987. 426 p. This catalog for an exhibition held at the Musée d'Art Moderne de la Ville de Paris, Dec. 1987-Feb. 1988, includes sculpture, paintings, poster art, and architecture, and the color reproductions are excellent. There is also a useful section of biographical/professional information about the artists, accompanied by their portraits, and a chronology of Brazilian modernism in the plastic arts, 1917-1985, which links it to Brazilian and world events in the arts, politics and other areas of activity.

359 Museu Nacional de Belas Artes. Arte brasileira século XX: Galeria Eliseu Visconti: pinturas e esculturas. Rio de Janeiro: 1984. 191 p. Reproductions of paintings and sculptures representative of the work of about 150 twentieth-century artists and sculptors are accompanied by brief biographical and critical notes and technical data about the works of art.

360 Museu Nacional de Belas Artes. Rio de Janeiro: Colorama, n.d. 226 p. Color reproductions of works of ninety artists represented in the collections of the museum, with biographical

and professional notes about each one. Most of the artists are Brazilians or foreigners who did significant work in Brazil.

361 Pontual, Roberto. Arte/Brasil/hoje: 50 anos depois. São Paulo: Collectio, 1973. 401 p. A publication based on an exhibition commemorating the fiftieth anniversary of the Semana de Arte Moderna (1922), a watershed event in Brazilian art history. Prepared by a well-known art and literary critic, this work includes about 175 contemporary artists, chiefly painters, although sculptors, creators of tapestries, and others are included. Each artist is represented by a portrait, biographical data including a summary of artistic achievements, brief critical commentary, a bibliography, and the reproduction of an example of his work. Although a work of this type must necessarily be highly selective in its inclusions, this is a very useful reference source, both for the number of artists that it includes, and for the quality of the information provided.

362 ______. Arte brasileira contemporânea: Coleção Gilberto Chateaubriand. Rio de Janeiro: Edições Jornal do Brasil, 1976. 478 p. Reproductions of Brazilian paintings and other art objects from the 1920's to the mid-1970's, with descriptive and critical commentary. Concludes with a biographical dictionary and portraits of the artists represented. Introduction and biographical dictionary in Portuguese and English.

363 ______. Dicionário das artes plásticas no Brasil. Rio: Editora Civilização Brasileira, 1969. 559 p. A biographical dictionary covering artists in the fields of painting, design, engraving, sculpture, wood-carving, gold work, jewelry design, tapestry, and cartoons. Illustrated with color and black-and-white reproductions of many works of art, although the quality of the illustrations is only fair.

364 Siqueira, Dylla Rodrigues de. 42 anos de premiações nos salões oficiais, 1934-1976. Rio de Janeiro: FUNARTE, 1980. 101 p. A chronological record of artists awarded prizes by the Salão Nacional de Belas-Artes and the Salao Nacional de Arte Moderna. Also provides information on the categories of prizes awarded.

365 Trevisan, Armindo. Escultores contemporâneos do Rio Grande do Sul. Porto Alegre: Editora da Universidade, 1983. 159 p. Covers eighteen contemporary sculptors in a well-illustrated work. In addition to examples of each sculptor's works the text provides personal and artistic biographical data, a list of exhibitions, and in some cases the location of works in private collections. This is an especially good example of a reference source devoted to regional art.

366 Valladares, Clarival do Prado. Análise iconográfica do barroco e neoclássico remanentes no Rio de Janeiro. 2 vols. Rio de Janeiro: Bloch, 1978. A rich source of visual documentation about the baroque and neo-classical heritage found in churches, monasteries, hospitals, fountains, statues, and parks of this beautiful city. The mostly color illustrations, accompanied by brief descriptive notes, both provide an overview and highlight many details of the buildings and monuments. An annotated bibliography in volume 2 directs the reader to additional sources.

POPULAR ART, HANDICRAFTS, AND ARTISANRY

Bibliography

367 Fundação Nacional de Arte. Centro de Documentação. Fotografia: levantamento bibliográfico. Série bibliografia, 2. Rio de Janeiro: FUNARTE, 1981. 70 leaves. An unannotated bibliography of 515 monographs and periodical articles dealing with photographs of Brazil and of other subjects, and with technical aspects of photography.

368 Salles, Vicente. Bibliografia analítica do artesanato brasileiro. Série referência, vol. 1. Rio de Janeiro: FUNARTE, 1984. 96 p. A well-annotated bibliography of 1400 entries covering all aspects of crafts and popular art.

369 Silvestre, Inalda Monteiro, and Sylvia Pereira de Holanda Cavalcanti. Artesanato brasileiro: uma contribuição à sua bibliografia. Recife: Fundação Joaquim Nabuco, 1981. 114 p. An unannotated bibliography of 723 references to books and periodical articles about handicrafts, artisans, the industrialization of handicrafts, and related topics.

Other Sources

370 Andrade, Geraldo Edson de. Aspectos da tapeçaria brasileira. Rio de Janeiro: FUNARTE, 1978. 134 p. The artistic careers of some fifty-five contemporary tapestry makers are outlined and illustrated in color reproductions and biographical data. This handsome publication, originally issued in 1977 by Spala Editora, was reissued under government sponsorship so that it could reach a wider audience. Indispensable for the study of this popular Brazilian art form.

371 Anuário de criação Brazilian Creative Annual. São Paulo: Clube de Criação de São Paulo. A yearbook illustrating the

best of Brazilian commercial art in the fields of advertising, merchandising, and publishing. Descriptive text in Portuguese and English. Editions examined: 13th, 1988; 14th, 1989.

372 Artesanato brasileiro. 3. ed. Rio de Janeiro: FUNARTE, 1986. 165 p. A primarily visual introduction to Brazilian folk art: ceramics, wood, fiber work, weaving, lace, metalwork, and other materials such as feathers. The excellent illustrations show examples of finished work and segments of the production process, enhanced by explanatory notes. Includes a glossary and a bibliography. 1st ed. published 1978; 2nd, 1980.

373 Artistas da cerâmica brasileira. n.p.: Volkswagen do Brasil, S.A., 1985. Unpaged. Excellent color photographs provide examples of the works of well-known ceramic artists who work in both popular and sophisticated contemporary styles.

374 Bardi, Pietro Maria. Arte da prata no Brasil. n.p.: Banco Sudameris Brasil, 1979. 135 p. Excellent color photographs of silverwork of the seventeenth, eighteenth, and nineteenth centuries, accompanied by an introductory essay about its development in Brazil. Presents a fascinating array of examples of the uses of silver pieces in religious and domestic life, as well as in other endeavors, such as cattle-raising in Rio Grande do Sul.

375 _______. O ouro no Brasil. Arte e cultura, no. 11. n.p.: Banco Sudameris Brasil, 1988. 102 p. Text and excellent color illustrations trace the history of the discovery and mining of gold in Brazil, and provide visual documentation of its use in jewelry, interior decoration, coins, religious objects, and other artifacts. Includes a bibliography.

376 Brasil: arte popular hoje. n.p.: Publicações e Comunicação, Ltda., 1987? 160 p. Excellent color photographs with descriptive notes, and text summarizing the current state of the popular arts in Brazil, comprise this work, written in Portuguese and English.

377 Brazilian Baroque: Decorative and Religious Objects of the Seventeenth and Eighteenth Century, from the Museum of Sacred Art of São Paulo, Brazil. São Paulo: Secretaria de Cultura, Esportes e Turismo do Estado de São Paulo, 1972? unpaged. This catalog of an exhibition held at the Renwick Gallery, Washington, D.C., in 1972-1973, is comprised of excellent color and black-and-white photographs of ninety-five religious objects in the baroque style. Statues, furniture, bells, candlesticks, crucifixes and oratories are some of the objects represented in various mediums: wood, silver, gold, brass, ivory, and clay, among others. Although information

about each piece is minimal--medium, size, and location--this is an excellent visual source from which to obtain an overview of the expression of baroque style in religious objects as well as to see fine examples of individual objects.

378 Brinquedos tradicionais brasileiros. São Paulo: Serviço Social do Comércio, 1983. 100 p. Excellent color photographs of traditional handmade toys, with explanatory text in English and Portuguese.

379 Canti, Tilde. O móvel do século XIX no Brasil. Rio de Janeiro: CGPM, 1988. 190 p. Provides history, descriptions, and excellent illustrations--some in color--of nineteenth-century Brazilian furniture. Includes a list of furniture makers and factories.

380 ______. O móvel no Brasil: origens, evolução e características. Rio de Janeiro: Cândido Guinle de Paula Machado, 1980. 340 p. Provides history, descriptions, and excellent illustrations of Brazilian furniture of the colonial period. Includes a glossary of terms.

381 Center for Inter-American Relations. Art Gallery. Gravadores brasileiros, September 25-November 2, 1969. New York: 1969? 16 p. An exhibition catalog of the works of twenty-one Brazilian printmakers which lists the works shown and provides the dates and places of their births. Illustrated with examples of the works exhibited.

382 Coimbra, Silvia Rodrigues, Flávia Martins, and Maria Letícia Duarte. O reinado da lua: escultores populares do Nordeste. Rio de Janeiro: Editora Salamandra, 1980. 305 p. A survey of the sculptured folk art of northeastern Brazil from Bahia to Maranhão in black-and-white photographs and text. Covers various types of sculpture from the carrancas (carved wooden figures of the prows of riverboats on the Rio São Francisco) to the tiny clay figures modeled in Caruarú. Provides biographical and artistic information about the principal artists of each form, with portraits of many of them. A geographical dictionary by state and city lists artists working in each city. Includes a bibliography.

383 Dreyfus, Jenny. Louça da aristocracia no Brasil. Rio de Janeiro: Monteiro Soares, 1982. 349 p. Identifies "louça brasonada brasileira," or china belonging to the Brazilian aristocracy from the sixteenth through the early twentieth centuries, with illustrations, sometimes enhanced by descriptive text. Also includes biographical notes on the owners of the pieces, and provides information on the types of china that made their way to Brazil. Excellent color illustrations.

384 Etzel, Eduardo. Imagem sacra brasileira. São Paulo: Edições Melhoramentos; Editora da Universidade de São Paulo, 1979. 157 p. The religious images of Brazil--"santinhos," crucifixes, creches, home oratories, and others--are described and illustrated with color photographs. Provides information on the regional characteristics of religious and popular images, and the falsification of images.

385 Franceschi, Humberto M. O ofício da prata no Brasil: Rio de Janeiro. Rio de Janeiro: Studio HMF, 1988. 325 p. Excellent illustrations and text trace the development of Brazilian silver-smithing in the seventeenth, eighteenth, and nineteenth centuries. Supplementary material includes a list of silversmiths in Rio de Janeiro during this period, with their dates and addresses, a glossary of terms associated with silver, and a bibliography.

386 Geisel, Amália Lucy, and Raul Lody. Artesanato brasileiro: teclagem. Rio de Janeiro: FUNARTE/Instituto Nacional do Folclore, 1983. 168 p. An introduction to Brazilian spinning and weaving through text and excellent, detailed illustrations, many in color. Covers all aspects: raw materials, the spinning and weaving processes, production, products, consumption, and commercialization. Includes a bibliography.

387 Girão, Valdelice Carneiro. Renda de bilros: coleção do Museu Arthur Ramos. Fortaleza: Edições Universidade do Ceará, 1984. 444 p. Photographs of 2187 examples of lace made in Ceará and most of the other states of Brazil, with accompanying descriptions. Introductory material discusses the techniques and vocabulary of lace-making. Includes a brief bibliography.

388 Kossoy, Boris. Origens e expansão da fotografia no Brasil: século XIX. Rio de Janeiro: FUNARTE, 1980. 125 p. Traces the development of photography in Brazil using many illustrations. Includes a list of nineteenth-century Brazilian photographers giving the cities where they worked, the approximate dates of their activity, and observations about their work. Concludes with a bibliography.

389 Lody, Raul, and Marina de Mello e Souza. Artesanato brasileiro: madeira. Rio de Janeiro: FUNARTE, Instituto Nacional do Folclore, 1988. 202 p. Treats traditional and contemporary artistic and utilitarian uses of wood through text and photographs. The excellent color and black-and-white illustrations depict the types of trees used, examples of the woodworker's art and craft, and well-known craftsmen. Includes a glossary of useful Brazilian trees, and a bibliography.

390 Montague, Rosie. Brazilian Three Dimensional Embroidery:

Instructions and Fifty Transfer Patterns. New York: Dover Publications, 1983. 15 p. 24 plates. Detailed instructions and patterns comprise this how-to-do-it book. It does not provide background information on this folk art.

391 Oiticica, Francisco de Paula Leite e. A arte da renda no Nordeste. Recife: Instituto do Açúcar e do Alcool, Museu do Açúcar, 1974. 41 p. A short work on the lacemaking art of the Northeast, enhanced with many drawings illustrating patterns, and with a glossary defining terms associated with lacemaking.

392 Rio de Janeiro (City). Casa de Rui Barbosa. Xilógrafos nordestinos. Rio de Janeiro: Fundação Casa de Rui Barbosa, 1977-. Reproductions of wood cuts that illustrate the covers of literatura de cordel by many of the better-known artists, accompanied by biographical information about each artist. This publication is planned to be issued in several volumes. Volume 1 was examined.

393 Rodman, Selden. Genius in the Backlands: Popular Artists of Brazil. Old Greenwich, CT: Devin-Adair, 1977. 150 p. Provides biographical data and descriptions of the work of twenty-one popular artists--painters, sculptors, woodcarvers, and others--based on interviews with them. Many informal portraits and photographs of the artists' works.

394 São Paulo (City). Museu de Arte. Artistas e artífices do Brasil, séculos xvi, xvii e xviii. São Paulo: Museu de Arte de São Paulo Assis Chateaubriand, 1977. unpaged. An exhibition catalog featuring furniture, silverwork, woodcarvings, stone carvings, and a few paintings of the colonial period, which provides excellent visual documentation and additional information about each piece--medium, date, location, size, and artisan, when known. A very good source for an overview of the decorative/applied arts of the period, as well as for information about specific arts.

395 Scheuer, Herta Loel. Estudo de cerâmica popular do Estado de São Paulo. Folclore, 3. São Paulo: Conselho Estadual de Cultura, 1976. 129 p. Describes and illustrates the pottery produced in eight municípios noted for that craft. Describes technique, typical measurements, and decoration of each product. Also includes photographs and a bibliography. The carefully systematized data can be applied to a wider universe of pottery than that which is specifically described.

396 Seraphico, Luiz. Arte colonial: mobiliário. Art colonial: mobilier. São Paulo: Ed. das Américas, Rhodia, 1977. 107 p. Includes 120 excellent color and black-and-white photographs of furniture of the colonial period with brief descriptions in Portuguese and with additional text in Portuguese and French.

Although this work is not intended to be a systematic catalog, it contains a variety of examples of domestic furniture of the period. Includes a bibliography and a list of experts in the field.

397 Silva, Orlando de. A arte maior da gravura. São Paulo: ESPADE/Escola Paulista de Arte e Decoração, 1976. 125 p. Covers engravings as an art form in its various manifestations: woodcuts, etchings, lithographs, etc. Some of the topics addressed are signatures, originals and reproductions, paper, proofs, numbering, the history and characteristics of various techniques, and the origins of engraving in Brazil. The index of names, extensive bibliography, and many reproductions illustrating the text contribute to the usefulness of this publication.

398 Simões, João Miguel dos Santos. Azulejaria portuguesa no Brasil, 1500-1822. Lisboa: Fundação Calouste Gulbenkian, 1965. 459 p. A state-by-state, município-by-município description of many of the Portuguese azulejos (ceramic tiles) used in Brazil during the colonial period. Excellent color illustrations, a bibliography, and several indexes enhance this fine work.

399 Talento, 1984-. São Paulo: Talento Publicações Editora e Gráfica. A commercial art directory listing production companies, illustrators, printers and engravers, models, special effects, studios, laboratories, and agencies. Well illustrated with examples of work. Volumes examined: 1, 1984; 2, 1985; 3, 1986; 4, 1988.

400 Teclagem manual no Triângulo Mineiro: uma abordagem tecnológica. Publicações da Subsecretaria do Patrimônio Histórico e Artístico Nacional, no. 36. Brasília: Fundação Nacional Pró-Memória, 1984. 124 p. A well-illustrated work presenting detailed information about weaving in a region where that craft is very important. Covers the technology of spinning and dying the yarn, implements used, examples of products with instructions for weaving, and many patterns. Includes a bibliography.

INDIGENOUS ART

401 Arte e corpo: pintura sobre a pele e adornos de povos indígenas brasileiros. Rio de Janeiro: FUNARTE, 1985. 108 p. Photographs and line drawings illustrate the body painting and ornaments used by a number of Indian tribes.

402 Exposição Arte Plumária do Brasil: 17ª Bienal de São Paulo,

14 de outubro a 16 de dezembro de 1983. São Paulo: 1983. 75 p. Color photographs of 375 feather ornaments worn by various Brazilian Indian tribes, complemented by written descriptions of each one.

403 Nicola, Norberto, and Sonia Ferraro Dorta. Aromerí: arte plumária do indígena brasileiro. Brazilian Indian Feather Art. São Bernardo do Campo: Mercedes-Benz do Brasil, 1986. 128 p. Line drawings, excellent color photographs, and text describe and illustrate in detail the feather art of many Indian tribes. A map of Brazil locates the tribes mentioned. Includes a bibliography. Text in Portuguese and English.

404 Ribeiro, Berta G. A arte de trançado dos Indios do Brasil: um estudo taxonômico. Belém: Museu Paraense Emilio Goeldi; Rio de Janeiro: Instituto Nacional do Folclore, 1985. 185 p. A well-illustrated study which classifies the types of weaving used by Brazilian Indians for utensils, such as baskets. Illustrates the patterns used and the shapes of utensils through line drawings and photographs. Defines terms and includes a bibliography and index.

405 _______. Dicionário do artesanato indígena. Coleção Reconquista do Brasil. 3. série especial, vol. 4. Belo Horizonte: Itatiaia; São Paulo: Editora da Universidade de São Paulo, 1988. 243 p. A dictionary of Indian artisanry covering ceramics, basket weaving, textiles, featherwork, costume, musical instruments, weapons, wooden utensils and implements, and ritual objects, illustrated with excellent line drawings. A glossary for each section elaborates upon the definitions and descriptions which accompany the illustrations. Includes a bibliography.

BIOGRAPHY

GENERAL SOURCES

The biographical sources included here are general in nature, encompassing persons in many fields of activity. Those covering people associated with specific fields are cited under those subjects. For example, biographical dictionaries of authors are listed under LITERATURE, and those covering musicians are cited under MUSIC. However, a few specialized sources are included here, because they do not fit elsewhere in this bibliography. The Brazilian custom, now much less prevalent than in the past, of listing persons in alphabetical order under their given names, is noted when it applies.

406 Almeida, Antônio da Rocha. Vultos da patria: os brasileiros mais ilustres do seu tempo. 4 vols. Rio de Janeiro: Editora Globo, 1961-1966. Biographical essays about Brazilian leaders of all periods. No portraits. Each volume contains thirty-five essays.

407 Behar, Eli. Vultos do Brasil: dicionário biobibliográfico. São Paulo: Livraria Exposição do Livro, 1967. 222 p. A biographical dictionary of prominent Brazilians prepared with the intention of providing information for young people. However, the substantial content of the entries makes it useful for a wider audience. Many of the subjects were authors, although others had primary careers in politics, religion, or other activities. Pen and ink portraits accompany many of the entries.

408 Bittencourt, Adalzira. Dicionário bio-bibliográfico de mulheres ilustres, notáveis e intelectuais do Brasil. Rio de Janeiro: Editora Pongetti, 1969-. Covers Brazilian women of all periods in entries varying in length from a sentence to short articles. Includes some portraits. The first three volumes, which were the only ones examined, covered only the A's and B's. Entries are arranged by first name.

409 Boutin, Leônidas. Dicionário biográfico brasileiro: 398 mini-biografias de Cabral a Pelé. Curitiba: Paperlaria Max Roesner, 197-? 127 p. Includes figures from the past and present: "políticos, soldados, eclesiásticos, trabalhadores, bandeirantes, artistas, pensadores, cientistas, professores, negociantes e industriais."

410 Dicionário biográfico universal Três. 4 vols. São Paulo: Três Livros e Fascículos, 1983-1984. Contains 4400 biographies and portraits of well-known persons, including many Brazilians and other Latin Americans. Although it covers past and present, it is especially useful for data on contemporary figures not readily found in other sources.

411 Grandes personagens da nossa história. 4 vols. São Paulo: Abril, 1969-1970. Biographies of sixty key figures in the history of Brazil from Cabral (sixteenth century) to Marechal Rondon (twentieth century), intended for a popular audience. Illustrated with color portraits, maps, and other illustrative matter. Originally issued in sixty fascicules. The first supplement, Mapas históricos brasileiros, reproduces fifty-six historic maps.

412 Holandeses no Brasil: verbetes do Novo dicionário holandês de biografias. Traduzido por Francisco José Moonen, com uma introdução por José Antônio Gonsalves de Mello. Recife: Universidade Federal de Pernambuco, 1968. 170 p. Biographical data about seventy-one Dutchmen important in Brazilian history. Many of them figured in Dutch attempts to establish themselves in Bahia and Pernambuco in the seventeenth centuries, although others are also included. The entries are translated from the Nieuw Nederlandsch Biografisch Woordenboek, edited by P. C. Molhuysen and published in ten volumes in Leiden, 1911-1937.

413 Montalvão, Alberto. 500 biografias dos maiores vultos da humanidade. São Paulo: Edições de Revistas e Atualidades, 1976. 211 p. The grandiose title of this work piques the reader's curiosity about which figures are worthy of inclusion, and, not unexpectedly, a disproportionate number of them are Brazilians or Portuguese. For example, ten persons with the surname "Almeida" are represented. Nevertheless, an interesting selection of past and contemporary figures--politicians, musicians, religious leaders, philosophers, and others--almost exclusively from the Western world are included. Useful to the foreign user as a source of biographical information about many well-known Brazilians.

414 Mulheres do Brasil: pensamento e ação. 2 vols. Fortaleza: Editora Henriqueta Galeno, 1971. Biographical essays about thirty-three well-known Brazilian women written by members

of the Ala Feminina da Casa de Juvenal Galeno. Also includes biographical sketches and portraits of the authors of the essays.

415 Pillar, Olyntho. Os patronos das Forças Armadas. Rio de Janeiro: Biblioteca do Exército, 1981. 381 p. Biographical information and accounts of the professional careers of seventeen outstanding Brazilian military leaders, past and present, with portraits of most of them.

416 Quem é quem nas artes e nas letras do Brasil: artistas e escritores contemporâneos ou falecidos depois de 1945. Rio de Janeiro: Ministério das Relações Exteriores, Departamento Cultural e de Informações, 1966. 352 p. Brief biographies of contemporary Brazilians involved in painting, architecture, classical and popular music, theater, cinema, and literature.

417 Sacramento Blake, Augusto Victorino Alves. Diccionario bibliographico brazileiro. 7 vols. 1883-1902. Reprint. Rio de Janeiro: Conselho Federal de Cultura, 1970. This classic nineteenth-century biographical dictionary, reprinted in 1970, concentrates on figures of that period, although it includes many from earlier times. Follows the custom of listing individuals by their given names.

418 Sociedade brasileira. Rio de Janeiro: Livraria São José. Lists socially prominent persons along with the names of their spouses and addresses, focusing on Rio de Janeiro and the Federal District. Also lists members of the Academia Brasileira de Letras and the diplomatic corps. Issues examined: 1974, 1978.

419 Súmulas biográficas de cidadãos prestantes. São Paulo: Ensil Publicações Culturais, 1975. 1258 p. Concentrates on rather long biographical articles complete with portraits, of contemporary Brazilians in all fields: politics, medicine, the arts, business, education, and others. The general tone of the work is laudatory, rather than objective. Arranged in alphabetical order by given name.

420 Who's Who in Brazil. São Paulo: Who's Who in Brazil Editorial, 1968/1969-. Biographical data for prominent people in many fields. Most entries include portraits. Arranged in alphabetical order by last name, but the use of this work is complicated by the inconsistent way in which the names are listed. Sometimes they are listed under the first element of a compound name, and other times under the second. The text is in Portuguese in spite of the English-language title. Edition examined: 1976/1977.

421 Who's Who in Latin America. 3d ed. 2 vols. 1945. Reprint.

Detroit: B. Ethridge, 1971. Vol. 2: Brazil, Bolivia, Chile, and Peru, Argentina, Paraguay, and Uruguay. Who's who-type information about people in a wide range of fields from journalism to engineering, very useful for the time period covered.

BIOGRAPHY--STATES

Acre

422 Brito, Natal Barbosa de, and Elzo Rodrigues da Silva. Vultos acreanos. Série novo Acre, vol. 1. Rio Branco: Serviço de Divulgação do Estado do Acre, 1974-. Portraits, biographical sketches, and texts of documents associated with the careers of prominent citizens of Acre. Volume 1 (102 pages), which was the only one examined, included five biographies.

Alagoas

423 Vaz Filho, Augusto. Alagoanos ilustres: esboços biográficos. 3 vols. Maceió: 1962-1965. Short biographies of prominent men and women of Alagoas.

Amazonas

424 Bittencourt, Agnello. Dicionário amazonense de biografias: vultos do passado. Academia Amazonense de Letras, Coleção Academia. Rio de Janeiro: Conquista, 1973. 517 p. Short biographical essays about important people in the life of the state of Amazonas--both those born there and those who made it the scene of their activities. Focuses on the nineteenth to mid-twentieth centuries. No portraits. Arranged in alphabetical order by first name.

Bahia

425 Souza, Antônio Loureiro de. Baianos ilustres: 1567-1925. 3. ed. revista. São Paulo: IBRASA; Brasilia: Instituto Nacional do Livro, 1979. 358 p. Biographical essays about more than 150 important men and women of Bahia from the sixteenth through the twentieth centuries. No portraits. The first edition of this work was published in 1949, and the second edition in 1973.

Ceará

426 Personalidades do Ceará. Fortaleza. A directory of current political, business, artistic, and institutional leaders of the state, with brief biographical data: address, name of spouse, birthday, etc. Volumes examined: 6, 1982; 7, 1983; 11, 1987/1988.

427 Studart, Guilherme. Dicionário bio-bibliographico cearense. 3 vols. 1910-1914. Reprint. Fortaleza: Imprensa Universitária, Universidade Federal do Ceará, 1980. This classic by the biographer of an era in Ceará is made widely available through this reprint, combining biographies of such well-known cearenses as João Capistrano de Abreu with those of his more obscure, but no less interesting compatriots. The addition of an index by last surname, providing access to the dictionary which is arranged by given name, greatly facilitates its use.

Goiás

428 Brito, Célia Coutinho Seixo de. A mulher, a história e Goiás. Goiânia: Departamento Estadual de Cultura, 1974. 362 p. Biographies of thirty-three women important in the life of Goiás from a slave in the early days of the province to a writer who died in 1971. Portraits in the form of line drawings, and drawings of the residences of many of the biographees contribute to the interest of this work.

429 Lôbo, José Ferreira de Souza. Goianos ilustres. Goiânia: Oriente, 1974. 208 p. Biographical essays about fifty-three eighteenth- and nineteenth- century goianos, which were originally published in a column by the same title in the Correio oficial in the early 1940's. No portraits.

Mato Grosso

430 Mendonça, Rubens de. Dicionário biográfico mato-grossense. 2. ed. Goiânia: Editora Rio Bonito, 1971. 165 p. Biographical data on prominent men and women of Mato Grosso from its early days to the present time. Does not include portraits. First edition published in 1953 and the second edition updates it.

Minas Gerais

431 Rivera, Bueno de. Pioneiros e expoentes de Minas Gerais. Belo Horizonte: Edições Guia Rivera, 1971. 217 p. Biographies

accompanied by portraits of mineiros and others who contributed to the economic, social, and cultural development of Minas Gerais from the mid-nineteenth century to the late 1960's.

Pará

432 Cunha, Raymundo Cyriaco Alves da. Parenses ilustres. 3. ed. Belém: Conselho Estadual de Cultura, 1970. 174 p. Short biographical essays about thirty prominent paraenses of the eighteenth and nineteenth centuries, illustrated with portraits in many cases.

433 Personalidades no Pará. 1. ed. Belém: Imprensa Oficial do Estado, 1987. 194 p. Biographical data and portraits for contemporary paraenses in politics, industry, the arts, and many other fields.

434 Silva, Ricardo Borges Ferreira e. Vultos notáveis do Pará. 2. ed. revista e aumentada. Belém: Edições CEJUP, 1986. 449 p. Biographical essays about prominent paraenses.

Paraíba

435 Cartaxo, Rosilda. As primeiras damas. Brasília: Senado Federal, Centro Gráfico, 1989. 205 p. Portraits of and brief biographical information about the "first ladies" of the state of Paraíba.

436 Odilon, Marcus. Pequeno dicionário de fatos e vultos da Paraíba. Rio de Janeiro: Cátedra, 1984. 231 p. Relatively brief identifications of important paraibanos, past and present, along with a few entries on important events, newspapers, and a variety of other topics. Nevertheless, the main utility of this publication is in its biographies.

Paraná

437 Almeida, Dino. Bandeirantes do progresso. Curitiba: 1968. 457 p. Biographies and portraits of leaders in government, business, industry, medicine, education, and other activities in the state of Paraná in the mid-1960s. Although the majority of subjects are from Curitiba, several cities of the interior are represented.

438 Nicolas, Maria. Vultos paranaenses. Curitiba. The only volume of this work examined was Volume 4 (1966), which provided biographies of more than fifty women of Paraná, whose

lives spanned the late nineteenth to the mid-twentieth centuries.

Pernambuco

439 Costa, Francisco Augusto Pereira da. Dicionário biográfico de pernambucanos célebres. Recife: Fundação de Cultura, Cidade do Recife, 1982. 816 p. Facsimile of the edition of 1882, with 200 biographies of notable pernambucanos from colonial times to the late nineteenth century. Arranged by first name.

440 Matos, Potiguar. Gente pernambucano. Rio de Janeiro: Tempo Brasileiro; Recife: Fundação do Patrimônio Histórico e Artístico do Pernambuco, 1986. 126 p. A series of biographical essays.

441 Wilson, Luiz. Roteiro de velhos e grandes sertanejos. 3 vols. Biblioteca pernambucana de história municipal, 6-8. Recife: Centro de Estudos de História Municipal, 1978. Biographies of more than 150 individuals prominent in the sertão of Pernambuco, many accompanied by portraits. They appear to be, for the most part, twentieth-century contemporaries of the author. In addition to the information provided about the lives of individual sertanejos engaged in a wide variety of activities, this work supplies valuable data about life in the small towns of the sertão in general.

Rio de Janeiro

442 Belchior, Elysio de Oliveira. Conquistadores e povoadores do Rio de Janeiro. Rio de Janeiro: Brasiliana, 1965. 528 p. An unillustrated biographical dictionary of sixteenth-century founders and leaders of Rio de Janeiro and the area around Guanabara Bay. Some entries are brief, while others are full length articles. There is an "Indice de cargos, ofícios, ocupações, títulos, etc." which lists the names of the individuals who held them during the sixteenth century. The 170 items in the bibliography are referred to in the entries for each individual.

443 Pimental, Luís Antônio. Eles nasceram em Niterói. Niterói: Instituto Niteroiense de Desenvolvimento Cultural, 1974. 102 p. Biographies of forty well-known niteroienses prominent in politics, entertainment, the arts, sports, and other activities. Covers past and present natives of that city, such as Benjamin Constant and Marcia Haydée.

444 Rheingantz, Carlos G. Primeiras famílias do Rio de Janeiro (séculos XVI e XVII). Rio de Janeiro: Brasiliense, 1965-. Volumes examined: 1: A-E; 2, F-M. The existence of volumes completing the alphabet was not confirmed.

Rio Grande do Norte

445 Medeiros Filho, João. Contribuição a história intelectual do Rio Grande do Norte. Natal: 1983-. Biographical or bio-bibliographical information on norte riograndenses in the fields of law, medicine, government, history, sociology, linguistics, education, literature, and general culture. Includes past and contemporary figures. Volume 1 was examined.

Rio Grande do Sul

446 Ferraz, João Machado. Os primeiros gaúchos da América portuguesa. Porto Alegre: Instituto Estadual do Livro; Caxias do Sul: Universidade de Caxias do Sul, 1980. 157 p. Transcriptions of baptismal records for the earliest days of Rio Grande do Sul up to 1753. Persons baptized are listed under the names of heads of families.

447 Porto Alegre, Aquiles. Homens ilustres do Rio Grande do Sul. 2. ed. 1917. Reprint. Porto Alegre: 1981. 235 p. Provides short biographical essays on nineteenth- and early twentieth-century leaders of Rio Grande do Sul. Although this work was originally published in 1916, the second edition of 1917 was expanded, and it was selected for reprinting.

448 Spalding, Walter. Construtores do Rio Grande do Sul. Porto Alegre: Livraria Sulina Editora, 1969-. A biographical dictionary, projected to comprise at least ten volumes, focusing on men and women who contributed to all aspects of life in Rio Grande do Sul from its beginnings to the twentieth century. Short essays, complete with bibliographical references to the sources used, and illustrated with line drawing portraits, provide information on cultural, business, educational, religious, and other leaders. Volumes 1 and 2 were examined. They are in alphabetical order by first name, and volume 2 contains an index by last name for both volumes.

São Paulo

449 Leme, Pedro Taques de Almeida Paes. Nobiliárquia paulistana histórica e genealógica. 3 vols. 5th ed. Belo Horizonte: Editora Itatiaia: São Paulo: Editora da Universidade de São Paulo, 1980. This work by an eighteenth-century author was first published in parts by the Revista of the Instituto Brasileiro de Geografia e Estatística beginning in 1869.

CINEMA

BIBLIOGRAPHY

450 Bernardet, Jean-Claude. Bibliografia brasileira do cinema brasileiro. Cadernos de pesquisa, 3. Rio de Janeiro: Embrafilme; Belo Horizonte: Centro de Pesquisas do Cinema Brasileiro, 1987. 98 p. An annotated bibliography citing books published in Brazil and those published elsewhere which deal with Brazilian cinema. It is arranged in chronological order, 1911-1986, and indexed by author, title, film title, and subject.

451 Cinema brasileiro. São Paulo: Museu Lasar Segall, Biblioteca Jenny K. Segall, no. 1-, 1974-. These unannotated bibliographies, issued periodically, cite books, pamphlets, and clippings related to Brazilian cinema, located in the library of the Museu Lasar Segall. They are indexed by directors, film titles, and subjects. The following numbers have been issued as parts of the series, Bibliografia cinema: Cinema brasileiro, 1. Bibliografia cinema, 2. 1974. 94 p. 397 entries. Cinema brasileiro, 2. Bibliografia cinema, 3. 1975. 81 p. 307 entries. Cinema brasileiro, 3. Bibliografia cinema, 4. 1977. 148 p. 538 entries. Cinema brasileiro, 4. 2 vols. Bibliografia cinema, 6. 1979-1980. Vol. 1: A-M, 153 p., 860 entries; vol. 2: N-Z, 197 p., 1226 entries. Cinema brasileiro, 5. Bibliografia cinema, 7. 1981. 284 p. 1314 entries. Cinema brasileiro, 6. Bibliografia cinema, 8. 1983. 237 p. 1059 entries. Cinema brasileiro, 7. Bibliografia cinema, 9. 1985. 205 p. 1084 entries. Cinema brasileiro, 8. Bibliografia cinema, 10. 1989. 158 p. 1268 entries.

452 Gerber, Raquel. O cinema brasileiro e o processo político e cultural (de 1950 a 1978): bibliografia e filmografia crítica e seletiva (ênfase no Cinema Novo e Glauber Rocha com entradas na área da política e da cultura. Rio de Janeiro: EMBRAFILME 1982. 290 p. The title of this work describes its content very well. The bibliography/filmography is preceded by

an introduction describing sources for research on Cinema Novo and Glauber Rocha, and an essay entitled "O processo cinemanovista: notas sobre a história e filmes." The bibliography is arranged in chronological order, and the lack of an index makes it awkward to use. In spite of this defect, this work is very useful.

453 Museu Lasar Segall. Biblioteca Jenny K. Segall. Roteiros, 2. Bibliografia cinema, 5. São Paulo: n.d. 139 p. A bibliography of film scripts (mostly unpublished) available at the library, including those for 101 Brazilian films. Supersedes the earlier publication, Cinema I: Roteiros (1973).

454 Nobre, F. Silva. Inventário do cinema brasileiro: bibliografia. Fortaleza: Gráfica Editorial Cearense, 1978. 256 p. A selected, annotated bibliography of books and magazine and newspaper articles published in Brazil about the Brazilian cinema. Citations are listed in alphabetical order under categories which are not mutually exclusive, and the lack of any kind of index makes the use of this work problematical. The last category, entitled "Filmes," lists films in alphabetical order by title, and cites one or more reviews of each one.

455 ______. O livro de cinema no Brasil. Fortaleza: Gráfica Editorial Cearense, 1976. 283 p. A bibliography of books about Brazilian cinema, with summaries of their content.

456 West, Dennis. Contemporary Brazilian Cinema. The Brazilian Curriculum Guide Specialized Bibliography. Albuquerque: Latin American Institute, University of New Mexico, 1986? 26 p. A short survey of contemporary Brazilian cinema is followed by an unannotated bibliography. Also provides information on distribution of Brazilian films in the United States.

FILMOGRAPHY

General filmographies are cited here. Those devoted to specific subjects are listed under those subjects.

457 Bernardet, Jean-Claude. Filmografia do cinema brasileiro, 1900-1935: jornal "O Estado de São Paulo." São Paulo: Governo do Estado de São Paulo, Secretaria de Cultura, Comissão de Cinema, 1979. ca. 600 p. A filmography of feature films, documentaries, and news features, arranged in chronological order of their exhibition. Information about each film varies, since it is limited to that which appeared in O Estado de São Paulo. Indexes of titles, names of individuals, names

of film companies, and exhibiting theaters provide many points of access to the filmography.

458 Brasil cinema. Rio de Janeiro: Empresa Brasileira de Filmes, no. 1-, 1968-. Basic information about Brazilian films produced each year, beginning with 1968. Includes those responsible for the production, direction, screenplay, photography, editing, and music; names of the cast; plot summaries in Portuguese, English, and Spanish; and stills. Numbers 1-4 issued semiannually (1968-1969); issued annually thereafter. Numbers examined: 2, July-Dec., 1968; 4, July-Dec., 1969; 5, 1970; 7, 1972; 8, 1973; 10, 1975; 11, 1976; 12, 1977. Issued 1968-1974 by the Instituto Nacional do Cinema, the predecessor of EMBRAFILME.

459 Cinémathèque Française, Paris. 80 ans de cinema brésilien. Paris?: 1978? 68 p. This work, covering 1913-1976 provides detailed information on one or two films per year. Based on an exhibition at the Cinématéque Française in 1978.

460 Empresa Brasileira de Filmes. Departamento do Filme Cultural. Catálogo de filmes. Rio de Janeiro: Diretoria de Operações Comerciais, 1978? 196 p. A catalog of educational and documentary films.

461 _______. Filmoteca/catálogo: catálogo do acervo da EMBRAFILME. Rio de Janeiro: 1985. 219 p. Lists films by title, with technical data, directors, and short plot summaries. Director, title, and subject indexes.

462 _______. Guia de filmes lançados no Rio de Janeiro e em São Paulo entre 1 de janeiro e 31 de dezembro de 1979. Rio de Janeiro: 1981. 75 p. Lists both foreign and domestic films, with detailed information on national films (director, technical information, cast, plot summary, date of release, and censorship status) and less on foreign films (director, cast, company, date of release, and censorship status).

463 _______. Guia de filmes produzidos entre 1 de janeiro e 31 de dezembro de 1981. Rio de Janeiro: Embrafilme, 1985. 118 p. Lists Brazilian feature films and short subjects produced in 1981, regardless of when they were exhibited, and foreign films released in Brazil in that year. Includes statistical tables.

464 Espírito Santo, Michel do. Filmes brasileiros, 1969: lançados comercialmente ou em festivais. n.p.: Instituto Nacional do Cinema, 197-? 52 leaves. A yearbook of Brazilian films. Although the brief time coverage limits the usefulness of this publication, the information for each film--producer, distributor, director, photographer, cinematographer, cast, music,

sound, continuity, makeup, duration, and date and place of premiere--make it a prototype for the kind of reference work needed to cover a longer time span.

465 Fundação Cinemateca Brasileira. Cinejornal brasileiro, 1938-1946: Departamento de Imprensa e Propaganda. São Paulo: Imprensa Oficial do Estado, 1982. 187 p. A filmography of more than 400 newsreels and documentaries produced by the Departamento de Imprensa e Propaganda, 1938-1946, providing visual documentation of the Brazil of the Estado Novo. Indexed by subject. Illustrated with stills from the films cited.

466 Galdino, Márcio da Rocha. Minas Gerais: ensaio de filmografia. Belo Horizonte: Prefeitura de Belo Horizonte, Secretaria Municipal de Cultura e Turismo, 1983. 430 p. A chronology of activity relating to cinema in the state of Minas Gerais, 1903-1983, with detailed information on films made there and brief plot summaries.

467 Guia de filmes produzidos no Brasil entre.... Série filmografia brasileira. Rio de Janeiro: Empresa Brasileira de Filmes, 1984-. Basic data on feature films arranged alphabetically by title, year-by-year. Includes sources of information about them. Issued in fascicules. The first fascicule (1984, 82 p.) covers 1897-1910. The second (1985, 94 p.) covers 1911-1920: the third (1987, 105 p.) covers 1921-1925.

468 Pereira, Araken Campos. ABC do cinema brasileiro, 1908-1978: longa metragem. Santos: Editora Cinema Brasileiro, n.d. 98 p. Lists 2111 Brazilian films alphabetically by title, giving director, location where filmed, and date. Also lists 774 directors and states the number of films that each directed.

469 _______. Cinema brasileiro, 1906-1968. n.p: n.d. 112 p. "Relação de filmes de ficção, documentários e semi-documentários, de longa metragem, lançados e inacabados, de 1906-1968, em ordem cronológica e alfabética. Lists 1120 films, with their directors, producers, and places of production.

470 _______. Cinema brasileiro (1908-1978): longa metragem. 2 vols. Santos: Casa do Cinema, 1979. Films are listed under their year of release in alphabetical order. Provides production, distribution, and cast information for each one.

471 Souza, José Ignácio de Melo. Retrospectiva do cinema brasileiro, 1975. São Paulo: 1976. 94 p. A chronological list of films released in São Paulo, which gives detailed information about them. Includes a bibliography of books and articles about cinema appearing that year.

472 Universidade Federal de Minas Gerais. Catálogo Centro Audio-visual UFMG: filmes, audiovisuais, video-tapes. Belo Horizonte: 1987? unpaged. Detailed information on the films, audio-visuals, and video-tapes in the Center's collection, arranged by medium and then by subject.

GENERAL WORKS

473 Bandeira, Roberto. Anuário de cinema, 1964-. Rio de Janeiro: Pongetti, 1967-. Critical comments on Brazilian and foreign films of the year. Editions examined: 1964, 1965.

474 Carrión, Luiz Carlos. Festival do Cinema Brasileiro de Gramado: levantamento dos seus primeiros anos: vencedores, críticas, biogilmografias, fotografias. Porto Alegre: Tchê, 1986. 567 p. Information on award-winning films and directors of this film festival from its beginning in 1973 through 1986. Also includes information on the festival's history and organization.

475 Centro de Pesquisa de Arte Brasileira. O filme curto. 2 vols. São Paulo: Secretaria Municipal de Cultura, Departamento de Informação e Documentação Artísticas, Centro de Pesquisa de Arte Brasileira, 1980. Focuses on short subject films, especially those produced in São Paulo. Includes information on individual production companies, associations and organizations, a filmography, a summary of legislation, and other topics. Illustrated with stills from films.

476 Les cinémas de l'Amérique Latine pays par pays: l'histoire, l'économie, les structures, les auteurs, les oeuvres. Paris: Lherminier, 1981. 543 p. The ninety-seven pages devoted to Brazilian cinema include an essay on its history, liberally interspersed with illustrations; a chronology; and biographical and artistic data about prominent filmmakers and some actors. Production statistics by date (1898-1978) and by city, and statistics for international co-productions are also included.

477 Empresa Brasileira de Filmes. Informações sobre a indústria cinematográfica brasileira, 1975. Rio de Janeiro: 1976? unpaged. Information on foreign and domestic films released, prizes, and statistics on prices, ticket sales, and number of theaters exhibiting films.

478 Mello, Alcino Teixeira de. Legislação do cinema brasileiro. 2 vols. Rio de Janeiro: EMBRAFILME, 1978. Vol. 1: Legislação básica, legislação complementar, resoluções do Conselho Nacional de Cinema (CONCINE); Vol. 2: Resoluções do INC (Instituto Nacional do Cinema), convênios, acordos, planos, instruções, circulares, portarias, apêndice.

479 Paiva, Salvyano Cavalcanti de. História ilustrada dos filmes brasileiros 1929-1988. Rio de Janeiro: Francisco Alves, 1989. 255 p. A decade-by-decade history of Brazilian sound films, liberally illustrated with stills. An index of film titles and a name index including artists, producers, directors, writers, composers, technicians and others greatly facilitate the use of this work.

480 Paranaguá, Paulo Antônio. Le cinema brésilien. Paris: Centre Georges Pompidou, 1987. 323 p. In addition to a series of essays on important aspects of Brazilian cinema, this work includes a chronology, a biographical dictionary of cineasts, basic information on 200 Brazilian films, 1912-1986, many illustrations, and a bibliography.

481 Pereira, Araken Campos. Astros brasileiros no cinema estrangeiro: cartazes. Santos: Editora Cinema Brasileiro, n.d. 122 p. Reproductions of posters advertising foreign films in which Brazilian actors and musicians appeared. Unfortunately, the quality of the reproductions is very poor.

482 ______. Cartazes, cinema brasileiro, A, B: 1929-1977. Santos: n.d. 155 p.

483 ______. Cartazes, cinema brasileiro, C: 1921-1977. Santos: n.d. 157 p.

484 ______. Cartazes, cinema brasileiro, D, E: 1916-1978. Santos: n.d. 167 p.

485 ______. Cartazes, cinema brasileiro, F, G, H: 1919-1978. Santos: n.d. 137 p.

486 ______. Cartazes, cinema brasileiro, I, J, K, L: 1923-1978. Santos: n.d. 79 p.

487 ______. Cartazes, cinema brasileiro, M: 1930-1978. Santos: Editora Cinema Brasileiro, n.d. 132 p.

488 ______. Cartazes, cinema brasileiro, N, O: 1926-1978. Santos: n.d. 79 p.

489 ______. Cartazes, cinema brasileiro, P: 1918-1978. Santos: n.d.: 125 p.

490 ______. Cartazes, cinema brasileiro, Q, R: 1925-1978. Santos: n.d. 78 p.

491 ______. Cartazes, cinema brasileiro, S: 1927-1978. Santos: n.d. 115 p.

492 ______. Cartazes, cinema brasileiro, T, U, V, X, Y, Z. Santos: n.d. 154 p. Each of the eleven publications on Brazilian film posters cited above covers certain letters of the alphabet. Reproductions of posters advertising the films are arranged alphabetically by title of the film. The quality of reproduction is poor.

493 ______. Cartazes: livro do ano de 1978. Santos: n.d. 178 p. Reproduction of posters for Brazilian films of 1978 arranged alphabetically by title. The verso of each page illustrating a poster gives data on the production of the film and on the cast.

494-96 ______. Cinema brasileiro: cartazes, curta metragem, 1928-1978. Santos: Editora Cinema Brasileiro, n.d. 146 p. Reproductions of posters and programs which provide information on Brazilian film "shorts," in alphabetical order by title.

497 Ramos, Fernando. História do cinema brasileiro. São Paulo: Art Editora, 1987. 555 p. A survey of Brazilian cinematic history in rough chronological order and by schools of filmmakers or genres. Includes a filmography. Well indexed by names of persons and by film titles. Each chapter concludes with notes and bibliography. Some illustrations.

498 Schumann, Peter B. Handbuch des brasilianischen Films. Frankfurt/M.: Vervuert: 1988. 160 p. An illustrated handbook of selected Brazilian films providing information about their casts, direction, and plots; chronologies of the careers of major directors; and a bibliography.

BIOGRAPHY

499 Bandeira, Roberto. Pequeno dicionário crítico do cinema brasileiro. Rio de Janeiro: Shogun Arte, 1983. 135 p. Briefly identifies actors, directors, and others associated with Brazilian cinema since 1960, listing the films with which they were associated. The word "crítico" in the title is misleading, since this work does not encompass film criticism. No portraits

500 Ewald Filho, Rubens. Dicionário de cineastas. São Paulo: Global, 1977. 469 p. An international directory of film producers, directors, technicians, and others prominent in the production of films. Data includes birth and death dates, nationality, major accomplishments, and a list of films with which the individual is associated. Includes some portraits. A good source of information on leaders in the Brazilian film world.

501 Neves, David E. Cinema novo no Brasil. Petrópolis: Vozes, 1966. 55 p. Includes a biographical section on film makers of cinema novo, which provides brief data about their lives and lists of their films.

COMMUNICATION

BIBLIOGRAPHY

502 Bibliografia brasileira de comunicação. São Paulo: INTERCOM--Sociedade Brasileira de Estudos Interdisciplinares da Comunicação no. 1-, 1977-. An annotated bibliography of books, articles, and theses in the field of communication, broadly defined. Some of the topics covered are: library science and documentation, cinema, communication theory, mass media, rural communication, creativity, popular culture, publishing, photography, cartoons, journalism, marketing, music, communication policy, radio, television, video, theater, sound, and telecommunications. Author and subject indexes. Volumes examined: 5, 1983; 7, 1987

503 Coura, Sonia Maria, and Aloísio de Arruda Pinto. Bibliografia sobre comunicação: adoção e difusão de inovações. Viçosa: Universidade Federal de Viçosa, Biblioteca Central, 1974. 77 p. An unannotated bibliography of 394 entries of Brazilian and other publications. Deals with such topics as literacy programs, technology transfer, agricultural extension, social action, etc.

504 Melo, José Marquês de. Inventário de pesquisas em comunicação no Brasil, 1883-1983. São Paulo: PORT-COM/INTERCOM/ALAIC/CIID/CNPq, 1984. 387 p. Cites 1312 annotated items published in Brazil and elsewhere. Includes books, articles, and unpublished theses and dissertations.

DICTIONARIES

505 Andrade, Cândido Teobaldo de. Dicionário profissional de relações públicas e comunicação, e glossário de termos anglo-americanos.

São Paulo: Saraiva, 1978. 139 p. A dictionary defining the specialized terms associated with public relations and communications. The supplementary glossary of Anglo-American terms related to the same fields is of fair quality, but it contains some errors.

506 Katz, Chaim Samuel; Francisco Antônio Doria; and Luiz Costa Lima. Dicionário básico de comunicação. 2. ed. Rio de Janeiro: Paz e Terra, 1975. 459 p. Defines terms and identifies people related to communication, thereby including terms from anthropology, philosophy, linguistics, psychology, sociology, information theory, and cybernetics. This is an expanded version of the authors' Dicionário crítico da comunicação (1971).

507 Rabaça, Carlos Alberto, and Gustavo Barbosa. Dicionário de comunicação. Rio de Janeiro: Editora Codecri, 1978. 498 p. Defines 4000 words used in mass communication including publishing, graphic arts, journalism, cinema, television, radio, advertising, public relations, and several other fields. Illustrated.

OTHER SOURCES

508 Anuário brasileiro de mídia. São Paulo: P.I.--Publicações Informativas, Ltda. Detailed information about media intended for use by potential advertisers, but helpful to anyone interested in mass communication. Covers radio and television stations, movie theaters, newspapers, and magazines. Includes data on advertising for large and small cities, state-by-state. Provides information on advertising costs in various media, and statistics on magazine sales, radio listeners, and television viewers. Issues examined: 1981/1982, 1983/1984, 1985/1986.

509 Anuário brasileiro de propaganda. São Paulo: PI--Publicações Informativas, Ltda. Provides information on the advertising business: agencies, market research firms, filmmakers, organizations, and print media. The state-by-state list of newspapers, giving address, publisher, and circulation provides hard-to-find information of interest to a wider public than potential advertisers. According to the introduction, this yearbook has been published regularly for sixteen years. Issues examined: 1981/1982, 1983/1984, 1985/1986.

510 Cascudo, Luís da Câmara. História dos nossos gestos. São Paulo: Melhoramentos, 1976. 248 p. An illustrated general history of gestures with comments on their use in Brazil. Includes an index of gestures.

511 Entidades cristãs de comunicação social no Brasil. São Paulo: Edições Paulinas, 1987. 199 p. A directory of Catholic and Protestant organizations in Brazil engaged in mass communication--print media, radio, and television. Arranged by state, with indexes of persons and institutions/titles.

512 Mercado brasileiro de comunicação. Brasília: Presidência da República, Secretaria da Imprensa e Divulgação, 1. ed.-, 1981-. A compilation of marketing statistics--population, income, literacy, and consumption potential in major markets--and of statistics about publishing and electronic media. Also lists radio and television stations and newspapers, and provides a directory of publicity and advertising professionals. Edition examined: 2nd, 1983.

513 Mídia no Brasil, 89/90. São Paulo: McCann-Erickson, n.d. 87 p. and 1 diskette. Provides data in charts statistical tables and diagrams on all forms of media in Brazil--television, radio, newspapers, magazines, cinema, theater, and outdoor advertising--as well as information on Brazilian market characteristics and the advertising industry in print and diskette formats.

514 Pequena cronologia das telecomunicações no Brasil. n.p.: EMBRATEL, 1982. 19 p. Important dates in the history of telecommunications, from the inauguration of the first telegraph (1852) to the beginning of the Rêde Nacional de Radiomonitoragem (1982) are listed in chronological order.

515 Quem é quem na pesquisa em comunicação. São Paulo: INTERCOM--Sociedade Brasileira de Estudos Interdisciplinares da Comunicação, 1983-. Bio-bibliographical and professional data about researchers in the field of communication. Biennial updating of this publication is planned. Issue examined: 1982/1983.

516 Rector, Mônica, and Aluizio R. Trinta. Comunicação não-verbal: a gestualidade brasileira. Petrópolis: Vozes, 1985. 184 p. In addition to the text which discusses the theory and practice of non-verbal communication, this work includes more than twenty-five pages of photographs illustrating common Brazilian gestures, and explaining their meanings.

DRAMA AND DANCE

BIBLIOGRAPHY

517 Associação Museu Lasar Segall. Bibliografia de dramaturgia brasileira. 2 vols. São Paulo: Escola de Comunicações e Artes da USP, 1981. 225 p. Locates the texts of plays by Brazilian authors in São Paulo libraries. Includes those published separately and in periodicals as well as unpublished scripts. Arranged by author with a title index and an index of the number of characters. A useful contribution to the bibliography of Brazilian theater.

518 _______. Bibliografia teatro. 4 vols. São Paulo: 1976. Vol 1: Textos com 4 personagems. 122 p. Cites 81 Brazilian plays. Vol. 2: Textos com 3 personagems. 103 p. Cites 63 Brazilian plays. Vol. 3: Textos com 2 personagems. 97 p. Cites 47 Brazilian plays. Vol. 4: Textos infanto-juvenis. 100 p. International in scope, although many Brazilian plays are included.

519 Brazil. Serviço Nacional de Teatro. Indice de autores e peças da dramaturgia brasileira. Rio de Janeiro: 1977-. An index of all Brazilian plays, including many unpublished ones, which could be located by the Banco de Peças of the Serviço Nacional de Teatro. Arranged alphabetically by author; information includes author's birth and death dates, title of the play, type of play (comedy, etc.), number of scenes, number and gender of characters, time period in which it is set, and central themes. A synopsis follows. No bibliographical information is given for published plays. Three volumes, covering the alphabet A-C, were examined. Citations in all of the volumes are unannotated.

OTHER SOURCES

520 Agenda de cultura popular. São Paulo: Centro de Pastoral Vergueiro, 1983. 33 p. A guide to popular theater groups in the city of São Paulo and the metropolitan area.

521 Anuário artes cênicas: teatro/dança. São Paulo: Departamento de Informação e Documentação Artísticas, Centro de Documentação e Informação sobre Arte Brasileira Contemporânea, 1980-. An inventory of theater and dance presentations in the city of São Paulo for the calendar year covered. Information for each show includes title, author, director, cast, opening and closing dates, location, times, prices, censorship status, number of performances given, and attendance statistics, as well as extracts from critical comments in the press. This publication provides an important overview of theater and related arts in Brazil's major cultural center. Editions examined: 1977, 1980, 1981. Title varies: 1977: Anuário artes cênicas; 1980: Anuário artes cênicas: dança/teatro.

522 Anuário do teatro brasileiro. 1-, 1974-. n.p.: Serviço Nacional de Teatro, 1976-. A state-by-state register of theater activity. Includes information on local productions, productions from other states and foreign countries, children's plays, musical shows, courses, conferences, competitions, and awards. Illustrated with scenes from plays, and reproductions of handbills and posters. The lack of indexes makes use of this yearbook awkward. Issues examined: 1976, 1977, 1978, 1979, 1980.

523 O cartaz no teatro. São Paulo: Imprensa Oficial do Estado, 198-?. 159 p. The history of Brazilian theater and the posters advertising it are reflected in 365 reproductions (many in color) of an exhibition of posters. Includes posters from 1917 to 1981, arranged in chronological order. Accompanying text provides historical background.

524 Castro, Cássia Nava Alves de. Imagens da dança em São Paulo. São Paulo: Imprensa Oficial do Estado, 1987. 287 p. A collection of photographs illustrates dance in São Paulo: ballet, modern dance, and contemporary dance. Brief text identifies each dance, date and place of performance, dancers, choreographer, and artistic director. Includes index of names and bibliography.

525 Duarte, Abelardo. Autores alagoanos, peças teatrais: contribuição para a história do Teatro das Alagoas. Maceió: Fundação Teatro Deodora, 1980. 82 p. The first part of this work is comprised of short essays on the history of theater in the state of Alagoas, while the second part,

entitled "Autores e suas peças," provides bio-bibliographical information for a number of playwrights.

526 Faró, Antônio José. A dança no Brasil e seus construtores. Rio de Janeiro: Ministério da Cultura, Fundação Nacional de Artes Cênicas, 1988. 115 p. Provides photographs of and biographical/artistic information about European artists who launched ballet in Brazil. Includes a list of ballets performed in Rio de Janeiro by choreographer.

527 Faró, Antonio José, and Luiz Paulo Sampaio. Dicionário de balé e dança. Rio de Janeiro: 1989. 426 p. A general dictionary of dance and ballet with some emphasis on Brazil. For example, preference is given to artists and works seen there. Includes many entries on Brazilian and other Latin American performers, dance companies, works, composers, and choreographers. Illustrated. Includes a bibliography.

528 Felícitas. Danças do Brasil. Rio de Janeiro: Ediouro, n.d. 163 p. Describes fifty-three indigenous dances and eighty-four folk dances of Brazil, and notes their significance. Includes photographs of poor to fair quality.

529 Fundação Japão. Empresários artísticos: São Paulo e Rio de Janeiro. Pesquisa 3. São Paulo: 1985. 60 p. Lists 180 impresarios and producers associated with the performing arts: theater for adults and children, dance, and classical and popular music, giving their names, addresses, telephone numbers, and principal field of activity.

530 Gonçalves, Augusto de Freitas Lopes. Dicionário histórico e literário do teatro no Brasil. Rio de Janeiro: Livraria Editora Cátedra, 1975-. A dictionary of the Brazilian theater from its beginnings through 1968. Includes plays, theatrical companies, musical scores, playwrights, actors, directors, technicians, theaters, and related topics. Four of the fifteen projected volumes, covering the letters A-E, were examined.

531 Kühner, Maria Elena. Teatro amador: radiografia de uma realidade (1974-1986). Rio de Janeiro: Instituto Nacional de Artes Cênicas, 1987. 374 p. A survey of amateur theater in Brazil, which presents information in easy-to-scan outline form. Appendix provides texts of documents related to the Federação Nacional do Teatro Amador (FENATA), the Confederação Nacional do Teatro Amador (CONFENAT), and other topics.

532 Lima, Mariângela Alves de. Imagens do teatro paulista. São Paulo: Imprensa Oficial do Estado de São Paulo; Centro Cultural de São Paulo, 1985. 288 p. Visual documentation

through 300 photographs and drawings of actors, scenes, and themes in the São Paulo theater world from 1900-1985, arranged in chronological order. "Estas imagens constituem um índice para um acervo de 60.000 fotogramas, reunido pela Equipe de Artes Cênicas da Divisão da Pesquisa do Centro Cultural São Paulo, da Secretaria Municipal de Cultura." The role of São Paulo as a major center of Brazilian cultural life enhances the importance of the documentation found in this publication.

533 Nossos autores através da crítica. São Paulo: Associação Museu Lasar Segall, Biblioteca Jenny K. Segall, 1980- . Provides photocopies of criticism and commentary about plays by Brazilian authors in a series of volumes of 150-200 pages. Clippings included are limited to those found in the files of the Biblioteca Jenny K. Segall, which specializes in cinema, theater, radio, television, communications, and photography. Volumes 1-5 (1980-1984), covering playwrights Antônio Abujamra through Artur Azevedo, were examined.

534 Teatro: 1973. Rio de Janeiro: Conselho Estadual de Cultura, 1974. 77 p. A yearbook of theater for the state of Guanabara (city of Rio de Janeiro) divided into three parts: data on plays subsidized by the Comissão Especial do Teatro; information on activities in the theater world, such as children's theater, amateur and experimental theater, and drama seminars; and statements by critics on the theater season of 1973. No yearbooks for other years were located.

ECONOMICS AND BUSINESS

This section focuses on contemporary economics and business. Works related to economic history are cited in the "History" section. Those focusing on industry are found in the "Labor and Industry" section.

BIBLIOGRAPHY

535 Banco Regional de Desenvolvimento do Extremo Sul. Agência de Porto Alegre. Bibliografia analítica de aspectos econômicos do Rio Grande do Sul, 1950-77. Porto Alegre: 1978. 182 p. An annotated bibliography of 1080 monographs, theses, pamphlets, and periodical articles about the economy of Rio Grande do Sul. Updates and expands the 1974 publication, Economia do Rio Grande do Sul: bibliografia (488 entries).

536 Bibliografia de cooperativismo. Brasília: BINAGRI--Biblioteca Nacional de Agricultura; INCRA--Instituto Nacional de Colonização e Reforma Agrária, 1982-. An unannotated bibliography of 1367 references to materials on the subject of cooperatives, published from 1912 to the early 1980's. Volume examined: 1.

537 Bibliografia de pequena e média empresa. Rio de Janeiro: Confederação Nacional da Indústria, Serviço Nacional de Aprendizagem Industrial, Departamento de Assistência à Média e Pequena Indústria, 1985. 180 p. An unannotated bibliography of 1225 entries related to all aspects of small business, international in coverage, but with many citations to Brazilian publications. Author/title indexes.

538 Brazil. Congresso. Câmara dos Deputados. Biblioteca. Bibliografia sobre empresas públicas. Brasília: 1966. 44 p. An unannotated bibliography of 363 items, international in coverage, about public enterprises. Cites many Brazilian publications, including government documents.

539 Confederação Nacional da Indústria. Departamento Econômico.

Divisão de Estatística e Documentação. Empresas multinacionais: Bibliografia seletiva, 1959-1975. Rio de Janeiro: CNI, 1975. 38 l. Citations to 457 journal articles and other publications published in Latin America, North America, and Europe, providing a historical approach to the recent past of multinationals. Includes many Brazilian publications.

540 Confederação Nacional do Comércio. Conselho Técnico. Indice cumulativo de autores e de assuntos das conferências publicadas na Carta mensal: período de abril de 1955 a março 1975, números 1 a 240, organizado por Renato Gaudie Ley Linhares. Rio de Janeiro: 1977. 71 p. An index of lectures and addresses given by members of the Conselho Técnico of the CNC, published in its monthly publication, Carta mensal. Although they deal with a variety of topics, the majority are on subjects related to economics and business.

541 Ferreira, Carmosina Novais. Planejamento econômico e social no Brasil de 1930 a 1974: uma análise bibliográfica. 3 vols. Rio de Janeiro: Programa Nacional de Pesquisa Econômica, 1983. Contains 3600 entries including primary sources such as planning documents and programs ("planos globais, sectoriais, regionais, estaduais, municipais, e de áreas metropolitanas"), as well as secondary literature about Brazilian economic and social planning. Covers the forty-five year period from Vargas through Geisel. The first two volumes comprise the bibliography, while the third is an index of authors and subjects.

542 Ferreira, Carmosina N., Lieny do Amaral Ferreira, and Elizabeth Tolomei Moletta. Bibliografia seletiva sobre desenvolvimento econômico no Brasil. Rio de Janeiro: Instituto de Planejamento Econômico e Social, Setor de Documentação, 1972. 96 p. An unannotated bibliography of almost 800 citations related to many aspects of economic development in Brazil. Government reports and plans, and legislation are well represented.

543 Furtado, Dilma Ribeiro. Indice de periódicos brasileiros de economia. Rio de Janeiro: Federação das Indústrias do Estado da Guanabara e Centro Industrial do Rio de Janeiro, 1968. 266 p. A subject index to two major periodicals in the field of economics: Conjuntura econômica and Desenvolvimento e conjuntura, for the period July 1957-June 1967.

544 Instituto Euvaldo Lodi. Política econômica. Série bibliografias, no. 14. Rio de Janeiro: 1985. 39 p. An unannotated bibliography of 128 entries on economic policy with the focus on Brazil.

545 Literatura econômica. Rio de Janeiro: IPEA--Instituto de

Planejamento Econômico e Social, vol. 1-, set./out. 1979-. A bimonthly publication focusing on the current bibliography of the field of economics, domestic and foreign. Includes book reviews and lists miscellaneous special studies as well as the contents of current issues of journals. Very useful for keeping abreast of Brazilian publishing activity and thought in this field. The current series of this publication was preceded by Literatura econômica: boletim bibliográfico bimensal, vol. 1-6, 1976-1979.

546 Literatura econômica: sumários de periódicos. Rio de Janeiro: IPEA--Instituto de Planejamento Econômico e Social, vol. 6, sup. 1, jun. 1984-. A bimonthly supplement to Literatura econômica. It provides copies of the tables of contents of more than sixty economics journals (foreign and domestic) most frequently consulted by Brazilian professionals in the field. Includes abstracts of selected articles from the Brazilian journals covered.

547 Sumários de periódicos correntes em estatística e economia. Rio de Janeiro: Fundação Instituto Brasileiro de Geografia e Estatística, vol. 1-, 1972-. Photocopies of the tables of contents of journals specializing in economics and statistics, including six Brazilian publications. Issues examined: vol. 1-6, 1972-1977.

DICTIONARIES

548 Altmann, Martin Rudolf. Dicionário técnico contábil inglês-português, português-inglês. Accounting Dictionary: English-Portuguese, Portuguese-English São Paulo: Editora Atlas, 1980. 126 p. A bilingual dictionary of equivalent terms in the field of accounting, and related terms from business, finance, and law.

549 Belchior, Elysio O. Vocabulário de termos econômicos e financeiros. Rio de Janeiro: Civilização Brasileira, 1987. 397 p. Defines terms associated with economics and finance with quotations from writers in the field. Quotations originally published in languages other than Portuguese are translated. A bibliography cites the works consulted.

550 Bolsa de Valores do Rio de Janeiro. Dicionário de mercado de capitais e bolsa de valores. 2. ed. Rio de Janeiro: 1981? 95 p. A dictionary of terms in use in the stock exchanges of Brazil and the United States. Portuguese and English terms are listed in separate alphabets. The Portuguese terms are defined, while the English alphabet gives equivalent terms in Portuguese. Identifies many acronyms associated with the Brazilian stock market.

551 Brunner, Victor. Dicionário brasileiro de siglas em comércio exterior. São Paulo: Livraria Nobel, 1977. 125 p. Identifies 3300 acronyms related to economic and administrative aspects of foreign trade. Although more than half of those included are Portuguese language acronyms, many in Spanish, English, and French are covered too. Includes a list of public and private Brazilian organizations related to foreign trade.

552 Cavalcante, José Cândido Marquês. Dicionário inglês-português de termos econômicos & comerciais. Petrópolis: Editora Vozes; Fortaleza: Banco do Nordeste do Brasil, 1979. 408 p. A dictionary designed for the use of the export sector--exporters, banks, businesses, and industries, covering the vocabulary of English language texts in publications specializing in economics and business. Entries are illustrated with quotations from contemporary texts. Very useful for English speakers searching for the right word in Portuguese, as well as for the Portuguese language user for whom it is primarily intended.

553 Chalhub, Melhim Namem. Glossário do Sistema Financeiro da Habitação, com um apêndice de expressões em uso no sistema norte-americano de poupança e empréstimo. Rio de Janeiro: ENHAP--Escola Nacional de Habitação e Poupança, 1982. 169 p. Defines terms and identifies acronyms and abbreviations associated with housing finance.

554 Florenzano, Zola. Dicionário do comércio exterior. Rio de Janeiro: Sugestões Literárias, 1973. 291 p. Terms related to imports and exports are listed, and legislation pertaining to them is cited along with commentary.

555 Glossário de termos técnicos de seguro. Rio de Janeiro: Home Insurance Company, 1978. unpaged. Defines words, phrases, and abbreviations associated with the insurance business.

556 Gottheim, Vera L. Dicionário prático de economia, finanças, e comércio: português, inglês, alemão, espanhol. São Paulo: Editora Atica, 1987. 503 p. A polyglot dictionary providing equivalents of terms used in economics, finance, and business in four languages. Each language represented is the base language in one of its four sections.

557 Krahenbuhl, Hélio Morato. Dicionário inglês-português para executivos: termos de economia, finanças e administração. São Paulo: Editora Resenha Universitária, 1979. 260 p. Terms in economics, finance and administration are translated from English to Portuguese. Includes a table of weights and measures equivalents.

558 Luna, Eury Pereira. Terminglês: glossário de expressões

inglesas de uso corrente no comércio exterior. 3. ed. Rio de Janeiro: Livros Técnicos e Científicos Editora, 1984. 116 p. Portuguese equivalents for English terms and abbreviations commonly used in international trade.

559 Mann, Everett J., and Alfred Weg. Dicionário inglês-português de economia e finanças. Rio de Janeiro: Edições Financeiras, 1969. 82 p. Portuguese equivalents of English terms associated with finance, accounting, and the stock market.

560 Mendonça, André Luiz Dumortout de. Dicionário de sociedades comerciais e mercado de capitais. Rio de Janeiro: Forense, 1983. 823 p. Defines terms and cites and quotes laws associated with corporations and the stock market.

561 Silva, Zander Campos da. Dicionário de marketing e propaganda. Rio de Janeiro: Pallas, 1976. 208 p. A useful reference work for the fields of marketing and advertising. In addition to brief definitions of terms and identification of acronyms, it contains information on associations and journals in the field, and the texts of documents such as the "Código de ética de propaganda brasileira."

562 Silveira, Omar de Brito. Dicionário de termos bancários e comerciais. Belo Horizonte: Editora do Brasil em Minas Gerais, 1969. 173 p. Definitions of banking and business terms by a former employee of the Banco do Brasil.

563 Strohschoen, Iris. Dicionário de termos comerciais em 4 línguas: português, inglês, francês, alemão. Termos e expressões usadas no comércio, indústria, finanças, economia, direito, exportação, importação, contabilidade, fraseologia da correspondência comercial. Rio de Janeiro: Editora Globo, 1966. 360 p.

564 Vocabulário de termos técnicos bancários para uso interno do Banco Nacional do Comércio, S.A.. n.p.: 196-? 41 leaves. A Portuguese/English, English/Portuguese dictionary of banking terms and phrases.

CENSUS MATERIALS

VIII recenseamento geral--1970

565 Fundação Instituto Brasileiro de Geografia e Estatística. Censo comercial. VIII recenseamento geral, 1970, Série nacional, vol. 6. Rio de Janeiro: Fundação IBGE, Departamento de Censos, 1975. 157 p. A summary of retail and wholesale

trade statistics at the national and state levels based on the census of 1970.

566 _______. Censo comercial. 24 vols. VIII recenseamento geral, 1970, Série regional, vol. 6. Rio de Janeiro: Departamento de Censos, 1975-. Detailed statistics for retail and wholesale business at the microregion and municípío levels, based on the census of 1970. The first volume summarizes statistics for the entire country and the others provide data for each state.

567 _______. Censo comercial, Brasil: inquéritos especiais, comércio e administração de imóveis, bancos comerciais, financeiras, seguros. VIII recenseamento geral, 1970. Rio de Janeiro: Departamento de Censos, 1975. 142 p. A statistical compilation on real estate, banking, finance, and insurance at the state and national levels, based on the census of 1970.

Censos econômicos de 1975

568 Fundação Instituto Brasileiro de Geografia e Estatística. Censo comercial. Censos econômicos de 1975, Série nacional, vol. 3. Rio de Janeiro: Fundação IBGE, 1981. 227 p. A summary of wholesale and retail trade statistics at the state and national levels, based on the economic census of 1975.

569 _______. Censo comercial. 24 vols. Censos econômicos de 1975, Série regional, vol. 3. Rio de Janeiro: Fundação IBGE, 1980. Detailed wholesale and retail business statistics at the microregion and muncípio levels, based on the economic census of 1975. The first volume summarizes statistics for the entire country and the others provide data for each state.

IX Recenseamento geral do Brasil--1980

570 Fundação Instituto Brasileiro de Geografia e Estatística. Censo comercial. 26 vols. IX Recenseamento geral do Brasil--1980, vol. 4. Rio de Janeiro: IBGE, 1984. Detailed wholesale and retail business statistics at the microregion and municípío levels, based on the census of 1980. The first volume summarizes statistics for the entire country and the others provide data for each state.

OTHER SOURCES

571 Andrade, Gilberto Osório de Oliveira. Panorama dos recursos

naturais do Nordeste. Recife: Universidade Federal de Pernambuco, Imprensa Universitária, 1968. 60 p. Surveys natural resources of the Northeast which have economic potential.

572 Annual Directory: Rio/Salvador. Rio de Janeiro: American Chamber of Commerce for Brazil, Rio de Janeiro Chamber. An alphabetical listing of the member firms of the Rio de Janeiro and Salvador American Chambers of Commerce giving their addresses, chief executive officers, nature of their businesses, registered capital, and other data. Editions examined: 1984, 1989.

573 Atlas financeiro do Brasil. Financial Atlas of Brazil. Rio de Janeiro: Interinvest Editora, 1984. 727 p. Analyzes 213 major Brazilian business groups listing the companies comprising them. Data for each company includes its name, recent name changes, address, amount of registered capital, capital composition, and officers. An equity chart for each group depicts the relationships among all companies that form it. An index of companies includes 4697 firms. This is a very important tool for information about individual firms and for understanding relationships between firms and their parent groups. An earlier edition was published in 1981.

574 Balanço anual. São Paulo: Gazeta Mercantil. An annual compilation of data on Brazil's largest companies: the 100 largest domestic private companies, state enterprises, foreign companies, and companies with mixed capital. Also provides information on many companies by sector. Edition examined: 1988.

575 Banas, Geraldo. Os donos do Brasil: múltis, estatais e nacionais. São Paulo: Editora Banas, 1984. 330 p. Analysis of twenty-two sectors of the economy through text and tables. Covers foreign capital and private and state enterprises. Index of companies and persons.

576 Banco do Brasil. International Division. Summary of the Investment Legislation in Brazil. 3d ed. Rio de Janeiro: 1982. 118 p. "The purpose of this publication ... is to provide firms interested in investing in Brazil with preliminary knowledge of the relevant laws and regulations...." Provides English translations of laws.

577 Banco do Estado de São Paulo. How to Import from Brazil. São Paulo: BANESPA, 1975. 26 p. General information about importing goods from Brazil, including a list of items subject to export restrictions.

578 Banco do Estado de São Paulo. How to Invest in Brazil. São

Paulo: 1974? 28 p. Outlines the ways and means of investing in Brazil.

579 Brasil dez mil. São Paulo: Dun & Bradstreet, Informações Comerciais, Divisão de Serviços de Marketing, 1982/1983-. Covers 10,000 major Brazilian firms--"líderes nacionais quanto a movimentação de negócios, investimentos e gastos." Provides address, activity, chief executive, etc. Editions examined: 1982/1983, 1985/1986, 1988/1989.

580 Brasil: sua indústria e exportação: cadastro Delta. São Paulo: Albeisa do Brasil Editores. Covers all states, providing information on products, companies, and tourism. Edition examined: 21st, 1977/1978 (3 vols.)

581 Brasile: informazioni economiche. Roma: Istituto Italo-Latino-Americano, Vice-Segreteria Affari Economici e Sociali, 1983. 83 p. Basic data for those interested in doing business with Brazil.

582 Brazil: Basic Comparative Data, 1982. Brasília: Presidency of the Republic, Planning Secretariat, 1983? 34 p. Compares Brazilian statistical data related to business and economics--national accounts, production of selected goods, energy resources, prices and wages, employment, transportation, foreign sector, and population--with eleven other countries.

583 Brazil Company Handbook: Data on Major Limited Companies. São Paulo: Bolsa de Valores do Estado de São Paulo--BOVESPA, 1987. 104 p. Profiles major Brazilian companies listed on the São Paulo stock exchange. Information on background, officers, major stockholders, number of shares outstanding, major markets, competition, main raw materials used and their sources.

584 Brazil. Ministério das Relações Exteriores. Divisão de Estudos e Pesquisas do Mercado. Mercados para produtos selecionados da exportação brasileira. Brasília: Instituto de Planejamento Econômico e Social, 1978. 526 p. A quantitative market analysis in tabular format, providing data on foreign markets for 240 non-traditional exportable products, with emphasis on manufactured and semi-manufactured goods. Arranged by product under the Standard International Trade Classification commodity classification, and then by the country which is being studied as a market. Information for each country is provided in twenty-one categories, such as its total importation of a given product, importation originating in Brazil, principal supplier countries, and tariff information.

585 Brazil. Secretaria da Receita Federal. Centro de Informações Econômico-Fiscais. Comércio exterior do Brasil: importação.

Brasília. Detailed statistical data about Brazilian imports by product and by country of origin. Published annually.

586 Business Yearbook of Brazil, Mexico & Venezuela. London: Graham & Trotman, 1980-. A handbook which provides an introduction to the economies of the countries mentioned in the title, and covers the transportation system, banking, corporate and personal taxation, foreign investment regulations, oil, gas, and petrochemicals, and import and export statistics for each one. Also lists useful addresses, gives business travel data and information on import regulations, customs, and tariffs, and summarizes development plans and the economic and financial background of each country. Issue examined: 1981.

587 Casagrande, Humberto. Abertura do capital de empresas no Brasil: um enfoque prático. São Paulo: Editora Atlantis, 1985. 143 p. A handbook outlining the procedures for listing stocks on Brazilian stock exchanges, identifying entities associated with them, and defining related terms.

588 Coopers & Lybrand. Profile of Banking and Finance in Brazil. São Paulo: 1987. 87 leaves. "This volume provides a comprehensive view of banking and finance in Brazil.... In addition to covering the historical development and the present structure of the nation's banking and finance, [it] examines issues relating to foreign involvement, regulations, principal products and standard practices in the Brazilian capital markets" (Foreword, p. 2). Includes a list of acronyms and abbreviations and a brief glossary of terms. Its detailed table of contents and well-organized format make it easy to consult for specific information.

589 Desempenho do comércio exterior brasileiro. Rio de Janeiro: Fundação Centro de Estudos do Comércio Exterior. Information on Brazil's exports and imports through statistics, graphs and text. The introduction implies that it has been published annually since 1979, although the only volume located was for 1982.

590 Directory of American Firms Operating in Foreign Countries. 11th ed. 3 vols. New York: Uniworld Business Publications, 1987. A worldwide directory which includes Brazil. Volume 1 lists American firms in alphabetical order followed by each firm's U.S. address, name of its chief executive officer and the officer in charge of foreign operations, its principal products or services, and the countries in which it has operations. Volumes 2 and 3 present a geographical approach--under each country are listed American firms operating there, with addresses of their subsidiaries or branches and of their home offices in the U.S., as well as brief descriptions of their products or services.

591 A economia brasileira e suas perspectivas. Rio de Janeiro: APEC--Associação Promotora de Estudos de Economia. An annual publication issued by a non-profit organization which analyzes the behavior of the Brazilian economy for the year in question and the outlook for the next year through macroeconomic conditions. Also includes special studies on relevant topics and a statistical appendix. Issues examined: 1983, 1984, 1988.

592 Exportação: análise estatística comparativa. Rio de Janeiro: Banco do Brasil, CACEX--Carteira do Comércio Exterior. A monthly publication providing statistics on export of principal products by sector, principal products in declining order by aggregate value, variations in prices, etc. Comparisons with previous years for up to ten years in some cases.

593 Exportação brasileira, empresas em ordem descrescente de valor. Rio de Janeiro? Banco do Brasil. A monthly publication presenting cumulative statistics from January of each year. Data for the current year are presented in comparison to data for the previous year. Issues examined: 1981, 1982, 1983, 1984.

594 Exportação e importação, balança comercial: principais empresas em ordem decrescente de importação. Rio de Janeiro? Banco do Brasil. A monthly publication presenting cumulative statistics from January of each year. Data for the current year are presented in comparison to data for the previous year. Issues examined: 1982, 1983, 1984, 1985.

595 Felsberg, Thomas Benes. Foreign Business in Brazil: A Practical Law Guide. 2. ed. São Paulo: Instituto Brasileiro de Direito Transnacional, 1976. 335 p. An overview of Brazilian business law of interest to foreigners. Deals with forms of business organization, foreign investment in the Brazilian stock exchange, foreign capital registration, control, and taxation, tax legislation, imports and exports, patents and trademarks, labor legislation, inflation and monetary correction, etc. The appendix contains English translations of pertinent laws and regulations.

596 Foreign Trade of Brazil. Brasília: Secretaria da Receita Federal. Coordenação do Sistema de Informações Econômico-Fiscais, 1970?-. Statistical data on foreign trade: merchandise imported/exported; countries and ports of destination and origin; quantities and values of imports and exports; and commodity classification according to the Standard International Trade Classification. Issued annually.

597 Garland, Paul Griffith. Doing Business In and With Brazil. Rio de Janeiro: Banco Lar Brasileiro, 1978. 484 p. A very

useful handbook for potential investors or businesses considering Brazilian branches, combining data on Brazilian politics and government, the economic system, and basic characteristics of Brazilian laws with specific information on such topics as incentives for investors, exchange controls, trading companies, taxation, industrial property agreements, and requirements for permanent residence. The translation into English of laws pertaining to these matters and forms which must be completed is an especially useful feature.

598 As grandes companhias. São Paulo: Banas. An annual publication providing information on Brazilian companies with capital over a specific amount, which varies with inflation and the economic situation. The companies are categorized in two ways: their overall ranking in terms of capitalization, and ranking within their sector of economic activity. The rest of the work profiles each company, giving date founded, headquarters, address, directors and chief executive officers, present capital and capital for each of the past several years, reserves, sales or receipts, profits, and area of activity if not evident from its name. Issues examined were for 1973/1974 and 1977/1978.

599 Guía bancaria latinoamericana. Latin American Banking Guide. Bogotá: Federación Latinoamericana de Bancos. A country-by-country listing of Latin American banks, including those in Brazil. Provides information in outline form: address, date founded, chief executive officer, number of branches and employees, and related financial institutions. Additional information about banking associations, the banking calendar, and basic economic indicators for each country. Volumes examined: 1984, 1986, 1990.

600 Guia do mercado brasileiro: páginas amarelas. Nacional. Rio de Janeiro: Confederação das Associações Comerciais do Brasil, Grupo Gilberto Huber, Empreendimentos Brasileiros de Informações Dirigidas, Ltda. National yellow pages of goods and services. Issues examined: 1984, 1986.

601 Guia Interinvest: O Brasil e o capital internacional. Interinvest Guide: Brazil and International Capital. Rio de Janeiro. A guide to foreign investment in Brazil providing detailed information. Lists investor countries and their fields of activity, as well as individual companies. The latter information includes firm name, address, registered capital, percentage of foreign capital, foreign exchange amounts registered with the Banco do Brasil, and balance sheet data. Charts show the relationships between companies, and indicate majority and minority holdings. Editions examined: 5th, 1983; 6th 1986.

602 Indice do Brasil. Brazilian Index Yearbook. Rio de Janeiro:

Indice--O Banco de Dados. A yearbook designed to promote Brazilian exports and investment in Brazil. The text, in Portuguese and English, addresses such subjects as energy, sectors of the economy, the labor force, the financial market, external and internal debt, and development in various regions. Statistical data about many aspects of the economy supplements the text. Unfortunately, this yearbook is difficult to use. There is no discernible logic to its arrangement, and the subjects included appear to have been selected at random. Issues examined: 1976-1977, 1977-1978, 1978-1979, 1979-1980.

603 Legal Aspects of Doing Business in Latin America: Mexico, Brazil, Argentina, Chile, and the Andean Common Market Countries. New York: Practising Law Institute, 1980. 296 p. Gives practical information on laws and regulations affecting foreign investment and the transfer of technology, on legal aspects of labor problems, the legal nature of business organizations, and other topics of interest to those wishing to do business in Latin America. The information is contained in articles by various authors which are, in general, easy to scan.

604 Os maiores mineradores do Brasil: perfil empresarial do setor mineral brasileiro. 3 vols. n.p.: Revista Minérios e Conselho Nacional de Desenvolvimento Científico e Tecnológico, 1982. Detailed information on the organization, mining activity, trade, etc., of the twenty-five major groups responsible for 80 percent of Brazil's mineral production, excluding petroleum, as well as much background on the Brazilian mining industry. Includes maps, charts, and statistical tables.

605 Major Companies of Argentina, Brazil, Mexico, and Venezuela. London: Graham & Trotman, 1979/1980-. The publisher describes this work as containing "more information on the major industrial and commercial companies than any other work," although no criteria for inclusion in the work are given. Information for each company listed includes address, chief executive, principal activities, branch offices, brief financial information, principal shareholder, and number of employees. Originally published under title: Major Companies of Argentina, Brazil, and Mexico. Editions examined: 1979/1980, 1982.

606 Manual de classificação de mercadorias. São Paulo: Edições Aduaneiras, 1983. 542 p. Covers various systems which classify merchandise for export/import and other purposes: NBM: Nomenclatura Brasileira de Mercadorias; TAB: Tarifa Aduaneira no Brasil; TIPI: Tabela de Incidência do I.P.I.; and NABALALC: Nomenclatura Aduaneira de Bruxelas para a Associação Latino-Americana de Livre Comércio.

607 Panorama. Rio de Janeiro: Bolsa de Valores do Rio de Janeiro, 1971-. An annual statistical record of stock market transactions and sectors of activity on one major stock exchange, which reflects what occurred on the Brazilian stock market for the year in question. Issue examined: 1972.

608 Perfil das empresas estatais. Brasília: Secretaria de Planejamento da Presidência da República, Secretaria de Orçamento e Controle de Empresas Estatais, 1986-. Profiles state business enterprises annually as a group and individually through statistical tables and graphics. Surveys them in the aggregate and in various rankings, and also presents detailed data on each one. Principal enterprises covered are PETROBRAS, CVRD, TELEBRAS, SIDERBRAS, ELETROBRAS, PORTOBRAS, and NUCLEBRAS, and many smaller ones are listed under the government ministries associated with them. This publication supersedes Cadastro das empresas estatais, published 1981-1985. Editions examined: 1986, 1988.

609 Price, Waterhouse and Company. Doing Business in Brazil. São Paulo: 1986. 119 p. "This guide has been prepared for the assistance of those interested in doing business in Brazil. It does not cover exhaustively the subjects it treats, but is intended to answer some of the important broad questions that might arise" (Foreword). Earlier editions were issued in 1970, 1972, and 1980.

610 Quem é quem na economia brasileira. São Paulo: Editora Visão, 1967-. An annual supplement to Visão (weekly news magazine), which analyzes the Brazilian economic-financial situation as it is reflected in the performance of companies. It provides statistical and financial information on companies by sector, including public enterprises, and lists the 1000 largest companies by profit and billings. The 20th edition (August, 1986) covered a total of 9299 companies.

611 São Paulo (State). Secretaria de Economia e Planejamento. Handbook for the Foreign Investor in Brazil. 3. ed. São Paulo, 1977. 239 p. A handbook of legal information necessary to the foreign investor in Brazil. Topics covered include foreign capital registration and money transfers, Brazilian company forms, company reorganizations, taxes, incentives to industry, incentives to foreign trade, trademark and patent rights, labor legislation, financing possibilities, foreign capital in the Brazilian stock market, and agrarian legislation.

612 São Paulo Yearbook. São Paulo: American Chamber of Commerce for Brazil, São Paulo Chamber. Combines a survey of current business conditions in Brazil with a membership directory which includes corporate and personal members.

Information for corporate members include their addresses, chief administrative officers, domestic sales, export sales, net worth, registered capital and number of employees, as well as the locations of their factories and branches, their products/services, and foreign affiliations. Editions examined: 1978, 1984, 1989.

613 Sinopsis Dun Brasil. São Paulo: Dun & Bradstreet Informações Comerciais Ltda. An annual compilation of financial and other information about Brazilian companies, arranged by state. Editions examined: 1982/1983; 1984/1985.

614 Statement of the Laws of Brazil in Matters Affecting Business. Supplement. No. 1-. Washington: Pan American Union, 1965-. Updates and supplements the third edition (1961).

615 U.S. Bureau of International Commerce. Brazil: Survey of U.S. Export Opportunities. Washington: Govt. Print. Off. "... designed as a market planning guide for American firms on capital goods export sales to Brazil. It is also intended to aid the business planning of suppliers of services, such as financial institutions, consultants, and engineers. The Survey provides both a ready reference of facts and figures and a guide to profitable growth potential in each of 14 areas, or sectors of the Brazilian economy." Issues examined: 1974, 1979.

616 Who's Who in Brazilian Economic Life: An Annual Biographical Dictionary of Men and Women Representing a Vital Force in Brazil's Drive for Economic Development. São Paulo: Sociedade Brasileira de Publicações Culturais e Econômicas, Ltda., 1967?-. Who's who-type biographical data and many portraits of contemporary business and industrial leaders. Volume 1, which was the only one located, appears to have been issued in about 1967, although it is not dated.

REGIONS

Center-West

617 Superintendência do Desenvolvimento da Região Centro-Oeste. Departamento de Promoções de Investimentos. Centro-Oeste: convite ao investidor. Brasília: SUDECO/SAO/DPI, 1986. 224 p. Basic information on the region of interest to prospective investors, much of it broken down by states and municípios. In addition to lists of investment opportunities, and information on fiscal incentives, credit programs, and legislation, there is detailed data on the infrastructure,

financial institutions, indigenous areas, and other topics. A publication with the same title was issued by SUDECO in 1983 (196 p.).

Northeast

618 Comércio exterior: exportações do Nordeste. Subsídios para análise econômica. Recife: Superintendência do Desenvolvimento do Nordeste, Superintendência Ajunta de Planejamento, Coordenação de Informática. Statistics on the value and quantity of products exported to foreign countries by the Northeast as a region, and by individual states. Editions examined: 1977, 1978, 1979.

619 Comércio exterior: importações do Nordeste. Subsídios para análise econômica. Recife: Superintendência do Desenvolvimento do Nordeste, Superintendência Ajunta de Planejamento, Coordenação de Informação. Statistics on the value and quantity of imports from foreign countries by the Northeast as a region and by specific states. Edition examined: 1980.

620 Importações e exportações do Nordeste do Brasil. Recife: Superintêndencia do Desenvolvimento do Nordeste. Statistical data on the region's trade. Published annually, although with a time lag of several years. Issues examined: 1975, 1976, 1977, 1978, 1980 (published 1979-1983).

621 Superintendência do Desenvolvimento do Nordeste. Divisão de Comércio. Nordeste: oportunidades de investimentos. 3. ed. Recife: 1977. 82 p. Focuses on factual information related to manufactured products and products of extractive industries needed in the Northeast.

622 Superintendência do Desenvolvimento do Nordeste. Superintendência Adjunta de Planejamento. Plan anual de trabalho, 1981. 2 vols. Recife: 1981? Vol. 2: Programas regionais especiais. A tabular presentation, program-by-program, of the activities of SUDENE. Includes financing of the programs.

STATES

The export directories cited under the states below are usually multilingual directories of a state's export products and the firms, banks, and government agencies that render import/export services, including Brazilian embassies, consulates, and trade bureaus worldwide. They also include background information on the state. Illustrated advertisements enhance these publications by providing interesting and colorful overviews of the products of the states. Other publications related to economics and business in specific states are also included here. Those focusing on industry in specific states are cited in the section on "Labor and Industry."

Amazonas

623 Brazil. Ministério das Minas e da Energia. Grande Carajás Program. n.p.: 1981. 35 p. Maps, charts, statistical tables, and brief text focus on the economic potential of the east Amazon region.

Bahia

624 Bahia's Export Directory. Salvador: Núcleo de Promoção de Exportações da Bahia--PROMOEXPORT Bahia. Edition examined: 1980/1981.

Goiás

625 Goiás: um convite ao investimento. Goiânia: Secretaria da Indústria e Comércio, 1972. unpaged. An overview of Goiás covering many aspects, with emphasis on those of interest to potential investors. Includes maps, charts, statistical tables, and color illustrations, as well as text.

Minas Gerais

626 Export Directory of Minas Gerais. Guia de exportación de Minas Gerais. São Paulo: EBID--Brazilian Targeted Information Publishing House; INDI--Industrial Development Institute of Minas Gerais; FIEMG--Minas Gerais State Industry Federation. Edition examined: 1985.

Paraná

627 Export and Tourism Directory of Paraná, Brazil. Guía de exportación y turismo del Paraná. Curitiba: Paraná Foreign Trade Center; n.p.: EBID--Brazilian Targeted Information Publishing House. Issued earlier under the title, Export Directory of Paraná, Brazil. Guía de exportación del Paraná. Editions examined: 1982/1983, 1985/1986.

628 Paraná: Investment Opportunities. Curitiba: Centro de Promoção Econômica do Paraná, 1973. 84 p. Provides general information about the state, as well as data about industry, agriculture,

services, utilities, education, the transportation and communications infrastructure, the economy, export corridors, and investment opportunities in text, tables, and maps. Text in English.

Pernambuco

629 The State of Pernambuco Export Directory. Recife: Núcleo de Promoção de Exportações de Pernambuco. Editions examined: 1975, 1987/1988.

Rio Grande do Sul

630 Brasil empresas: cadastro socio-econômico. n.p.: Braempel Editorial, 197-? Vol. 1: Rio Grande do Sul: Região Nordeste. Basic data on specific municípios: their history, industry, taxes, exports, tourism. Detailed information on many local companies. This volume covers Caxias do Sul, Bento Gonçalves, Flores da Cunha, Farroupilha, Antônio Prado, Nova Prata, Carlos Barbosa, Veranópolis, Garibaldi, and Gramado.

631 Desempenho da economia do RS. Porto Alegre: Governo do Estado do Rio Grande do Sul, Secretaria de Coordenação e Planejamento, 1978-. An annual publication which documents in text and statistical tables the principal regional macroeconomic aggregates and economic indicators of the gaúcho economy. Editions examined: 1978, 1979, 1981, 1982, 1983, 1984.

632 Rio Grande do Sul Export and Tourism Directory. Guía de exportación y turismo del Rio Grande do Sul. Fuhrer fur export und turismus fur Rio Grande do Sul. Porto Alegre? State Secretariat of Industry and Commerce of Rio Grande do Sul; n.p.: EBID--Brazilian Targeted Information Publishing House. Issued earlier under the title, Export Directory of Rio Grande do Sul. Guía de exportación del Rio Grande do Sul. Editions examined: 1982/1983, 1985/1986.

633 Rio Grande do Sul. Secretaria da Indústria e Comércio. Investor's Handbook: Rio Grande do Sul, Brazil. Porto Alegre: 197-? unpaged. Economic facts and figures, well presented in text, statistical tables, maps, and other graphics. Additional information on the state's transportation and communications infrastructure, commercial legislation, taxes, and other matters of concern to investors.

Santa Catarina

634 Export and Tourism Directory of Santa Catarina, Brazil. São Paulo: Editora Páginas Amarelas--EBID, Foreign Trade Publications Division--EBIDEX; Florianópolis? Santa Catarina Foreign Trade Centre--CECESC. Editions examined: 1st, 1982/1983; 1987. 1st edition issued under the title, Export Directory of Santa Catarina, Brazil.

Sergipe

635 Manual do investidor: Sergipe. Aracajú: Companhia de Desenvolvimento Industrial e de Recursos Minerais de Sergipe, 1980. 145 p. Basic information about Sergipe for potential investors, enhanced with statistics, maps, and charts.

EDUCATION

Reference materials related to the field of education were limited to those of a general nature, which might be useful to social scientists and other non-specialists, for purposes of this bibliography. No attempt was made to identify materials primarily of interest to professionals in the field, such as bibliographies on pedagogy.

BIBLIOGRAPHY

636 Associação Nacional de Pós-Graduação e Pesquisa em Educação. Teses em educação, 1985. Rio de Janeiro: 1987. 134 p. Bibliographic data about and abstracts of 262 master's theses and doctoral dissertations in all fields of education, based on information provided by the data bank of the Coordenação de Aperfeiçoamento de Pessoal de Nível Superior (CAPES). Author and subject indexes.

637 Conselho de Reitores das Universidades Brasileiras. Catálogo das publicações do Conselho de Reitores das Universidades Brasileiras: subsídios para uma bibliografia sobre educação superior. Brasília: 1987. 408 p. A bibliography with 503 entries and many descriptive annotations. Covers monographs, periodical articles, and proceedings of meetings.

638 "Educação especial: bibliografia." Boletim do Centro de Documentação [Fundação Getúlio Vargas]. Instituto de Estudos Avançados em Educação. Centro de Documentacão, vol. 18, no. 1 (1989): 1-178. An entire issue of this journal is comprised of 307 annotated entries citing books and periodical articles devoted to special education, plus a separate list of 168 unannotated titles. The majority of publications cited are Brazilian in origin. Includes a subject index.

639 "Formação e orientação profissional: bibliografia." Boletim do Centro de Documentação, no. 1 (July 1984), pp. 1-247. A bibliography of about 500 items focusing on professional

education with abstracts summarizing the content of each one. Includes journal articles, monographs, and theses. Comprises the entire first issue of the Boletim do Centro de Documentação of the Instituto de Estudos Avançados em Educação of the Fundação Getúlio Vargas.

640 Fundação Getúlio Vargas. Instituto de Estudos Avançados em Educação. Catálogo de pesquisas, 1975-1983. Rio de Janeiro: 1984. 90 p. Bibliographic data and abstracts of studies in the field of education--many of them related to the social and economic aspects--by researchers of the Fundação Getúlio Vargas. Expands a catalog of master's theses produced 1976-1980, also published by the Institute.

641 Fundação Movimento Brasileiro de Alfabetização MOBRAL. Publicações do MOBRAL: um estudo preliminar. n.p.: 1975. 173 p. Detailed information about the publications of MOBRAL, through statistics, maps, and other graphics, and in a bibliography of its teaching, cultural, informational, and promotional materials.

642 McNeill, Malvina Rosat. Guidelines to Problems of Education in Brazil: A Review and Selected Bibliography. New York: Teachers College Press, 1970. 66 p. Covers publications concerned with "contemporary developments and problems in Brazilian education." Cites those published since 1955 in the fields of education, educational statistics, values and society, educational psychology, educational economics, planning and research, elementary, secondary, and higher education, and statutes and regulations. Addresses many of the social aspects of education, and is therefore a useful tool for social scientists as well as educators.

643 Oliveira, Regina Maria Soares de. Pós-graduação: levantamento bibliográfico. 2. ed. Brasília: Coordenação do Aperfeiçoamento de Pessoal de Nível Superior, 1978. 57 p. An unannotated bibliography of 515 books, newspaper and periodical articles, government documents, proceedings of conferences, and other publications related to graduate education in Brazil. This revised edition of a bibliography first published in 1974 more than doubles the number of publications cited in the earlier work.

OTHER SOURCES

644 Brazil. Coordenação de Aperfeiçoamento de Pessoal de Nível Superior. Catálogo dos cursos de pós-graduação no Brasil. Brasília: 1975. 1215 p. Lists graduate courses in all disciplines offered in forty institutions of higher education.

645 Brazil Coordenação de Aperfeiçoamento de Pessoal do Nivel

Superior. Coordenação de Acompanhamento e Avaliação. Catálogo de cursos de mestrado e doutorado. Brasília: 1989: 234 p. Graduate courses throughout Brazil are listed under subjects. Information includes name of university or institute, course name, level, areas covered by course, address, and telephone.

646 Brazil. Departamento de Ensino Supletivo. Catálogo do entidades de ensino supletivo. Brasília. A detailed guide to adult education programs in Brazil. Issue examined: 1978.

647 Brazil. Secretaria da Educação Superior. Catálogo das instituições do ensino superior. Brasília: 1983. 476 p. Basic data on institutions of higher learning, listed state-by-state.

648 Brazil. Serviço de Estatística da Educação e Cultura. Estatísticas da educação nacional. Rio de Janeiro: 1960-71-. Educational statistics for pre-primary, primary, secondary, and university levels. Issues examined: 1960-1971; 1971-1973.

649 Cadastro de entidades fontes de informações em educação no Brasil. Brasília: Instituto Nacional de Estudos e Pesquisas Educacionais, Coordenaria do Sistema de Informações Bibliográficas em Educação, Cultura, e Desporto, 1984-. Information on institutions which produce or collect sources of information in the field of education. Edition examined: 1984. A preliminary edition was issued in 1982.

650 Catálogo de entidades financiadoras de bolsas de pós-graduação: Brasil e exterior. 5 vols. n.p.: CAPES/CNPq, 1975. Specific information on groups and institutions offering post-graduate fellowships in all fields. vol. 1: Instituições nacionais; Vol. 2-3: Instituições estrangeiras; Vol. 4: Organizações internacionais; Vol. 5: Referências (index).

651 Duarte, Sérgio Guerra. Dicionário brasileiro de educação. Rio de Janeiro: Edições Antares, 1986. 175 p. Defines educational terms as they are used in Brazil, including legal terms, and identifies specific educational institutions. Includes a chronology of education in Brazil.

652 Guia do estudante: cursos e profissões. São Paulo: Editora Abril. A guide intended to assist the prospective student in selecting the appropriate university or faculty for the major chosen. Edition examined: 1988.

653 Indicadores educacionais. Brasília: Ministério da Educação, Serviço de Estatística da Educação e Cultura, 1982/1983-. Provides statistics on pre-school, elementary, and secondary education. Edition examined: 1982/1983.

654 I glossário de termos utilizados na estatística educacional. Rio de Janeiro: Fundação MUDES/Movimento Universitário de Desenvolvimento Econômico e Social, 1980. 142 p. Defines 471 terms in the field of education as they are used in statistical tables. An alphabetical list of the terms included refers the user to the actual glossary, which is inconveniently arranged in "ordem semântica." Lists of the same terms in Spanish, French, and English also refer to the terms in the glossary.

655 Sinopse estatística da educação pré-escolar, 1984-. Série sinóptica. Brasília: Ministério da Educação, Serviço de Estatística da Educação e Cultura, 1986-. Statistical profile of pre-school education: number of establishments, teachers, students enrolled, and other data. Issue examined: 1984.

656 Willadino, Gildo. Atlas da educação no Brasil. Rio de Janeiro: Fundação de Assistência ao Estudante, 1985. 153 p. Detailed maps and statistical tables provide information on levels of education completed and literacy for Brazil as a whole and for each of the states and territories and their microregions, enabling the user to visualize Brazilian educational problems and achievements.

ETHNIC GROUPS

GENERAL SOURCES

657 História da imigração no Brasil: as famílias. São Paulo: Editora Cultura Brasileira, 1976. 376 p. Summarizes the history of the immigration of many nationalities to Brazil through text and statistical tables. Provides information about important families of each nationality.

658 Levine, Robert M. Race and Ethnic Relations in Latin America and the Caribbean: An Historical Dictionary and Bibliography. Metuchen, NJ: Scarecrow Press, 1980. 252 p. A dictionary of "terms, names, and events related to racial and ethnic questions," covering the geographic area described in the title with emphasis on "countries where racial themes have played unusually important roles"--including Brazil. Some of the major themes yielding terms for definition are slavery, race relations, prejudice and discrimination, and the role of race in formal and popular culture. Twenty pages of the ninety-five-page bibliography are devoted to race and ethnic relations in Brazil.

BLACKS

659 Alves, Henrique L. Bibliografia afro-brasileira: estudos sobre o negro. 2. ed. Rio de Janeiro: Editora Cátedra, 1979. 181 p. An unannotated bibliography of 2283 citations to monographs, conference proceedings, and periodical and newspaper articles, encompassing such topics as history, including abolition, physical anthropology, religion, music, race relations, linguistics, folklore, medicine, and literature published in Brazil. The arrangement in alphabetical order by author's name, with no index to provide subject access,

is a limiting factor in the use of this work. First edition: 1976.

660 Araújo, Emanoel. A mão afro-brasileira: significado da contribuição artística e histórica. São Paulo: Tenenge, 1988. 398 p. Técnica Nacional de Engenharia, S.A. Records black contributions to the plastic arts, literature, and the performing arts through excellent reproductions of art works and visual documentation (excellent reproductions of art works and photographs) and text, including biographical information about the artists. Includes bibliography for the plastic arts.

661 Bahia. Secretaria de Cultura. Departamento de Bibliotecas. Bibliografia sobre o negro: livros de acervo das bibliotecas do DEPAB. Salvador: 1987. 13 p. An unannotated bibliography with 158 entries.

662 Bibliografia da cultura negra. Rio de Janeiro: Departamento Geral de Cultura, Divisão de Documentação e Biblioteca, 1984. 56 p. An unannotated bibliography of 279 books on black culture, located in libraries of the regional system.

663 Carise, Iracy. Arte-mitologia: orixás, deuses iorubanos. n.p.: 198-? 121 p. Art and mythology of blacks in Brazil who originated in Nigeria (iorubanos or nagôs) in many black and white photographs accompanied by explanatory text. A glossary of African terms and a map depicting distribution of the tribes in Africa are also useful.

664 Couceiro, Solange Martins. Bibliografia sobre o negro brasileiro. São Paulo: Universidade de São Paulo, Escola de Comunicações e Artes, 1971. 66 p. An unannotated bibliography of 881 items related to sociological or anthropological aspects of blacks in Brazil. Omits history, folklore, and fiction.

665 Damesceno, Caetana; Micenio Santos, and Sonia Giacomini. Catálogo de entidades do movimento negro no Brasil precedido de um perfil das entidades dedicadas à questão do negro no Brasil. Comunicacões do ISER, 29. Rio de Janeiro: Instituto de Estudos da Religião--ISER, Programa Religião e Negritude Brasileira, 1988. 89 p. A state-by-state list of names and addresses of organizations concerned with racism and discrimination. Also lists serials associated with these issues and provides a profile of black organizations by state.

666 Fundação Cultural do Maranhão. O negro no Maranhão. São Luís: 1978. 19 p. An annotated bibliography with fifty-five entries.

667 Hasenbalg, Carlos A. Race Relations in Modern Brazil. The

Brazilian Curriculum Guide Specialized Bibliography. Albuquerque: Latin American Institute, University of New Mexico, 1985 or 1986. 22 p. An essay surveying contemporary race relations in Brazil, focusing on the black-white color continuum that characterizes them. An annotated bibliography provides many suggestions for further reading.

668 Instituto Nacional do Folclore. Biblioteca Amadeu Amaral. Bibliografia afro-brasileira. Série referência, 2. Rio de Janeiro: FUNARTE, 1988. 105 p. An unannotated bibliography of 953 entries in alphabetical order by author or title with a subject index.

669 Maggie, Yvonne. Catálogo: centenário da abolição. Publicações avulsas no. 2. Rio de Janeiro: Universidade Federal do Rio de Janeiro, Centro Interdisciplinar de Estudos Contemporâneos--Ciec, Núcleo da Cor, 1989. 265 p. A catalog listing 1702 events commemorating the 1988 centennial of the abolition of slavery in Brazil, with emphasis on Rio de Janeiro, São Paulo, and Salvador. There are thirty categories of events, such as "acontecimento cívico," "passeata," "publicação," and "visita diplomática."

670 Moura, Antônio de Paiva. A cultura afro-brasileira em Minas: catálogo bibliográfico. Belo Horizonte: Edição Carranca; Comissão Mineira de Folclore, 1987. 59 p. An unannotated bibliography of books, pamphlets, clippings, unpublished works, photographs, recordings, and other items related to blacks in Minas Gerais in the collection of the Centro de Informações Folclóricas. arranged by broad subject with an author/detailed subject index.

671 Museu Lasar Segall. O negro no cinema. São Paulo: 1988. 93 p. An annotated bibliography and filmography of 170 items related to blacks in films. The bibliography includes books and journal articles, published in Brazil and elsewhere, while the filmography lists only Brazilian films. Indexes of subjects, directors and films.

672 Nuñez, Benjamin. Dictionary of Afro-Latin American Civilization. Westport, CT: Greenwood Press, 1980. 525 p. Described by the author as "a historical and descriptive dictionary of terms and phrases, with selected biographies of Afro-Latin political leaders, writers, and other important personalities caught in the complex neo-African sociocultural evolution in the New World," the 4500 entries in this dictionary are taken from English, French, Portuguese, and Spanish sources. The emphasis on the Caribbean islands reflects their importance as "the focal point in the African Diaspora," although this work is also a very useful source of information about Afro-Brazilian civilization. A good bibliography, a subject index,

and a name index by country enhance its usefulness. Often cites the source of the information supplied in a definition.

673 Porter, Dorothy B. Afro-Braziliana: A Working Bibliography. Boston: G. K. Hall, 1978. 294 p. A partially annotated, selective bibliography of monographs, pamphlets, and periodical articles by or about Afro-Brazilians.

674 Querino, Manuel. Costumes africanos no Brasil. 2. ed. ampliada e comentada. Série Abolição, 20. Recife: Fundação Joaquim Nabuco; Editora Massangana, 1988. 251 p. Describes African customs in Brazil related to religion, food, folklore, festivals, and other observances. Includes a bibliography. First published in 1938.

675 Sant'Ana, Moacir Medeiros de. Bibliografia sobre o negro. Maceió: Secretaria de Comunicação Social, 1989. unpaged. An unannotated bibliography of 340 books in the personal library of the author. The vast majority are concerned with blacks in Brazil.

676 Soares, Francisco Sérgio Mota; Henriette Ferreira Gomes; Jeane dos Reis Passos. Documentação jurídica sobre o negro no Brasil, 1800-1888: índice analítico. Salvador: Secretaria da Cultura, Departamento de Bibliotecas, 1988. 270 p. Cites and describes the contents of 1472 legal documents in the collection of the Departmento de Bibliotecas related to blacks in Brazil during most of the nineteenth century. Since it lists printed sources, rather than unique manuscripts, this work serves as a general guide to the subject. Includes a useful subject index and a bibliography.

GERMANS

677 Oberacker, Carlos H. A contribuição teuta à formação da nação brasileira. 2 vols. 2. ed. em língua portuguesa, revista e aumentada. Rio de Janeiro: Presença, 1985. Biographies of Germans prominent in Brazilian history, arranged chronologically. Includes an extensive bibliography and a good index.

INDIANS

678 Baldus, Herbert. Bibliografia crítica da etnologia brasileira. 2 vols. São Paulo and Hannover: 1954-1968. An annotated bibliography of some 2835 publications--books, pamphlets,

periodical articles, and conference proceedings--about past and present groups of Indians of Brazil. The second volume updates the first one. Each volume has author and subject indexes.

679 Catálogo de filmes etnológicos. Encyclopaedia cinematographica, vol. 1, Brasil. São Paulo: Universidade de São Paulo, Escola de Comunicações e Artes, Serviço de Biblioteca e Documentação, Seção Técnica de Filmoteca, 1987. 43 p. "Os filmes deste catálogo são parte de uma coleção denominada 'Encyclopaedia Cinematographica,' editada desde 1952 pelo Instituto do Filme Científico de Gottinger, na Alemanha" [p. 1]. The catalog lists all films on Brazilian Indians in the German collection, copies of which are available at the Filmoteca cited in the bibliographic description above. Information about each silent, 16 mm. film includes a summary of its content, translation of title into Portuguese, director, duration, color, and date. Arranged by subject with an index of Indian tribes and a bibliography.

680 Emiri, Loretta. Levantamento bibliográfico yanomami. n.p.: Território Federal de Roraima, Secretaria de Educação e Cultura, Departamento de Assuntos Culturais, Divisão de Etnografia e Folclore, 1984. 26 leaves. An unannotated bibliography of materials related to the Yanomami in the areas of health, land, language, and culture.

681 Empresas de mineração e terras indígenas no Amazonas. Edição revista e atualizada. São Paulo: Centro Ecumênico de Documentação e Informação--CEDI; Coordenação Nacional de Geólogos, 1987. 82 p. Locates charters for mineral exploration in indigenous areas of Amazonas. Provides name of area, name of company, registration number with the Departamento Nacional de Pesquisa Mineral, charter number, date of publication in the Diário oficial da União, size of lot, and observations.

682 Fundação Cultural do Maranhão. Indios do Maranhão: bibliografia. São Luís: 1977. 19 p. A partially annotated bibliography with sixty-five entries of books and journal articles published in Brazil and elsewhere.

683 Fundação Instituto Brasileiro de Geografia e Estatística. Mapa etno-histórico de Curt Nimuendaju. Rio de Janeiro: 1981. 97 p. 1 folded map in pocket. Locates linguistic families of Indian languages throughout Brazil. Based on research done 1905-1944. Indexed by tribes. Includes an extensive bibliography.

684 Gregório, Irmão José. Contribuição indígena ao Brasil: lendas e tradições, usos e costumes, fauna e flora, língua, raízes, toponímia, vocabulário. 3 vols. Belo Horizonte: União

Brasileira de Educação e Ensino, 1980. Much of this work (volumes 2-3) is devoted to a dictionary of words derived from Indian languages, illustrated with 850 line drawings. Volume 1 consists of "Notas preliminares" on a wide range of topics beginning with the names of many Indian tribes and groups, the significance of the names, and nicknames of the tribes. It also includes a useful index of illustrations, other indexes, and an extensive bibliography. An important reference work for those interested in Brazilian Indians, and for students of Brazilian Portuguese and its many words of Indian origin.

685 Grünberg, Georg, and René Fuerst. Kritische Bibliographie zum Genozid in Brasilien (1957-1969). Veroffentlichungen des Seminars fur Ethnologie der Universitat Bern, Nr. 1. Bern: Seminar fur Ethnologie, 1969. 16 p. An annotated bibliography of works published 1957-1969 on genocide and Brazilian Indians.

686 Meliã, Bartomeu; Marcos Vinícios de Almeida Saul, and Valmir Francisco Muraro. O guarani: uma bibliografia etnológica. Santo Angelo: Fundação Missioneira de Ensino Superior, 1987. 448 p. An unannotated bibliography of 1163 entries of ethnological writings about the Guarani Indians from 1528 through 1986, preceded by an essay on the ethnology of various periods of their history. Thorough indexing by subject, tribes, places, author, chronology, and illustrations provides excellent access to this valuable work.

687 Povos indígenas no Brasil. São Paulo: Centro Ecumênico de Documentação e Informação, 1981-. A series of eighteen projected volumes about indigenous peoples of contemporary Brazil giving basic factual information and summarizing the history of their contacts with the outside world. They contain many photographs, drawings, maps, and bibliographies. Coverage of the planned volumes is as follows. Starred (*) volumes were examined: 1: Noroeste da Amazônia; 2. Roraima *3. Amapá/Norte do Pará; 4. Solimões; *5: Javari; 6: Juruá; 7: Tapajós/Madeira; *8: Sudeste do Pará; 9: Maranhão; 10: Nordeste; 11: Acre/Purus; 12: Rondônia; 13: Oeste do Mato Grosso; 14: Parque Indígena do Xingú; 15: Leste do Mato Grosso; 16: Leste; 17: Mato Grosso do Sul; and 18: Sul.

688 Povos indígenas no Brasil, 1985/1986. Aconteceu especial, 17. São Paulo: Centro Ecumênico de Documentação e Informação--CEDI, n.d., 448 p. A collection of news stories about indigenous peoples, which appeared in 1985/1986. Arranged by geographic areas. Includes useful maps and photographs. Similar publications for 1980, 1981, 1982, 1983, and 1984 (Aconteceu especial, 6, 10, 12, 14, and 15 respectively) were also examined.

689 Steward, Julian Haynes. Handbook of South American Indians. 7 vols. New York: Cooper Square Publishers, 1963. Volumes 1-4 of this guide deal with specific tribes, presenting geographical, environmental, historical, and cultural data as well as the principal sources of anthropological data and a bibliography about each one. Volumes 1, The Marginal Tribes and 3, The Tropical Forest Tribes, cover Brazilian Indians. Volume 5 deals with the comparative ethnology of South American Indians. Volume 6 covers physical anthropology, linguistics, and cultural geography. Volume 7 is a detailed subject index to the set.

690 Terras indígenas no Brasil. Rio de Janeiro: Centro Ecumênico de Documentação e Informação; Museu Nacional, Projeto Estudo sobre Terras Indígenas no Brasil, 1987. 148 p. A survey of officially recognized Indian lands. Gives Indian name of area, tribe, legal status, município where located, population, source of data, and observations. Includes maps and other graphics.

ITALIANS

691 Costa, Rovílio, and Itálico Marcon. Imigração italiana no Rio Grande do Sul: fontes históricos. Porto Alegre: Escola Superior de Teologia e Espiritualidade Franciscana; Caxias do Sul: Editora da Universidade de Caxias do Sul, 1988. 223 p. An annotated bibliography of monographs, periodical and newspaper articles, almanacs, pamphlets, and unpublished materials associated with Italian immigration to southern Brazil. Includes a useful name index.

692 Mellafe R., Rolando. Inmigración italiana a la Argentina, Brasil y Uruguay: bibliografia selectiva. Santiago de Chile: Centro Latino-americano de Demografía, 1978. 47 p. A partially annotated bibliography of Italian inmigration to three South American countries, including Brazil, with a topical approach, such as general effects of immigration in the receiving country, assimilation of the immigrants, and agriculture and colonization.

JAPANESE

693 Aliança Cultural Brasil-Japão. Guia da cultura japonêsa em São Paulo. São Paulo: 1989. unpaged. A guide designed to acquaint Brazilians of other ethnic groups with Japanese

culture. Provides information on customs, organizations, courses, and activities associated with Japan and Japanese-Brazilians (nipo-brasileiros).

694 Centro de Estudos Nipo-Brasileiros. The Japanese and Their Descendents in Brazil: An Annotated Bibliography. São Paulo: 1967. 188 p. The 658 entries in this bibliography are annotated in English. They cover materials in Japanese, Portuguese, and other European languages.

695 Estudos japoneses no Brasil. Pesquisa 2. São Paulo: Fundação Japão; Assessoria Cultural do Consulado Geral do Japão, 1988. 91 p. A directory of corporate entities and individual researchers engaged in Japanese and Japanese-Brazilian studies in Brazil.

696 Fundacão Japão. Catálogo de livros sobre assuntos japoneses editadas em língua portuguesa. Pesquisa, 1. São Paulo: Fundação Japonesa, 1984. 57 p. Concentrates on books about Japan, but also deals with Brazilian subjects, including nine pages devoted to Japanese immigration to Brazil.

JEWS

697 Comunidades judías de Latinoamerica. Buenos Aires: Oficina Sudamericana del Comité Judío Americano, Instituto de Relaciones Humanas, 1966-. Basic information about the Jewish communities in each country of Latin America, including Brazil: history, population, education, the press, community life, religion, relations with other groups, civil rights, and prominent persons. A separate section serves as a country-by-country directory of Jewish institutions and organizations. Editions examined: 1966, 1968, 1970, 1971/1972.

698 Instituto Cultural Judaico Marc Chagall. Projeto Preservação de Memória Judaica. Imigração judaica no Rio Grande do Sul: histórias de vida. Jewish Immigration in Rio Grande do Sul: Life Stories. Porto Alegre: 1989. 104 p. Summaries of eighty interviews with Jewish immigrants to Rio Grande do Sul, which were part of an oral history project. Text in Portuguese and English.

699 Kleiner, Alberto. Atlas de los territorios de la Jewish Colonization Association en Argentina y Brasil, 1913-1941. Buenos Aires: Libreros y Editores del Polígono, 1983. 65 leaves. Depicts the development of a colonization group in South America. Locates and provides plans for two colonies in Rio Grande do Sul.

700 Margulies, Marcos. Iudaica brasiliensis: repertório bibliográfico comentado dos livros relacionados com o judaísmo e questões afins, publicados no Brasil desde os primórdios das atividades editoriais no país até o presente momento. Rio de Janeiro: Editora Documentário, 1974. 159 p. An annotated bibliography covering such topics as Jews, Judaism, Israel, Zionism, ecumenicism, and anti-Semitism. Arranged by author, with a subject index. Continued by nos. 702 and 703.

701 Mello, José Antônio Gonsalves de. Gente da nação: judeus residentes no Brasil holandês, 1630-54. Recife: 1979. 233 p. "Separata do vol. 51 da Revista do Instituto Arqueológico, Histórico e Geográfico Pernambucano."

702 Schlesinger, Hugo. Iudaica brasiliensis, 1974-1984: repertório bibliográfico das publicações relacionadas com o judaísmo e questões afins. São Paulo: Federação Israelita do Estado de São Paulo, 1984? 239 p. Continues the bibliography of books in Portuguese published in Brazil related to Jews and Judaism (no. 700).

703 ______. Iudaica brasiliensis III, 1984-1988: Repertório bibliográfico das publicações relacionadas com o judaismo e questões afins. São Paulo: Federação Israelita do Estado de São Paulo, 1989? 165 p. A unannotated bibliography of 697 entries, continuing the bibliographies described in nos. 700 and 702.

704 Wolff, Egon, and Frieda Wolff. Contratos comerciais. Documentos, 1-2. 2 vols. Rio de Janeiro: 1988. "Este volume contém transcrições de contratos sociais particulares ou feitos em tabelionatos registrados no Tribunal do Comércio e na Junta Comercial do Rio de Janeiro entre 1869 e 1900, guardados hoje em dia no Arquivo Nacional." Vol. 1: A-K, século XIX; vol. 2: L-Z, século XIX.

705 ______, and ______. Dicionário biográfico. Rio de Janeiro: 1986- . Subjects of the six volumes published 1986-1990 include 1: Judaizantes e judeus no Brasil 1500-1808; 2: Judeus no Brasil, século XIX; 3: Testamentos e inventários; 4: Processos de naturalização de israelitas, século XIX; 5: Judaísmo e judeus na bibliografia em língua portuguesa; and 6: Genealogias judaicas.

706 ______, and ______. Guia histórico da comunidade judaica de São Paulo. São Paulo: Editora B'nei B'rith, 1988. 151 p. This guide of the Jewish community in São Paulo includes organizations, persons, commercial firms, street names, and other topics associated with the subject. Emphasis is on the nineteenth to mid-twentieth centuries. Many portraits and other illustrations. The lack of an index is an unfortunate omission, since the text is partially in narrative format, arranged by broad topics.

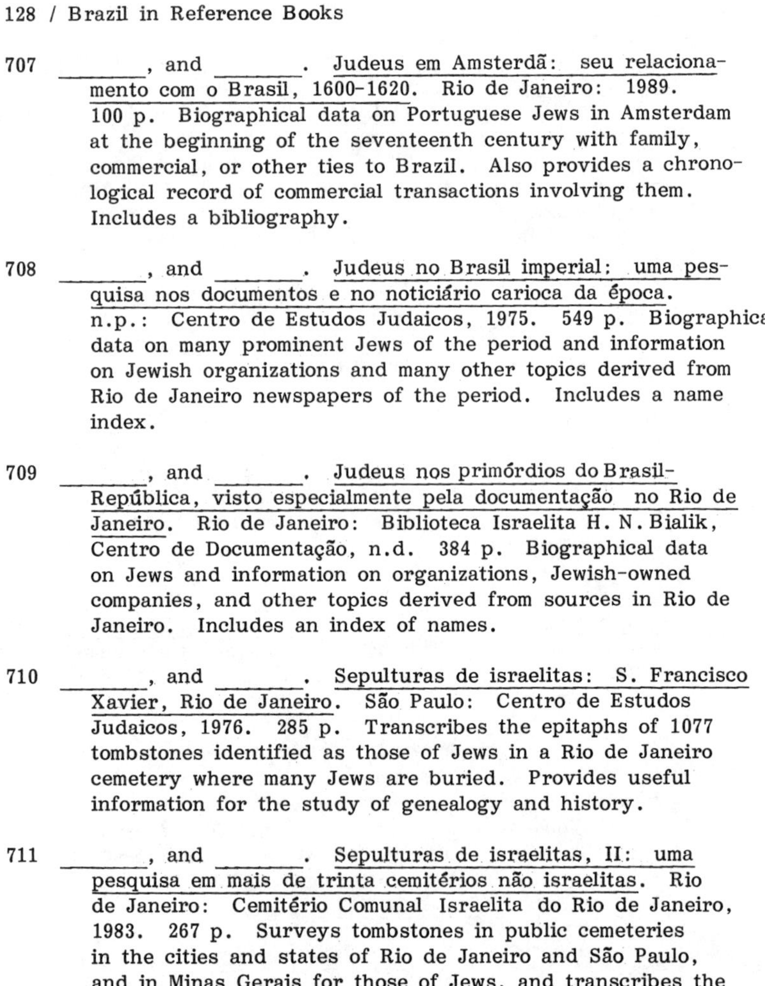

707 ______, and ______. *Judeus em Amsterdã: seu relacionamento com o Brasil, 1600-1620.* Rio de Janeiro: 1989. 100 p. Biographical data on Portuguese Jews in Amsterdam at the beginning of the seventeenth century with family, commercial, or other ties to Brazil. Also provides a chronological record of commercial transactions involving them. Includes a bibliography.

708 ______, and ______. *Judeus no Brasil imperial: uma pesquisa nos documentos e no noticiário carioca da época.* n.p.: Centro de Estudos Judaicos, 1975. 549 p. Biographical data on many prominent Jews of the period and information on Jewish organizations and many other topics derived from Rio de Janeiro newspapers of the period. Includes a name index.

709 ______, and ______. *Judeus nos primórdios do Brasil-República, visto especialmente pela documentação no Rio de Janeiro.* Rio de Janeiro: Biblioteca Israelita H. N. Bialik, Centro de Documentação, n.d. 384 p. Biographical data on Jews and information on organizations, Jewish-owned companies, and other topics derived from sources in Rio de Janeiro. Includes an index of names.

710 ______, and ______. *Sepulturas de israelitas: S. Francisco Xavier, Rio de Janeiro.* São Paulo: Centro de Estudos Judaicos, 1976. 285 p. Transcribes the epitaphs of 1077 tombstones identified as those of Jews in a Rio de Janeiro cemetery where many Jews are buried. Provides useful information for the study of genealogy and history.

711 ______, and ______. *Sepulturas de israelitas, II: uma pesquisa em mais de trinta cemitérios não israelitas.* Rio de Janeiro: Cemitério Comunal Israelita do Rio de Janeiro, 1983. 267 p. Surveys tombstones in public cemeteries in the cities and states of Rio de Janeiro and São Paulo, and in Minas Gerais for those of Jews, and transcribes the epitaphs. Arranged by cemetery with a name index. Includes a section of brief obituaries for Jews known to have died in the nineteenth century whose burial places were not located.

712 ______, and ______. *Sepulturas de israelitas III: as mishpakot de Belém.* Rio de Janeiro, 1987. 107 p. Transcribes the epitaphs on the tombstones of Jews in two cemeteries of Belém.

LEBANESE

713 *O libanês no Brasil.* São Paulo: Hekmat Khodr, 1987. unpaged.

Biographical information and portraits of prominent contemporary Brazilians of Lebanese descent. Although there is no general title, this book is referred to as "Vol. 3--Brasil." According to the introduction, volumes 1 and 2 are devoted to France and the United States, respectively.

NORTH AMERICANS

714 American Society of Rio de Janeiro. *Yearbook*. Rio de Janeiro. Lists members of the organization, and gives other information about the society's history, and about other organizations in Rio of interest to the American community. Edition examined: 1988.

715 Oliveira, Betty Antunes de. *North American Immigration to Brazil: Tombstone Records of the "Campo" Cemetery, Santa Bárbara d'Oeste, São Paulo State, Brazil*. Brasília: Centro Gráfico do Senado Federal, 1978. 66 p. A record of tombstone inscriptions in a cemetery begun by American southerners who immigrated to Brazil after the Civil War, and maintained by their descendants.

FOLKLORE AND POPULAR CULTURE

BIBLIOGRAPHY

716 Bibliografia do folclore brasileiro: fontes para o estudo existentes em Minas Gerais. Belo Horizonte: Grupo de Bibliotecários de Ciencias Sociais e Humanidades da Associação dos Bibliotecários de Minas Gerais, 1. parte-. 1983-. An unannotated bibliography which focuses on the folklore of Minas Gerais while including many items of general interest. Part I, which was examined, includes 445 citations.

717 Bibliografia folclórica. Rio de Janeiro: FUNARTE, Instituto Nacional do Folclore, no. 1-, 1977-. An unannotated bibliography listing material on folklore and popular culture added to the Biblioteca Amadeu Amaral of the Instituto Nacional do Folclore. Although two issues were published in 1977, it has been published annually since 1978. Numbers examined: 1-13; 1977-1988.

718 Colonelli, Cristina Argenton. Bibliografia do folclore brasileiro. São Paulo: Conselho Estadual de Artes e Ciências Humanas, 1979. 294 p. An unannotated bibliography of more than 4900 items about Brazilian folklore published in Brazil and abroad through 1978. It includes monographs, periodical articles, exposition catalogs, and conference proceedings.

719 Nascimento, Braulio do. Bibliografia do folclore brasileiro. Rio de Janeiro: Biblioteca Nacional, 1971. 353 p. An unannotated bibliography of 2468 books, pamphlets, and periodical articles about Brazilian folklore published 1762-1970. Covers beliefs and superstitions, customs, popular language, games, dances, festivals, folk arts, folk music, oral literature, children's folklore, and folklore research.

720 Rio de Janeiro (State). Departamento de Cultura. Divisão de Folclore. Acervo da Divisão de Folclore. Rio de Janeiro:

1987. 116 leaves. Lists books, periodicals, sound recordings, photographs, artifacts, and other items related to folklore in the state of Rio de Janeiro in the collection of the Division of Folklore.

721 Vieira Filho, Domingos. Populário maranhense: bibliografia. Rio de Janeiro: Civilização Brasileira; São Luis: Secretaria de Cultura do Maranhão, 1982. 72 p. Has 438 unannotated references to publications about the folklore of Maranhão. Includes a brief discography.

GENERAL SOURCES

722 Almeida, Bira. Capoeira: A Brazilian Art Form. Richmond, CA: North Atlantic Books; Palo Alto, CA: Sun Wave, 1982. 152 p. Describes capoeira techniques and movements and illustrates them with photographs. Provides information on the accompanying rhythms and gives the lyrics of songs, complete with English translations. Includes a bibliography.

723 Almeida, Renato. Manual de coleta folclórica. Rio de Janeiro: Campanha de Defesa do Folclore Brasileiro, 1965. 216 p. Summarizes major elements and aspects to consider in collecting folklore data, with particular attention to Brazil. Among the many types of folklore covered are superstitions, religious beliefs, oral literature, foods, and the folklore of animals, water, minerals, and fire.

724 Antologia de folclore e cultura popular nordestina. Recife: Editora ASA Pernambuco, 1985. 92 p. Brief descriptions of important festivals and other folklore practices in the Northeast. Intended for a popular audience.

725 Araújo, Alceu Maynard. Cultura popular brasileira. 3. ed. São Paulo: Melhoramentos, 1977. 198 p. Divided for easy reference into chapters of festivals, dances, games, music, rituals, wisdom, language, myths and legends, and folk arts and crafts. Illustrated with photographs and line drawings. No bibliography. The third edition appears to be a reprint of the 1973 edition.

726 Atlas folklórico do Brasil: artesanato, danças, e folguedos. Rio de Janeiro: Edições FUNARTE, 1982-. A projected multi-volume publication issued by the Instituto Nacional de Folclore, surveying popular arts, folk dance, and popular theatre on a município-by-município basis. Text, photographs, maps, and tables provide the data, and a bibliography supplies references for further reading. The first volume covers the municípios in the state of Espírito Santo.

727 Bastos, Wilson de Lima. Danças no registro do folclore brasileiro. Juiz de Fora: Centro de Estudos Sociológicos de Juiz de Fora, 1977. 35 p. Identifies Brazilian folk dances with their geographic areas of origin and provides additional information about them which varies in extent of coverage from one sentence to several paragraphs.

728 Campos, Eduardo. Medicina popular: superstições, crendices e meizinhas. 3. ed. Rio de Janeiro: Edições O Cruzeiro, 1967. 145 p. A compilation of popular remedies, arranged by type of illness. Includes a useful bibliography. First ed.: Fortaleza: 1951.

729 Carneiro, Edison. Folguedos tradicionais. 2. ed. Rio de Janeiro: Conquista, 1982. 176 p. Covers popular celebrations and entertainment: traditional holiday observances, dances, parades, games, and folk drama. Includes lyrics and scores of some folk songs, and pen and ink sketches and a few photographs as illustrations.

730 Cascudo, Luis da Câmara. Antologia do folclore brasileiro. 4. ed. São Paulo: Martins, 1971. 675 p. Excerpts from the writings of 100 authors associated with Brazilian folklore--chroniclers, travelers, and scholars--and valuable biobibliographical notes about them. Divided into three major sections: "Séculos XVI, XVII, XVIII: cronistas;" "Séculos XIX, XX: viajantes estrangeiros;" and "Séculos XIX e XX: os estudiosos brasileiros." First edition: 1943; second, 1956; third, 1965 (2 vols.)]

731 ______. Contos tradicionais do Brasil (folclore). Rio de Janeiro: 1967. 480 p. A compilation of about 100 Brazilian folk tales.

732 ______. Dicionário do folclore brasileiro. 6. ed. Coleção Reconquista do Brasil, 2. série; vol. 151. Belo Horizonte: Editora Itatiaia; São Paulo: Editora da Universidade de São Paulo, 1988. 811 p. The terms associated with Brazilian folklore are identified, described, and explained in entries ranging in length from a few lines to more than a page, with many entries including bibliographic citations. According to the author's note, the text of the fifth edition of this classic work was not revised, unlike earlier editions in which entries were added and the bibliography updated. Later editions of this dictionary omit the illustrations found in the first (1954) and second (1962) editions. Therefore the earlier ones are still useful, although the quality of the illustrations--mostly photographs--is poor.

733 ______. Geografia dos mitos brasileiros. Belo Horizonte: Editora Itatiaia; São Paulo: Editora da Universidade de São Paulo, 1983. 345 p. A state-by-state-summary of the

ethnic groups and sociological factors influencing local folklore comprises the first part of this work. The second part discusses indigenous, European, African, and local myths such as the lobishomem and the mula-semcabeça, in terms of their content, origins, regional variations, etc. A detailed table of contents provides access to individual myths.

734 Delorme, Renée Jeanne, and Hermes Miolla. Pronto socorro do sertão: a cura pelas plantas. Porto Alegre: Escola Superior de Teologia de São Lourenço de Brindes, 1979. 208 p. Identifies popular medicinal plants, gives their scientific and popular names, indications for their use, and efficacious parts. A second alphabet lists illnesses and ailments and gives instructions for preparing remedies from plants.

735 Folclore brasileiro. Rio de Janeiro: Fundação Nacional de Arte--FUNARTE. A series of publications issued by FUNARTE on the major elements of the folklore of Brazilian states. Chapters on such topics as oral literature, popular language, folk dances, folk art, popular religion, and traditional cookery provide a useful but brief overview of each state's folkloric traditions. A calendar of traditional festivals, the scores and lyrics of well-known folk songs, and photographs illustrating events and objects, combine with a bibliography to make these publications useful reference works. The following publications in the series were examined:

Alagoas, by José Maria Tenório Rocha, 1977. 79 p.
Bahia, by Hildegardes Vianna, 1981. 79 p.
Ceará, by Florival Seraine, 1978. 64 p.
Espírito Santo, by Guilherme Santos Neves, 1978. 77 p.
Goiás, by Regina Lacerda, 1977. 75 p.
Maranhão, by Domingos Vieira Filho, 1977. 65 p.
Paraná, by Roselys Vellozo Roderjan, 1981. 87 p.
Pernambuco, by Waldemar Valente, 1979. 94 p.
Piauí, by Noé Mendes de Oliveira, 1977. 77 p.
Rio de Janeiro, by Cáscia Frade, 1979. 101 p.
Rio Grande do Norte, by Veríssimo de Melo, 1977. 77 p.
Santa Catarina, by Doralécio Soares, 1979. 77 p.
São Paulo, by Hélio Damante, 1980. 65 p.

736 Donato, Hernâni. Dicionário de mitologia: asteca, maia, aruaque e caraíba, inca, tupi, diauita, banto, ioruba, ere e fanti-ashanti, negro-maometana. São Paulo: Editora Cultrix, 1982. 275 p. A dictionary of the mythology of the Amerindians and Africans of the Americas, including Brazil. Reprint of the first edition (1973) entitled Dicionário das mitologias americanas.

737 Lenko, Karol, and Nelson Papavero. Insetos no folclore. São

Paulo: Conselho Estadual de Artes e Ciências Humanas, 1979. 518 p. Information on the folklore of insects, by type of insect, including superstitions, uses in folk medicine, rhymes and sayings, myths and legends, uses as food, common names, and other topics. Very well indexed. Good bibliography.

738 Lima, Rossini Tavares de. Abecê do folclore. 5. ed. São Paulo: Ricordi, 1972. 262 p. Covers the basics of folklore research supplying facts about folklore and its collection in Brazil. About 100 pages are devoted to a "Pequeno dicionário musical," which provides the scores and lyrics of folk songs.

739 Maior, Mário Souto. Alimentação e folclore. Rio de Janeiro: FUNARTE, Instituto Nacional do Folclore, 1988. 196 p. Defines the meanings of food terms in Brazilian idiomatic usage and folklore. Cites written examples, which refer to the bibliography.

740 _______. Território da danação: o diabo na cultura popular do Nordeste. Rio de Janeiro: Livraria São José, 1975. 102 p. A glossary of terms of the Northeast associated with the devil, a chapter on the devil in literatura de cordel, information on other regional literature in which the devil figures, and a bibliography contribute to the usefulness of this work.

741 Marconi, Marina de Andrade. Folclore do café. São Paulo: Secretaria da Cultura, Ciência e Tecnologia, Conselho Estadual de Cultura, 1976. 134 p. Covers the folklore of coffee culture and processing, medicinal uses of coffee, games, songs, riddles, and other aspects of this important commodity.

742 Meireles, Cecília. Batuque, samba, e macumba: estudos de gesto e ritmo, 1926-1934. Rio de Janeiro: Instituto Nacional do Folclore--FUNARTE, 1983. 105 p. A collection of watercolors and drawings by the well-known poet, who was also knowledgable about folklore. They illustrate beautifully the costumes and many of the movements associated with batuque, samba, and macumba during the period covered.

743 Mello Moraes, Alexandre José de. Festas e tradições populares do Brasil. Coleção Reconquista do Brasil, vol. 55. São Paulo: Editora da Universidade de São Paulo; Belo Horizonte: Livraria Itatiaia, 1979. 312 p. Descriptions and illustrations of popular and religious holidays, festivals, and observances, such as weddings in nineteenth-century Brazil. This work was first published in 1895 with a second edition in 1901. An edition with revision and notes by Luis da Câmara Cascudo was published in 1967 in Rio de Janeiro.

744 Muniz Júnior, José. Do batuque a escola de samba: subsídios

para a história do samba. São Paulo, Edições Símbolo, 1976. 207 p. Traces the development of the samba from its African origins to its present prominence in Brazilian culture. An appendix covers the escolas de samba: their organization, legal aspects, and regulations for the desfiles de carnaval. Includes a good bibliography. Illustrated.

745 Rezende, Angélica de. Lembrando o Natal e suas tradições. Belo Horizonte: Gráfica Editora Sion, 1967. 110 p. Information on the celebration of Christmas including the scripts of traditional plays, and the scores and words of songs.

746 Ribeiro, Joaquim. Folclore do açúcar. Rio de Janeiro: Campanha de Defesa do Folclore Brasileiro, 1977. 227 p. Provides a wealth of information about the myths, dances, festivals, superstitions, popular medicine, and other folklore associated with sugar--a major factor in the Brazilian economy and social life since colonial days. Includes a useful bibliography. Although this book is not in reference format, its short chapters, preceded by detailed summaries of their content, lend themselves readily to reference use.

747 Rodrigues, Anna Augusta. Rodas, brincadeiras e costumes. Rio de Janeiro: Plurarte; Brasília: Instituto Nacional do Livro, Fundação Nacional Pró-Memória, 1984. 336 p. A collection of the traditional games and customs of children, which includes musical scores and lyrics, diagrams of games, and other illustrations. A good source for this type of information.

748 Romero, Sílvio. Folclore brasileiro: cantos populares do Brasil. Coleção Reconquista do Brasil (Nova série), vol. 86. Belo Horizonte: Editora Itatiaia; São Paulo; Editora da Universidade de São Paulo, 1985. 306 p. This work, published in two earlier editions (Lisboa: Nova Livraria Internacional, 1883 and Rio de Janeiro: Livraria Classica de Alves & Comp., 1897), provides the lyrics of folk songs under four major headings: "Romances e xácaras," "Bailes, cheganças e reisados," "Versos gerais," and "Orações e parlendas." Useful notes supply historical and other information.

749 Trigueiros, Edilberto. A língua e o folclore da Bacia do São Francisco. Rio de Janeiro: Campanha de Defesa do Folclore Brasileiro, 1977. 192 p. This compilation, based on research completed in 1963, provides brief definitions of local language usage with terms related to the folklore of the area--the São Francisco River valley which includes parts of the states of Alagoas, Bahia, Minas Gerais, Pernambuco, and Sergipe. Includes the scores and lyrics of many folk songs and a few illustrations.

750 Xidich, Osvaldo Elias. Narrativas pias populares. São Paulo: Universidade de São Paulo, Instituto de Estudos Brasileiros, 1967. 145 p. A compilation of short, traditional religious legends and folktales.

STATES

Additional publications on the folklore of specific states are listed under the series, Folclore brasileiro in the "General Sources" section.

Amazonas

751 Monteiro, Mário Ypiranga. Cultos de santos & festas profano-religiosas. Manaus: Imprensa Oficial do Estado do Amazonas, 1983. 349 p. Information on the observance of religious holidays and popular festivals in the state of Amazonas. Includes a calendar of observances, many illustrations, lyrics of songs and a wide variety of other data.

Ceará

752 Instituto Nacional do Folclore. Pequeno atlas de cultura popular do Ceará: Juazeiro do Norte. Rio de Janeiro: FUNARTE/INF; Fortaleza: Universidade Federal do Ceará, 1985. 89 p. A potpourri of data about the popular culture of an area rich in that tradition. Covers Juazeiro as a regional religious center, gives a chronology of the life of Padre Cícero, discusses types of housing, poesia de bancada, artisanry, and folk rituals. Illustrated with photographs of poor to fair quality. Includes a brief bibliography.

753 Seraine, Florival. Antologia do folclore cearense. 2. ed. Fortaleza: Edições UFC, 1983. 356 p. Excerpts from the writings of twenty-five nineteenth and twentieth century students of folklore of Ceará, and examples of the works of eight popular poets (principally authors of literatura de cordel). Provides biobibliographic notes for authors included.

Espírito Santo

754 Cláudio, Affonso. Trovas e cantares capixabas. Introdução e notas de Guilherme Santos Neves. 2. ed. Rio de Janeiro: Instituto Nacional do Folclore, 1980. 120 p. This second edition of a pioneer work first published in 1923 (Rio de Janeiro), preserves some of the oral tradition in the folklore

and popular culture of the state of Espírito Santo. It includes the texts of nursery rhymes, popular religious poetry and prayers, improvised poetry, proverbs, riddles, and folk tales.

755 Teixeira, Fausto. Crendices & superstições. Vitória: Fundação Cultural do Espírito Santo, 1975. 123 p. A collection of beliefs, superstitions, and the practice of magic in Espírito Santo, based on material collected over a ten-year period, 1958-1967.

Minas Gerais

756 Ambrósio Júnior, Manoel. No meu rio tem mãe d'água: folclore do Vale São Franciscano. Belo Horizonte: Imprensa Oficial, 1987. 181 p. Covers the myths, festivals, superstitions, folksongs, customs, and other aspects of an area of Minas Gerais rich in folklore.

Pernambuco

757 Empresa de Turismo de Pernambuco. Vamos festejar juntos: Santo Antônio, São João, São Pedro. Recife?: 1977. 19 p. A schedule of events associated with the "festas juninas," so important in the Northeast. Includes recipes for the traditional dishes of the season.

758 Maior, Mário Souto, and Waldemar Valente. Antologia pernambucana de folclore. Série monografias, 31. Recife: Fundação Joaquim Nabuco, Editora Massangana, 1988. 345 p. Excerpts from the writings of past and contemporary Pernambucan folklorists are preceded by biobibliographical information.

Piauí

759 Silva, Pedro. O Piauí no folclore. Teresina: Fundação Cultural Monsenhor Chaves, 1988. 133 p. Detailed descriptions of many religious festivals and observances, the festas juninas, holiday celebrations, folk dances, types of folk music and other aspects of the folklore of Piauí.

Rio de Janeiro

760 Guia do folclore fluminense. Rio de Janeiro: Presença, 1985. 253 p. Entries in dictionary format describe and define contemporary folklore practices in the state of Rio de Janeiro. Includes text and scores of many folk songs, a few illustrations, and a bibliography.

Rio Grande do Sul

761 Cortês, J. C. Paixão. Folclore gaúcho: festas, bailes, música, e religiosidade rural. Porto Alegre: Cia Riograndense de Artes Gráficas--CORAG, 1987. 351 p. Describes and illustrates many aspects of the folklore of Rio Grande do Sul, each festival, myth, etc. being listed under its name. Includes photographs of poor quality.

762 Laytano, Dante de. Folclore do Rio Grande do Sul: levantamento dos costumes e tradições gaúchas. Porto Alegre: Escola Superior de Teologia São Lourenço de Brindes; Caxias do Sul: Editora da Universidade de Caxias do Sul, 1984. 350 p. Topics summarized are ethnic groups contributing to regional folklore, the gaúcho, and the horse; folklore research and teaching; the Church and African religions; myths and legends; and folklore in an agricultural setting. Useful bibliography is interspersed throughout the text.

763 Meyer, Augusto. Guia do folclore gaúcho. 2. ed. Rio de Janeiro: Presença; Instituto Nacional do Livro; Instituto Estadual do Livro--RS, 1975. 277 p. A revised and expanded edition of a work on the folklore of Rio Grande do Sul, first published in 1951. The dictionary format includes brief identifications and longer articles on such subjects as popular sayings, places, herbs, folk heroes and villains, folk dances, and folk songs. There are detailed descriptions of the steps of many folk dances. The lyrics, and occasionally the scores, of many folk songs are included. No illustrations or bibliography.

São Paulo

764 Lima, Rossini Tavares de. Folclore das festas cíclicas: Carnaval, Semana Santa, Festa de Santa Cruz, São João, Natal. São Paulo: Irmãos Vitale Editores, 1971. 185 p. Descriptions, photographs, and music and text of songs provide data about the observance of the festivals listed in the title, focusing on São Paulo. The last third of the book is devoted to folk literature--tales, legends, and poetry collected in the state of São Paulo.

765 Maia, Tom, and Thereza Regina de Camargo Maia. O folclore das tropas, tropeiros e cargueiros no Vale do Paraíba. Rio de Janeiro: Instituto Nacional do Folclore; São Paulo: Secretaria de Estado da Cultura, Universidade de Taubaté, 1981. 125 p. An illustrated compilation of the folklore of mule drivers and their animals in this mountainous region of the state of São Paulo. Includes a glossary of terms and a bibliography.

766 Pellegrini, Américo. *Folclore paulista: calendário & documentário*. 2. ed. São Paulo: Cortez Editora, 1985. 240 p. Provides a calendar of folk festivals in the state of São Paulo and describes the observances as they have been practiced from the 1960's to the present. Includes the lyrics and scores of many folk songs and some folk dance choreography, along with a few photographs. First published in 1975 under the title, *Calendário e documentário de folclore paulista*.

767 Quental, Daisy Soares. *Pecuária folclórica: o boi*. São Paulo: Escola de Folclore, 1979. 67 p. Covers the folklore and terms associated with oxen in the area of Andradina, São Paulo, although much of the information provided would be valid for a wider geographic area.

GEOGRAPHY

BIBLIOGRAPHY

768 Boeckel, Denise Obino, and Hespéria Zuma de Rosso. Fontes de informação em geodésia, cartografia e sensoriamento remoto. 2. ed. revista e ampliada. Rio de Janeiro: Fundação Instituto Brasileiro de Geografia e Estatística, Centro de Documentação e Disseminação de Informações, Gerência de Documentação e Biblioteca, 1989. 77 p. Combines an unannotated bibliography of 334 citations, international in scope, plus a directory of 114 Brazilian organizations, government agencies, libraries, institutions of higher education, and other entities in the field of coverage. A similar directory of foreign entities, more limited in scope, and subject, author, and title indexes complete the work.

769 Brazil. Exército. Diretoria do Serviço Geográfico. Catálogo de cartas e publicações. Rio de Janeiro: 1965. 104 p. Information on the types of maps issued by this agency and a list of the maps and its other publications.

770 Brazil. Ministério das Relações Exteriores. Mapoteca. Bibliografia cartográfica. Rio de Janeiro: 1960-. A bibliography of maps and atlases in the map library of the Ministry of Foreign Relations, which is international in scope but includes many of Brazil. Title varies: 1960-? Bibliografia cartográfica. Série A. Published monthly, 1960-? and later at irregular intervals. Issues examined: vol. 1-5, 1960-1964; 1970-1973.

771 Fundação Instituto Brasileiro de Geografia e Estatística. Biblioteca Central. Mapas e outros materiais cartográficos na Biblioteca Central do IBGE. 3 vols. Rio de Janeiro: 1983-1989. Cites maps, charts, atlases, and other cartographic materials about Brazil. An excellent source for locating maps of obscure locations. Vol. 1: Editados pelo IBGE (1983); Vol. 2: Editados por outros órgãos brasileiros (1984); Vol. 3: Editados por órgãos estrangeiros (1989).

772 Pan American Union. Department of Economic Affairs. Indice anotado de los trabajos aerofotográficos y los mapas topográficos y de recursos naturales. Annotated Index of Aerial Photographic Coverage Mapping of Topography and Natural Resources. Washington: Pan American Union, 1965. Vol. 3: Brazil. An index of aerial photography, topographic and planimetric mapping, geologic mapping, soils and land capability mapping, and vegetation, ecology, land use, and forest inventory mapping done in Brazil. Information about each map cited includes scale, date, institution preparing it, and a brief description of its content.

773 Salmito, Adeilda Rigaud. Catálogo das cartas topográficas do Nordeste: escala 1.100.000. Recife: Superintendência do Desenvolvimento do Nordeste, 1980. 196 p. Catalogs the topographic maps of the Northeast prepared by SUDENE. Detailed cartographic description is followed by annotations noting the political-administrative units that each map includes, the physical features found there, and the development programs operating in that area. There is a place name index, and a map index locating quadrants, both very useful in providing access to these detailed maps of the Northeast.

774 Silveira, Daury de. Bibliografia toponímica e lingüística nacionais. Recife: Editora Universitaria, Universidade Federal de Pernambuco, 1983. 59 p. A bibliography of articles related to place names and the language of geography appearing chiefly in the Boletim geográfico and the Revista brasileira de geografia.

775 Superintendência do Desenvolvimento do Nordeste. Departamento de Recursos Naturais. Bibliografia cartográfica do Nordeste. Recife: Divisão de Documentação, 1965. 209 p. A bibliography of maps in the map collection of SUDENE, including many cities and municípios in the Northeast. An index of place names identifies the corresponding maps.

DICTIONARIES

776 Dicionário de geografia do Brasil com terminologia geográfica. 2. ed. São Paulo: Edições Melhoramentos, 1976. 544 p. A dictionary of places, agricultural products, economic activities, government agencies, geographical features, and other terms related to geography, broadly defined. Entries vary in length from a few lines to short essays.

777 Dicionário geográfico brasileiro. 2. ed. Porto Alegre: Globo, 1972. 622 p. A dictionary supplying brief data about

Brazilian geopolitical features. Originally published in 1966, this edition is updated with information from the preliminary synopsis of the 1970 census. Includes maps and photographs of poor to fair quality.

778 Florenzano, Everton. Dicionário de termos geográficos. Rio de Janeiro: Fundação Instituto Brasileiro de Geografia e Estatística, 1983. 781 p. A dictionary of geographical terms with many verbal and pictorial examples from the geography of Brazil.

779 Oliveira, Cêurio de. Dicionário cartográfico. 2. ed. Rio de Janeiro: Fundação Instituto Brasileiro do Geografia e Estatística, 1983. 781 p. An illustrated dictionary defining geographic and cartographic terms and identifying geographers and map-makers associated with colonial, nineteenth century, and contemporary Brazil, as well as many from other parts of the world. Appendix 3 provides the text of "Legislação cartográfica brasileira." The first edition was published in 1981.

780 Palmerlee, Albert Earl, and Mary Killgore Gade. A Glossary of Portuguese & Brazilian Map Terms & Abbreviations. Cleveland: Micro Photo Division, Bell & Howell Company, 1968. 109 p. "This glossary has been prepared to facilitate the study of Portuguese and Brazilian maps by an English-speaking person.... Included ... are terms and abbreviations from ... maps and atlases, including specialized economic, geologic, climatic and vegetation maps" (Introduction, p. i).

781 Tibiriçá, Luiz Caldas. Dicionário de topônimos brasileiros de origem tupi: significação dos nomes geográficos de origem tupi. São Paulo: Traço, 1985. 197 p. Locates geographic features with Tupi names and gives the meanings of the names.

GENERAL WORKS

782 Castro, Therezinha de. Atlas-texto de geopolítica do Brasil. Rio de Janeiro: Capemi, 1982. 58 p. Maps and corresponding text illustrate and explain Brazilian geopolitics from the Accord of Tordezilhas to contemporary international relations in twelve chapters. "Geoestratégia da Amazônia" and "Geopolítica nacional" are of particular interest to students of contemporary Brazil, while those interested in history will find the chapters on Brazil's territorial evolution, the development of nationality, and other useful ones.

783 Fundação Instituto Brasileiro de Geografia e Estatística. Divisão

territorial do Brasil: relação de municípios e distritos em 1-1-1979; apêndice com atualizações até 31-12-1979. 9. ed. Rio de Janeiro: 1980. 459 p. Identifies and locates all the municipalities and the districts within them at the end of 1979. Information on developments between 1964 and 1979 include such things as name changes, the creation of new municípios and districts, and status changes in existing ones. A table charting the numbers of municípios in each state, year-by-year for the time period covered provides a survey of the growth and development of certain areas in terms of the increase in administrative units, although population data is not included. This edition is the first widely available update of this information since 1965, although two mimeographed editions of limited circulation were published in the interim.

784 ______. Divisão territorial do Brasil, suplemento: atualização à 9.ª edição até 1.º de julho de 1983. Série Obras de referência da Biblioteca Central do IBGE, 1. Rio de Janeiro: 1984. 87 p. Notes changes and additions to the information provided in the ninth edition described above.

785 ______. Departamento de Geografia. Geografia do Brasil. 5 vols. Rio de Janeiro: 1977. A five-volume set covering the geology, climate, vegetation, hydrology, population, transportation, energy, agriculture, industry, and urbanization of the regions of Brazil. It is well illustrated with maps, diagrams, and photographs, and a bibliography concludes each chapter. Vol. 1: Região Norte; Vol. 2: Região Nordeste; Vol. 3: Região Sudeste; Vol. 4: Região Centro-Oeste; and Vol. 5: Região Sul.

ATLASES

Only general atlases covering Brazil as a whole or large regions of it are cited here. State atlases are listed along with other publications about the geography of specific states under state names.

786 Atlas enciclopédico brasileiro. 2 vols. 2. ed. São Paulo: Ed. Pedagógica Brasileira, n.d. An atlas intended for students illustrating Brazilian geography, politics, history, and the economy.

787 Fundação Instituto Brasileiro de Geografia e Estatística. Atlas nacional do Brasil: Região Nordeste. Rio de Janeiro: 1985. 110 p., 53 colored maps. The first volume in a projected series of detailed atlases of the regions of Brasil. In addition

to the usual geopolitical maps, there are those relating to social, economic, and health aspects, as well as to demographics and the infrastructure.

788 Rêde Ferroviária Federal, S.A. Mapa das linhas: sistema ferroviário nacional. Rio de Janeiro: 1976. 19 leaves. Maps of railroad routes in the six administrative districts of the national railway system. Includes some detailed maps, such as one of the railways serving the suburbs of Rio de Janeiro.

789 Rodrigues, João Antônio. Atlas para estudos sociais. Rio de Janeiro, Ao Livro Técnico, 1977. 98 p. A world atlas featuring historical and political maps. Includes maps of Brazil depicting its history, beginning with Cabral's voyage; the distribution of indigenous groups at the time of discovery; economic activities during the colonial period and later; jurisdictions of contemporary development agencies; and others.

STATES

Amazonas

790 Mello, Octaviano. Topônimos amazonenses: nomes das cidades amazonenses, sua origem e significação. Série Torquato Tapajós, v. 13. Manaus: Edições Govêrno do Estado do Amazonas, 1967. 163 p. Brief information about the origins and meanings of the names of twenty-eight cities of Amazonas, accompanied by simple maps of each city locating principal streets and landmarks.

Bahia

791 Centro de Planejamento da Bahia. Atlas do estado da Bahia: 2^{a}. etapa. Salvador: 19--? unpaged. Scale of maps: 1:2,500,000.

Ceará

792 Superintendência do Desenvolvimento do Estado do Ceará. Departamento de Recursos Naturais. Atlas do Ceará. Fortaleza: 1986. 57 p. Scale of maps: 1:1,500,000.

Distrito Federal

793 Companhia do Desenvolvimento do Planalto Central. Atlas do Distrito Federal. 3 vols. Brasília: 1984.

Maranhão

794 Fundação Instituto Brasileiro de Geografia e Estatística. Atlas do Maranhão. Rio de Janeiro: 1984. 104 p., 170 maps. A detailed atlas illustrating political divisions, geographical and geological features, hydrology, population, extractive industries, agriculture, industry, commerce, the transportation and communications infrastructure, education, health, housing conditions, and spatial organization.

Minas Gerais

795 Barbosa, Waldemar de Almeida. Dicionário histórico geográfico de Minas Gerais. Belo Horizonte: 1971. 549 p. Identifies 3350 populated places in Minas Gerais, including "cidades, vilas, alguns povoados e uma ou outra paragem," providing information about their founding and history, partly based on historical documents. A useful feature for the researcher is the identification of places no longer existing, which are mentioned in documents of centuries past. Does not identify natural geographic features.

796 Costa, Joaquim Ribeiro. Toponímia de Minas Gerais: com estudo histórico da divisão territorial administrativa. Belo Horizonte: Imprensa Oficial do Estado, 1970. 429 p. In addition to an alphabetical list of districts and municípios identifying and summarizing their history as legal entities, this work includes a "Genealogia dos municípios" outlining their history in tabular form, and a history of administrative divisions, which also presents much of the information in outlines.

Pernambuco

797 Instituto de Desenvolvimento de Pernambuco. Catálogo de mapas e de outros materiais especiais. Recife: 1985. 157 p. A catalog of 866 maps, slides, photographs and other special materials related to Pernambuco and the Northeast in the collection of the Institute. Indexed by subject, author, and title.

Piauí

798 Baptista, João Gabriel. Geografia física do Piauí. 3. ed. revista e aumentada. Teresina: Academia Piauiense de Letras, 1988?-. This work will be issued in three volumes according to the introduction. Volume 1, As terras, which was examined, includes general information and data on boundaries, geological structure, latitude and longitude, relief, and coastal characteristics.

Rio de Janeiro

799 Fundação de Amparo à Pesquisa do Estado do Rio de Janeiro. Atlas do estado do Rio de Janeiro: referências gerais. Rio de Janeiro: 1982. 1 atlas (6, [16] p.) Scales vary.

799A Peixoto, Dídima de Castro. Geografia fluminense: subsídios aos estudos sociais. 3. ed. Rio de Janeiro: 1973. 389 p. Basic information and description of each município of the state of Rio de Janeiro, as well as background material on its physical setting, political organization, transportation, communications, religions, and educational system.

800 Teixeira, Alvaro. Roteiro cartográfico da Baia da Guanabara e cidade do Rio de Janeiro: século XVI e XVII. Coleção histórica e cultural de Rio de Janeiro, 1. Rio de Janeiro: Livraria São José, 1975. 151 p. Identifies, describes, and reproduces thirty-eight sixteenth and seventeenth century maps of Guanabara Bay and Rio de Janeiro. Information about the cartographer and the circumstances under which each map was made is included along with bibliographic data related to it. A bibliography, and name and subject indexes are useful additions.

Rio Grande do Norte

801 Cascudo, Luís da Câmara. Nomes da terra: história e toponímia do Rio Grande do Norte. n.p.: Fundação José Augusto, 1968. 321 p. Information on place names including their meanings and brief historical data. Includes political and geographic units.

Roraima

802 Fundação Instituto Brasileiro de Geografia e Estatística. Atlas de Roraima. Rio de Janeiro: 1981. 44 p. Scales vary.

Santa Catarina

803 Santa Catarina. Gabinete de Planejamento e Coordenação Geral. Subchefia de Estatística, Geografia e Informática. Atlas de Santa Catarina. Florianópolis: 1986. 173 p. Scale: 1:1,200,000-1:100,000. Transverse Mercator projection.

São Paulo

804 Santos, Maria do Carmo Soares Rodrigues dos. Inventário cartográfico do Estado de São Paulo. São Paulo: Programa de Desenvolvimento de Recursos Minerais--Pró-Minério; Companhia de Promoção de Pesquisa Científica e Tecnológica do Estado de São Paulo--PROMOCET, 1981. 339 p. A well-indexed

series of maps of the state of São Paulo showing topography, geology, mineral deposits, water resources, vegetation, climate, geomorphology, land use, and others, including nautical charts, and various scales.

HISTORY

In addition to reference sources related to Brazilian history published since 1965, this section includes several reprints or new editions of reference works originally published in the nineteenth century and reissued since 1965. These almanacs, chronologies, dictionaries and other reference works of the past are thus made widely available for today's researchers.

GENERAL BIBLIOGRAPHY

805 Archives Nationales (France). Catálogo dos documentos referentes ao Brasil. Brasília? Ministério das Relações Exteriores, 1975. 335 p. A catalog of 1630 documents related to Brazil, located in the French National Archives. The focus is on correspondence received from the French embassy and consulate in Lisbon in the seventeenth and eighteenth centuries.

806 Assis, Edvaldo de. Uma contribuição à história social: os almanaques. João Pessoa: Ed. Universitária, Universidade Federal de Paraíba, 1979. 15 p. An inventory of almanacs in the holdings of the Biblioteca Pública "Epiphanio Dórea" in Aracajú, which has an almanac collection representing many Brazilian states, from the mid-nineteenth to the mid-twentieth centuries. Since almanacs contain much information of interest to social and economic historians, this inventory is a valuable source of bibliographic data.

807 Barbosa, Nilda Sampaio, and Laura de Oliveira Guedes. Catálogo do acervo sonoro da Agência Nacional. Rio de Janeiro: Arquivo Nacional, 1987. 79 p. A catalog of recordings made between 1939 and 1979, available on tape at the Divisão de Documentação Audiovisual of the Arquivo Nacional. The material encompassed by the collection is quite diverse according to the introduction: "discursos de presidentes da

República, ministros de Estado, senadores, deputados e de muitas otras personalidades que desempenharam funções públicas; reportagens sobre inaugurações oficiais, campanhas e comemorações cívicas; noticiários referentes à II Guerra Mundial e, ainda, radioteatros de contrapropaganda à ideologia nazista...."

808 Berger, Paulo. Bibliografia do Rio de Janeiro de viajantes e autores estrangeiros, 1531-1900. 2. ed. Rio de Janeiro: SEEC-RJ, 1980. 478 p. This unannotated bibliography of travel literature about the best-known Brazilian city actually cites much of the travel literature about Brazil in general for the time period described in the title.

809 Boschi, Caio César. Roteiro sumário dos arquivos portugueses de interesse para o pesquisador da história do Brasil. São Paulo: Edições Arquivo do Estado, 1986. 113 p. A bibliography of general works on archives and libraries in Portugal with manuscript collections is followed by specific information on those in ten Portuguese cities and towns. Includes name, address, telephone number, brief descriptions of major manuscript collections related to Brazil, and published finding aids or descriptive material.

810 Brazil. Arquivo Nacional. Departamento de Imprensa Nacional. Guia brasileiro de fontes para a história da Africa, da escravidão negra, e do negro na sociedade atual: fontes arquivísticas. Guia de fontes para a história das nações: 8, Africa; 11, Brasil. 2 vols. Rio de Janeiro: Arquivo Nacional; Brasília: Ministério da Justiça, 1988. Volume 1: Alagoas-Rio Grande do Sul; Volume 2: Rio de Janeiro-Sergipe. A guide to archival resources throughout Brazil on the subjects of African history, slavery, and blacks in contemporary society. This two-volume work, totaling 1296 pages, identifies and describes resources on a state-by-state, município-by-município basis. There are indexes of municípios, informants (institutions reporting archival material) and subjects.

811 Catálogo da documentação referente ao negro no Brasil, século XVII ao XX. Rio de Janeiro: Museu Histórico Nacional, Departamento de Acervo, Divisão de Arquivo Histórico, 1988. unpaged. The 274 citations list and briefly describe visual and textual documentation related to blacks in Brazil in the collection of the National Historical Museum. Indexes of collections and of names.

812 Centro de Pesquisa e Documentação de História Contemporânea do Brasil. Bibliografia: tenentismo. Rio de Janeiro: CPDOC, 1978. 37 p. A selective, unannotated bibliography of books, theses, and periodical articles related to tenentismo, an important theme in twentieth-century Brazilian history.

Includes a brief description of primary sources, such as manuscript materials which are in the CPDOC collection. Photographs provide visual documentation for major tenentista movements and add an extra dimension to the bibliography.

813 Chambolle, Monique. Les voyageurs français au Brésil au XIX° siècle. Paris: Université des Hautes Etudes de L'Amérique Latine, 196-? 58 leaves. An unannotated bibliography of 260 items citing accounts by French travelers to Brazil (sixteenth through nineteenth centuries) and biographies of them. Includes a chronology of travelers.

814 Coelho, Beatriz Amaral de Salles, and Maria Lúcia Horta Ludolf de Mello. Bibliografia sobre escravidão negro no Brasil. Papéis avulsos, no. 6. Rio de Janeiro: Fundação Casa de Rui Barbosa, 1988. 71 leaves. A list of books, chapters of books, periodical articles, and manuscript materials about slavery in Brazil in the collections of the Arquivo Histórico and the Biblioteca of the Casa de Rui Barbosa. Information about the manuscripts includes descriptive notes, but annotations for other materials are lacking.

815 Conrad, Robert. Brazilian Slavery: An Annotated Research Bibliography. Boston: G. K. Hall, 1977. 163 p. Includes monographs and periodical articles, as well as "selected newspapers, travel accounts, law collections, propaganda pamphlets, speeches, censuses, professional journals, official publications, agricultural manuals, legal handbooks, medical dissertations and treatises."

816 Corrêa, Carlos Humberto. Catálogo das dissertações e teses dos cursos de pós-graduação em história, 1973-1985. Florianópolis: Editora da Universidade Federal de Santa Catarina, 1987. 400 p. Lists 770 theses and dissertations produced 1973-1985 at fourteen Brazilian universities with graduate programs in history, arranged by university. Information given includes author, title, date, advisor, and examining committee. Indexes of authors, advisors, and subjects.

817 Dutra, Francis A. A Guide to the History of Brazil, 1500-1822: The Literature in English. Santa Barbara, CA: ABC-Clio, 1980. 625 p. An annotated bibliography of 939 citations to books, articles, and dissertations in English, in the fields of art, literature, geography, sociology, anthropology, and archeology related to the history of the colonial period. Additional useful features include a chronology of the colonial period, a biographical index, and a glossary of Portuguese terms related to the period.

818 Even, Pascal. Guide des sources de l'histoire du Brésil aux

archives du Ministère Français des Affaires Etrangères. Travaux & mémoires de l'Institut des Hautes Etudes de Amérique Latine, no. 38; Collection "textes & documents" 1. Paris: 1987. 64 p. General descriptions of manuscript collections related to Brazilian history found in the archive. The appendix includes a list of French representatives to Brazil in chronological order.

819 Fundação Casa de Rui Barbosa. Bibliografia sobre a Campanha Civilista. Bibliografias, 1. Rio de Janeiro: 1981. 117 p. A partially annotated bibliography of books, pamphlets, periodicals, cartoons, correspondence, iconography, and documents associated with the Campanha Civilista, both contemporary (1908-1910) or written later. Limited to materials in libraries and archives in Rio de Janeiro. The appendix includes a chronology of the campaign.

820 Griffin, Charles Carroll. Latin America: A Guide to the Historical Literature. Austin: Published for the Conference on Latin American History by the University of Texas Press, 1971. 700 p. This selective bibliography with critical annotations includes several sections devoted to Brazilian history.

821 Grupo de Trabalho em Ciências Sociais e Humanas de Minas Gerais. Bibliografia de D. Pedro II e sua época, 1840-1889: levantamento realizado em Minas Gerais por ocasião das comemorações do sesquicentenário de nascimento do Imperador. Belo Horizonte: 1977. 162 p. A bibliography of books and articles related to the period of the reign of Dom Pedro II found in libraries in Minas Gerais.

822 Guerra, Flávio. Alguns documentos de arquivos portuguêses de interêsse para a história de Pernambuco: Arquivo Nacional da Tôrre do Tombo e Arquivo Histórico Ultramarino. Recife: Arquivo Público Estadual, 1969. 309 p. Cites and summarizes the contents of 1317 documents related to the history of Pernambuco in two Portuguese archives. Includes facsimiles of a few maps, but the quality of reproduction is not good. The introduction discusses other archives in Brazil and Portugal with materials about Pernambuco. An analytical index includes names of persons, places, organizations, and subjects.

823 Horch, Rosemarie Erika. Bibliografia do domínio holandês no Brasil. São Paulo: 1967. 19 p. An unannotated bibliography of ninety-seven works about the Dutch occupation of Brazil to be found in the library of the Instituto dos Estudos Brasileiros of the Universidade de São Paulo. Reprinted from Revista do Instituto dos Estudos Brasileiros, no. 2.

824 Latin America: A Guide to Economic History, 1830-1930, Roberto Cortés Conde and Stanley J. Stein, editors. Berkeley:

University of California Press, 1977. 685 p. More than 100 pages is devoted to Brazil in Part 4 of this excellent bibliography. An interpretive essay by Nícia Villela Luz is followed by an annotated bibliography with 646 entries focusing on economic history, although many are relevant to other aspects of Brazilian history. Essay and annotations are in Portuguese.

825 Leite, Míriam Moreira; Maria Lúcia de Barros Mott; and Bertha Kauffman Appenzeller. A mulher no Rio de Janeiro no século XIX: um índice de referências em livros de viajantes estrangeiros. São Paulo: Fundação Carlos Chagas, 1982. 167 p. Travel books by foreigners visiting Brazil in the nineteenth century are indexed for their content referring to women. Arranged by subject, then chronologically by author. A bibliography gives complete citations for the 152 books indexed.

826 Levine, Robert M. Brazil, 1822-1930: An Annotated Bibliography for Social Historians. Garland Reference Library of Social Science, vol. 132. New York: Garland, 1983. 487 p. An annotated bibliography of materials useful for social history, broadly defined, covering the 108 years from independence to the end of the República Velha.

827 Medeiros, Ana Lígia Silva, and Mônica Hirst. Bibliografia histórica: 1930-45. Coleção Temas brasileiros, vol. 28. Brasília: Editora Universidade de Brasília: 1982. 226 p. An unannotated bibliography of secondary sources about the Vargas era, published through 1980. Includes a variety of sources: books, periodical articles, theses, papers, and research reports.

828 ________ and Maria Celina Soares D'Araújo. Vargas e os anos cinquenta: bibliografia. Rio de Janeiro: Editora da Fundação Getúlio Vargas, 1983. 155 p. An unannotated bibliography of selected works about the second administration of Getúlio Vargas. Deals with a variety of topics such as his speeches, the crisis of 1954, Petrobrás, political parties, populism, and nationalism.

829 Neves, Fernanda Ivo. Fontes para o estudo da história do Nordeste. Coleção pernambucana, 2. fase, vol. 20. Recife: Fundação do Patrimônio Histórico e Artístico de Pernambuco, 1986. 486 p. Entries for 4880 articles from 100 periodicals published in Brazil and elsewhere through 1979. Arranged by state, then by century. Author and title indexes.

830 Oliveira, Lúcia Lippi, Eduardo Rodrigues Gomes, and Maria Celina Whately. Elite intelectual e debate político nos anos 30: uma bibliografia comentada da Revolução de 1930. Rio de Janeiro: Fundação Getúlio Vargas and Instituto Nacional do Livro,

1980. 355 p. Studies 143 works associated with the political debate accompanying the Revolution of 1930, which ushered in the Vargas era. Provides biographical data about each author, and summarizes the contents of the book and the author's interpretation of the events described or the facts presented.

831 Samara, Eni de Mesquita, and Iraci del Nero da Costa. Demografia histórica: bibliografia brasileira. São Paulo: Instituto de Pesquisas Econômicas, 1984. 75 p. An unannotated bibliography of books, articles, theses, and dissertations on Brazilian historical demography. Some of them are abstracted in a separate section, and another section lists works in progress. Although no specific time frame is defined, most of the works cited deal with the sixteenth through nineteenth centuries.

832 Sant'Anna, Rizio Bruno, and Iraci del Nero da Costa. A escravidão brasileira nos artigos de revistas (1976-1985). São Paulo: Fundação Instituto de Pesquisas Econômicas, 1988. 94 p. This publication, which summarizes the content of 276 articles, is intended to update Robert Conrad's Brazilian Slavery: An Annotated Research Bibliography (no. 814). Includes both Brazilian and foreign publications.

833 Souza, Amaury de. Annotated Bibliography of the Brazilian Political Movement of 1964. Bibliography Series Report No. 2. Riverside, CA: University of California, Latin American Research Program, 1966. 15 p. An annotated bibliography of 103 books and articles about the Brazilian Revolution of 1964 published before August, 1966.

834 Spain. Archivo General de Indias. O Arquivo das Indias e o Brasil: documentos para a história do Brasil existentes no Arquivo das Indias de Sevilha. Rio de Janeiro: Ministério das Relações Exteriores, Comissão de Estudos de Textos da História do Brasil, 1966. 779 p. Documents related to Brazil in the Archive of the Indies are listed in chronological order and described. This massive work is divided into four sections: 1493-1599, and those representing the seventeenth, eighteenth, and nineteenth centuries. There is no index.

835 U.S. Library of Congress. The Portuguese Manuscripts Collection of the Library of Congress: A Guide, compiled by Christopher C. Lund and Mary Ellis Kahler, edited by Mary Ellis Kahler. Washington, DC: 1980. 187 p. Although the majority of manuscripts in this collection deals with strictly Portuguese topics, a number of manuscripts dealing with a variety of subjects related to colonial and nineteenth century Brazil are cited.

836 Waters, Paul E. A Bibliography of Brazilian Railway History. Bromley, England: P. E. Waters & Associates, 1984. 30 p. 500 unannotated citations to materials related to the history of rail transportation in Brazil, many of them published in the nineteenth and early twentieth centuries. An index by railway serves the double purpose of locating published materials about them, and providing a list of Brazilian railways in alphabetical order.

STATES

Bahia

837 Arquivo Público do Estado da Bahia. Guia de fontes para a história da escravidão negra na Bahia. Publicações APEB, Série Ordens Régias, 1. Salvador: 1988. 218 p. More than half of this guide is devoted to summaries of the Ordens Régias and Avisos Régios, 1648-1822, related to slavery, in the collection of the Arquivo Público do Estado da Bahia. The rest is an unannotated bibliography of books and journal articles on slavery in the collections of several public and private libraries in Salvador.

Distrito Federal

838 Arquivo Público do Distrito Federal. Guia preliminar de fontes para a história de Brasília. Brasília: 1988. 145 p. Brief descriptions of archival collections related to the history of Brasília including those of the federal government, the government of the Federal District, private institutions, and personal archives. Supplementary information includes a chronology of the move of the capital from Rio de Janeiro to Brasília, a list of prefeitos and governadores of the District, lists of museums and libraries located there, and a bibliography.

839 Bueno, Vera Americano. Os cine-jornais sobre o período da construção de Brasília. 2. ed. Brasília: Fundação Nacional Pró-Memória, 1988. 63 p. A catalog of twenty-four newsreels documenting the construction of Brasília in the collection of the Memorial JK [Juscelino Kubitschek]. Besides basic technical information about each film, there is a detailed outline of its content.

Espírito Santo

840 Bittencourt, Gabriel. Literatura e história: historiografia capixaba (bibliografia da 1. República). Vitória: Instituto Histórico e Geográfico do Espírito Santo, 1984. 109 p. Chapter 3 of this work is a historical bibliography, "Informações bibliográficas: O Espírito Santo (1889/1930)." The texts of speeches and essays comprising the other chapters also include much bibliographical information about the history of the state.

Mato Grosso

841 Randazzo, Vera. Catálogo de documentos históricos de Mato Grosso. Cuiabá: Fundação Cultural de Mato Grosso, 1977. 80 p. Briefly describes 146 eighteenth century documents related to the history of Mato Grosso in the collection of the Arquivo Público de Mato Grosso, and provides a glossary defining archaic words used during that period. Also lists ninety-four local newspapers in the holdings of the Hemeroteca Mato-Grossense.

Minas Gerais

842 Boschi, Caio César. Fontes primárias para a história de Minas Gerais em Portugal. Belo Horizonte: Conselho Estadual de Cultura de Minas Gerais, 1979. 193 p. Cites documents located in Portuguese archives and libraries in Lisbon, Coimbra, Porto, Evora, and Muge, related to the colonial history of Brazil, and therefore of Minas Gerais, one of the most important colonial centers.

Pará

843 Souza, Denise Helena Farias de; Maria de Nazareth Moreira Martins de Barros; and Luiza Castro das Chagas. Estado do Pará: pesquisa histórico-bibliográfica. 4 vols. Belém: Governo do Estado do Pará; Universidade Federal do Pará. 1986. A major bibliography and review of sources for the study of the history of Pará, based on materials located in public and private libraries in Belém. Its 1227 entries cover 1616 to the present, providing bibliographic data and annotations summarizing the content of the publications, which include monographs, government publications, journal articles, and others. Appendices indicate where each title can be found and provide a list of chief executives of Pará, 1616-1983. Includes author and title indexes and a bibliography of works consulted.

Pernambuco

844 Silva, Genny da Costa e, and Maria do Carmo Rodrigues. Bibliografia sobre Goiana: aspectos históricos e geográficos. Recife: Comissão Organizadora e Executiva das Comemorações do IV Centenário do Povoamento de Goiana, 1972. 423 p. An annotated bibliography which summarizes the contents of books, periodical articles, government reports, and other material associated with the history of Goiana on the occasion of its 400th anniversary, "em sua dupla função de 'fronteiro,' efetivando a presença de Pernambuco nos confins com a Paraíba, e de núcleo de uma civilização açucareira e quase aristocrática, rural e urbana...."

Rio Grande do Sul

845 Arquivo Histórico do Rio Grande do Sul. Falas e relatórios dos presidentes da Província do Rio Grande do Sul. Porto Alegre: 1982-. A list of speeches and reports of the presidents of the province of Rio Grande do Sul, followed by a list of the contents of each one, and the page where each item cited is located. Volumes examined: 1: 1835-1869; 2: 1870-1899. Vol. 2 is entitled, Fintes da Revolução Farroupilha: falas e relatórios dos presidentes da Provincia do Rio Grande do Sul.

846 Bandeira, Pedro Silveira, and Marli M. Mertz. Manual bibliográfico de história do Rio Grande do Sul e temas afins. 2 vols. Porto Alegre: Fundação de Economia e Estatística; Conselho de Desenvolvimento do Extremo Sul, 1986. An annotated bibliography of 1727 entries citing books, theses, conference proceedings, government documents, and other publications related to the economic history of Rio Grande do Sul.

847 Cortés, Carlos E., and Richard Kronweibel. Bibliografia da história do Rio Grande do Sul: período republicano. Porto Alegre: Faculdade de Filosofia, Universidade Federal do Rio Grande do Sul, 1967. 58 p. An unannotated bibliography of books and pamphlets about the history of Rio Grande do Sul through 1967. General sections on national, state, and local history are followed by chronological sections. The lack of an author index is a drawback to this work.

848 Laytano, Dante de. Manual de fontes bibliográficos para o estudo da história do Rio Grande do Sul: levantamento crítico. Porto Alegre: Gabinete de Pesquisa de História do Rio Grande do Sul, Instituto de Filosofia e Ciências Humana Universidade Federal do Rio Grande do Sul, 1979. 293 p. A bibliography of the printed sources related to the history of this important state. Citations are accompanied by extensiv

descriptions and critical comments, as well as background information on the authors.

849 Levantamento de fontes sobre a Revolução Farroupilha. Porto Alegre: Secretaria da Educação e Cultura, Subsecretaria de Cultura; Instituto Estadual do Livro, 1983? 192 p. Describes archival and published sources for the study of the Farroupilha Revolution, 1835-1845 in the Arquivo Histórico do Rio Grande do Sul, the Museu "Júlio de Castilhos," the Biblioteca Pública do Estado and to a lesser degree, other institutions.

São Paulo

850 Camargo, Ana Maria de Almeida. Os primeiros almanaques de São Paulo: introdução à edição facsimilar dos almanaques de 1857 e 1858. São Paulo: IMESP, 1983. 62 p. A bibliography of 113 almanacs published in São Paulo in the last half of the nineteenth century. Accompanies two facsimile editions of Almanak administrativo, mercantil e industrial da Provincia de São Paulo.

851 Fernandes, Rofran. Relatórios dos presidentes da Província de São Paulo, 1836-1889, coleção microfilmada pelo Plano Nacional de Microfilmagem de Periódicos Brasileiros: pesquisa, descrição catalográfica, catálogo coletivo e notas informativas. São Paulo: Imprensa Oficial; Arquivo do Estado, 1982. 85 p. 110 reports of the presidents of the Province of São Paulo from the earliest one located to the end of the Empire are cataloged in detail, with bibliographic descriptions and lists of the contents of the appendixes. In addition to the regular annual reports to the legislature, this work lists other reports, most often those made at the time that an administration changed hands.

852 São Paulo (State). Arquivo do Estado. Catálogo das publicações do Arquivo do Estado. São Paulo: 1984. 52 p. An unannotated list of the publications of this important state archive, including basic historical sources, monographic studies, periodical bulletins, commemorative editions, and others.

GENERAL SOURCES

853 Almeida, Antônio da Rocha. Dicionário de história do Brasil. Porto Alegre: Editora Globo, 1967. 531 p. This historical dictionary, intended for secondary school students, provides good coverage of people and events, fleshing out with considerable detail the more superficial information found in secondary textbooks. No illustrations.

854 Brazil. Arquivo Nacional. Catálogo da exposição de modelos de brasões e de cartas de nobreza e fidalguia: colônia, Reino Unido, Império. Rio de Janeiro: 1965. 135 p. Descriptions of the coats of arms of the Brazilian nobility, with some illustrations in color.

855 Brazil: Empire and Republic, 1822-1930, edited by Leslie Bethell. Cambridge; New York: Cambridge University Press, 1989. 353 p. "The contents of this book were previously published as part of volumes III and V of the Cambridge History of Latin America ... 1985 and 1986"--verso, title page (see no. 857).

856 Brazil. Ministério da Justiça. Dom Pedro II e a cultura. Publicações históricas, 82. Rio de Janeiro: Centro de Serviços Gráficos do IBGE, 1977. 478 p. A collection of the acts of the emperor related to culture and education, 1840-1889, which gives an overview of activities in these areas and their support by the head of state. Some of the acts were declarations of the acquisitions of art works by official entities, acknowledgements of gifts of literary or art works, prizes awarded, educational and cultural institutions created, and others.

857 The Cambridge History of Latin America, edited by Leslie Bethell. 8 vols. Cambridge, England: Cambridge University Press, 1984-. This authoritative work is comprised of a series of essays on Latin American history from colonial times to the present, complemented by bibliographical essays discussing the secondary literature. Several chapters are devoted to Brazil, and other general chapters include it. Contents: Vols. 1-2: Colonial Latin America; Vol. 3: Latin America, Independence, and Post-Independence, c.1790-1870/80; Vols. 4-5: Latin America, 1870/80-1930; Vols. 6-8: Latin America, 1930 to the Present.

858 O clero no Parlamento brasileiro. Brasília: Câmara dos Deputados, Centro de Documentação e Informação; Rio de Janeiro: Centro João XIII; Instituto Brasileiro de Desenvolvimento; e Fundação Casa de Rui Barbosa, Centro de Estudos Históricos, 1978-. Traces the participation of the clergy in Brazilian political life. The first five volumes, published between 1978 and 1980, cover their activities in the Assembléia Geral Constituinte e Legislativa of 1823, and in the Câmara dos Deputados from 1836 through 1889. This work is arranged in chronological order and brief summaries of the events in Congress in which individual clergymen were involved are accompanied by excerpts from their speeches or writings. Detailed name and subject indexes in volume 5 provide access to this rather unwieldy arrangement. These five volumes complete the part devoted to the Câmara dos Deputados, but more volumes covering the Senate are planned.

859 Colonial Brazil, edited by Leslie Bethell. Cambridge; New York: Cambridge University Press, 1987. 398 p. "The contents of this book were previously published as part of volumes I and II of the Cambridge History of Latin America"--verso, title page (see no. 857).

860 Dicionário de história do Brasil, moral e civismo. 4th ed. São Paulo: Edições Melhoramentos, 1976. 618 p. A dictionary identifying significant individuals in Brazilian history, social and political movements, organizations and government agencies, and civic and patriotic concepts. Includes a table which links related entries, a bibliography, and a table of important dates--historic, religious, and patriotic.

861 Dicionário histórico-biográfico brasileiro, 1930-1983. 4 vols. Rio de Janeiro: Ed. Forense-Universitária; Fundação Getúlio Vargas; Centro de Pesquisa e Documentação de História Contemporânea do Brasil, 1984. A major contribution to the history of Brazilian politics and public administration. Covers the period from the Revolution of 1930 through 1975, with coverage extended to 1983 for a limited number of important figures and events. Some 3740 of its 4500 entries are biographical, while the remainder cover institutions, events, publications, and political concepts. The articles are well-researched, substantial, and accompanied by bibliographical references. Many of them are signed. This is an invaluable reference tool for twentieth century Brazilian history and politics.

862 Donato, Hernâni. Dicionário das batalhas brasileiras. São Paulo: IBRASA--Instituição Brasileira de Difusão Cultural, Ltda., 1987. 542 p. The main body of this work identifies, dates, and describes battles in Brazilian history. Also provides chronologies, a list of battles with more than one name, a bibliography, and other information.

863 Duarte, Paulo de Queiroz. Os voluntários da Pátria na Guerra do Paraguai. Rio de Janeiro: Biblioteca do Exército, 1981-. Presents the history of the Paraguayan War in a systematic, easy-to-scan format. Provides information on the organization of each batallion, its trip to Rio Grande do Sul, battles in which it participated, and its principal officers, including portraits of chief officers and illustrations of uniforms, some in color. Each volume includes a bibliography. Volumes examined: vol. 1: O Imperador, os chefes militares, a mobilização e o quadro militar da época; vol. 2, tomos 1-5: O Comando de Osório; vol. 3, tomo 1: O Comando de Caxias.

864 Fitzgibbon, Russell H. Brazil: A Chronology and Fact Book, 1488-1973. Dobbs Ferry, NY: Oceana Publications, 1974. 150 p. Contains a chronology of significant events in Brazilian

history; a list of rulers, 1808-1974; and translations of the texts of a number of historically important documents. Includes a bibliography of books about Brazil in English.

865 Flexor, Maria Helena Ochi. Abreviaturas: manuscritos dos séculos XVI ao XIX. São Paulo: Arquivo do Estado, 1979. 391 p. Identifies more than 15,000 abbreviations used in Brazilian and Portuguese documents from the sixteenth through the nineteenth centuries.

866 Franco, Francisco de Assis Carvalho. Dicionário de bandeirantes e sertanistas do Brasil: séculos XVI, XVII, XVIII. Belo Horizonte: Editora Itatiaia; São Paulo: Editora da Universidade de São Paulo, 1989. 443 p. Coleção Reconquista do Brasil, 3ª série, vol. 6. A biographical dictionary of Brazilian pioneers and explorers. The source of the data is included. Originally published in 1953.

867 Komissarov, Boris Nicolaevich. Russkie istochniki po istorii Brazilii pervoi tretí 19. Leningrad: Izd-vo Leningr. un-ta, 1977. 168 p. Information on archival resources for the study of Brazilian history in the Soviet Union, which includes bibliographical references. Although the title is romanized for purposes of this bibliography, the title page and text are in Russian.

868 Levine, Robert M. Historical Dictionary of Brazil. Metuchen, NJ: Scarecrow Press, 1979. 297 p. "Entries in this dictionary ... treat not only people and events but Brazilian civilization in several dimensions: popular and folk culture as well as the fine arts, slang as well as established terminology, women as well as men, popular as well as erudite culture, sports, as well as politics...." Covers contemporary and historical Brazil.

869 Lima, José Ignácio de Abreu e. Sinopse ou dedução cronológica dos fatos mais notáveis da história do Brasil. 2. ed. Recife: Fundação de Cultura Cidade do Recife, 1983. 436 p. A new edition of a work first published in 1845, which provides a chronological summary of the history of Brazil from 1492 to 1843. Name/subject index.

870 Lyra, Heitor. Efemérides luso brasileiros, 1807/1970. Lisboa: 1971. 351 p. A calendar of important events in Brazil and Portugal on each day of the year from the early nineteenth century to 1970.

871 Menezes, José Luiz Mota, and Maria do Rosário Rosa Rodrigues. Fortificações portuguesas no Nordeste do Brasil, séculos XVI, XVII e XVIII. Recife: Pool Editora, 1986. 157 p. Basic data in outline form on the historic forts of Alagoas, Bahia,

Ceará, Fernando de Noronha, Maranhão, Paraíba, Pernambuco, Rio Grande do Norte, and Sergipe. Includes reproductions of the plans of some of them, and a bibliography.

872 Nôvo dicionário de história do Brasil, ilustrado. 2. ed. São Paulo: Melhoramentos, 1971. 645 p. Entries varying in length from short paragraphs to several pages cover biography, political movements, historical events, organizations, and general topics, such as science in Brazil. Includes many color illustrations and a list of topics, with related topics indicated.

873 Rodrigues, José Honório. A pesquisa histórica no Brasil. 3. ed. São Paulo: Editora Nacional/MEC, 1978. 306 p. A wealth of basic information for the historical researcher, treating such topics as documentary sources, archives and libraries, institutions promoting research such as the Instituto Histórico e Geográfico Brasileiro, and the Instituto Nacional de Pesquisa Histórica, prominent early historians, and similar subjects. Includes appropriate bibliography interspersed throughout the text.

874 Young, Jordan M. Brazil, 1954-1964: End of a Civilian Cycle. New York: Facts on File, 1972. 197 p. Chronicles major events in Brazilian political life from the fall of Getúlio Vargas in 1954 to the fall of his protegé, João Goulart in 1964, in a year-by-year format. Includes English translations of important documents and excerpts from speeches. Indexed by name and subject. Provides a good overview of this important period in recent Brazilian history.

STATES

Bahia

875 Almanach para a cidade da Bahia: anno 1812. Edição facsimilar. Salvador: Secretaria de Educação e Cultura; Conselho Estadual de Cultura, 1973. unpaged. Information on business, educational, religious, governmental, military, and other activities in this facsimile edition of an early nineteenth century almanac.

876 Bahia. Secretaria do Planejamento, Ciência e Tecnologia. Fundação de Pesquisas. A inserção da Bahia na evolução nacional: 1ª. etapa, 1850-1889. 4 vols. Salvador: 1978-1979. A series of publications tracing Bahia's economic development from the mid-nineteenth century to the end of the Empire, through text, statistical tables, graphs, and lists. It is divided into four volumes, with subsections as follows:

Vol. 1: A economia baiana no século XIX: síntese.

Vol. 2: Atividades produtivas.
2:1 Cana de açúcar
2:2 Pecuária
2:3 Fumo
2:4 Diamante
2:5 Café
2:6 Cacau
2:7 Algodão e textil
2:8 Indústria

Vol. 3: Atividades não produtivas
3:1 Banco
3:2 Finanças
3:3 Intermediação comercial

Vol. 4: Anexos
4:1 Anexo estatístico
4:2 Anexo biográfico: agentes econômicos na Bahia no século XIX.

877 Cartilha histórica da Bahia: a República e seus governadores: municípios, prefeitos, câmaras municipais, vereadores, riqueza, economia, desenvolvimento industrial. 2. ed. Salvador: 197-? 329 p. Although rather superficial in its approach, this historical dictionary is useful for its many portraits and other illustrations.

Ceará

878 Braga, Renato. Dicionário geográfico e histórico do Ceará. Fortaleza: Imprensa Universitária do Ceará, 1964-. Identifies the geographic features of Ceará, and gives information about its municípios--history, physical description, population, and economic data. A section under most municípios entitled "Filhos ilustres" identifies its favorite sons. Volume 1 (1964) and 2 (1967), covering the letters A-C, were examined.

879 Ribeiro, Francisco Moreira. Breve cronologia política do Ceará: 1890-1948. Série idéias, no. 4. Fortaleza: Universidade Federal do Ceará, Núcleo de Documentação Cultural--NUDOC, 1987. 19 leaves. A chronology of formal political events and others, such as strikes, affecting politics.

Goiás

880 Brandão, A. J. Costa. Almanach da Provincia de Goyaz para o anno de 1886. Coleção documentos goianos, 1. Goiânia: UFG Editora, 1978. 157 p. Information about the province of Goiás in the late nineteenth century. This is the first

publication in a series planned to re-issue works of cultural importance that are long out-of-print, or in some cases to publish works which exist only in manuscript.

Maranhão

881 Marques, César Augusto. Dicionário histórico-geográfico da Província do Maranhão. 3. ed. Coleção São Luís, 3. Rio de Janeiro: Editora Fon-Fon e Seleta, 1970. 634 p. The third edition of this scholarly work, first published in 1870 and reissued in 1970 under the auspices of the Superintendência do Desenvolvimento do Maranhão includes much detail about life in the province, covering geographical locations, people, institutions, important buildings, agricultural products and other subjects. Entries range from brief to long articles.

882 Meireles, Mário M. História do Maranhão. 2. ed. São Luís: Fundação Cultural do Maranhão, 1980. 430 p. A history of Maranhão from the beginning of the sixteenth century through 1977 in easy-to-scan chronological order enhanced by a detailed table of contents. Contains much information on the administrations of its presidentes da província, governors of the state, and chief executives during the early colonial period. Provides a bibliography, but no index.

Minas Gerais

883 "Catálogo de sesmarias." Revista do Arquivo Público Mineiro, ano 37, vol. 1-2, 1988, pp. 13-363 and [5]-230, respectively. "Este trabalho relaciona as sesmarias concedidas em Minas Gerais, nos períodos colonial e provincial, tendo por base os 7.985 registros existentes nos códices do Arquivo Público Mineiro, que contém índice publicado nesta Revista, ano xxviii de 1977, as págs. 36, 123, e 212." The entire volumes are devoted to this catalog. Volume 1 covers A-L, and volume 2 covers M-Z.

884 As constituintes mineiras de 1891, 1935, e 1947: uma análise histórica. Belo Horizonte: Assembléia Legislativa do Estado de Minas Gerais, 1989. 313 p. An analysis of three state constitutional conventions, with brief biographical data about each delegate, statistical profiles, bibliography, and other information.

885 Matos, Raimundo José da Cunha. Corografia histórica da Província de Minas Gerais (1837). 2 vols. Reconquista do Brasil, nova série, vol. 61-62. Belo Horizonte: Ed. Itatiaia; São Paulo: Editora Universidade de São Paulo, 1981. Provides detailed information about colonial days in the Province of Minas Gerais

in concise form: the discovery and mining of gold and gemstones, geographic features, cities, vilas, and other political divisions, religious life, Indians, economic activity, and statistics. This work, first published in 1837, makes fascinating browsing at the same time that it provides data for the study of the history of this period.

Pará

886 Baena, Antônio Ladislau Monteiro. Compêndio das eras da Província do Pará. Belém: Universidade Federal do Pará, 1969. 395 p. Summarizes the history of the Province of Pará in chronological order from 1615-1823. It is unfortunate that this edition of the work, originally published in 1838, was not indexed for access to names of the individuals and places that it includes.

Paraíba

887 Pinto, Irineu Ferreira. Datas e notas para a história da Paraíba. Reprodução da edição de 1908, com estudo introdutório do prof. José Pedro Nicodemos. João Pessôa: Editora Universitária, 1977-. Reprint of notes on the history of Paraíba, arranged chronologically, with an index of documents found in the text. The first volume, which was examined, covers 1501-1820.

Paraná

888 Cardoso, Jayme Antônio, and Cecília Maria Westphalen. Atlas histórico do Paraná. 2. ed. revista e ampliada. Curitiba: Editora do Chain, 1986. 71 p. A series of maps with accompanying text illustrating and describing the waves of migration and colonization which characterize the history of Paraná.

Pernambuco

889 Barbalho, Nelson. Cronologia pernambucana: subsídios para a história do agreste e do sertão. Recife: Fundação de Desenvolvimento Municipal do Interior de Pernambuco, 1982-. Summarizes the history of the Pernambucan interior in chronological order. As of 1983, ten volumes, covering the pre-1600 period through 1810 had been published. The lack of an index thus far makes the use of this work difficult.

890 Honorato, Manoel da Costa. Dicionário topográfico, estatístico, e histórico da Província de Pernambuco. 2. ed. Recife: Secretaria da Educação e Cultura, 1976. 150 p. New edition of a work first published in 1863.

Piauí

891 Costa, Francisco Augusto Pereira da. Cronologia histórica do Estado do Piauí. 2 vols. 2. ed. Rio de Janeiro: Artenova, 1974. A chronological history by a Pernambucan historian who participated in the administration of Piauí in 1884-1885. It covers the period from the beginning of the province in 1735 to the proclamation of the Republic in 1889. Volume 1 covers 1735-1800, while the second volume covers 1801-1889. The first edition was published in Recife in 1909.

892 Nascimento, Francisco Alcides, and Geraldo Almeida Borges. Cronologia do Piauí republicano, 1889-1930. Teresina: Fundação Centro de Pesquisas Ecônomicas e Sociais do Piauí--CEPRO, 1988. 297 p. Separate chronologies for political developments, administration, the economy and finance, culture, and education comprise this contribution to the history of the state.

Rio de Janeiro

893 Berger, Paulo. Dicionário histórico das ruas de Botafogo: IV Região Administrativa. Rio de Janeiro: Fundação Casa de Rua Barbosa, 1987. 67 p.

894 ______. Dicionário histórico das ruas do Rio de Janeiro da Glória ao Cosme Velho: IV Região Administrativa. Rio de Janeiro: Fundação Casa de Rui Barbosa, 1989. 63 p.

895 ______. Dicionário histórico das ruas do Rio de Janeiro: I e II regiões administrativas (Centro). Rio de Janeiro: Gráfica Olímpica Editora, 1974. 145 p. These historical dictionaries of streets in the older districts of Rio de Janeiro give their current and former names, location, number of the decree which established or changed the name, and history of the name. In the case of streets named after persons, brief biographical information is included.

896 Brazil. Arquivo Nacional. Relação de algumas cartas das sesmarias concedidas em território da Capitania do Rio de Janeiro, 1714-1800. Rio de Janeiro: 1968. 74 p. Land grants in the province of Rio de Janeiro are listed in chronological order by name of recipients and by place name.

897 Cavalcanti, J. Cruvello. Nova numeração dos prédios da Cidade do Rio de Janeiro. Coleção Memória do Rio, 6. 2 vols. 1878. Reprint. Rio de Janeiro: Departamento de Imprensa Oficial da Secretaria Municipal de Administração, 1979. A valuable source for the study of the urban development of Rio de Janeiro in the late nineteenth century. Information is provided about each street in a tabular format, including old and new building

numbers, owners of the buildings, number of floors, and other observations in some cases, which provide additional information. Also includes a brief history of each street, with name changes.

898 Frota, Guilherme de Andréa. Apontamentos para um guia histórico do Rio de Janeiro. Rio de Janeiro: Companhia Editora Americana, 1971. 199 p. Concise, factual information about major points of historic interest in the city of Rio de Janeiro, written by a teacher of history in the Curso de Guia de Turista of the Escola de Serviço Público do Estado de Guanabara. Photographs of poor to fair quality illustrate this work.

899 Rosa, Ferreira da. Rio de Janeiro: notícia histórica e descritiva de capital do Brasil. Coleção Memória do Rio, 3. 1924. Reprint. Rio de Janeiro: Departamento de Imprensa Oficial de Secretaria Municipal de Administração, 1978. 222 p. Describes Rio de Janeiro in the early 1920's, with entries for its main avenues, suburbs, educational, scientific, and cultural institutions, monuments, hospitals, and much more. Third in a series of reprints intended to provide reference materials for the study of the history of Rio de Janeiro. An index provides access to the text, which is only partially arranged in an easy reference format.

900 Rio de Janeiro (City). Secretaria Municipal de Obras e Serviços Públicos. Departamento Geral de Edificações. As ruas do Rio: 31 de outubro de 1917 a 30 de setembro de 1977. 3 vols. Rio de Janeiro: 197-? A directory and gazetteer of 11,000 street names which were recognized or changed between 1917 and 1977, a period of constant urban development. The data included is useful for current reference and for historical research. Presented in tabular format, it includes the present name of the street, its designation as a rua, praça, ladeira, etc., the decrees that first recognized its existence and that fixed its current boundaries, the locations where it begins and ends, and miscellaneous observations. Many of the latter are historical notes, including former names, origins of names, changes in locations, etc.

Rio Grande do Norte

901 Lemos, Vicente, and Tarcísio Medeiros. Capitães-mores e governadores do Rio Grande do Norte: 2º volume, 1701-1822. Natal: Instituto Histórico e Geográfico do Rio Grande do Norte; Brasília: Conselho Federal de Cultura, 1980. 170 p. Biographical data about the chief administrative officials representing the Portuguese government in Rio Grande do Norte from the date that it was subordinate to Pernambuco to Independence. Includes texts of related documents and a section

listing the terms used for officials and defining their responsibilities.

902 Medeiros Filho, Olavo de. Naufrâgios no litoral potiguar. Natal: Instituto Histôrico e Geogrâfico do Rio Grande do Norte, 1988. 60 p. Summaries of nine ship wrecks which took place 1678-1724 on the coast of Rio Grande do Norte, compiled from documents in the archives of the Instituto Histôrico e Geogrâfico do Rio Grande do Norte. Includes inventories of cargo salvaged.

903 Soares, Antônio. Diccionario historico e geographico do Rio Grande do Norte. Reprint. Natal: Imprensa Official, 1930. Mossorô: Escola Superior de Agricultura de Mossorô; Fundação Guimarães Duque, 1988. 107 p. A dictionary of persons and places of Rio Grande do Norte. Individuals are listed under their given names. This facsimile edition comprises vol. 417 of the series Coleção mossoroense, and is vol. 1 (A-E) of the dictionary, which was presented to the Congresso Econômico do Rio Grande do Norte, which met in January, 1930.

Rio Grande do Sul

904 Arquivo Histôrico do Rio Grande do Sul. Cronologia da Revolução Farroupilha. Porto Alegre: 1984. 33 p. Lists the events of 1834-1845 in Rio Grande do Sul in chronological order.

905 Flores, Moacyr. Historiografia estudos. n.p.: Nova Dimensão, 1989. 94 p. Bio-bibliographical information and notes on the historical perspectives of twenty-seven past and present historians of Rio Grande do Sul.

906 Franco, Sêrgio da Costa. Porto Alegre: guia histôrico. Porto Alegre: Editora da Universidade, Universidade Federal do Rio Grande do Sul; Prefeitura Municipal de Porto Alegre, 1988. 441 p. A historical dictionary of street and other place names in Porto Alegre which besides giving the history of places, often identifies persons for whom they are named. Includes bibliography.

Santa Catarina

907 Meirinho, Jali. Datas histôricas de Santa Catarina, 1500-1985. Florianôpolis: Editora da Universidade Federal de Santa Catarina e Assemblêia Legislativa do Estado de Santa Catarina, 1985. 264 p. A historical chronology of Santa Catarina with a name index.

São Paulo

908 Almanak da Provincia de São Paulo para 1873, organisado e publicado por Antonio José Baptista de Luné e Paulo Delfino da Fonseca. Edição facsimilar. São Paulo: Imprensa Oficial do Estado, 1985. 932 p. Detailed information about each município, statistics, lists of government officials, and other data, make this almanac an important historical source for nineteenth century São Paulo.

909 Amaral, Antônio Barreto do. Dicionário de história de São Paulo. Coleção paulística, vol. 19. São Paulo: Imprensa Oficial, 1981. 481 p. Covers people, places, events, organizations, and institutions associated with the history of the state. Although most entries are brief, there are some fairly long articles on topics of major importance, such as immigration.

910 Empresa Metropolitana de Planejamento de Grande São Paulo. Reconstituição da memória estatística da Grande São Paulo. São Paulo: EMPLASA, 1980-. A series of maps and statistical tables tracing the demographic and economic growth and the development of the infrastructure of greater São Paulo from 1765 through the mid-twentieth century. Volumes examined: 1 (1980) 256 p.; 2 (1983) 208 p.

911 Godoy, Joaquim Floriano de. A Província de S. Paulo: trabalho estatístico, histórico e noticioso. 2. ed. facsimilada. Coleção paulística, vol. 12. São Paulo: Governo do Estado, 1978. 157 p. A compilation of facts about nineteenth century São Paulo originally published in 1875 and designed to provide information about the province at the Philadelphia Exposition of 1876.

912 Marques, Abílio A. S. Indicadores de São Paulo: administrativo, judicial, industrial, profissional e commercial para o ano de 1878. Ed. facsimilar. São Paulo: Convênio IMESP-DAESP, 1983. 256 p. Provides a variety of statistical and other information on the subjects listed in the title.

913 Marques, Manuel Eufrâsio de Azevedo. Apontamentos históricos, geográficos, biográficos, estatísticos e noticiosos da Província de São Paulo seguidos da cronologia dos acontecimentos mais notáveis desde a fundação da Capitania de São Vicente até o ano de 1876. 2 vols. Coleção Reconquista do Brasil, nova série, no. 3-4. Belo Horizonte: Ed. Itatiaia; São Paulo.: Ed. da Universidade de São Paulo, 1980. A new edition of a classic first published in 1879. Its author was an official in the Secretaria do Governo da Província de São Paulo, and much of the information it contains was derived from documents to which he had access. Its dictionary format covers people, places, institutions, companies such as railroads, statistics,

and much more, and is followed by a chronology of significant dates in the life of the province. It follows the practice of alphabetizing persons' names under their given names. Although some of the information contained in this work is now known to be inaccurate, it is still a valuable source for the history of São Paulo.

LABOR AND INDUSTRY

BIBLIOGRAPHY

914 Centro de Pastoral Vergueiro. Setor de Documentação e Pesquisa. Informe bibliográfico: trabalhador rural. São Paulo: 1988. 20 p. A partially annotated bibliography of 338 entries (chiefly articles from the alternative press) about rural workers.

915 ______. ______. Informe bibliográfico: 1º de maio. São Paulo: 1988. 42 p. A partially annotated bibliography of 563 items related to the labor movement: the history of the observance of May 1, salaries, automation, the work week, and others. Concentrates on articles, including those in the labor press.

916 Confederação Nacional da Indústria. Departamento Econômico. Divisão de Documentação e Informação Bibliográfica. Política industrial: bibliografia seletiva, 1950-1978. Rio de Janeiro: 1979. 54 l. An unannotated bibliography of books, pamphlets, theses, and periodical articles about Brazilian industrial policy over a period of almost thirty years, published in Brazil and elsewhere.

917 ______. ______. ______. Política salarial e salários no Brasil de 1964 a 1983: guia bibliográfico. 2 vols. Rio de Janeiro: 1983. Covers wage policy from 1964 when the government began to use it as an anti-inflationary measure, through June of 1983, thus including much polemic writing following a policy change in October, 1979. The unannotated list includes books, pamphlets, theses, periodical and newspaper articles, and pertinent legislation.

918 Fontes para o estudo da industrialização no Brasil, 1889/1945. Campinas: IFCH-UNICAMP, 1983? 117 p. A report on resources available in the Arquivo Edgard Leuenroth of the Universidade Estadual de Campinas, in the fields of industrial

legislation, industrialization and technology, and living and working conditions for industrial workers. The archive surveyed is well known for its materials related to the labor movement.

919 Instituto Euvaldo Lodi. Centro de Documentação e Informação. Formação profissional. Série bibliografias, 15. Rio de Janeiro: 1986. 28 leaves. An unannotated list of 112 books and articles, international in scope, but with emphasis on Brazil.

920 ______. ______. Mercado de trabalho. Série bibliografias, 9. Rio de Janeiro: 1985. 35 leaves. Cites 124 books and articles about the labor market, with emphasis on Brazil. Title index.

921 ______. ______. Política de emprego. Série bibliografias, 7-. Rio de Janeiro: 1985-. An unannotated bibliography of 166 books, pamphlets, and periodical articles associated with employment policy. All of the materials cited are in the library of the Institute, which is described as the "órgão de estudos e pesquisas da Confederação Nacional da Indústria." Part 1 (43 p.) was examined; a second part, covering the holdings of the Fundação Getúlio Vargas, is projected.

922 ______. ______. Relações industriais. Ed. ampliada e atualizada. Série bibliografias, no. 12. Rio de Janeiro: 1985. 60 p. An unannotated bibliography of 211 entries on industrial relations, universal in scope, but focusing on Brazil.

923 Projeto de Pesquisa UFRGS-FINEP "Processo de Industrialização no Rio Grande do Sul (1889-1945)". Guia preliminar de fontes para o estudo de processo de industrialização no Rio Grande do Sul (1889-1945). Porto Alegre: Editora da Universidade; Fundação de Economia e Estatística, 1986. 220 p. An important annotated bibliography covering the economic history of Rio Grande do Sul, which includes a variety of sources: government documents such as laws, official communications, bulletins, reports, statistical compilations, and exposition catalogs; and non-official publications, such as those of political parties and associations; registrations of firms and trademarks, conference proceedings, biographies, commemorative editions, labor movement periodicals, almanacs, yearbooks, pamphlets, broadsides, theses, and monographs.

CENSUS MATERIALS

VIII Recenseamento geral--1970

924 Fundação Instituto Brasileiro de Geografia e Estatística. Censo

industrial. VIII Recenseamento geral--1970. Série regional. 24 vols. Rio de Janeiro: 1973-1974. Provides detailed data about industrial activity in each state, territory, and the Federal District.

925 _______. Censo industrial, Brasil. VIII recenseamento geral--1970. Série nacional. Rio de Janeiro: 1974. 287 p. Statistical data regarding industrial activity in the country as a whole. Includes sample census questionnaire.

926 _______. Censo industrial, Brasil: produção física. VIII recenseamento geral--1970. Série nacional. Rio de Janeiro: 1975. 303 p. Statistics on quantity and value of goods produced.

Censos economicos de 1975

927 Fundação Instituto Brasileiro de Geografia e Estatística. Censo industrial, Brasil. Censos econômicos de 1975. Série nacional, vol, 2, pt. 1. Rio de Janeiro: 1981. 381 p. Summarizes statistical data about industrial activity for the country as a whole.

928 _______. Censo industrial, Brasil. Censos econômicos de 1975. Série regional. 24 vols. Rio de Janeiro: 1979. Detailed information about industrial activity in each of the states, territories, and the Federal District.

929 _______. Censo industrial, Brasil: produção física. Censos econômicos de 1975, Série nacional, vol. 2, pt. 2. Rio de Janeiro: 1981. 628 p. Statistical data about production by types of industries and by states, including the value (in cruzeiros) of goods produced.

IX Recenseamento geral do Brasil--1980

930 Fundação Instituto Brasileiro de Geografia e Estatística. Censo industrial, Brasil: dados gerais. IX Recenseamento geral do Brasil--1980, tomo 2, pt. 1. 28 vols. Rio de Janeiro: 1984. Statistical data for industrial activities related to extraction of minerals, processing of raw materials, manufacturing, and industrial services such as packaging and maintenance of equipment. Volume 1 covers Brazil as a whole, and the others provide detailed data for the states, territories, and the Federal District.

931 _______. Censo industrial: produção física, Brasil. IX Recenseamento geral do Brasil--1980. Rio de Janeiro: 1984. 583 p. Statistical data about production by types of industries and

by states, including the value of goods produced. Includes a sample questionnaire used for data collection.

OTHER SOURCES

932 Anuário brasileiro de recursos humanos, 1.-. São Paulo: Embranews, 1984-. Data related to employers, employee organizations, and government agencies dealing with labor issues and problems. Tables provide information on strikes, unemployment, consumption, the labor force, salary adjustments (indexing), etc. A section for each major city provides a directory of such services as labor lawyers, medical assistance, uniforms, and industrial cleaning. Editions examined: 1984, 1985.

933 Anuário da propriedade industrial. São Paulo: Edições Loyala, vol. 1-, 1977-. An annual publication concerned with court and administrative decisions, legislation, and other aspects of patents and trademarks.

934 Anuário das indústrias. São Paulo: Editora Pesquisa e Indústria, Ltda. An industrial catalog, arranged by type of producer or service, with name, address, and telephone/telex provided. Edition examined: 24th, 1989/1990.

935 Anuário do trabalho e da previdência. Rio de Janeiro: Editas. A yearbook which summarizes labor and social legislation, provides statistics on the labor market, salaries, and employment; lists labor unions state-by-state, and summarizes court decisions dealing with labor law. Edition examined: 1973.

936 Anuário RAIS: [relação anual de informações sociais] 1985-. Brasília: Ministério do Trabalho. A detailed compilation of statistics related to employment, remuneration, and reporting establishments, issued annually in a six-volume set covering Brazil as a whole and each of its five macroregions. Similar information was published earlier under the title, RAIS: relação anual de informações sociais (no. 943). Editions examined: 1985, 1986.

937 Banas clasificado industrial brasileiro. Who Produces What in Brazil. São Paulo: Editora Banas, 1974-. Lists 4300 products in alphabetical order with the names and addresses of companies producing them. Alphabetical indexes of products in English, German, French, and Spanish facilitate access for foreigners. Also lists industrial associations, chambers of commerce, and workers syndicates. A separately published index of the companies listed and their telephone numbers

accompanies this work: Indice alfabético das empresas e seus telefones. Editions examined: 1975, 1976.

938 Cadastro brasileiro das entidades sindicais. Brasília. A list of all the urban labor unions in Brazil by major categories of activity, subdivided by states. Provides brief, basic information about each one. Edition examined: 1985.

939 Cadastro brasileiro das entidades sindicais: rural. Curitiba: Editora Decisório Trabalhista. This list of rural sindicatos is divided into two parts: sindicatos of rural workers and of rural employers. Each part is arranged by state, and provides basic information about each sindicato: name, address, telephone number, president, and registration number. Published annually. Edition examined: 1987.

940 Companhia de Distritos Industriais do Estado de Rio de Janeiro. Industrialização no Brasil e os distritos industriais. Rio de Janeiro: 1977. 68 p. Information on official industrial districts in each region of Brazil in brief texts and charts which provide such data as distance from the state capital, status (existing or projected), space allocated, number of industries, predominant industries, and average number of workers per industry.

941 Greenfield, Gerald Michael, and Sheldon L. Maram. Latin American Labor Organizations. New York: Greenwood Press, 1987. 929 p. This basic reference source in English for Latin American labor history includes a sixty-five page chapter on Brazil. In addition to an essay surveying the history of the Brazilian labor movement and its current status, it identifies and describes many labor organizations in an alphabetical listing. Appendix 2 provides a brief chronology of Brazilian labor history, and Appendix 3, "Glossary of Terms, People, and Events," has a section devoted to Brazil.

942 Pesquisa industrial: dados gerais. Rio de Janeiro: Fundação Instituto Brasileiro de Geografia e Estatística, vol. 7-, 1979-? Provides statistical data pertaining to mining and mineral industries, industries which process raw materials, and others. Covers such aspects as the number of establishments, acquisition of real estate and equipment, number of persons employed, salaries, and value of production. Published annually except for years ending in "0" or "5" when the same data is published in the Censo industrial. Continues Produção industrial, which was published 1972-1978 (volumes 1-6).

943 RAIS: relação anual de informações sociais. Brasília: Ministério do Trabalho. Reports annually on employment in general, changes in the labor force, and wages, through text and graphics, with statistical tables in the appendix. Editions

examined: 1980 (published 1984, 5 vols.); 1981 (published 1984, 4 vols.); 1982 (published 1984, 4 vols.); 1983 (published 1985, 4 volumes). Anuário RAIS (no. 936) has provided similar information since 1985.

944 Revista da propriedade industrial. n.p.: Instituto Nacional da Propriedade Industrial. This monthly periodical is divided into two sections: the first cites patents and contracts registered, and the second illustrates new trademarks.

945 Serviço Nacional de Aprendizagem Industrial. Departamento Regional de São Paulo. Divisão de Pesquisas, Estudos e Avaliação. Relação de ocupações industriais. São Paulo: 1983. 212 p. Lists 2282 industrial job titles which require professional preparation provided by SENAI.

946 Trabalhadores urbanos no Brasil 82/84. Aconteceu especial, 16. Rio de Janeiro: Centro Ecumênico de Documentação e Informação--CIDE, n.d. 198 p. Summarizes significant facts concerning urban workers through newspaper clippings arranged by subject. Also lists strikes and summarizes other information in tabular format. A similar publication was issued under the title Trabalhadores urbanos no Brasil 1981 (Especial, 11).

947 Valle, Gerson. Vocabulário trabalhista: direito de trabalho, processo de trabalho, previdência social. Rio de Janeiro: Editora Rio, 1975. 290 p. Defines terms related to labor law and social security in the Brazilian context.

STATES

The industrial yearbooks and surveys cited under the states below usually supply information about industrial and service industries in the state in listings by product or service and by município. Extractive, processing, manufacturing, and construction industries, financial services, transportation, and other services supporting industry and exportation are the types of activities covered. Maps and other illustrative matter are sometimes included, as are indexes in English and Spanish.

Alagoas

948 Cadastro industrial de Alagoas. Maceió: Federação das Indústrias do Estado de Alagoas. Edition examined: 1979, 1980.

Amapá

949 Cadastro industrial do Território Federal do Amapá. Macapá: Coordenaria de Indústria e do Comércio. Edition examined: 1978.

Amazonas

950 Cadastro industrial do Amazonas. Manaus: Governo do Estado do Amazonas; CEBRAE; SUFRAMA; SUDAN. Editions examined: 1975, 1984, 1986/1987.

Bahia

951 Cadastro industrial da Bahia. Salvador: Federação das Indústrias da Bahia. Edition examined: 1973.

952 As 200 maiores indústrias da Bahia. Salvador: Federação das Indústrias da Bahia, 1973?-. Lists industries by name, and type, with statistical tables summarizing data and comparing several years. Additional information on the ten largest industries. This publication appears to have begun in 1973 under the title, 100 grandes empresas industriais da Bahia. Editions examined: 1979, 1980, 1983, 1985.

Ceará

953 Cadastro industrial do Ceará. Fortaleza: Secretaria de Indústria e do Comércio; Federação das Indústrias do Estado do Ceará. Editions examined: 1973/1974, 1980, 1981, 1984.

Distrito Federal

954 Cadastro industrial do Distrito Federal. Brasília: Companhia do Desenvolvimento do Planalto Central. Edition examined: 1974.

Espírito Santo

955 Anuário industrial: Espírito Santo. Vitória. Edition examined: 1980/1981.

956 Cadastro industrial do Espírito Santo. Vitória: Federação das Indústrias do Estado do Espírito Santo, Instituto de Desenvolvimento Industrial do Espírito Santo. Edition examined: 1985/1986. Introductory information refers to this publication as the "Anuário industrial, edição 1985" (see also no. 955).

957 100 maiores empresas do estado do Espírito Santo. Vitória: Secretaria de Estado da Indústria e do Comércio, Instituto de Desenvolvimento Industrial do Espírito Santo. Statistical and other information about the largest businesses in the state, presented in tabular and graphic formats. Title varies slightly: As 100 maiores empresas do Espírito Santo (1976). Editions examined: 1976, 1983, 1985, 1986, 1987.

Goiás

958 Anuário industrial de Goiás. Goiânia: Federação das Indústrias do Estado de Goiás; SENAI, Departamento Regional de Estado de Goiás. Editions examined: 1973/1974, 1976.

Guanabara
(See also Rio de Janeiro)

959 Anuário industrial da Guanabara. Rio de Janeiro: Federação das Indústrias do Estado da Guanabara; Centro Industrial do Rio de Janeiro; Instituto de Desenvolvimento, 1.-, 1968-. Edition examined: 3rd, 1972.

Maranhão

960 Cadastro industrial do Maranhão. 2 vols. São Luís: Núcleo de Assistência Empresarial do Maranhão--NAE/MA, 1973-1974. Vol. 1: Ilha de São Luís; vol. 2: Região de Bacabal, Pedreiras.

Mato Grosso

961 Anuário das indústrias: Mato Grosso. São Paulo: Editora Pesquisa e Indústria, 1. ed.- 1989-. Lists of business and industry in the state by type of goods/services offered and by name of company. Also provides detailed information on the Federação das Indústrias no Estado de Mato Grosso. Edition examined: 1st, 1989.

962 Cadastro industrial do Mato Grosso. Cuiabá: Federação das Indústrias no Estado de Mato Grosso, 1. ed.-, 1983-. Edition examined: 1st, 1983.

Mato Grosso do Sul

963 Cadastro industrial de Mato Grosso do Sul. Campo Grande: Federação das Indústrias do Mato Grosso do Sul. Editions examined: 1981/1982; 1983/1984.

Minas Gerais

964 Anuário industrial de Minas Gerais FIEMG. Belo Horizonte: Federação das Indústrias do Estado de Minas Gerais, 1972?-. Edition examined: 1972/1973.

Pará

965 Cadastro industrial do Pará. Belém: Federação das Indústrias do Estado do Pará; Instituto de Desenvolvimento Empresarial do Estado do Pará. Editions examined: 1974/1975, 1976/1977, 1980/1981, 1984/1985.

Paraíba

966 Cadastro industrial do Estado da Paraíba. Campina Grande: Federação das Indústrias do Estado da Paraíba. Edition examined: 1985.

Paraná

967 Anuário das indústrias Paraná, Brasil. Curitiba: Federação das Indústrias do Estado do Paraná e Centro das Indústrias do Estado do Paraná. Edition examined: 1986/1987.

Pernambuco

968 Cadastro industrial Pernambuco. Recife: Federação das Indústrias do Estado de Pernambuco. Editions examined: 1980, 1983, 1987, 1988/89.

Piauí

969 Cadastro industrial Estado do Piauí. Teresina? Federação das Indústrias do Estado do Piauí; Estado do Piauí, Secretaria de Indústria e Comércio. Edition examined: 1981.

Rio de Janeiro

970 Cadastro industrial do Estado do Rio de Janeiro. Rio de Janeiro: Federação das Indústrias do Estado do Rio de Janeiro; Centro Industrial do Rio de Janeiro. Edition examined: 1979.

Rio Grande do Norte

971 Cadastro industrial do Rio Grande do Norte. Natal: Federação

das Industrias do Estado do Rio Grande do Norte. Editions examined: 1979, 1988.

Rio Grande do Sul

972 Anuário das indústrias do Estado do Rio Grande do Sul. Porto Alegre: Secretaria da Indústria e Comércio do Estado do Rio Grande do Sul e Federação das Indústrias do Estado do Rio Grande do Sul. Editions examined: 1976/1977, 1979.

973 Cadastro industrial: relação das indústrias com mais de 50 empregados no Estado do Rio Grande do Sul. Porto Alegre: Federação das Indústrias do Estado do Rio Grande do Sul; Centro das Indústrias do Estado do Rio Grande do Sul. Edition examined: 1972.

974 Cadastro industrial. Porto Alegre: Compannia de Desenvolvimento Industrial e Comercial do Rio Grande do Sul, Banco de Informações. Edition examined: 1975.

Santa Catarina

975 Cadastro industrial. Florianópolis: Federação das Indústrias do Estado de Santa Catarina. Edition examined: 1973/1974.

São Paulo

976 Anuário das indústrias. São Paulo: Federação e Centro das Indústrias do Estado de São Paulo. Editions examined: 1973/1974, 1982. (See also Guanabara.)

LANGUAGE

BIBLIOGRAPHY

977 Almeida, Atila. Dicionários parentes & aderentes: uma bibliografia de dicionários, enciclopédias, glossários, vocabulários e livros afins em que entra a língua portuguesa. João Pessoa: FUNAPE--Fundação de Apoio à Pesquisa e Extensão; Nova Stela Editora, 1988. 349 p. A partially annotated bibliography arranged alphabetically by title, with indexes by subject and date of publication. Includes those published in Brazil, Portugal, and elsewhere in the Portuguese language.

978 Almeida, Horácio de. Catálogo de dicionários portugueses e brasileiros. Rio de Janeiro: 1983. 132 p. An unannotated bibliography of about 1000 Portuguese and Brazilian dictionaries--general, specialized and bilingual.

979 Aragão, Maria do Socorro Silva de. Bibliografia dialetal brasileira. João Pessoa: Centro de Ciências Humanas, Letras e Artes, Universidade Federal da Paraíba, 1988. 60 p. An unannotated bibliography with 536 entries covering dialects, sociolinguistics, ethnolinguistics and lexicology of the Portuguese language in Brazil. Includes books, journal articles, theses, papers presented at conferences, and other works. Indexed by author and subject.

980 Dietrich, Wolf. Bibliografia da língua portuguesa do Brasil. Tubingen: Gunter Narr Verlag, 1980. 292 p. Focuses on works dealing with the differences between the Portuguese of Portugal and that of Brazil, and those studying Brazilian Portuguese. Its 1465 entries--many with annotations--include books, journal articles, conference proceedings, and other items.

981 Magalhães, Erasmo d'Almeida. Bibliografia de lingüística indígena brasileira, 1954-1974. São Paulo: U.S.P., F.F.L.C.H., 1975. 35 p. An unannotated bibliography of 478 books, periodical articles, and conference papers related to Indian

languages of Brazil, with emphasis on the Tupinambá and Guarani languages. "Separata de Língua e literatura, 4: p. 149-184, 1975."

GENERAL SOURCES

982 Autuori, Luiz. Nos garimpos da linguagem. 7. ed. Rio de Janeiro: Distribuidora Record, 1976. 407 p. A manual of the Portuguese language. Lists common spelling errors, Portuguese equivalents of foreign geographic names, antonyms and synonyms, abbreviations, and other useful information.

983 Beltrão, Odacir. Correspondência: linguagem & comunicação, oficial, comercial, bancária, particular. 13. ed. São Paulo: Editora Atlas, 1973. 322 p. A manual providing models and commentary on official, business, and private correspondence.

984 _______. A pontuação hoje: normas, comentários, histórias e estórias. Porto Alegre: Livraria Sulina Editora, 1976. 120 p. A manual of punctuation for contemporary Portuguese.

985 Brazil. Secretaria de Tecnologia Industrial. Tradutores: cadastro. Brasília: 1985. 215 p. Directory of translators of various languages and their subject specialties in all subject areas.

986 British Council. Directory of English Courses in Brazil. Rio de Janeiro: 1980. 185 p. A directory intended to provide information on the potential market for English language publications in Brazil, which also serves other purposes. Its lists of addresses include those of universities, English language schools, English studies associations, publishers interested in English language materials, book importers, and others.

987 Grimes, Barbara F. Ethnologue: Languages of the World. 10th ed. Dallas: Wycliffe Bible Translators, 1984. 592 p. Identifies the languages in use in each country of the world, including Brazil, for which 136 languages are listed. Information about each one includes name and alternate names, approximate number of speakers, location, dialects, linguistic affiliation, bilingualism of its speakers, and other data. A language map of Brazil pinpoints the location where each language is spoken. A separately published Index to the Tenth Edition of Ethnologue (1984) lists the "more than 26,000 names that are associated with the 5,445 languages listed in the Ethnologue. It identifies all the language names and their alternates, and all the dialect names and their alternates."

988 Handbook of Amazonian Languages, edited by Desmond C. Derbyshire and Geoffrey K. Pullum. Berlin: Mouton de Gruyter,

1986-. Covers the languages spoken by the indigenous peoples of the region known as Amazonia. Provides introductory information about each language and detailed coverage of the grammatical structures: syntax, phonology, morphology, and ideophones. Includes notes about the gathering of data and bibliographic references. Volumes examined: 1 (1986); 2 (1990).

989 International Center for Research on Bilingualism. Linguistic Composition of the Nations of the World. Composition linguistique des nations du monde. Québec: Les Presses de l'Université Laval, 1979. vol. 3: Central and South America. L'Amérique Centrale et l'Amérique du Sud. Statistics and brief explanatory notes on the languages spoken in the countries of the world are provided in a seven-volume set. Forty-six pages of Volume 3 are devoted to Brazil and they cover Amerindian, European, Oriental, Arabic, and Creole of the Caribbean languages.

GENERAL DICTIONARIES

990 Bueno, Francisco da Silveira. Grande dicionário etimológico-prosódico da língua portuguesa: vocábulos, expressões da língua geral e científica, sinônimos, contribuições do tupi-guarani. 8 vols. São Paulo: Saraiva, 1963-1967. A scholarly dictionary of the Portuguese language.

991 Dictionário brasileiro da língua portuguesa. 9. ed. 3 vols. São Paulo: Encyclopaedia Britannica do Brasil Publicações, 1987. An updated version of a standard dictionary.

992 Fernandes, Francisco; Celso Pedro Luft, and F. Marques Guimarães. Dicionário brasileiro Globo. Porto Alegre: Editora Globo, 1984. unpaged. A general dictionary.

993 Fernandes, Francisco. Dicionário brasileiro contemporâneo, com a colaboração de F. Marques Guimarães e Celso Pedro Luft. 4. ed. Porto Alegre: Editora Globo, 1975. 1392 p. A general Portuguese language dictionary.

994 Ferreira, Aurélio Buarque de Holanda. Novo dicionário da língua portuguêsa. 2. ed. Rio de Janeiro: Editora Nova Fronteira, 1986. 1838 p. This dictionary, commonly known as the "Novo Aurélio," is the authoritative dictionary of contemporary Brazilian Portuguese.

DICTIONARIES--INDIGENOUS LANGUAGES

995 Bontkes, Willem Dicionário preliminar sururí-português, português-sururí. Edição preliminar. Porto Velho, Rondônia:

Summer Institute of Linguistics, 1978. 30 p.

996 Boudin, Max H. Dicionário de tupi moderno: dialeto tembé-ténêtéhar do alto do Rio Gurupi. 2 vols. São Paulo: Conselho Estadual de Artes e Ciências Humanas, 1978. Equivalents in Portuguese. The etymology of words is traced through citations to the works of early writers, providing a historical dimension as well as a contemporary one.

997 Bueno, Francisco da Silveira. Vocabulário tupi-guarani/português. 3. ed. São Paulo: Brasilivros Editora, 1984. 629 p. Equivalents in Tupi-Guarani and Portuguese, and a useful section defining the meanings of place names with indigenous origins. Also includes the text of the Dicionario da lingua tupy, chamada lingua geral dos indígenas do Brazil, by Antonio Gonçalves Dias (1858). See no. 999.

998 Cunha, Antônio Geraldo da. Dicionário histórico das palavras portuguêsas de origem tupi. 3. ed. São Paulo: Editora Universidade de São Paulo, 1989. 357 p. A scholarly dictionary in which each entry includes the word's grammatical category, variants, etymology, definition, and examples of its usage in written texts. Length of entries varies from a few lines to two pages. Includes a good bibliography. First published in 1978.

999 Dias, Antônio Gonçalves. Dicionário da língua tupi, chamada língua geral dos indígenas do Brasil: tupi-português. Rio de Janeiro: Livraria São José, 1965. 72 p. Facsimile edition of an 1858 dictionary of Tupi words with equivalents in Portuguese (see also no. 997).

1000 Dicionário bilíngüe em português e mundurukú. Brasília: Fundação Nacional do Indio, Programa de Educação Bilíngüe, 1977. 47 p. Equivalents of basic vocabulary with many drawings of objects as illustrations. An experimental publication in the bilingual education program of FUNAI.

1001 Emiri, Loretta. Dicionário yanomame-portugues: (dialeto wakathautheri). Boa Vista: Comissão Pró-Indio, 1987. 93 p. Equivalents in Yanomami and Portuguese.

1002 Masucci, Oberdan. Dicionário tupi-português e vice versa, com um dicionário de nomes topográficos. São Paulo: Brasilivros, 1979. 146 p. A dictionary of equivalents in Tupi-Portuguese/Portuguese-Tupi. A section devoted to the meanings of place names which are Tupi in origin is of particular interest, given the importance of that language in Brazilian geography.

1003 Mello, Octaviano. Dicionário tupi (nheengatu)-português e vice-versa, com um dicionário de rimas tupi. São Paulo: Editora Folco Masucco, 1967. 123 p. A dictionary of equivalents in Tupi-Portuguese/Portuguese-Tupi.

1004 Melo, Anísio Taumaturga Soriano de. Vocabulário etimológico tupi do folklore amazônico. Manaus: SUFRA--Superintendência da Zona Franca de Manaus; FUNCOMIZ--Fundo Comunitário das Indústrias da Zona Franca de Manaus, 1983. 99 p. Defines words of Tupi origin associated with Amazonian folklore and gives their etymology.

1005 Sampaio, Mário Arnaud. Vocabulário guarani-português. Porto Alegre: L & PM, 1986. 223 p. Guarani with equivalents in Portuguese.

BILINGUAL DICTIONARIES

This list of bilingual dictionaries is not intended to be comprehensive, since such dictionaries abound, but it is representative of the dictionaries available. It excludes those covering Portuguese/indigenous languages. They are included in the section, "Dictionaries--Indigenous Languages."

English

1006 Almeida, Dauster C. Dicionário de expressões idiomáticas inglês-português. São Paulo: Atlas, 1979. 198 p. A more accurate dictionary of idioms than that by Subkoff (no. 1022), although spelling errors and inaccuracies in translation have crept in. For example, "stooges" is defined as "assistente profissional," a designation that many such assistants would find alarming. Nevertheless, this is the exception rather than the rule.

1007 Chamberlain, Bobby J., and Ronald M. Harmon. A Dictionary of Informal Brazilian Portuguese with English Index. Washington: Georgetown University Press, 1983. 701 p. The introduction states that this dictionary is designed as a reference tool especially for English speakers to bridge the gap "between the basic, generally simple language learned in the classroom and the preponderance of nonformal and idiomatic language used in Brazilian society on all levels and in contemporary Brazilian literature." Includes 7500 entries.

1008 Chiquetto, Oswaldo. Inglês: mil erros que você deve evitar. 3 ed. São Paulo: Editora Resenha Universitário, 1983. The meaning of English words which might be misunderstood by Portuguese speakers is explained. Also instructive for English speakers.

1009 Collins, Donald E., and Luiz L. Gomes. Dicionário de gíria americana contemporânea. A Dictionary of American Slang. São Paulo: Livraria Pioneira, 1972. 250 p. Defines American slang for Portuguese speakers, and illustrates usage in sentences.

1010 Dennis, Ronald D. 2200 Brazilian Idioms. Provo, UT: Brigham Young University, 1979. 171 p. Brazilian Portuguese idioms and their English equivalents are presented under their key words in alphabetical order.

1011 Downes, Leonard S. Palavras amigas-da-onça. A Vocabulary of False Friends in English and Portuguese. Rio de Janeiro: Ao Livro Técnico, 1984. 241 p. Lists words in English which appear similar to Portuguese words, "but which differ, often widely, in meaning and/or usage." Emphasizes British and Brazilian usage, but often explains differences in American or Portuguese usage.

1012 Fraenkel, Benjamin Bevilaqua. English Portuguese Technical and Idiomatic Dictionary. São Paulo: Livraria Nobel, 1980. 471 p. A dictionary with an odd combination of purposes: to provide equivalents in English and Portuguese for technical terms and for slang. In fact, some words which could be considered neither have crept in--"cousin" being one example. Although this dictionary has fewer errors of spelling or translation in comparison to some of the others which are available, its lack of focus detracts from its usefulness.

1013 Gomes, Luiz L. Dicionário inglês-português ilustrado. São Paulo: Livraria Pioneira, 1981. 186 p. Pictures in color illustrate 1200 basic words in English. Sentences give examples of words in context. A basic reference source for the beginner.

1014 Grossklags, Carlos. Glossário de termos militares: inglês-português. 2 ed. [n.p.] 1987. 22 p. Equivalents in English and Portuguese.

1015 Houaiss, Antônio. Dicionário inglês-português. Rio de Janeiro: Record, 1982. 925 p. Portuguese equivalents of English words and abbreviations.

1016 The New Appleton Dictionary of the English and Portuguese Languages, edited by Antônio Houaiss and Catherine B. Avery. New York: Appleton-Century-Crofts, 1967. 636 p. A bilingual dictionary of English-Portuguese/Portuguese-English equivalents.

1017 Novo dicionário Oxford inglês-português/português-inglês. 5 vols. 2. ed. Rio de Janeiro: Edições Babilônia, 1978. Equivalents in the two languages. 1st edition: 1977.

1018 Novo Michaelis dicionário illustrado. The New Michaelis Illustrated Dictionary. 2 vols. 36th ed. São Paulo: Melhoramentos, 1984 (copyright 1961). A bilingual dictionary which illustrates many objects. The visual identification that it provides is a very useful feature.

1019 Pându, Pandiá. Dicionário brasileiro da língua inglesa: inglês-português. 4 vols. Rio de Janeiro: Editora Fase. n.d. Many illustrations and examples of usage in addition to equivalents.

1020 Santos, Agenor Soares dos. Guia prático de tradução inglesa: comparação semântica e estilística entre os cognatos de sentido diferente em inglês e português. São Paulo: Editora Cultrix, 1983. 511 p. Good comparisons of English and Portuguese words with the same cognates, but different meanings.

1021 Serpa, Oswaldo. Dicionário de expressões idiomáticas: inglês-português/português-inglês. 4. ed. Rio de Janeiro: FENAME--Fundação Nacional de Material Escolar, 1982. 373 p. A useful bilingual dictionary of idioms.

1022 Subkoff, Cecile. Guia fácil para traduzir inglês-português: cerca de 8.000 expressões idiomáticas inglesas sobre os mais variados assuntos para ajudar a estudantes, correspondentes, secretarias e tradutores. Rio de Janeiro: Livraria Editora Cátedra, 1980. 231 p. Portuguese equivalents for English idiomatic phrases. Its accuracy in English leaves much to be desired: awkward phrases and misspellings abound.

1023 Taylor, James Lumpkin. A Portuguese-English Dictionary. Rev. ed. Stanford, CA: Stanford University Press, 1982. 655 p. An excellent Portuguese-English dictionary of equivalents which includes many idiomatic phrases.

1024 Tito Filho, Arimatéia. Anglo-norte americanismos no português do Brasil. Rio de Janeiro: Nórdica, 1986. 430 p. Identifies and defines words from the English language which have become part of Portuguese. Originally published in 1981 under the title, Chico's Bar: a solução.

French

1025 Burtin Vinholes, S. Dicionário francês-português/português-francês. 31. ed. Porto Alegre; Rio de Janeiro: Editora Globo, 1986. 838 p. Equivalents in the two languages.

1026 Campos, Aluizio Mendes. Dicionário francês-português de locuções. São Paulo: Editora Atica, 1980. 301 p. 4000 French idiomatic phrases are defined in French and Portuguese, and examples of their usage in French literature are quoted.

1027 Rónai, Paulo. Dicionário francês-português/português-francês. Rio de Janeiro: Editora Nova Fronteira, 1989. 574 p. Equivalent terms.

1028 Scartezzini, César, and Maria José Marcondes Pestana. Dicionário francês-português/português-francês. São Paulo: Hemus, 1980. 831 p. Equivalents in the two languages.

German

1029 Tochtrop, Leonardo. Dicionário alemão-português. 6. ed. Porto Alegre: Editora Globo, 1984. 686 p. Equivalents in German and Portuguese, but not vice-versa.

Hebrew

1030 Dicionário hebraico-português & aramaico-português. São Leopoldo: Editora Sinodal; Petrópolis: Editora Vozes, 1988. 305 p. A dictionary designed to facilitate biblical exegesis.

1031 Zlochevsky, Huzeff. Dicionário básico português-hebraico. 4. ed. revisada e ampliada. São Paulo: 1988. 150, 197 p. Equivalents in Portuguese/Hebrew and Hebrew/Portuguese.

Italian

1032 Masucci, Oberdan. Dicionário italiano-português. São Paulo: Editora Folco Masucci, 1971. 322 p. Portuguese equivalents of Italian words.

1033 Spinelli, Vincenzo, and Mario Casasanta. Dizionario completo, italiano-portoghese (brasiliano) e portoghese (brasiliano)-italiano. 2. ed. 2 vols. Milano: Editore Ulrico Hoepli, 1983-1985. Equivalents in Italian/Brazilian Portuguese and vice-versa.

1034 Stawinski, Alberto Vitor. Dicionário vêneto sul-riograndense-português: com breves noções gramaticais do idioma veneto sul-rio-grandense. Caxias do Sul, EDUCS; Porto Alegre: ESTEF; Correio Riograndense; n.p.: Fondazione Giovanni Agnelli, 1987. 321 p. Dictionary of an Italian dialect used by immigrants to southern Brazil, estimated to be spoken by one million persons in Rio Grande do Sul, with equivalents in Portuguese and examples of usage in sentences and phrases.

Spanish

1035 Becker, Idel. Dicionário espanhol-português e português-espanhol: termos técnicos, vozes familiares e populares, questões gramaticais, locuções idiomáticas, hispanoamericanismos, expressões de gíria, estrangeirismos usuais, neologismos. 5. ed. São Paulo: Livraria Nobel, 1976. 371 p. A bilingual dictionary of Spanish-Portuguese/Portuguese-Spanish equivalents.

1036 _______. Grande dicionário latino-americano português-espanhol. São Paulo: Livraria Nobel, 1983. 499 p. A Portuguese-

Spanish dictionary of equivalents, concentrating on Brazilian Portuguese, including regionalisms.

OTHER LANGUAGES

1037 Mello, William Agel de. Dicionário catalão-português. Goiânia: Oriente, 1975. 282 p. Equivalents in Catalan and Portuguese.

1038 _______. Dicionário galego-português. Goiânia: Oriente, 1979. 261 p. Equivalents in Galician and Portuguese.

1039 _______. Dicionário português-romeno. Goiânia: Oriente, 1979. 160 p. Equivalents in Rumanian and Portuguese.

1040 Sansone, Gaetano. Dicionário poliglota: português, italiano, francês, espanhol, inglês, alemão. Belo Horizonte: Editora Vega, 1972. unpaged. Equivalents in six languages.

1041 Starets, S., and N. Voinova. Dicionário prático português-russo: 7000 palavras. 3. ed. Moscovo: Edições "Russi Yazik," 1986. 471 p. Equivalents in Portuguese and Russian, but not vice-versa.

SPECIALIZED DICTIONARIES

1042 Almeida, Horácio de. Dicionário de termos eróticos e afins. 2. ed. Rio de Janeiro: Civilização Brasileira, 1981. 285 p. Defines 4300 words with erotic connotations, noting regional usage. First published under the title: Dicionário erótico da língua portuguesa (1980).

1043 Almeida, Napoleão Mendes de. Dicionário de questões vernáculas. São Paulo: Caminho Suave, 1981. 351 p. Defines and comments on idioms in Brazilian Portuguese.

1044 Barbosa, Osmar. Dicionário de nomes próprios, indígenas e afro-brasileiros. Rio de Janeiro: Ediouro, 1986. 124 p. Provides the meanings of given names of Indian and Afro-Brazilian origins.

1045 Bergo, Vittorio. Pequeno dicionário brasileiro de gramática portuguesa (adstrito a Nomenclatura Gramatical Brasileira). 2. ed. revista e ampliada. Rio de Janeiro: Francisco Alves, 1986. 219 p. This edition was prepared in order to explain the terms of the Nomenclatura Gramatical Brasileira which was officially instituted by the Ministério da Educação e Cultura. First edition: 1960.

1046 Câmara, Joaquim Mattoso. Dicionário de lingüística e gramática referente à língua portuguesa. 7. ed. Petrópolis: Vozes, 1977. 266 p. This linguistic and grammatical dictionary has been published under various titles. The first edition was issued in 1956 by the Casa de Rui Barbosa (Rio de Janeiro) under the title, Dicionário de fatos gramaticais, while the second through sixth editions were entitled Dicionário de filologia e gramática.

1047 Carneiro, W. Soares. Novo dicionário enciclopédico-humorístico. Belém: Edições CEJUP, 1987. 167 p. Contains 1300 words which have humorous connotations when parts of them are slightly altered or distorted or when their pronunciations are similar to other words. Expands an earlier work by the same author, Disse-o-nário (1952) which had 330 entries.

1048 Carvalho, Bárbara de Vasconcelos. Dicionário de conjugação de verbos. São Paulo: Editora Lotus, 1975. 352 p. Conjugations of regular and irregular verbs.

1049 Cascudo, Luís da Câmara. Locuções tradicionais no Brasil. Coisas que o povo diz. Coleção Reconquista do Brasil, 2. série, vol. 93. Belo Horizonte: Editora Itatiaia; São Paulo: Editora da Universidade de São Paulo, 1986. 314 p. Combines two earlier works of the author in one volume. Locuções tradicionais no Brasil, first published in Recife in 1970, gives the meaning and history of 505 idiomatic phrases used in contemporary Brazilian Portuguese. Coisas que o povo diz, originally published in Rio de Janeiro in 1968, identifies and explains sixty popular ideas, customs, and phrases.

1050 Cherubim, Sebastião. Dicionário de figuras de linguagem. São Paulo: Livraria Pioneira Editora, 1989. 74 p. Defines terms associated with figures of speech, giving examples from literature in the Portuguese language.

1051 Costa, Agenor. Dicionário de palavras homônimas e parônimas para estudantes dos cursos primário e ginasial. Rio de Janeiro: 1972. 139 p. Defines words with the same pronunciations, but different spellings, and words which sound similar to others and which therefore are easily misunderstood. A useful dictionary for non-native speakers of Portuguese.

1052 Cunha, Antônio Geraldo da. Vocabulário ortográfico Nova Fronteira da língua portuguesa. Rio de Janeiro: Nova Fronteira, 1983. 890 p. Includes syllabification and pronunciation for some 100,000 words; spellings for irregular plurals, superlatives, etc.; and gender, variants, and other information needed for correct spelling and speech.

1053 *Dicionário de palavras cruzadas*. n.p.: Ediouro, 1983. 832 p. A cross-word puzzle dictionary.

1054 *Dicionário ilustrado do futebol*. São Paulo: Placar, 1972. 127 p. A dictionary of soccer terms illustrated with photographs. Includes the rules of the game, and a glossary of the names and nicknames of soccer teams, stadiums, etc.

1055 Fernandes, Francisco. *Dicionário de regimes de substantivos e adjetivos*. 17. ed. Porto Alegre: Editora Globo, 1980. 384 p. "Mais de 1.859 substantivos e 2.105 adjetivos com cerca de 9.000 regimes." First edition published in 1949.

1056 ______. *Dicionário de sinônimos e antônimos da língua portuguesa*. 3. ed. revista e ampliada por Celso Pedro Luft. Porto Alegre: Editora Globo, 1980. 870 p. An updated edition of a work first published in 1945, containing synonyms, and in some cases antonyms for 30,000 words, including neologisms, Brazilianisms, and some foreign words in common usage.

1057 ______. *Dicionário de verbos e regimes*. 4. ed. Porto Alegre: Editora Globo, 1974. 603 p. "Mais de 11,000 verbos em suas diversas acepções e regências." First published in 1940. The fourth edition was published in 1954 and its eighteenth printing was issued in 1974.

1058 Fernandes, José Augusto. *Dicionário de rimas da língua portuguesa*. Rio de Janeiro: Editora Record, 1985. 428 p. A dictionary of rhymes.

1059 Ferreira, Fernando Luiz Vièira. *Dicionário brasileiro de turismo*. Rio de Janeiro: Colorama, 1975? 90 p. A dictionary defining the specialized terms used in the tourist industry. Includes many acronyms. An appendix gives equivalent terms in Portuguese, French, German, and Spanish.

1060 Franco, Cid. *Dicionário de expressões populares brasileiras*. 3 vols. São Paulo: Editoras Unidas, 1971. A dictionary of Portuguese idioms combining definitions and examples of their usage. Volume 3 includes a bibliography of "Autores e livros relacionados com expressões e temas populares brasileiros."

1061 Gianella, Antônio. *A gíria do automóvel*. São Paulo: 1976. 135 p. Defines slang terms associated with automobiles. Originally written as a master's thesis.

1062 Gonçalves, Maxamiano Augusto. *Dicionário de estrangeirismos*. Rio de Janeiro: Editora Fundo de Cultura, 1968. 317 p. Defines foreign words and phrases used in Portuguese and gives their origins.

1063 Guérios, Rosário Farâni Mansur. Dicionário etimológico de nomes e sobrenomes. 2. ed. São Paulo: Editora Ave Maria, 1973. 231 p. A dictionary of the origins and meanings of given names and surnames, with emphasis on those common in Brazil. First published in Curitiba in 1949 (179 p.) and reprinted in 1967.

1064 Heckler, Evaldo; Sebald Back, and Egon Ricardo Massing. Dicionário morfológico da língua portuguesa. 5 vols. São Leopoldo: Universidade do Vale do Rio dos Sinos, 1984-1985. A dictionary of word formation. Includes, origin, family, variants, etc. Volumes examined: 1, 2.

1065 Jota, Zélio dos Santos. Dicionário de lingüística. 2. ed. Rio de Janeiro: Presença, 1981. 353 p. Defines terms associated with linguistics. First published in 1976. Both editions have the same copyright date (1975).

1066 Knapp, Carlos H., and José Francisco Quirino. Grossário: pequeno dicionário brasileiro de palavras feias. n.p.: H. Knapp Editora, 1986. 256 p. "Apenas palavras feias, vulgares, pernósticas, anacrônicas, tecnocratas, estrangeirismos, ignorância. Ou palavras que simplesmente soam mal." Defines more than 250 "bad words."

1067 Magalhães, Raimundo. Dicionário de provérbios, locuções, curiosidades verbais, frases feitas, etimologias pitorescas, citações (em ordem alfabética). Rio de Janeiro: Ediouro, 1983. 366 p. Defines the meanings of proverbs and sayings, cites their use in literature, and discusses their etymology, when known. This edition is described in the preface as being in "forma definitiva." It is an enlarged version of Dicionário brasileiro de provérbios, frases feitas, ditos históricos e citações literárias, de curso corrente na língua falada e escrita (1960).

1068 Maior, Mário Souto. Dicionário do palavrão e termos afins. 4. ed. Rio de Janeiro: Editora Record, 1988. 173 p. A dictionary of "cuss words" and erotic words in the Portuguese language, with citations documenting their use in the written language in many cases, and indications of regional usage.

1069 _______. Galalaus & batorés. Recife: Editora Universitária, Universidade Federal de Pernambuco, 1981. 73 p. Slang and regional terms for tallness and shortness of stature in Brazilian Portuguese.

1070 _______. Dicionário folclórico da cachaça. 3. ed. Recife: Fundação Joaquim Nabuco, Editora Massangana, 1985. 152 p. A dictionary of popular terms related to cachaça. Each entry includes a definition of the term, the geographic area in which it is used, and a bibliographical reference to the source of the information. The first edition was published in 1973, and the second in 1980.

1071 _______. A morte na boca do povo. Rio de Janeiro: Livraria São José, 1974. 50 p. Lists words and phrases referring to death in slang and regional Brazilian Portuguese.

1072 Mazurkiewicz, Anselmo. Dicionário de têrmos próprios e relativos. Petrópolis: Editora Vozes, 1968. 729 p. A dictionary of related terms and concepts.

1073 Miranda, Nicanor. Dicionário de parônimos. Belo Horizonte: Editora Itatiaia. 1989. 184 p. A dictionary of pairs or groups of words which sound similar, but which have different meanings. Includes definitions of each word.

1074 Morais, Orlando. Dicionário de sinônimos e antônimos pela nova ortografia. 10. ed. corrigida e aumentada. Rio de Janeiro: Anaconda Cultural Edições, 1986. 445 p. A dictionary of synonyms and antonyms which incorporates the latest revisions in Portuguese language spelling.

1075 Mota, Mauro. Os bichos na fala da gente. 2. ed. Rio de Janeiro: Tempo Brasileiro; Brasília: Instituto Nacional do Livro, 1978. 204 p. Defines idiomatic meanings of the names of animals or of phrases including them, and quotes adages associated with animals. First edition: Recife, 1969.

1076 Nascentes, Antenor. Dicionário de dúvidas e dificuldades do idioma nacional de acordo com a Nomenclatura Gramatical Brasileira. 5. ed. Rio de Janeiro: Livraria Freitas Bastos, 1967. 197 p. A dictionary of idioms, usage, and common errors in Brazilian Portuguese. Earlier editions: 1941, 1944, 1952, 1962 under the title, Dicionário de dúvidas e dificuldades do idioma nacional.

1077 _______. Dicionário de sinônimos. 3. ed. Rio de Janeiro: Editora Nova Fronteira, 1981. 485 p. A dictionary which lists not only synonyms in groups, but explains the nuances of meanings.

1078 _______. Dicionário etimológico resumido. Rio de Janeiro: Instituto Nacional do Livro, 1966. 791 p. A condensed and updated etymological dictionary based on the author's two-volume work, Dicionário etimológico da língua portuguesa (1932-1952).

1079 _______. Tesouro de fraseologia brasileira. 3. ed. revista por Olavo Anibal Nascentes. Rio de Janeiro: Nova Fronteira,

1986. 431 p. Defines idiomatic expressions and identifies the regions where they are used. Sometimes gives examples of usage in literature.

1080 Obata, Regina. O livro dos nomes. São Paulo: Círculo do Livro, 1986. 208 p. Lists given names, their origins, and meanings. Includes bibliography.

1081 Pându, Pandiá. Novo dicionário de acentuação das palavras homógrafas e heterófonas: complementado com regras práticas de ortografia e acentuação gráfica. Rio de Janeiro: Livros do Mundo Inteiro, 1972. 76 p. A dictionary designed to explain and illustrate certain changes in the spelling of Portuguese with regard to diacritics enacted in a 1971 law.

1082 Pena, Leonam de Azeredo. Novo vocabulário ortográfico brasileiro da língua portuguesa. 2 vols. Rio de Janeiro: Editora Científica, 1966. "Enriquecido com milhares de vocábulos na publicação oficial feita pela Academia de Letras em 1945."

1083 Penalva, Gastão. Gíria maruja. Coleção Jaceguay, 13. 1. ed. Rio de Janeiro: Serviço de Documentação da Marinha, 1982. 110 p. Defines the slang words and phrases used by seamen.

1084 Pontes, Joel. Palavras luso-brasileiras do futebol. Recife: Editora Universitária, 1974. 125 p. Defines soccer terms used in Brazil and Portugal.

1085 Pugliesi, Márcio. Dicionário de expressões idiomáticas: locuções usuais da língua portuguesa. São Paulo: Editora Parma, 1981. 205 p. Brief definitions of Brazilian Portuguese idioms.

1086 São Paulo, Fernando. Linguagem médica popular no Brasil. 2 vols. Salvador: Editora Itapuã, 1970. Defines terms used in popular and folk medicine. Quotes from writings which use them, and sometimes identifies the locality in which they are used and gives their etymology.

1087 Schwab, Artur. Locuções adverbiais. Curitiba: Gráfica Ribeirão Preto, 1976. 206 p. "Mais de 3.000 locuções adverbiais, assim antigas que modernas, em suas diversas acepções, com farta exemplificação para seu correto uso."

1088 Silva, Euclides Carneiro da. Dicionário da gíria brasileira. Rio de Janeiro: Bloch Editores, 1973. 217 p. Contains 3000 slang words and expressions with citations from contemporary authors. Included are terms not appearing in standard dictionaries, but frequently used in oral expression, and in the texts of books, magazines, and newspapers.

1089 ______. Dicionário de locuções da língua portuguesa. Rio de Janeiro: Editora Bloch, 1975. 419 p. A dictionary of some 3000 idiomatic expressions with definitions and examples from written Portuguese.

1090 Silva, Felisbelo da. Dicionário de gíria: gíria policial, gíria dos marginais, gíria humorística. São Paulo: Papelivros, 1969? 112 p. This dictionary of slang includes many currently used expressions.

1091 Sousa, Paulo José de. Moderno dicionário de antônimos. João Pessoa: Editora Universitária, UFPb, 1978-. The first fascicule (ABA-ACABAVEL) of a projected dictionary of antonyms and synonyms of the Portuguese language. Many entries include examples of usage from the written language.

1092 Spalding, Tassilo Orpheu. Dicionário brasileiro de gramática, de acordo com a Nomenclatura Gramatical Brasileira. São Paulo: Editora Cultrix, 1971. 278 p. Defines terms related to grammar, punctuation, speech, and related topics with many useful and interesting examples.

1093 ______. Dicionário de coletivos. Belo Horizonte: Editora Itatiaia, 1966. 63 p. A dictionary of collective nouns with entries under the individual term followed by collective terms referring to it. Identifies regional usage.

1094 Spina, Segismundo. Dicionário prático de verbos conjugados. 2. ed. São Paulo: Editora F.T.D., S.A., 1969. 153 p. Conjugations of regular and irregular verbs.

1095 Tacla, Ariel. Dicionário dos marginais. Rio de Janeiro: Forense-Universitária, 1981. 99 p. A dictionary of the language used by those who live on the fringes of Brazilian society.

1096 Victória, Luiz A. P. Dicionário da origem e da evolução das palavras. 4. ed., revista, aumentada e atualizada. Rio de Janeiro: Editora Científica, 1965. 260 p. An etymological dictionary intended for quick reference by the lay person.

1097 ______. Dicionário de dificuldades, erros e definições de português. 4. ed. Rio de Janeiro: Tridente, 1969. 247 p. Includes 2000 entries dealing with problems or errors in Portuguese, such as solecisms, foreign words, irregular verbs, unusual collective terms, placement of pronouns, punctuation, and diacritics.

1098 Villar, Mauro. Dicionário contrastivo luso-brasileiro. Rio de Janeiro: Editora Guanabara, 1989. 318 p. "Alguns lusismos, brasileirismos, regionalismos, expressões idiomáticas, ortografias, ortoépias, particularidades gramaticais, regenciais, fonêmicas, toponímia e outras peculiaridades confrontadas ou explicadas" (Subtitle).

1099 Vitor, Edgar d'Almeida. Pequeno dicionário de gíria entre delinquentes: pesquisa em torno da linguagem de um sub-grupo social. Rio de Janeiro: Pongetti, 1969. 39 p. Defines words and phrases used by delinquents and others living on the fringes of society.

1100 Vocabulário ortográfico da língua portuguesa. 1. ed. n.p.: Academia Brasileira de Letras, 1981. 795 p. Reflects changes in Brazilian spelling.

1101 Ximenes, Sérgio Barcellos. Vocabulário de rimas. Rio de Janeiro: Ediouro, 1983. 334 p. A rhyming dictionary.

DICTIONARIES--REGIONS AND STATES

North

1103 Jacob, Paulo and Herban Maciel. Dicionário da língua popular da Amazônia. Rio de Janeiro: Livraria Editora Cátedra; Brasília: Instituto Nacional do Livro, Fundação Pró-Memória, 1985. 159 p. Defines words as they are used in the Amazon region, and illustrates their usage by in-context examples.

1102 Miranda, Vicente Chermont de. Glossário paraense: coleção de vocábulos peculiares à Amazônia e especialmente à Ilha do Marajó. Belém. Universidade Federal do Pará, 1968. 98 p. Defines words in common usage in Amazônia, especially those of Tupi origin. New edition of a classic first published in 1905.

Northeast

1104 Azevedo, Teó. Abecedário matuto. São Paulo: Global, 1982. 128 p. Defines terms used in northern Minas Gerais, the sertão of Bahia, and northeastern Brazil.

Bahia

1105 Passos, Alexandre. A gíria baiana. Rio de Janeiro: Livraria São José, 1973. 102 p. A dictionary of words and expressions as they are used in Bahia.

Ceará

1106 Cabral, Tomé. Novo dicionário de termos e expressões populares. 2. ed. Fortaleza: Edições UFC, 1982. 786 p. A dictionary of the expressions of the sertanejo of Ceará, especially of the area around Cariri. The expressions are defined, and examples of them found in literature, including literatura de cordel, are cited. Updates Dicionário de termos e expressões populares, published in 1972.

1107 Chaves, Euripedes. Nomes e expressões vulgares da medicina no Ceará. Fortaleza: Edição Centro Médico Cearense, 1985. 192 p. Defines regionalisms associated with medicine. Cites sources of information and includes a bibliography.

1108 Girão, Raimundo. Vocabulário popular cearense. Fortaleza: Imprensa Universitária do Ceará, 1967. 238 p. A dictionary of common terms and slang used in Ceará, excluding terms for animals and plants, except those meaning something other than their original significance. The entries define each word and sometimes supply etymological information. A bibliography concludes the work.

Goiás

1109 Ortêncio, Waldomiro Bariani. Dicionário do Brasil Central, subsídios à filologia: linguagem, usos e costumes, folclore, toponímia dos municípios goianos. São Paulo: Editora Atica, 1983. 472 p. Defines words and expressions as they are used in Goiás. Includes examples of their use in writing, and bibliographical citations for the works in which the examples can be found.

Maranhão

1110 Vieira Filho, Domingos. A linguagem popular do Maranhão. 3. ed. São Luís, 1979. 105 p. Defines terms used in popular speech in Maranhão.

Minas Gerais

1111 Barbosa, Waldemar de Almeida. Dicionário da terra e da gente de Minas. Belo Horizonte: Arquivo Público Mineiro, 1985. 208 p. Defines and explains terms used in Minas Gerais, including many associated with its history. Quotes from writings which use the words. The bibliography cites many sources of information about this state.

Paraíba

1112 Almeida, Horácio de. Dicionário popular paraibano. João Pessoa: Editora Universitária/UFPb, 1979. 180 p. A dictionary of the colloquialisms of Paraíba. Entries sometimes include examples of usage in literature.

1113 Aragão, Maria do Socorro Silva de, and Cleusa Palmeira Bezerra de Menezes. Atlas lingüístico da Paraíba. Vol. 1: Cartas léxicas e fonéticas. Vol. 2: Análise das formas e estruturas lingüísticas encontradas. 2 vols. Brasília: UFPB--Universidade Federal da Paraíba: CNPq--Conselho Nacional de Desenvolvimento Científico e Tecnológico, 1985. According to the abstract, this linguistic atlas consists of two volumes: the first "containing [149] lexical and phonetic maps based on primary data, and the second one presenting the methodology, the phonetic-phonological analysis, the morpho-syntactic analysis and a glossary of basic data obtained through a general questionnaire."

Pernambuco

1114 Costa, Francisco Augusto Pereira da. Vocabulário pernambucano. 2. ed. Recife: Secretaria da Educação e Cultura, 1976. 814 p. A dictionary of regionalisms, first published in 1916 as an issue the Revista do Instituto Arqueológico, Histórico e Geográfico Pernambucano.

Rio Grande do Norte

1115 Faria, Oswaldo Lamartine de, and Guilherme de Azevedo. Vocabulário do criatório norte-riograndense. Estudos brasileiros, no. 23. Rio de Janeiro: Serviço de Informação Agrícola, 1966. 92 p. Defines the vocabulary of the vaqueiros of Rio Grande do Norte, often using descriptions from literature to elaborate upon a simple definition.

1116 Nonato, Raimundo. Calepino potiguar: gíria rio-grandense. Mossoró? 1980. 496 p. A dictionary of local terms and usage.

Rio Grande do Sul

1117 Braun, Jayme Caetano. Vocabulário pampeano: pátrias, fogões e legendas. Porto Alegre: Edigal, 1988. 358 p. Defines terms used on the pampas of Rio Grande do Sul. Includes a bibliography.

1118 Castillo, Carlos. O cavalo gaúcho. Porto Alegre: Grafosul, 1983. 164 p. The main part of this interesting work is a glossary of local expressions related to horses. The definitions are enhanced by whimsical illustrative line drawings. Other sections are devoted to a glossary of terms describing the coloration and markings of horse hides, and to poetry about horses.

1119 Corrêa, Piaguaçú. Antigos e novos vocábulos gaúchos. Canôas: Editora LaSalle, 1965. 105 p. Defines words used in rural Rio Grande do Sul.

1120 Echenique, Sylvio da Cunha. Bruaca: adagiário gauchesco. 2. ed. Bagé: 1980. 224 p. Identifies and defines proverbs and slang terms of Rio Grande do Sul. First edition published in 1954.

1121 Herrlein, Natálio. Peçuelos: adágios, ditos e expressões gauchescas. Porto Alegre: Martins Livreiro, 1986. 174 p. Explains the meanings of idiomatic expressions used in Rio Grande do Sul.

1122 Nunes, Zeno Cardoso, and Rui Cardoso Nunes. Dicionário de regionalismos do Rio Grande do Sul. 3. ed. Porto Alegre: Martins Livreiro, 1986. 552 p. Defines words and expressions as they are used in Rio Grande do Sul. Many entries include examples of usage from written sources.

1123 ________, and ________. Minidicionário guasca. Porto Alegre: Martins Livreiro, 1986. 160 p. An abridged dictionary of regionalisms based on the Dicionário de regionalismos by the same authors (see above).

1124 Porto Alegre, Apolinário. Popularum sul-rio-grandense: estudo de filologia e folclore. Porto Alegre: Co-edições UFRGS e Instituto Estadual do Livro, 1980. 492 p. This work, written more than 100 years ago, was first published in 1980. It lists, defines, and discusses the vocabulary of Rio Grande do Sul, including words of German and Tupi-Guarani origin, and proverbs and sayings in common use.

Roraima

1125 Rocha, Luiz Cláudio Ribeiro da. Pequeno glossário do garimpo. n.p.: Museu Integrado de Roraíma: 1985. unpaged. A glossary defining terms associated with panning for gold and other activities of the garimpeiros in Roraíma.

São Paulo

1126 Amaral, Amadeu. O dialeto caipira: gramática, vocabulário. 3. ed. São Paulo: HUCITEC, em co-edição com a Secretaria da Cultura, Ciência e Tecnologia do Estado de São Paulo, 1976. 195 p. A glossary of words as they are used in the caipira dialect in São Paulo comprises more than half of this work, with other chapters on phonetics and syntax. First published in 1920. The third edition is a reprint of the second (1955).

LAW

Reference works abound in the field of Brazilian law, and a lengthy list could be compiled. The publications cited here represent a basic selection intended to assist the non-specialist in defining terms, locating laws and material written on legal topics, and determining the requirements of common legal situations.

BIBLIOGRAPHY

1127 Bibliografia brasileira de direito, vol. 1-9; 1967/1968-1979; Rio de Janeiro: Instituto Brasileiro de Informação em Ciência e Tecnologia, 1967/1968-1979; nova série, vol. 1-, 1980/1981-, Brasília: Senado Federal, Subsecretaria da Biblioteca. An unannotated bibliography of monographs and journal articles produced in Brazil. The volumes of the new series were published out of sequence beginning with volume 3 (1984/1985) which was issued in 1986. Volumes 1 (1980/1981) and 4 (1986) were published in 1987, and volume 2 (1982/1983) was published in 1988. Volumes examined: 4, 1986; 5, 1987 (published 1989).

1128 Brazil. Congresso. Câmara dos Deputados. Biblioteca. Seção de Referencia e Circulação. Direito romano. Bibliografias, 2. Brasília: 1970. 439 p. An unannotated bibliography of 2628 book-length works (monographs, theses, etc.) on Roman law, which is the basis of the Brazilian legal system.

1129 Dallari, Dalmo de Abreu. Bibliografia brasileira de direito constitucional. Série bibliografias especializadas, no. 1. São Paulo: Centro de Documentação Jurídica da Faculdade de Direito da Universidade de São Paulo, 1972. 46 p. An unannotated bibliography of 424 publications referring to the constitutions of Brazil, 1824-1969.

1130 United States. Library of Congress. Hispanic Law Division. Index to Latin American Legislation, 1950-1960. 2 vols. Boston: G. K. Hall, 1961.

1131 ______. ______. ______. Index to Latin American Legislation, 1961-1965: First Supplement. 2 vols. Boston: G. K. Hall, 1970.

1132 ______. ______. ______. Index to Latin American Legislation, 1966-1970: Second Supplement. 2 vols. Boston: G. K. Hall, 1973.

1133 ______. ______. ______. Index to Latin American Legislation, 1971-1975: Third Supplement. 2 vols. Boston: G. K. Hall, 1978. Reproduces cards prepared in the Hispanic Law Division of the Library of Congress, indexing national legislation which appears in the official gazettes of twenty Latin American republics. Legislation printed in Brazil's Diário oficial is included.

1134 Villalón Galdames, Alberto. Bibliografia jurídica: Latin American Legal Bibliography, 1810-1965. Vol. II: Brazil, Colombia, Costa Rica, Cuba. Boston: G. K. Hall, 1984. 820 p. An unannotated bibliographv of publications related to Latin American law. The extensive section devoted to Brazil contains about 2500 entries. Subject and author indexes, and a useful index of authors by country.

DICTIONARIES

1135 Barros, Orlando Mara de. Dicionário de classificação de crimes. Rio de Janeiro: Editora Rio, 1980. 174 p. Defines and categorizes crimes covered in the Brazilian penal code. This work, prepared by a professor of law, is written in a manner that makes it understandable to legal experts and laypersons alike.

1136 Magalhães, Humberto Piragibe, and Cristovão Piragibe Tostes. Dicionário jurídico. 4. ed. 2 vols. Rio de Janeiro: Edições Trabalhistas, 1984. Definitions of legal terms and a list of abbreviations commonly used in legal writing.

1137 Mello, Maria Chaves de. Dicionário jurídico português-inglês/inglês-português. Portuguese-English/English-Portuguese Law Dictionary. 3. ed. Rio de Janeiro: Barrister's Editora, 1987. 513 p. A bilingual dictionary of equivalent legal terms.

1138 Nunes, Pedro dos Reis. Dicionário de tecnologia jurídica. 9. ed.

2 vols. Rio de Janeiro: Livraria Freitas Bastos, 1976. "Definições de termos, locuções, expressões e abreviaturas de direito romano, civil, comercial (terrestre, marítimo, industrial, cambial, e aeronáutico), criminal, penal, militar, fiscal, trabalhista, público, parlamentar, canônico, administrativo, internacional (público e privado), judiciário (civil e penal), constitucional, político, diplomático e financeiro, e, ainda, dos que são comuns na vida mercantil e econômica, na sociologia, na medicina legal, na psicologia e na psiquiatria" (subtitle).

1139 Soibelman, Leib. Enciclopédia do advogado. 3. ed. Rio de Janeiro: Editora Rio, 1981. 520 p. A dictionary of 9500 entries, defining legal terms, and those from related fields such as philosophy and the social sciences, which are closely associated with the law.

OTHER SOURCES

1140 Luz, Valdemar P. da. Manual prático da elaboração de contratos e documentos. Porto Alegre: Editora Síntese, 197-? 181 p. A manual designed for the layperson with information about the technicalities of common legal situations and the texts of the forms used in them. Treats such matters as purchase or sale of automobiles, leases, registration of trademarks or patents, and divorce. Very helpful for understanding some of the basics of an unfamiliar legal system.

LIBRARIES, ARCHIVES, MUSEUMS, INFORMATION SCIENCE

BIBLIOGRAPHIES

1141 Bibliografia brasileira de ciência da informação. Vol. 6-, 1980/1983-. Brasília: Instituto Brasileiro de Informação em Ciência e Tecnologia, 1984-. An irregularly published bibliography supplying bibliographic data about and abstracts of publications in information science including library science. Cites articles, monographs, conference proceedings, and theses. Arranged by subject, with indexes of authors, corporate authors, and detailed subjects. Continues Bibliografia brasileira de documentação, which covered the years 1811-1980 in five volumes. Volumes examined: 6, 1980/1983; 7, 1984-1986.

1142 Brazil. Arquivo Nacional. Arquivo: bibliografia de publicações periódicas. Rio de Janeiro: 1979. 30 p. A list of holdings of the Arquivo Nacional of periodicals published by archives or specializing in the subject of archives. Although it is universal in scope, the list of sixty-nine titles includes twenty-two published by Brazilian archives.

1143 Indice geral da RBBD. São Paulo: Federação Brasileira de Associações de Bibliotecários Brasileiros, 1981. 352 p. Indexes more than 1300 articles, laws, speeches, etc. related to library science and documentation published in the Revista brasileira de biblioteconomia e documentação from 1960 through 1977, by author and subject.

1144 Mattos, Doroty Francischelli. Bibliografia seletiva, retrospectiva, analítica especializada em bibliotecas públicas (1979-1984). São Paulo: Secretaria Municipal de Cultura, Departamento de Bibliotecas Públicas, 1985. 97 p. An annotated bibliography with 332 entries, covering forty journals including seven published in Brazil.

GENERAL SOURCES

1145 Albuquerque, Vera Lúcia Lellis. Linguagens documentárias utilizadas no Brasil: construídas, traduzidas ou adaptadas. Brasília: Conselho Nacional de Desenvolvimento Científico e Tecnológico--CNPq; Instituto Brasileiro de Informação em Ciência e Tecnologia--IBICT; Centro de Informação em Ciência da Informação--CCI, 1984. 126 p. Brief descriptions of the means of accessing the printed material available in 162 research institutes, libraries, government agencies, and other entities, in all subject areas. Information for each includes type of documentary language used (subject headings, thesauri, etc.), the types of documents accessed, state of development of the method of accessing them, physical presentation (cards, printed catalog, etc.), and scope of the material held by the institution.

1146 Instituto Brasileiro de Bibliografia e Documentação. Quem é quem na biblioteconomia e documentação no Brasil. Fontes de informação, vol. 5. Rio de Janeiro: 1971. 544 p. Who's who-type information for 1386 professionals in the fields of library science and documentation. Arranged by state, and indexed by names of persons.

1147 Instituto Brasileiro de Informação em Ciência e Tecnologia. Quem informa no Brasil: guia de bibliotecas, centros e serviços de documentação e informação. Brasília: 1987. 195 p. Information on entities registered in the data base, Unidade de Informações (UNIR), of IBICT. Emphasis is on science and technology, but it includes the social sciences, humanities, arts, and multidisciplinary topics. Arranged by subject, then geographically.

1148 Jurasek, Sonia Regina Gonçalves. Pequeno glossário de termos técnicos em biblioteconomia e documentação: inglês-português. 2. ed. Rio de Janeiro: Delegacia do Ministério da Fazenda no Estado do Rio de Janeiro, Divisão de Administração, Seção de Documentação, Biblioteca, 1987. 142 p. A glossary of more than three hundred equivalent terms in English and Portuguese associated with library science and documentation. First edition issued in 1984.

ARCHIVES

1149 Achiamé, Fernando A. M. Guia preliminar do Arquivo Público Estadual. Vitória: Arquivo Público Estadual, 1981. 62 p.

A guide to document collections of the Public Archive of the State of Espírito Santo, including public records of the state, private collections, and the archive of the Câmara Municipal de Itapemirim.

1150 Brazil. Arquivo Nacional. Guia dos arquivos de instituições religiosas e beneficentes. Série Instrumentos de trabalho. Rio de Janeiro: 1975. 44 p. Lists archives of religious institutions throughout Brazil, briefly summarizing their holdings.

1151 _______. _______. Guia preliminar dos arquivos estaduais. Rio de Janeiro: 1987. 78 p. Basic information about twenty-three state archives which includes name, address, founding date, availability to the public, publications, and names of collections in the holdings.

1152 Centro de Pesquisa e Documentação de História Contemporânea do Brasil. Guia dos arquivos CPDOC, 1979. Rio de Janeiro: 1979? 99 p. A guide to the archival holdings of this center which specializes in the period from 1930 to the present. Provides general descriptions of forty-one collections related to participants in Brazilian public life: government officials, leaders of political parties, military men, technocrats, businessmen, and journalists, among others. Includes the papers of three presidents: Getúlio Vargas, Arthur da Costa e Silva, and Humberto de Alencar Castello Branco.

1153 Guia preliminar de fontes para a história do Brasil: instituições governamentais no município do Rio de Janeiro. Rio de Janeiro: Fundação Casa de Rui Barbosa; Fundação Getúlio Vargas, 1979. 128 p. The first in what is intended to be a series of publications identifying and describing archival sources for historical research in government agencies and institutions in each município of Brazil. Federal, state, and municipal entities are covered. Also lists institutions contacted which do not have archives, those with archives located outside of Rio de Janeiro, and institutions with archives closed to the public. This is a valuable reference tool providing information about a city rich in archival resources.

LIBRARIES

1154 Brazil. Coordenação de Aperfeiçoamento de Pessoal de Nível Superior. Guia de bibliotecas universitárias brasileiras. Brasília: 1979-. Provides data on university libraries--federal, state, and private. Vol. 1: Regiões norte, nordeste, centro-oeste; vol. 2: Região sudeste.

1155 Deransart, Pierre. Bibliothèques et systèmes documentaires en Argentine et au Brésil. Le Chasnay: Institut de Recherche d'Informatique et d'Automatique, 1977? 145 p. A guide to selected Argentine and Brazilian libraries and documentation centers considered to be the most important of their kinds. Covers approximately seventy-five Brazilian libraries in Belo Horizonte, Brasília, Porto Alegre, Recife, Rio de Janeiro, São Paulo, and Salvador.

1156 Fundação Instituto Brasileiro de Geografia e Estatística. Bibliotecas brasileiras. Rio de Janeiro: 1980. 75 p. The data collected for the Guia das bibliotecas brasileiras, 1976 (below) is summarized in charts and statistical tables.

1157 Guia das bibliotecas brasileiras, 1976. Rio de Janeiro: Fundação Instituto Brasileiro de Geografia e Estatística; Instituto Nacional do Livro, 1979. 1017 p. A guide to all types of libraries in Brazil with collections of 300 or more volumes. Arranged geographically, first by state, then by city. Information for each library includes address, type, year founded, number of volumes, classification system, user statistics, and space.

1158 Guia das bibliotecas do Estado de São Paulo. São Paulo: Departamento de Artes e Ciências Humanas, Divisão de Bibliotecas, 1978. 399 p. The 1061 libraries in the state of São Paulo are described in sections devoted to public, school, university, and special libraries. Indexed by name of library and name of city.

1159 Guia das bibliotecas e bibliotecários do Recife. 2. ed. Recife: Associação Profissional de Bibliotecários de Pernambuco, 1971. 120 p. Basic data about all types of libraries in Recife. First edition issued in 1964.

1160 Guia de bibliotecas e serviços de documentação do Estado do Rio de Janeiro, 1984. 3. ed. Rio de Janeiro: Grupo de Bibliotecários em Informação e Documentação Tecnológica do Rio de Janeiro, 1984. 105 p. Focuses on special libraries, providing address, speciality, services, and size of collection and staff.

1161 Habitat: guia de bibliotecas e centros de documentação. Brasília: Conselho Nacional de Desenvolvimento Científico e Tecnológico, 1982. 95 p. Data on libraries and other information centers specializing in urban development and housing. Includes address, hours, subjects of specialization, services, and publications.

1162 Instituto Brasileiro de Bibliografia e Documentação. Bibliotecas especializadas brasileiras. 2. ed. Rio de Janeiro: 1969. 605 p. A directory of special libraries, broadly defined, in all subject areas. Arranged by state, with indexes by subject and name of institution.

1163 Instituto Brasileiro de Informação em Ciência e Tecnologia. Lista geral de cabeçalhos de assunto. 4 vols. Rio de Janeiro: 1977.

1164 ______. Lista geral de cabaçalhos de assunto. Suplemento. Rio de Janeiro: 1978. 638 p. A list of standard subject headings to be used in library card catalogs, updated with a supplement.

1165 Instituto Nacional do Livro. Guia das bibliotecas públicas brasileiras conveniadas com o Instituto Nacional do Livro. Brasília: Fundação Nacional Pró-Memória, Ministério da Educação e Cultura, 1983. 341 p. Basic information about public libraries all over Brazil for the year 1981: address, date founded, size of collection, number of volumes purchased. This guide serves to update the information about public libraries covered in Guia das bibliotecas brasileiras (no. 1157).

MUSEUMS

1166 Carrazzoni, Maria Elisa. Guia dos museus do Brasil. 2. ed. Rio de Janeiro: Expressão e Cultura, 1978. 167 p. This guide to both public and private museums is arranged alphabetically by state. Information given for each museum varies, the minimum being its name and address. Other data provided when possible includes purpose, hours, a brief description of the building housing the museum, history, and publications. First edition edited by Fernanda de Camargo e Almeida, published in 1972.

1167 Coleção museus brasileiros. Rio de Janeiro: Fundação Nacional de Arte, 1979-. A series of beautifully illustrated books describing the collections and narrating the history and present status of important Brazilian museums. The publications examined for inclusion in this bibliography were:

no. 1: Museu Nacional de Belas Artes (1979). 193 p.
no. 2: Museu de Imagens do Inconsciente (1980). 191 p.
no. 3: Museu de Arte de São Paulo (1981). 193 p.
no. 4: Museu Paraense Emílio Goeldi (1981). 205 p.
no. 5: Museu do Folclore Edison Carneiro (1981). 205 p.
no. 6: Pinacoteca do Estado de São Paulo (1982). 202 p.
no. 7: Museu da Inconfidência (1984). 159 p.

1168 Ferrez, Helena Dodd, and Maria Helena S. Bianchini. Thesaurus para acervos museológicos. Série técnica, 1. 2 vols. Rio de Janeiro: Fundação Nacional Pró-Memória, Coordenadoria Geral de Acervos Museológicos, 1987. A thesaurus of the terminology to be used in identifying/labeling artifacts.

Volume 1 lists them in systematic order, and volume 2 in alphabetical order.

1169 Santos, Fausto Henrique dos; Fernando Menezes de Moura; and Neusa Fernandes. Catálogo dos museus do Brasil. Rio de Janeiro: Associação dos Museus do Brasil, 1984. 50 p. A state-by-state listing of museums and their addresses. In addition to traditional museums, it includes aquariums, zoos, botanical gardens, national parks, and certain other parks.

1170 Vieira, Lícia Margareth da Silva, and Marília Colnago Coelho. Museus e casas de cultura do Piauí. Teresina: Academia Piauense de Letras, 1989. 73 p. Summarizes the history, describes the collections, and provides photographs of twelve state-supported museums and lists an additional eleven private collections with their addresses.

INFORMATION SCIENCE

1171 Bases de dados: catálogo. Rio de Janeiro: INFO; EMBRATEL. This issue of Revista INFO (no. 57, Oct. 1987) supplies basic information about data bases in all fields.

1172 Brazil. Sistema de Informações Organizacionais da Administração Federal. Catálogo dos sistemas de informação. Brasília: 1983: 95 p. A catalog of government agencies which maintain data bases, registers, and other types of information systems, and the subjects which they cover. No information about their accessibility to the public is included.

1173 Guia de bases de dados no Brasil: saiba onde encontrar as informações que você precisa. Rio de Janeiro: Companhia Brasileira de Trens Urbanos, Diretoria de Recursos Humanos e Organizacionais, Centro de Documentação, 1986. 36 p. A guide to data bases arranged by subject. Describes each data base and provides its address and information on access to it. Includes a name/subject index.

LITERATURE

BIBLIOGRAPHY AND BIOBIBLIOGRAPHY

This section includes only collective bibliographies and bio-bibliographies; those devoted to individual authors are excluded.

1174 Brasil, Francisco de Assis Almeida. Dicionário prático de literatura brasileira. Rio de Janeiro: Edições de Ouro, 1979. 324 p. A biobibliographical dictionary focusing on living authors, although many from the past are also included. Entries include biographical data, lists of works and brief critical assessments of each one. Includes only novelists, poets, short story writers, and literary critics and essayists; writers in other fields are excluded. Entries are arranged alphabetically by given name.

1175 Brazil. Biblioteca Nacional. O romance brasileiro: catálogo da exposição organizada pela Seção de Exposições e inaugurada em dezembro de 1974. Rio de Janeiro: Divisão de Publicações e Divulgação, 1974. 86 p. A bibliography of 385 Brazilian novels which comprised an exhibit intended to provide an overview of this genre from its beginnings to the contemporary period. Partially annotated with brief notes.

1176 Brazil. Ministério da Cultura. Brazilian Literature Today: Novels, 30 Authors. Brasília: Instituto Nacional do Livro, 1987. unpaged. This catalog in English, prepared for the Frankfort International Book Fair, summarizes the content of thirty contemporary Brazilian novels, provides biographical data on the authors, and lists their other literary works.

1177 Brinches, Victor. Dicionário biobibliográfico luso-brasileiro. Rio de Janeiro: Editora Fundo de Cultura, 1965. 509 p. A biobibliographical dictionary covering more than 400 literary figures, one-third Portuguese and two-thirds Brazilian, past and present. Although the work was designed for secondary school students, the basic and often extensive information that it provides would be helpful to others interested in this field.

1178 Carpeaux, Otto Maria. Pequena bibliografia crítica da literatura brasileira. Nova ed. Com um apêndice de Assis Brasil, incluindo 47 novos escritores. Rio de Janeiro: Edições de Ouro, 1979 or 1980. 470 p. Lists the principal works of more than 250 past and contemporary authors along with selected bibliography of critical works about them. The main body of this work was completed in the 1940's (there were four editions, 1949-1967), but the appendix which includes contemporary writers cites articles dated as late as 1978. Birth and death dates and place of birth of authors are given when known.

1179 Catálogo de publicações: literatura brasileira. São Paulo: Nobel, 1985. 215 p. A catalog citing 3000 Brazilian literary works, derived from the publisher's Catálogo brasileiro de publicações, formerly available only on microfiche. Serves as a "books in print" tool for the subject, providing author, title, place of publication, date, type of binding, publisher, number of pages, illustrations, size, and International Standard Book Number. Covers popular literature, folklore, poetry, novels, stories, satire, humor, and drama.

1180 Faria, Francisco Leite de. Os impressos quinhentistas portugueses referentes exclusivamente ao Brasil. Lourenço Marques: Universidade de Lourenço Marques, 1972. 52 p. Detailed bibliographical and physical descriptions and historical notes on seven very rare sixteenth-century Portuguese imprints with Brazilian subjects, which includes facsimiles of title pages or illustrations. "Separata da Revista de ciências do homem, vol. IV, Série A, 1972."

1181 Foster, David William, and Roberto Reis. A Dictionary of Contemporary Brazilian Authors. Tempe: Center for Latin American Studies, Arizona State University, 1981. 152 p. A dictionary concentrating on living authors, although a few others who profoundly affected twentieth-century literature are included. Provides brief biographical information, a listing of principal works, and commentary on some of them.

1182 Gomes, Celuta Moreira. O conto brasileiro e sua crítica: bibliografia (1841-1974). 2 vols. Rio de Janeiro: Biblioteca Nacional, 1977. An exhaustive bibliography citing 2844 collections of short stories by individual authors, 146 anthologies, and 2250 references to literary criticism of the works. Does not include single stories published in periodicals.

1183 Hulet, Claude Lyle. Brazilian Literature. 3 vols. Washington: Georgetown University Press, 1974-1975. A survey of literature through short biographies of important authors, bibliographies of their writings, and excerpts from their works. Volume 1: 1500-1880: Renaissance, Baroque, Neo-classicism, Romanticism; Volume 2: 1880-1920: Naturalism, Realism/Parnassianism, Symbolism; Volume 3: Since 1920: Modernism.

1184 Menezes, Raimundo de. Dicionário literário brasileiro. 2. ed. Rio de Janeiro: Livros Técnicos e Científicos, 1978. 803 p. Covers authors from colonial times to the 1970's, providing biographical data, bibliographies, and criticism. A separate alphabet defines "Ismos literários, escolas, e academias," while a dictionary of pseudonyms comprises a third alphabet. A general bibliography concludes the work.

1185 Pérez, Renard. Escritores brasileiros contemporâneos. 2. ed. 2 vols. Rio de Janeiro: Editora Civilização Brasileira, 1970-1971. Biobibliographies and portraits of well-known contemporary authors, with excerpts from their works. Volume 1 contains information about twenty-seven literary figures, while Volume 2 covers another twenty-two.

1186 Placer, Xavier. Modernismo brasileiro: bibliografia (1918-1971). Rio de Janeiro: Biblioteca Nacional, 1972. 401 p. An unannotated bibliography of 2900 books, pamphlets, periodicals, and newspaper and periodical articles relating to Brazilian modernism reflected in literature, the fine arts, and architecture.

1187 Reis, Antônio Simões dos. Bibliografia da crítica literária em 1907 através dos jornais cariocas. Rio de Janeiro: Casa de Rui Barbosa, 1968. 210 p. A bibliography of literary criticism appearing in newspapers in Rio de Janeiro in 1907, which was intended to serve as a prototype for future annual volumes. One section is devoted to brief biographical notes and bibliographical references about the critics and authors covered. This work is useful, in spite of its limited time coverage, because of the important writers and critics that it includes.

1188 Souza, Sebastião de. Discografia da literatura brasileira. Rio de Janeiro: Livraria Editora Cátedra em convênio com o Instituto Nacional do Livro, 1977. 85 p. A selective discography of sixty-six sound recordings of Brazilian literature. Information for each recording includes author, title, recording company, catalog number, date if known, size, and speed of the recording. The content of each side is also listed. The author index lists each literary work of a particular author which has been recorded.

1189 Tolman, John, and Ricardo Paiva. Brazilian Literature and Language Outlines. The Brazilian Curriculum Guide Specialized Bibliography. Albuquerque: Latin American Institute, University of New Mexico, 1985 or 1986. 49 p. An essay outlining the development of Brazilian literature is followed by a bibliography citing the works of recent authors, undocumented in the literary histories cited in the bibliography of Brazilian literary history which concludes the work. A short section is devoted to a bibliography of Portuguese language teaching materials.

GENERAL WORKS

1190 Abdala, Benjamin, and Samira Youssef Campedelli. Tempos da literatura brasileira. São Paulo: Atica, 1985. 304 p. A summary of Brazilian literature from 1500 to the present. In addition to narrative, each chapter includes biographical notes on authors mentioned, and a literary chronology of the period. A bibliography concludes the work.

1191 Anuário de poetas do Brasil. Rio de Janeiro: Folha Carioca Editora, 1976-. This yearbook, reported to be a vanity publication, provides biographical information, address, and examples of the poetry of the contemporary authors included in it. Interest in publishing in it has increased. From its beginning in 1976 to the 1979 edition the publication expanded from two to four volumes, although major poets are conspicuously absent from its pages.

1192 Brasil, Francisco de Assis Almeida. Vocabulário técnico de literatura. Rio de Janeiro: Edições de Ouro, 1979. 232 p. Brief articles define and explain the meanings of about 150 terms in current use in literary historiography, criticism, and essays. Pictures, illustrating the meaning of such terms as "poema/processo" as well as portraits of authors associated with literary movements are valuable additions. Sources of information are included in most entries.

1193 Camargo, Oswaldo de. O negro escrito: apontamentos sobre a presença do negro na literatura brasileira. São Paulo: Imprensa Oficial do Estado, S.A.--IMESP, 1987. 214 p. An anthology of works dealing with black themes by forty-three black or mulatto Brazilian literary figures--past and contemporary, which includes biobibliographical information about them and portraits of some. Also provides various lists, such as Brazilian fiction, poetry, and drama with themes or major characters associated with blacks.

1194 Campos, Geir. Pequeno dicionário de arte poética. 3. ed. São Paulo: Cultrix, 1978. 181 p. Defines 618 terms from Portuguese and other languages related to poetry. Quotations from Brazilian and Portuguese poetry illustrate many of the definitions. Includes a bibliography.

1195 Coelho, Jacinto do Prado. Dicionário de literatura: literatura portuguesa, literatura brasileira, literatura galega, estilística literária. 3. ed. 3 vols. Porto: Figuerinhas, 1976. Substantial articles cover individuals, literary movements, publications, and topics related to literature, such as philosophy, history, and culture. Articles include bibliography. First edition, 1956-1960 has title, Dicionário das literaturas portuguesa, galega e brasileira. Second edition published in 1969 in Rio de Janeiro.

1196 Doyle, Plínio. História de revistas e jornais literários. Coleção de estudos bibliográficos, vol. 1. Rio de Janeiro: Ministério de Educação e Cultura, 1976-. Fourteen rare nineteenth- and twentieth-century Brazilian literary journals, or those published abroad in Portuguese for Brazilian readers are covered in the first of several projected volumes. In addition to bibliographic information, a history of the journal, and a listing of the table of contents for each issue, there is a facsimile of the title page of the first number of each title. A useful name index refers to individuals associated with the journals, including authors of works published in them. Journals included in the first volume and their beginning dates of publication are: Niterói, revista brasiliense (1836), Revista da Sociedade Fênix Literária (1878), Gazeta literária (1884), Revista Sulamericana (1889), A nova revista (1896), Klaxon (1922), Estética (1924), A revista (1925), Festa (1927), Verde (1927), Revista de antropofagia (1928), Revista nova (1931), Literatura (1946).

1197 Enciclopédia de literatura brasileira. 2 vols. Rio de Janeiro: Ministério da Educação, Fundação de Assistência ao Estudante, 1990. This encyclopedia, compiled under the auspices of the Oficina Literária Afrânio Coutinho, provides exhaustive coverage of the authors, periods, genres, movements, literary magazines, and other topics associated with Brazilian literature. Entries range in length from one line to several pages. Includes extensive bibliography and many portraits and other illustrations.

1198 Grupo Gente Nova. Dicionário crítico do moderno romance brasileiro. 2 vols. Belo Horizonte: 1970. Provides critical commentary, including excerpts from the writings of literary critics about 335 past and contemporary novelists. Includes bibliography.

1199 _______. Dicionário crítico do moderno romance brasileiro. Suplemento 1: Brasil, Ficção 70. Belo Horizonte: 1971. 71 p. The first part of this work lists some of the fiction published in 1970, accompanied by quotations from critical reviews. The second section cites works of literary criticism, describing and excerpting them.

1200 Igreja, Francisco. Dicionário de poetas contemporâneos. Rio de Janeiro: Oficina Letras & Artes, 1988. 148 p. A bio-bibliographical dictionary of living Brazilian poets, based on responses to a questionnaire. Also lists periodicals which publish literary news and gives the names and addresses of the Brazilian academies of letters.

1201 Luft, Celso Pedro. Dicionário de literatura portuguesa e brasileira. 2. ed. Porto Alegre: Editora Globo, 1969. 406 p. Biographical, critical and bibliographical data about Brazilian and Portuguese authors, as well as discussions of important movements, well-known anonymous works, etc., comprise this work. It is intended for secondary school teachers and students, and the authors and topics selected reflect that aim, although the information presented is useful for a wider audience. First published in 1967.

1202 Magalhães, Raimundo. Dicionário de citações brasileiras. São Paulo: Editora Didática Irradiante, 1971. 232 p. Summarizes the thought of principal Brazilian intellectuals on specific topics through excerpts from their writings. Arranged by topic.

1203 Masucci, Folco. Dicionário de pensamentos, máximas, aforismos, paradoxos, provérbios, etc. de autores clássicos e modernos, nacionais e estrangeiros. 6. ed. revista e aumentada. São Paulo: Edições Leia, 1968. 685 p. A dictionary of "familiar quotations," with 6132 entries. Provides an index which briefly identifies the authors cited, including many Brazilians. First edition published in 1946.

1204 Meira, Cécil. A sabedoria popular. 2. ed. ampliada, atualizada. Belém: Editora Grafisa, 1988. 235 p. "Ditos, dizeres, ditados, aforismos, lemas, curiosidades, anexins, adágios, refrões, frases feitas, sentenças, chavões e provérbios antigos e modernos, em Portugal e no Brasil."

1205 Moises, Massaud. Dicionário de termos literários. São Paulo: Cultrix, 1974. 520 p. A dictionary of the etymology and meaning of literary terms, with attention given to their relationship to Brazilian literature when relevant.

1206 Mota, Leonardo. Adagiário brasileiro. Coleção Reconquista do Brasil, 2. série, vol. 115. Belo Horizonte: Itatiaia; São Paulo: Editora da Universidade de São Paulo, 1987.

403 p. Part 1 of this book is a compilation of proverbs based on research completed in 1935, which was lost at the time of the author's death, and was later reconstructed by his sons. The proverbs, in alphabetical order by first word, are sometimes accompanied by explanations, or by their equivalents in other languages, including English. Part 2 reprints the concluding chapters of four other books by the same author, which also cite proverbs and rhymes, sometimes defining their meanings. Part 1 was first published in 1982 under the same title (Fortaleza: Edições Universidade Federal do Ceará; Rio de Janeiro: J. Olympio).

1207 Muricy, José Cândido de Andrade. Panorama do movimento simbolista brasileiro. 2. ed. 2 vols. Rio de Janeiro: Instituto Nacional do Livro, 1973. Biographical data and excerpts from the works of 131 poets representative of the symbolist movement in Brazilian literature. Includes an introductory essay, portraits of many of the poets and other illustrations, lists of the members of symbolist groups, bibliographic information on symbolist journals, a glossary, and a good index.

1208 Pequeno dicionário de literatura brasileira, organizado y dirigido por José Paulo Paes and Massaud Moíses. 2.ed. revista e ampliada. São Paulo: Cultrix, 1980. 462 p. An important source providing the general reader with basic information on principal authors, works, historical periods, literary movements, forms, and themes of Brazilian literature, from its beginnings to the present. The signed entries, prepared by well-qualified specialists, contain bibliographical data and other information about their subjects. Indexes of authors, titles, and subjects enhance the usefulness of this work. First edition: 1967.

1209 Rónai, Paulo. Dicionário universal Nova Fronteira de citações. Rio de Janeiro: Editora Nova Fronteira, 1985. 1020 p. Includes many quotations originating from the Portuguese language.

1210 Síntese da nossa literatura: vade-mecum das literaturas brasileiras e portuguesas. Curitiba: Editora Educacional Brasileira, 198-? Summarizes plots and lists characters of classic Brazilian literary works. Volume 2 (1982) was examined.

1211 Steinberg, Martha. 1001 provérbios em contraste: provérbios ingleses e brasileiros. São Paulo: Editora Atica, 1985. 127 p. Provides literal Portuguese translations for English language proverbs as well as the equivalents in Portuguese, which may be similar to or quite different from their English counterparts.

1212 Stern, Irwin. Dictionary of Brazilian Literature. New York: Greenwood Press, 1988. 402 p. Contains about 300 entries "covering the most significant writers, literary schools, and related cultural movements in Brazilian literary history, with an emphasis on twentieth century and very contemporary figures" (p. xv) prepared by American, British, and Brazilian literary scholars and intended for English language readers. Also includes a chronology of Brazilian history, literature, and foreign literature in parallel columns and a glossary of frequently used Brazilian terms. An introductory essay places Brazilian literature in cultural perspective. The entries include bibliography.

1213 Xavier, Raul. Vocabulário de poesia. Rio de Janeiro: Imago Editora; Brasília: Instituto Nacional do Livro, 1978. 226 p. Defines the terms of poetics used in Portuguese and other languages, with quotations to illustrate many of the definitions. Includes a bibliography. This dictionary, and that of Campos (no. 1194) cited above are complementary, since each one includes many terms omitted by the other.

POPULAR LITERATURE

1214 Almeida, Atila Augusto F. de, and José Alves Sobrinho. Dicionário bio-bibliográfico de repentistas e poetas de bancada. 2 vols. João Pessoa: Editora Universitária, 1978. A bio-bibliographical dictionary of poets and minstrels of literatura de cordel and other popular poetry of the Northeast. An especially useful feature is the identification of the acrostics frequently used by authors in place of their full names in printed literatura de cordel. Volume 1 is an alphabetical listing of persons and acrostics, and Volume 2 is an alphabetical list of titles, followed by the names of their authors.

1215 Batista, Sebastião Nunes. Antologia da literatura de cordel. Natal: Fundação José Augusto, 1977. 388 p. An anthology of works of forty-four popular authors of literatura de cordel. The illustrated cover of a work by each author precedes the biobibliographical information, and the latter is followed by an example of his work. Very useful to anyone studying this important popular genre.

1216 Cavalcanti, Ionaldo A. O mundo dos quadrinhos. São Paulo: Símbolo, 1977. 254 p. Identifies more than 1800 Brazilian and foreign "heróis, superheróis, e vilões," in past and present comic books and comic strips. Listed by name in dictionary format, the information about them includes their creators, dates of existence, and, in the case of foreign characters, their publishers. Illustrations complement many of the entries.

1217 O cordel do Grande Rio. Rio de Janeiro: Secretaria Estadual de Educação e Cultura, Departamento de Cultura; Instituto Estadual do Livro; Instituto Estadual do Patrimônio Artístico e Cultural, 1978. 23 p. Biobibliography covering eight cordelistas.

1218 Curran, Mark J. Selected Bibliography of History and Politics in Brazilian Popular Poetry. Special Study no. 8. Tempe: Center for Latin American Studies, Arizona State University, 1971. 26 p. A bibliographic essay about literatura de cordel dealing with historical and political events: disasters and unusual phenomena, war (both international and internal strife), internal economic conditions, foreign interests and intervention, communism, politics, and banditry. The author has located and cited a number of interesting examples of these types of literature. Unfortunately for the use of scholars, all of the titles of the works have been translated into English and their original Portuguese titles omitted.

1219 Hallewell, Laurence, and Cavan McCarthy. "Bibliography of Brazilian Chapbook Literature" in Latin American Masses and Minorities: Their Images and Realities: Papers of the Thirtieth Annual Meeting of the Seminar on the Acquisition of Latin American Library Materials, Princeton University, Princeton, New Jersey, June 19-23, 1985, edited by Dan C. Hazen, vol. 2, pp. 683-707. Madison: SALALM Secretariat, University of Wisconsin--Madison, 1987. A partially annotated bibliography of 251 entries citing publications on all aspects of literatura de cordel: history, criticism, origins, geography, production, publication and distribution, illustrations and covers, subjects and themes, individual artists and authors, and others. Does not list the literature itself. This bibliography was originally prepared as an appendix to the authors' paper, "Brazilian Chapbook Literature," which appears in Volume 1 (pp. 361-379) of the same publication.

1220 Luyten, Joseph Maria. Bibliografia especializada sobre literatura popular em verso. São Paulo: Escola de Comunicações e Artes da Universidade de São Paulo, 1981. 104 p. An unannotated bibliography of publications on critical works and histories of literatura de cordel and other popular literature in verse.

1221 Mota, Leonardo. Cantadores: poesia e linguagem de sertão cearense. 6. ed. Belo Horizonte: Editora Itatiaia, 1987. 323 p. Brief biographical data and examples of the verse of well-known cantadores of the sertão of Ceará. Includes glossary of words and phrases used in the verse.

1222 Trovadores brasileiros. Rio de Janeiro: Shogun Editora e Arte; Clube dos Trovadores Capixabas, 1984. 97 p. Brief biographical information and examples of the works of some eighty contemporary authors of trovas, a form of poetry which took hold in Brazil about thirty years ago, was especially popular in the 1960's, and continues today.

CHILDREN'S LITERATURE

1223 Bibliografia da literatura infantil em língua portuguesa. 2. ed. São Paulo: Prefeitura do Município de São Paulo, Departamento de Bibliotecas Infanto-Juvenis, 1955-. An excellent annotated bibliography of children's literature arranged by age groups, with author, title, and subject indexes. First published in 1953 with a second edition in 1955 and periodic supplements at irregular intervals. Ten supplements had been published as of mid-1988: 1955-1957, 1958-1962, 1962-1968, 1968-1970, 1970-1973, 1973-1976, 1976-1979, 1983, 1984-1985, and 1985. The supplement covering 1979-1982 was reported to be in preparation.

1224 Bibliografia sobre literatura infantil. São Paulo: Secretaria Municipal de Cultura, Departamento de Bibliotecas Infanto-Juvenis, Sub-Divisão Biblioteca "Monteiro Lobato," 1984. 38 p. An unannotated bibliography of books, articles, conference proceedings, and other works on the subject of children's literature.

1225 Brazil. Biblioteca Nacional. Literatura infanto-juvenil brasileira: catálogo da exposição comemorativa do Ano Internacional da Criança. Rio de Janeiro: 1979. 126 p. A partially annotated bibliography of 755 items of twentieth-century children's literature including stories, biography, poetry, drama, songs, and periodicals. Most of the annotations identify books awarded literary prizes.

1226 Catálogo de publicações: literatura infanto-juvenil. São Paulo: Nobel, 1985. 238 p. Lists 3000 children's and juvenile literature titles, giving basic information: author, title, place and date of publication, publisher, size, illustrations. Extracted from the publisher's Catálogo brasileiro de publicações (microfiche).

1227 Coelho, Nelly Novaes. Dicionário crítico da literatura infantil/juvenil brasileira: 1882/1982. São Paulo: Edições Quiron, 1983. 963 p. Traces the development of children's literature in Brazil from the writings of Monteiro Lobato to the present, through biobibliography and critical commentary.

1228 Fundação Nacional do Livro Infantil e Juvenil. Bibliografia analítica da literatura infantil e juvenil publicada no Brasil: 1965-1974. São Paulo: Melhoramentos, 1977. 384 p. A bibliography of about 1200 children's books with critical annotations.

1229 Literatura infantil e juvenil: obras e autores premiados. Série bibliografia, 8. Rio de Janeiro: FUNARTE, Centro de Documentação, 1985. 85 p. A list of award-winning children's literature, listed under the names of the prizes, covering the years 1937-1982. Includes Brazilian authors and illustrators winning Brazilian and foreign prizes, and includes works translated into languages other than Portuguese. Indexed by authors, illustrators, and prizes.

STATES

Amazonas

1230 Poetas do Amazonas: antologia, UBE. Manaus: UBE--União Brasileira de Escritores, 1982. 148 p. Brief biographical data, and selected poems for sixteen poets of Amazonas. Includes line-drawing portraits.

Bahia

1231 Castro, Renato Berbert de. Breviário da Academia de Letras da Bahia, 7.3.1917-7.3.1985. Salvador: Bureau Gráfica e Editora, 1985. 196 p. Lists former and current occupants of each chair of the Academy of Letters of Bahia, providing brief biographical notes of erratic quality and information about the date of election. Includes portraits of the incumbents.

Ceará

1232 Girão, Raimundo, and Maria da Conceição Souza. Dicionário da literatura cearense. Fortaleza: Imprensa Oficial do Ceará--IOCE, 1987. 233 p. Supplies biobibliographical information and sources of literary criticism about past and present authors of Ceará.

1233 Nobre, F. Silva. Cronologia da cultura cearense. Rio de Janeiro: Academia Cearense de Ciências, Letras e Artes do Rio de Janeiro, 1988. 334 p. A chronology of events associated with culture in the state of Ceará, which emphasizes literature and publishing, but includes other types of cultural activity. Notes birth dates and other biographical data for authors and other individuals. Unfortunately, the lack of an index makes the use of this work difficult.

1234 Souza, Maria da Conceição. Autor cearense: índice de bio-bibliografias. Fortaleza: Edições UFC; Academia Cearense de Letras, 1982. 104 p. Indexes sixty sources of bio-bibliographical information, locating data for about 973 literary figures of Ceará.

Distrito Federal

1235 Gomes, Danilo. Escritores brasileiros ao vivo. Belo Horizonte: Editora Comunicação, 1979-. Interviews, preceded by bio-bibliographical data, about contemporary authors, conducted by a reporter for the Suplemento literário de Minas Gerais. The first two volumes concentrate on writers of Brasília. Volume 2, which was examined, contained thirty-seven interviews with recognized poets, essayists, storytellers, and novelists.

Espírito Santo

1236 Cláudio, Affonso. Historia da litteratura espirito-santense. Edição fac-similar. Porto: 1912. Rio de Janeiro: Xerox, 1981. 556 p. Biobibliographical information and excerpts from the works of twenty-nine capixaba writers of the nineteenth and early twentieth centuries, and briefer mention of others.

1237 Elton, Elmo. Poetas do Espírito Santo. Vitória: Universidade Federal do Espírito Santo; Fundação Ceciliano Abel de Almeida, Prefeitura Municipal de Vitória, 1982. 280 p. Biographical data about, and excerpts from the poetry of 117 capixaba poets, from Padre José de Anchieta (born 1534) to the present.

Goiás

1238 Barbosa, Alaor. Pequena história da literatura goiana (1799-1983). Goiânia: 1984. 134 p. Brief information about many authors of Goiás in narrative format with a name index.

1239 Teles, José Mendonça. Gente & literatura. Goiânia: UCG, 1983. 185 p. Biobibliographical essays about thirty-five past and present goiano authors.

Maranhão

1240 Moraes, Jomar. Apontamentos de literatura maranhense. São Luís: Edições SIOGE, 1976. 187 p. Biobibliographical data about writers of Maranhão from the colonial period through 1930 is presented in chapters devoted to literary periods and movements. Includes information on literary societies. The lack of an index makes use of this work more difficult than it should be, but the chapters are fairly easy to scan.

1241 Leal, Antônio Henriques. Pantheon maranhense: ensaios biográficos dos maranhenses ilustres já falecidos. 2. ed. Rio de Janeiro: Editorial Alhambra, 1987-. This edition of a work first published 1873-1875 (4 volumes; Lisboa: Imprensa Nacional), is a collection of biographical essays about nineteenth century literary figures of Maranhão. Includes portraits of each biographee. Volumes examined: 1, 2.

Mato Grosso

1242 Mendonça, Rubens de. Bibliografia mato-grossense. Rio de Janeiro: Universidade Federal de Mato Grosso; Secretaria de Educação e Cultura, 1975. 126 p. A biobibliography of uneven quality of authors born in Mato Grosso, and those who wrote about Mato Grosso. Biographical information is usually limited to birth and death dates when known, place of birth, and profession; frequently it is omitted altogether. In spite of its weaknesses this is a helpful bibliography for this state which is little-known on the literary/cultural scene.

Pernambuco

1243 Nascimento, Luiz do. Dicionário de pseudônimos de jornalistas pernambucanos. Recife: Universidade Federal de Pernambuco, Editora Universitária, 1983. 231 p. Lists pseudonyms used by journalists in Pernambuco in the nineteenth and twentieth centuries, under the full names of the individuals. Entries often include brief biographical data, and cite the publications where the pseudonyms appeared. Unfortunately, there is no index by pseudonym, unnecessarily complicating the task of identifying a writer when only the pseudonym is known.

Piauí

1244 Moraes, Herculano. A nova literatura piauiense. Rio de Janeiro

Editora Artenova, 1965. 174 p. Biographical data, critical commentary, and excerpts from the works of novelists, poets, historians, folklorists, and other writers of Piauí, who have become prominent since 1965. The quality of information provided is uneven.

Rio de Janeiro

1245 Ribeiro, João de Sousa. Dicionário biobibliográfico de escritores cariocas, 1565-1965. Rio de Janeiro: Brasiliana, 1965. 285 p. Authors of creative literature and works on all subjects born in the city of Rio de Janeiro are included in this bibliography. Biographical information is relatively brief, often consisting of birth and death dates and profession, although activities and memberships are sometimes included. The bibliographic portion of each entry excludes periodical articles, citing only single works of forty-nine or more pages. Information given includes only the title and date of publication.

1246 Trotta, Frederico. Poetas cariocas em 400 anos. Rio de Janeiro: Casa Editora Vecchi, 1966. 414 p. Biobibliographical data and excerpts from the works of Rio de Janeiro poets over four centuries.

Rio Grande do Sul

1247 Faraco, Sérgio, and Blásio H. Hickman. Quem é quem nas letras riograndenses. 2. ed. Porto Alegre: Secretaria Municipal de Educação e Cultura, 1983. 270 p. Biobibliography of information and references to critical commentary about contemporary authors of Rio Grande do Sul. Not limited to authors of creative literature; includes writers of all types. The second edition updates and expands the first, which was published in 1982, and annual editions are planned.

1248 Gardelin, Mário. Imigração italiana no Rio Grande do Sul: fontes literárias. Coleção imigração italiana, 90. Porto Alegre: Escola Superior de Teologia e Espiritualidade Franciscana; Caxias do Sul: Editora da Universidade de Caxias do Sul; Torino, Itália: Fondazione Giovanni Agnelli, 1988. 133 p. Surveys key works of Italian literature of Rio Grande do Sul, summarizing their histories, plots, and characters, and providing bibliographies of critical works about them.

1249 Leite, Lígia Chiappini Moraes. Modernismo no Rio Grande do Sul. Publicação do Instituto de Estudos Brasileiros, 20. São Paulo: Instituto de Estudos Brasileiros, Universidade de São Paulo, 1972. 358 p. A scholarly bibliography studying modernism in the literature of Rio Grande do Sul, and its links to the modernist movement in São Paulo and Rio de Janeiro. In addition to the unannotated list of books and periodicals related to the subject, there is a bibliography of articles appearing in newspapers, with extensive summaries of them. There are also summaries of personal interviews about modernism with a number of well-known gaucho authors. The work concludes with a chronology of modernism in Rio Grande do Sul, its effect on music and the plastic arts, an analysis of the theoretical positions of individual authors, and general conclusions. Very valuable as a source for research in this major aspect of twentieth-century Brazilian literature.

1250 Martins, Ary. Escritores do Rio Grande do Sul. Porto Alegre: Universidade Federal do Rio Grande do Sul, 1978. 633 p. A biobibliographical dictionary of Rio Grande do Sul authors, past and present. Includes authors of creative literature as well as writers in other fields such as journalism and literature. Identifies authors who use pseudonyms.

1251 Villas-Bôas, Pedro. Notas de bibliografia sul-riograndense: autores. Porto Alegre: A Nação; Instituto Estadual do Livro, 1974. 615 p. A biobibliographical dictionary of Rio Grande do Sul, including gáucho authors and those who wrote about the state. Biographical data are generally brief, limited to dates of birth and death, place of birth, type of writing, and pseudonym, if applicable. The bibliographical section of each entry includes books and articles. There is an index of pseudonyms. An important contribution to the study of gaúcho literature.

1252 ______. Pseudônimos de regionalistas e abreviaturas. Porto Alegre: Impressora Moliterni, 1967. 26 p. Identifies past and contemporary writers of Rio Grande do Sul who wrote under pseudonyms and initialisms.

Santa Catarina

1253 Junkes, Lauro. Presença da poesia em Santa Catarina. Florianópolis: Lunardelli, 1979. 272 p. Biographical data and excerpts from the works of more than seventy past and contemporary poets of Santa Catarina.

1254 Sachet, Celestino. A literatura de Santa Catarina. Florianópolis: Lunardelli, 1971. 291 p. Biobibliographical information about Santa Catarina authors, past and contemporary, is presented in a series of chapters devoted to various literary schools or forms. Information for each author is not uniform, but there is often a biographical sketch, a list of works and excerpts from works and criticism. Three brief chapters focus on litarary figures from cities of the interior, authors of privately published books, and new authors who have published chiefly in local newspapers or literary journals. Although the overall quality of this work leaves something to be desired, it contains much information that is unavailable elsewhere.

Sergipe

1255 Horta, Maria Helena de Castro. Indice do Dicionário bio-bibliográfico sergipiano do Dr. Armindo Guaraná. Aracajú: Governo do Estado do Sergipe, Departamento de Cultura e Patrimônio Histórico, 1975. 45 p. An index to facilitate the use of a biobibliographical dictionary of Sergipe, published in 1925, entering individuals under their given names, and lacking standardization in the entry of pseudonyms, initialisms, etc. This index lists persons under the last element of their surnames. Also lists authors and their pseudonyms.

1256 Lima, Jackson da Silva. História da literatura sergipana. Coleção Ofenísia Freire. Aracajú: Secretaria de Estado da Educação e Cultura, Fundação Estadual de Cultura, 198?-. Volume 2, Fase romântica (1986), which was the only one examined, provides biobibliography, critical commentary, and examples of the work of twenty-six authors who lived from the middle of the nineteenth century through the early twentieth century. Several introductory chapters discuss the romantic period as it evolved in Sergipe. A general bibliography concludes the work.

MUSIC

BIBLIOGRAPHY AND DISCOGRAPHY

1257 Barbosa, Elmer C. Corrêa. _O ciclo do ouro, o tempo, e a música do barroco católico_. Rio de Janeiro: Fundação Nacional de Arte; Ministério da Educação e Cultura; Xerox, 1979. 454 p. This publication is the catalog of an archive of microfilm of eighteenth-century sacred music and of books and documents related to it. The materials microfilmed were widely dispersed in different museums and archives, and were collected on microfilm by the Pontifícia Universidade Católica do Rio de Janeiro. Although the eighteenth century, when Minas Gerais was in its cultural ascendency, is emphasized, it also covers nineteenth-century music.

1258 _Bibliografia da música brasileira, 1977-1984_. São Paulo: Universidade de São Paulo, Escola de Comunicações e Artes, Serviço de Biblioteca e Documentação; Centro Cultural São Paulo, Divisão de Pesquisas, 1988. 275 p. An unannotated bibliography of 2239 entries listing books and periodicals about Brazilian music for the period mentioned in the title, published in Brazil and elsewhere. A companion volume citing materials published up to 1976 is planned, as is a current bibliography, beginning with 1985.

1259 Brazil. Biblioteca Nacional. _Rio musical, crônica de uma cidade: exposição comemorativa do IV centenário da cidade do Rio de Janeiro_. Rio de Janeiro: Biblioteca Nacional, Divisão de Publicações e Divulgação, 1965. 51 p. A partially annotated bibliography of 290 songs and other types of music about the city of Rio de Janeiro from the nineteenth and twentieth centuries. Covers many aspects of life: carnival, political events, forms of transportation, epidemics, neighborhoods, and others.

1260 _Catálogo das músicas sob controle do SDDA (Serviço de Defesa_ do Direito Autoral): repertório do Brasil, do mundo, de todos os gêneros e todas as épocas. Vol. 1: Música brasileira. Rio de Janeiro: 1972-. unpaged. Lists some 50,000 compositions falling under Brazilian copyright law, as well as music publishers, composers, and pseudonyms of composers whose compositions are protected by copyright. Also serves as an incomplete but useful bibliography of Brazilian music.

1261 Discografia brasileira 78 rpm: 1902-1964. 5 vols. Rio de Janeiro: FUNARTE, 1982. Lists recordings issued commercially over a period of sixty-two years, providing title, company, identifying number, composer(s), performer(s), and date. The vast majority of titles listed are Brazilian popular music, although música erudita is also included.

1262 Fundação Cultural do Maranhão. A música no Maranhão. São Luís: 1978. 12 p. Cites eighty-two books and articles about music and musicians in Maranhão.

1263 Instituto Nacional do Folclore. Núcleo de Música. Catálogo das gravações do Núcleo de Música do Instituto Nacional de Folclore: música folclórica e literatura oral. Rio de Janeiro: 1986. 111 p. Cites folk music and literature from all over Brazil recorded and preserved on magnetic tape in collections maintained by the Instituto Nacional de Folclore.

1264 Rangel, Lúcio. Bibliografia da música brasileira. Rio de Janeiro: Livraria São José, 1976. 20 p. An unannotated bibliography of about 220 entries citing writings about Brazilian popular music. Arranged by first name of author.

1265 Rego, Enylton de Sá, and Charles A. Perrone. MPB: Contemporary Brazilian Popular Music. The Brazilian Curriculum Guide Specialized Bibliography. Albuquerque: Latin American Institute, University of New Mexico, 1985? 29 p. A summary of developments in Brazilian popular music from the emergence of the Bossa Nova in the late 1950's to the present is followed by a discography and bibliography.

1266 Ripper, João Guilherme. Música brasileira para orquestra: catálogo geral. Rio de Janeiro: FUNARTE, Instituto Nacional de Música, Projeto Orquestra, 1988. 132 p. A catalog of published and unpublished compositions for orchestra by past and contemporary Brazilian composers, listed under their names. Information provided includes title, date and duration of the composition, instrumentation, and publisher or place where the material can be obtained. "Anexos" include the names and addresses of living composers, of musicologists responsible for compiling information on composers who are dead, and of publishers issuing the scores.

1267 Schoenbach, Peter J. Classical Music of Brazil. The Brazilian Curriculum Guide Specialized Bibliography. Albuquerque: Latin American Institute, University of New Mexico, 1985? 19 p. An essay touching on the highlights of Brazilian classical music is followed by an annotated bibliography. The lack of a discography is an unfortunate omission.

1268 Schwab, Alceu. Bibliografia da MPB (Música popular brasileira). Curitiba: 1984. 81 p. An unannotated bibliography of 471 current and retrospective publications related to Brazilian popular music. The introduction describes it as complementing the Bibliografia de música brasileira by Rangel (no. 1264).

1269 Sumários periódicos de música. São Paulo: Universidade de São Paulo, Escola de Comunicações e Artes, Dec. 1978-. This semiannual publication reproduces the title pages of major music journals, worldwide. The most recent issue examined (July/Dec. 1984) covered twenty-eight journals, including two from Brazil.

1270 Universidade de São Paulo. Escola de Comunicações e Artes. Biblioteca. Setor de Documentação Musical. Catálogo de partituras por autor e título: autores brasileiros. São Paulo: 1984. 174 p. A list of 1756 published and unpublished compositions by Brazilian composers available at the library.

1271 Universidade de São Paulo. Escola de Comunicações e Artes. Serviço de Difusão de Partituras. Catálogo de Serviço de Difusão de Partituras. São Paulo: 1983-. A catalog of unpublished, contemporary musical scores available for copying by the Serviço de Difusão de Partituras. Updated catalogs are planned as more scores are added to the collection.

OTHER SOURCES

1272 Alencar, Edigar de. O carnaval carioca através da música. 2 vols. 5. ed. corrigida, ampliada e atualizada. Rio de Janeiro F. Alves, 1985. A chronological account of the history of carnaval in Rio de Janeiro, from its beginnings in 1835 through 1984. Musicians and songs of the past are highlighted; the elusive lyrics of many songs are included. Indexes of names of persons and of song titles provide access to the text. A song index provides date and a brief discography for each title.

1273 _______. A modinha cearense. Fortaleza: Imprensa Universitária do Ceará, 1967, 256 p. Contains biographies of twenty-two composers and lyricists of modinhas, along with portraits of some of them, and the scores and lyrics of some of their most popular songs. An index of song titles is a useful feature.

1274 Andrade, Mário de. Danças dramáticas do Brasil. 2. ed. 3 vols. Obras completas de Mário de Andrade, 18-B. Belo Horizonte: Editora Itatiaia; Brasília: Instituto Nacional do Livro [e] Fundação Nacional Pró-Memória, 1982. This important work in the field of Brazilian ethnomusicology provides the musical scores, lyrics, characters and in many cases the choreography of the folk dances of Brazil (including regional variations), accompanied by copious notes about their cultural background. Volume 3 contains a bibliography with 337 entries. First published in 1959.

1275 ______. Dicionário musical brasileiro. Coleção Reconquista do Brasil, 2. série, v. 162. Belo Horizonte: Itatiaia; Brasília: Ministério da Cultura; São Paulo: Instituto de Estudos Brasileiros da Universidade de São Paulo, 1989. 701 p. This major contribution to Brazilian musicology, based on research by the eminent musicologist, folklorist, and literary figure, Mário de Andrade (1893-1945), but left unfinished at his death, was completed by a team of researchers and editors in 1989. It defines terms associated with all types of Brazilian music--popular, religious, classical, and folk music and dance. Many definitions include illustrations in the form of sketches or musical notations and they all cite printed sources which can be found in the extensive bibliography. The bibliography has not been updated; it includes only works available at the time that Andrade did the research for the dictionary. This work is an important source for those interested in music, anthropology, folklore, dance, and history.

1276 Appleby, David P. The Music of Brazil. Austin: University of Texas Press, 1983. 209 p. This survey of music from colonial days to the present is replete with information about composers, performing artists, forms of music, and instruments. Many musical examples illustrate themes and types of music. A glossary of musical terms peculiar to Brazil, a thorough bibliography, and an excellent index enhance the value of this work as a reference source.

1277 Baroncelli, Nilcéia Cleide da Silva. Mulheres compositoras. São Paulo: Roswitha Kempf, 1987. 331 p. Biographical data about women composers of popular and art music, international in scope. Includes many Brazilians.

1278 Bastos, Wilson de Lima. Instrumentos de música no registro do folclore brasileiro. Arquivos de folclore, trabalho 7.

Juiz de Fora: Centro de Estudos Sociológicos de Juiz de Fora, 1980. 27 p. Verbal descriptions of more than 200 instruments related to folk music. The type of information provided about each one is not consistent so that the informational value of the entries is erratic. The lack of illustrations is a serious fault in a work of this type, but it provides minimal information about many instruments in one place.

1279 Béhague, Gerard. Music in Latin America: An Introduction. Englewood Cliffs, NJ: Prentice-Hall, 1979. 369 p. Brazilian music is well covered in this survey of Latin American music. Each of its three major sections, "The Colonial Period," "The Rise of Nationalism," and "Counter Currents in the Twentieth Century" devotes sub-sections to Brazil. Includes many musical examples. Bibliographic notes conclude each section. A good index facilitates access.

1280 Brasil musical. Musical Brazil. Rio de Janeiro: Arte Bureau Representações e Edições de Arte, 1988. 304 p. A well-illustrated overview of Brazilian popular music arranged by type of music with text in Portuguese or English. Includes many brief biographical sketches and portraits of composers, performers, and others. A good name index facilitates its use.

1281 Camêu, Helza. Instrumentos musicais dos indígenas brasileiros: catálogo da exposição. Rio de Janeiro: Biblioteca Nacional, 1979. 69 p. An exhibition catalog of twenty-eight drawings of Brazilian Indian musical instruments, executed by José Coelho. The drawings are accompanied by excellent descriptive and bibliographic notes. A general bibliography concludes the work.

1282 _______. Introdução ao estudo da música indígena brasileira. Rio de Janeiro: Conselho Federal de Cultura, 1977. 295 p. Although not strictly in reference format, this book is easy to scan for the desired information. It is especially useful for its descriptions and photographs of musical instruments, its "Suplemento musical," which provides the scores of music discussed in the text, and an extensive bibliography.

1283 Cardoso, Sylvio Tullio. Dicionário biográfico de música popular. Rio de Janeiro: 1965. 351 p. An international "who's who" of popular music, although more than half of the text is devoted to Brazilian composers, artists and performing groups. It is especially useful for persons associated with bossa nova. Each entry includes brief biographical data, a list of the major compositions of composers, and a partial discography for performers. Although it was published in 1965, many of the artists and groups included are still popular in Brazil.

1284 Dicionário de música. Rio de Janeiro: Zahar, 1985. 424 p. This work, translated and adapted for Brazilian users from Dictionary of Music (London: 1982), includes many entries related to Brazilian music. Cover title: Dicionário de música Zahar.

1285 Diniz, Jaime C. Músicos pernambucanos do pasado. 3 vols. Recife: Universidade Federal de Pernambuco, 1969-1979. Biographical data on composers and performers of Pernambuco from colonial times through the nineteenth century.

1286 _______. Notas sobre o piano e seus compositores em Pernambuco: contribuição so I Ciclo de Música para Piano--Popular, de Salão e de Testro, Recife, 1980. Recife: Coro Guararapes do Recife, 1980. 54 p. Biographical and artistic data on nineteenth and twentieth century Pernambucan composers of piano music, arranged alphabetically by given name.

1287 _______. Organistas da Bahia: 1750-1850. Rio de Janeiro: Tempo Brasileiro; Salvador: Fundação Cultural do Estado da Bahia, 1986. 172 p. Detailed biographical data on thirty-three organists, organ builders, and composers of organ music in the churches of Bahia from the mid-eighteenth to mid-nineteenth centuries. Includes a useful bibliography and a list of archival collections consulted.

1288 Enciclopédia da música brasileira: erudita, folclórica, popular. 2 vols. São Paulo: Art Editora, 1977. Provides good coverage of classical, folk, and popular music with in-depth coverage of the more important individuals, organizations, and types of music. The appendix includes a discography of Brazilian classical music and a useful alphabetical list of the titles of all of the compositions mentioned in the text, with their composers and dates of composition.

1289 Freitag, Léa Vinocur. Momentos de música brasileira. São Paulo: Nobel, 1985. 175 p. A monograph studying sociological aspects of Brazilian music, including opera, with brief biographies of important composers in tabular format, and a chronology of significant compositions. Includes many portraits of figures in the Brazilian music world.

1290 Gomes, João Ferreira. Figuras e coisas da música popular brasileira. 2 vols. Rio de Janeiro: Fundação Nacional de Arte, 1978-1980. A collection of articles on popular music, written between 1940 and 1978 by Jota Efegê, pseudonym of João Ferreira Gomes, which appeared in various newspapers and magazines in Rio de Janeiro. The articles cover artists, musical forms and themes, Carnaval, and similar topics, appearing in chronological order. Access to specific topics is through the table of contents, and through the name index in each volume. Includes a limited number of illustrations, mainly portraits.

1291 Guia de corais brasileiros. São Paulo: Universidade de São Paulo, Escola de Comunicações e Artes, 1981- . A state-by-state directory of choral groups.

1292 Hinos e canções nacionais. 2. ed. Rio de Janeiro? Comando de Transporte Aéreo, Seção de Relações Públicas, 1967. 19 p. Lyrics only of several patriotic anthems and songs, including military songs not included in Marques' Hinos oficiais (below).

1293 Instrumentos musicais brasileiros. Coordenação, Ricardo Ohtake; texto, João Gabriel de Lima; fotos, Rômulo Fialdini. n.p.: Projeto Cultural Rhodia, 1988. 213 p. Outstanding color and black-and-white illustrations of Brazilian musical instruments used for folk, indigenous, and popular music are accompanied by explanatory text.

1294 Mariz, Vasco. A canção brasileira: erudita, folclórica, popular. 5. ed. Rio de Janeiro: Nova Fronteira; Brasília: Instituto Nacional do Livro, 1985. 380 p. Biographies of composers and artists of Brazilian songs, and many other facts are packed into the easily scanned chapters of this work. A selected list of the songs of major composers is appended.

1295 ______. Dicionário biográfico musical: compositores, intérpretes e musicólogos. 2. ed. Rio de Janeiro: Philobiblion, 1985. 286 p. This biobibliographical dictionary is international in scope, although it naturally includes many figures from the Brazilian music world. Entries, although usually brief, contain useful information. No portraits or other illustrations. Revision of Dicionário bio-bibliográfico musical (1949).

1296 ______. Figuras da música brasileira contemporânea. 2. ed. Brasília: Universidade de Brasília, 1970. 209 p. The lives and works of twenty-two contemporary Brazilian composers are the focus of this work. An appendix lists the complete works of several of them.

1297 ______. História da música no Brasil. Rio: Civilização Brasileira; Brasília: Instituto Nacional do Livro, 1981. 331 p. Narrative interspersed with biographical sketches and portraits of composers comprises this history of music in Brazil, covering the period from colonial days to the present. A bibliography concludes each chapter.

1298 Marques, Alvonira. Hinos oficiais e canções patrióticas do Brasil. Santa Cruz do Sul: Rigel Editora, 197-? 80 p. Words and music of the "Hino nacional brasileiro," the "Hino da Independência," the "Hino da Proclamação da República," and the "Hino a bandeira nacional," as well as biographical information about their authors and composers. Includes lyrics only of several other patriotic and folk songs. Concludes with the text of the law on national symbols of September 1, 1971.

1299 Mohana, João. A grande música do Maranhão. Rio de Janeiro: Agir, 1974. 135 p. Lists the compositions of 169 composers of Maranhão.

1300 Muniz, J. Sambistas imortais: dados biográficos de 50 figuras do mundo do samba. São Paulo: Cia. Brasileira de Impressão e Propaganda, 1976-. Vol. 1: 1850-1914. Biographical data and portraits of leading figures in the world of samba. According to the introduction the biographees include "verdadeiros bambas, compositores, ritmistas, puxadores de samba, intérpretes,e mesmo dirigentes." The sambistas are listed in chronological order by date of birth under the names or nicknames by which they are commonly known, and each one is the subject of a two- or three-page biography. A brief bibliography concludes the work. A second volume, covering 1915 to the mid-1970s was projected, but was not located.

1301 Osborne, Charles. Dicionário de opera. Tradução de Júlio Castañón Guimarães; verbetes brasileiros de Marcus Goés. Rio de Janeiro: Editora Guanabara, 1987. 465 p. This translation of the Dictionary of Opera (1983) has been adapted to the needs of those interested in Brazilian opera, with the addition of a number of entries covering Brazilian composers, performers, and opera houses.

1302 Passos, Claribalte. Vultos e temas da música brasileira. Rio de Janeiro: Paralelo, 1972. 335 p. "Levantamento cronológico e histórico do popular." Biographical data, portraits, discography, and criticism of Brazilian composers and performing artists, including such diverse figures as Vila Lobos, Carmen Miranda, and Dorival Caymmi.

1303 Ribeiro, Wagner. Folclore musical. 5 vols. São Paulo: Editora Coleção F.T.D. Ltda., 1965. In spite of the title emphasizing folk music, this work includes information about other types of Brazilian music: patriotic, choral, and children's songs, among them. Volume 3 contains a section devoted to biographies of Brazilian composers, Vol. 1: Elementos de teoria da música; vol. 2: História da música no antigo continente; vol. 3: História da música na América; vol. 4: Antologia de cantos orfeônicos e folclóricos, parte I; vol. 5: Antologia de cantos orfeônicos e folclóricos, parte II.

1304 Salles, Vicente. Música e músicos do Pará. Belém: Conselho Estadual de Cultura, 1970. 297 p. An introductory essay entitled "Quatro séculos de música no Pará," is followed by a biographical dictionary of almost 500 past and contemporary musicians of Pará: composers, performing artists, and teachers. Includes a few portraits.

1305 São Luís, Maranhão. Departamento de Cultura do Município. A festa dos sons. São Luís: 1972. 43 p. Biographical notes on musicians and composers of Maranhão.

1306 Saraiva, Gumercindo. Adágios, provérbios e termos musicais. Belo Horizonte: Editora Itatiaia, 1985. 126 p. Covers "adágios, axiomas, aforismos, apotegmas, brocardos, ditos, parêmias, provérbios, rifões, sentenças e termos," which are associated with music.

1307 ______. A canção popular brasileira em tres tempos. São Paulo: Indústria Gráfica Saraiva, 1968. 156 p. Provides the lyrics of many Brazilian popular songs, past and contemporary. The lack of an index makes locating specific songs more difficult than it should be.

1308 Schreiner, Claus. Música popular brasileira: Anthologisches Handbuch der popularen und folkloristischen Musik Brasiliens. Darmstadt: Verlag Tropical Music GMBH, 1978. 276 p. A survey of Brazilian popular and folk music with musical notations illustrating different types, portraits of individual musicians and performing groups, and illustrations of indigenous instruments.

1309 Silva, Osmar. Música popular capixaba, 1900-1980. Vitória: DEC - SEDU, 1986. 64 p. Information on popular music in the state of Espírito Santo: performers and performing groups, composers, escolas de samba, radio programs, and other aspects of the subject.

1310 Sinzig, Petrus. Dicionário musical. 2. ed. Rio de Janeiro: Kosmos: 1976. 612 p. An illustrated dictionary that includes terms related to Brazilian instruments, musical forms, dances, etc., in addition to general terms.

1311 Souza, Oswaldo de. Música folclórica do médio São Francisco. 2 vols. Rio de Janeiro: Conselho Federal de Cultura, 1979-1980. A collection of folk music from the São Francisco River Valley illustrating its melodic forms and rhythmic characteristics, based on research done in 1949. Volume 1, devoted to dramatic dances and religious music, includes the scores and lyrics of 137 folk songs. Volume 2 contains 201 folk songs from sambas to a-bê-cês. It also includes limited biographical data on some of the informants. The occasional notes about particular songs are usually superficial.

1312 Souza Lima, . Guia temático selecionado e classificado por ordem do dificuldade e alfabética de autores. n.p.: Irmãos Vitale, n.d. 356 p. A guide to musical themes, half of which is devoted to music by Brazilian composers. Title index.

1313 Tinhorão, José Ramos. Música popular: teatro e cinema. Petrópolis: Editora Vozes, 1972. 284 p. A history of musical theater and movies, containing much information in lists interspersed throughout the text. These include the shows of eight major composers of musical reviews, and a list of silent films "com aproveitamento de temas, denças e músicas populares."

1314 Vasconcelos, Ary. Carinhosos etc.: história e inventário do choro. n.p.: 1984. 271 p. An introduction to the history of the choro is followed by the major part of this work: "Repertório e discografia (A-D)," a list of choros by title (instrumental pieces only), and the recordings of them. This volume covers the letters A-D. Additional volumes are planned.

1315 _______. A nova música da Velha República. Rio de Janeiro: 1984. 276 p. Biographical data, discography, and bibliography related to composers and performers, 1889-1930, arranged in chronological order by birth dates of the individuals. An index of names provides easier access. According to the text (p. 44), a second volume is planned in order to complete this work.

1316 _______. Panorama da música popular brasileira na "Belle Epoque." Rio de Janeiro: Livraria Sant' Anna, 1977. 454 p. Covers popular music from 1870 to 1919, focusing on biographical data for composers and artists. Includes lists of their compositions, discographies, bibliography, and in some cases photographs of individuals and groups. An appendix lists the musical hits of Carnaval, 1900-1977.

1317 _______. Raízes da música popular brasileira, 1500-1889. São Paulo: Livraria Martins Editora, 1977. 362 p. Biographical information on composers and performers is arranged in broad chronological order with a name index to facilitate access. Entries include bibliography and a discography when applicable. Coverage is uneven--for example, lists of the compositions of some composers are included, as are the lyrics of some popular songs--but this is not done consistently.

NATURAL HISTORY

The publications cited in this section are representative of a large group of materials devoted to Brazilian natural history. They are intended to provide a few useful fact sources for the non-specialist seeking basic information on flora, fauna, geology, and minerals. No bibliographies of the extensive literature covering these subjects are included.

FAUNA

1318 Amaral, Afrânio de. Serpentes do Brasil: iconografia colorida. Brazilian Snakes: A Color Iconography. São Paulo: Edições Melhoramentos, 1977. 246 p. A well-illustrated guide with text in Portuguese and English. Information includes scientific and common names of each snake, its geographical distribution, and its habits.

1319 Atlas da fauna brasileira. São Paulo: MA/IBDF-MEC/FENAME, 1978. 128 p. An atlas of Brazilian fauna with many color illustrations, intended for a popular audience. Includes sections on legislation related to fauna and on national parks and biological reserves.

1320 Carvalho, Cory T. de. Dicionário dos mamíferos do Brasil. 2. ed. São Paulo: Livraria Nobel, 1979. 135 p. This dictionary of Brazilian mammals is uneven in the information that it supplies. Animals are sometimes identified by genus, and information about their habits, physical descriptions, and drawings of them are included on an unpredictable basis. This work is most useful for its historical and etymological data about the names of mammals: the first use of a name in written form and its development as a word in common usage is covered. Glossaries give Portuguese equivalents for English, French, German, and Spanish animal names.

1321 Frisch, Johan Dalgas. Aves brasileiras. São Paulo: Dalgas-Ecotec Ecologia Técnica e Comércio, 1981-. An identification guide to Brazilian birds, with each one represented in a color plate. Captions and indexes give the Latin name, and the popular names of birds in Portuguese, Spanish, and English. Volume examined: 1.

1322 Nomura, Hitoshi. Dicionário dos peixes do Brasil. Brasília: Editerra Editorial, 1984. 482 p. The main body of this work lists Brazilian fresh- and salt-water fish by their common names followed by their scientific names and families, and other information such as size and other physical characteristics, habitat, food, and in some cases line drawings or black-and-white photographs of poor quality. Another section lists them by scientific names with corresponding common names. Includes a bibliography.

1323 Ruschi, Augusto. Aves do Brasil. 2 vols. São Paulo: Editora Rios, 1979-1981. This useful work in Portuguese and English classifies Brazilian birds, and provides general information on them. The text is enhanced by many line drawings and color plates. An illustrated "Topography of the Bird" in Volume 1 identifies the anatomical parts of a bird in both languages. Includes a bibliography. The subtitle of Volume 2 is: "Chaves artificiais e analíticas."

1324 Santos, Eurico. Nossos peixes marinhos: vida e costumes dos peixes do Brasil. Coleção zoologia brasílica, vol. 1. Belo Horizonte: Editora Itatiaia, 1982. 265 p. Salt-water fish of Brazil are listed under their common names, with scientific name and family following. Additional notes on their habitats, physical characteristics, and habits, as well as line drawings and color plates provide further information. A glossary of commonly used ichthyological terms and a bibliography further enhance this work.

1325 ________. Peixes da água doce: vida e costumes dos peixes do Brasil. Coleção zoologia brasílica, vol. 2. Belo Horizonte: Editora Itatiaia, 1981. 267 p. Fresh-water fish of Brazil, including ornamental and exotic fish are listed under their common names, with scientific name, family, and descriptive notes following. Line drawings, color plates, and bibliography provide additional information.

1326 Sick, Helmut. Ornitologia brasileira. 2 vols. Brasília: Editora Universidade de Brasília, 1985. In addition to descriptions and illustrations of all species of birds found in Brazil, this work includes background information on such topics as the history of ornithology there, maps, and an extensive bibliography.

FLORA

1327 Arvores no Brasil. São Paulo: Duratex, 1989. 119 p. Information in Portuguese and English on forty-three Brazilian trees, accompanied by excellent color photographs of each one and close-ups of significant features of many (blossoms, bark, trunk, etc.). Includes a glossary and a vegetation map of Brazil.

1328 Cruz, G. L. Dicionário das plantas úteis do Brasil. Rio de Janeiro: Civilização Brasileira, 1979. 599 p. This work is limited to coverage of the medicinal uses of plants, although the introduction describes it as covering their industrial uses as well. Arranged in alphabetical order by popular name of plant, each entry includes its scientific name, the area in which it grows, its uses, and variant names. Unfortunately, the main alphabet includes no cross-references from the variant names to the name under which information is given. An index of physical ailments, with plants used to treat them, concludes the work.

1329 Eiten, George. Classificação da vegetação do Brasil. Brasília: Conselho Nacional de Desenvolvimento Científico e Tecnológico, 1983. 305 p. Photographs of the variety of vegetation types found in Brazil are accompanied by brief notes identifying them. This work is useful for the non-specialist, enabling the visualization of types of vegetation frequently referred to in speech and writings, such as "caatinga," or "restinga." The quality of the photographs is only fair.

1330 Gomes, Raymundo Pimental. Fruticultura brasileira. 2. ed. São Paulo: Livraria Nobel, 1975. 446 p. Information on the botany and cultivation of Brazilian fruits and identification of some which are not presently under large-scale cultivation. Arranged in alphabetical order by common name of the fruit, most entries include data on varieties, climate and soils suitable for cultivation, planting, fertilization, harvesting, pests, diseases, and related matters. Although there are some illustrations, their quality is poor; the lack of a picture of each fruit treated is a major flaw of this work. Nevertheless, its approach is such that the non-specialist needing information on the subject would find it helpful.

1331 Joly, Aylthon Brandão, and Hermógenes de Freitas Leitão. Botânica econômica: as principais culturas brasileiras. São Paulo: Editora da Universidade de São Paulo; Editora de Humanismo, Ciência e Tecnologia--HUCITEC, 1979. 114 p. This reference work, intended to provide the general public with information about Brazilian plants of economic significance includes plants in such categories as cereals, fibers, fruits, woods, oil and fat-yielding plants, roots, spice-producing plants, and others. A brief botanical description of each plant, and information on its economic uses comprise each entry. Photographs of mediocre quality illustrate the text. The index of common and scientific plant names provides easy access to the groupings of plants under the categories described above.

1332 Rizzini, Carlos Toledo. Arvores e madeiras úteis do Brasil: manual de dendrologia brasileira. São Paulo: Editora Edgard Blücher, 1971. 294 p. An illustrated guide to 278 Brazilian trees of economic value. Information for each tree includes its common names, its distinctive characteristics, its uses, the geographic area in which it grows, and related species. A glossary of technical terms related to trees facilitates the use of this work. Arranged in alphabetical order by scientific name, with a common name index. Includes a bibliography.

MINERALS

1333 Franco, Rui Ribeiro, et al. Minerais do Brasil. Minerals of Brazil. 3 vols. São Paulo: E. Blücher, 1972. A guide to Brazilian minerals with excellent color photographs illustrating each one. Text in Portuguese and English.

1334 Principais depósitos minerais do Brasil. Brasília: Departamento Nacional da Produção Mineral em convênio com a Companhia Vale do Rio Doce, 1985-. Detailed information on Brazilian mineral deposits with abstracts in English, illustrated with line drawings and photographs. Includes bibliographies. Volumes examined were 1, Recursos minerais energéticos; 2, Ferro e metais da indústria do aço, and 3, Metais básicos não-ferrosos, ouro e alumínio; while volume 4, Rochas e minerais industriais, was referred to in volume 1, but not located.

1335 Silva, Jair Carvalho da, and César Mendonça Ferreira. Gemas do Brasil. Gems of Brazil. São Bernardo do Campo: Mercedes-Benz do Brasil, 1987. 130 p. Excellent color photographs of Brazil's precious and semi-precious gemstones are accompanied by descriptive parallel text in Portuguese and English.

GEOLOGY

1336 Lima, Murilo Rodolfo de. Fósseis do Brasil. São Paulo: T. A. Queiroz; Editora da Universidade de São Paulo, 1989. 118 p. Text and excellent color photographs describe and illustrate Brazilian fossils in chapters arranged chronologically by geologic period.

1337 Mendes, Josué Camargo, and Setembrino Petri. Geologia do Brasil. Enciclopédia brasileira. Biblioteca universitária. Geociências. Geologia, 9. Rio de Janeiro: Instituto Nacional do Livro, 1971. 207 p. An overview of the geology of Brazil for a lay audience, with many photographs, maps, bibliographies at the end of each chapter, and an index.

1338 Oliveira, Avelino Ignácio de, and Othon Henry Leonardos. Geologia do Brasil. 3. ed. Coleção Mossoroense, vol. 72. Mossoró: 1978. 813 p. This reprint, first published in 1940 by the Imprensa Nacional, Rio de Janeiro, discusses each geologic eon in general terms and then takes a state-by-state approach to it. It is illustrated with maps, diagrams, and photographs. Bibliographic citations are in footnote form. Indexed.

1339 Petri, Setembrino, and Vicente José Fúlfaro. Geologia do Brasil: fanerozóico. Biblioteca de ciências naturais, vol. 9. São Paulo: Editora Universidade de São Paulo, 1983. 631 p. A geology of the Paleozoic, Mesozoic, and Cenozoic eons well illustrated with maps, diagrams, photographs, and comparative charts. Includes an extensive bibliography.

OTHER SOURCES

1340 Glossário de ecologia. 1. ed. (definitiva). Publicações ACIESP, no. 57. São Paulo: Academia de Ciências do Estado de São Paulo; Conselho Nacional de Desenvolvimento Científico e Tecnológico; Fundação de Amparo à Pesquisa do Estado de São Paulo; Secretaria da Ciência e Tecnologia, 1987. 271 p. A dictionary defining more than 4500 terms associated with all aspects of ecology. Appendices provide additional information about soils, ocean currents, climate, legislation, and many other subjects through maps, tables, diagrams, and text. Includes bibliography.

NUMISMATICS AND PHILATELY

STAMPS

1341 Catálogo de selos: Brasil. São Paulo: Editora RHM. This illustrated catalog gives descriptive detail for each stamp and the current value of each one. The edition examined, 47th, 1989, is divided into two volumes: I: 1843-1967; this volume, published later than Volume II, has the date of publication, 1989/90; II: 1967-1988.

COINS, PAPER MONEY, AND MEDALS

1342 Amaral, José Vinícius Vieira do. Moedas do Brasil. São Paulo. J.V.V. do Amaral, 1989-. Provides descriptions and photographs of Brazilian coins, arranged in chronological order, as well as their current average prices. Volume 2, which was the only one available for examination, is entitled Prata, níquel: Colôna, Reino Unido, Imperio, Republica.

1343 Brazil. Marinha. Serviço de Documentação Geral. Medalhas e condecorações. Rio de Janeiro: 1983. 67 p. History, description, and excellent color and black-and-white photographs of Brazilian naval decorations and medals from 1822 to the present. Includes a brief bibliography.

1344 Brazil. Ministério do Exército. Medalhística militar brasileira. Rio de Janeiro: 1968. unpaged. Provides descriptions, significance, citations to enabling legislation, and color illustrations of Brazilian military medals and decorations.

1345 Catálogo Vieira: moedas brasileiras. 1. ed. Rio de Janeiro: Numismática Vieira, 1989. 253 p. This catalog, which covers the period 1662-1988, identifies and illustrates each coin and gives the current value of pieces in good condition.

1346 O ciclo do ouro: Brasil, século XVIII. The Gold Cycle: Brazil, XVIII Century. Die Goldperiode: Brasilien, XVIII Jahrhundert. Rio de Janeiro: Banco Central do Brasil, Divisão de Museu de Valores, 1980. 78 p. Excellent color photographs of gold coins minted in Brazil between 1683 and 1805, with information on location where minted, their values, and sizes.

1347 Costa, Ney Chrysostomo da. História das moedas do Brasil. Porto Alegre: Instituto Estadual do Livro, 1973. 561 p. A history of Brazilian coins with much of the data presented in a reference format--tables and alphabetical lists--rather than narrative. Sections on metals, markings, values, mints, and many other topics, make this illustrated history a useful and interesting work.

1348 Ferreira, Lupércio Gonçalves. Catálogo descritivo das moedas de 640 reis: 1695 a 1833. Recife: Indústrias Gráficas Barreto, 1986. 381 p. Provides detailed descriptions and illustrations of these colonial period coins, in chronological order.

1349 Iconografia de valores impressos do Brasil. Brasília: Banco Central do Brasil, 1979. 313 p. A handsome work featuring excellent color plates which illustrate the development of printed monetary instruments in Brazil from the eighteenth century to the present. Introductory chapters providing background information on the beginnings of paper monetary instruments and on the national financial system, are followed by others on paper money, actions and debentures, stock certificates, instruments used by savings and credit institutions, fiscal stamps, and the like. In addition to providing visual documentation of Brazil's economic and financial development, this work reflects the evolution of its culture and its artistic tastes.

1350 Lissa, Violo Idolo. Catálogo do papel-moeda do Brasil, 1771-1980: emissões oficiais, bancárias e regionais. 2. ed. Brasília: Editora Gráfica Brasiliana, 1981. 300 p. A work which aims to catalog all issues of paper money in Brazil originating from the national and regional governments, and banks, in the form of notes, bonds, and certificates. Information provided includes the period of circulation, issuing agency, value, physical description, and an illustration of each example of currency.

1351 Museu Imperial, Petrópolis. Catálogo das medalhas comemorativas referentes ao Brasil, da colônia à regência. Série Cadernos museológicos, 1. Petrópolis, 1973. 62 p. A descriptive and illustrated catalog of Brazilian and foreign medals in the collection of the Imperial Museum commemorating persons, organizations, and events during the colonial period and the Empire. In addition to photographs of the medals accompanied by detailed physical descriptions, there are separate sections of notes on the events and organizations and brief biographies of persons honored.

1352 Musso Ambrosi, Luís Alberto. Uruguay-Brasil y sus medallas. Montevideo: Instituto de Cultura Uruguaya-Brasileiro, 1976. 195 p. Describes and illustrates "las medallas conmemorativas de acontecimientos históricos en que actuaron, como protagonistas, uruguayos y brasileños." Includes military medals. Bibliography.

1353 Prober, Kurt. Catálogo das medalhas da República. Rio de Janeiro: 1965. 209 p. A catalog in tabular format of medals struck in Brazil from November 15, 1889 to 1965, arranged in chronological order. Each medal is fully described, but illustrations are totally lacking.

1354 _______. Catálogo das medalhas maçônicas brasileiras. 2. ed. ampliada. Paquetá: K. Prober, 1988/925. 200 p. in various pagings. Photographs and line drawings of the medals of Brazilian Masonic lodges, along with the history of each lodge.

1355 _______. Catálogo das moedas brasileiras. 3. ed. Rio de Janeiro: Livraria Kosmos Editora, 1981. 233 p. A catalog of Brazilian coins with illustrations of fair quality and much detailed information. Includes a numismatic glossary.

1356 _______. Obsidionais, as primeiras moedas do Brasil: falsificadas, autênticas. Monografias numismáticas, 13. Paquetá: K. Prober, 1987. 92 p. Identifies, describes, and illustrates the emergency florins and struivers struck by the beseiged Dutch government in Recife in 1645, 1646, and 1654. Prepared in response to a spate of counterfeit coins on the numismatic market. Preface in Portuguese and English.

1357 Russo, Arnaldo. Livro das moedas do Brasil. 2. ed. São Paulo: A. Russo, 1981. 394 p. A catalog of Brazilian coins intended for numismatists, with fairly good illustrations of each coin included. First edition published in 1978 under the title, Catálogo de moedas do Brasil.

1358 Silveira, Enzo. Breviário heráldico, medalhístico e nobiliário. Edição comemorativa do sesquicentenário da Independência do Brasil, 1822-1972. São Paulo: Edições Ensil, 1972. 332 p. Outlines the basic principles and protocol of heraldry, medals, and the nobility, defines terms, and provides many illustrations, drawing on Brazilian examples. Includes bibliography.

1359 Souza, Dimas S. Catálogo de cédulas brasileiras: cruzeiro-cruzado novo, 1942-1989. 2. ed. São Paulo? 1989. 100 p. An illustrated catalog of paper currency with technical descriptions of each bill.

PHILOSOPHY

BIBLIOGRAPHIES

1360 Centro de Documentação do Pensamento Brasileiro. Catálogo de obras filosóficas. Salvador: 1983. 156 p. Lists 1200 titles related to philosophy in the collection of the Center, arranged by subject, with an author index.

1361 Paim, Antônio. Bibliografia filosófica brasileira, 1808/1930. Salvador: 1983. 96 p. A partially annotated bibliography of books on philosophy published in Brazil, 1808-1930, arranged by subject, with no author index. Includes useful appendices on early professors of philosophy and the teaching of philosophy in specific faculdades.

1362 ______. Bibliografia filosófica brasileira: período contemporâneo, 1931-1977. São Paulo: GRD, 1979. 248 p. This unannotated bibliography covers books only--no journal articles are cited--and its chronological arrangement calls attention to the increase in publishing in the field of philosophy in Brazil over the time period covered, from an average of thirty titles per year in the 1930's to eighty per year in the period 1967-1976. A preliminary version of this work, "Bibliografia filosófica brasileira, período contemporaneo (1931/1971)," appeared in Verbum 29 (1972): 1-218.

1363 ______. Bibliografia filosófica brasileira: periodo contemporâneo, 1931/1980. Salvador: 1987. 123 p. An updated version of Bibliografia filosófica brasileira: período contemporâneo, 1931-1977 (no. 1362) arranged by subject rather than chronologically. Like its predecessor, it includes books and theses, but no journal articles. Cites many theses not listed in the earlier version. Periodic updates are planned.

1364 ______. Bibliografia filosófica brasileira: período contemporâneo, 1981/1985. Salvador: Centro de Documentação do Pensamento Brasileiro, 1988. 31 p. An update continuing numbers 1361, 1362, and 1363. Arranged by subject.

DICTIONARIES

1365 Castanha, César Arruda. Dicionário universal das idéias. São Paulo: Ed. Meca, n.d. 530 p. Discusses ideas and philosophical concepts, putting them into a Brazilian context when appropriate--"espiritismo," for example. Also includes concepts specific to Brazil, such as "getulismo."

1366 Pugliesi, Márcio, and Edson Bini. Pequeno dicionário filosófico. São Paulo: Hemus, 1977. 414 p. Defines the basic terms associated with philosophy.

OTHER SOURCES

1367 As idéias filosóficas no Brasil. Coordenador: Adolpho Crippa. 3 vols. São Paulo: Editora Convívio, 1978. The ideas of more than 1200 philosophers, thinkers, scholars, and writers covered in this survey of Brazilian thought from the eighteenth through the twentieth centuries are accessed through a name index in Volume 3. Vol. 1: Séculos XVIII e XIX; Vol. 2: Século XX, parte 1; Vol. 3: Século XX parte 2.

1368 Machado, Geraldo Pinheiro. A filosofia no Brasil. 3. ed. São Paulo: Cortez e Moraes, 1976. 121 p. A summary of Brazilian philosophical thought from the sixteenth century to the middle of the twentieth century, containing biobibliographical data about many individuals and information about philosophical schools. Includes a chronology of Brazilian positivism. Although it is not in a reference format, a detailed name index provides easy access to the text. Includes bibliography.

POLITICS AND GOVERNMENT

BIBLIOGRAPHY

Only general bibliographies related to politics and government are cited in this section. Those about the politics and governments of specific states are listed under the appropriate state.

1369 Bibliografia de publicações oficiais brasileiras, área federal: livros e folhetos, 1975/1977-. Brasília: Câmara dos Deputados, Centro de Documentação e Informação, 1981-. Cites publications of federal government agencies, arranged by agency, with indexes by author, title, series, and subject. Some entries include annotations and acquisitions information. Volume 1, 1975/1977, entitled Bibliografia de publicações oficiais brasileiras with no subtitle, included serials, but they are excluded from subsequent volumes. Volumes examined: 1, 1975/1977; 2, 1978/1980; 3, 1981/1982; 4, 1983/1984; 5, 1985/1986.

1370 "Brazil," in Latin American Politics: A Historical Bibliography. Santa Barbara, CA: ABC-Clio, 1984, pp. 155-176. Abstracts of journal articles about modern Brazilian politics (beginning in 1914) which appeared in a variety of Brazilian and foreign journals between 1973 and 1982. About 300 citations are divided into the following groupings: "General," "Interwar Years, 1914-1945," "The Democratic Governments, 1945-1964," and "The Military Regime Since 1964."

1371 Brazil. Congresso. Senado. Subsecretaria de Biblioteca. Eleições e partidos políticos: bibliografia. Brasília: 1980. 92 p. The 804 unannotated citations identify Brazilian and foreign publications about political parties and elections, with emphasis on Brazil.

1372 ______. ______. ______. ______. Tributação: reforma

tributária. Bibliografia, 3. Brasília: 1983. 84 leaves. An unannotated bibliography of 802 entries about tax reform. Although it is international in scope, citations of Brazilian publications predominate.

1373 _______. _______. _______. _______. Parlamentarismo: presidencialismo, funções dos pariamentos. Bibliografia, 4. Brasília: 1983. 36 leaves. An unannotated bibliography of 218 books, chapters of books, and periodical articles on legislative branches of governments and their relationship to the executives. Emphasizes Brazilian publications, although others are included.

1374 Brazil. Congresso. Senado. Subsecretaria de Edições Técnicas. Catálogo de publicações. Brasília: 1974. 167 p. This publication provides a complete listing of issues of the Revista de informação legislativa, 1964-1973, and other publications of the Subsecretariat of Technical Publications for approximately the same period. However, 143 of its 167 pages are devoted to subject and author indexes of the above-mentioned Revista, and lists of the contents of each issue.

1375 Brazil. Departamento de Imprensa Nacional. Relação das obras. Rio de Janeiro: 1966. 46 p. A list of the publications of the Imprensa Nacional, most of which are directly related to government or to the political process.

1376 Brazil. Ministério da Fazenda. Divisão de Documentação. Indicador das publicações do Ministério da Fazenda, 1968-1974. Guias de biblioteconomia, documentação, informática e editoração, 1. Rio de Janeiro: 1975. 143 p. An unannotated bibliography of the publications of this government agency, focusing on public finance from contemporary and historical points of view.

1377 Brazil. Ministério do Interior. Secretaria de Planejamento. Coordenaria de Documentação. Bibliografia publicações oficiais do MINTER. Brasília: 1987. various pagings. Lists the past and present publications of the Ministry with bibliographical data, but no annotations. Author, title, and subject indexes. Cover title: MINTER: 20 anos.

1378 Centro de Estudos e Pesquisas de Administração Municipal. Bibliografia sobre administração municipal e poder local. São Paulo: Fundação Prefeito Faria Lima; Centro de Estudos e Pesquisas de Administração Municipal--CEPAM, 1986. 339 p. An annotated bibliography of 1000 entries covering a broad range of topics related to municipal administration: personnel administration, culture and recreation, rural development, metropolitan, urban, and regional planning, sanitation, education, and others. The majority of publications cited are Brazilian.

1379 Chilcote, Ronald H. Brazil and Its Radical Left: An Annotated Bibliography on the Communist Movement and the Rise of Marxism, 1922-1972. Milwood, NY: Kraus International Publications, 1980. 455 p. The author describes this list of books, pamphlets, articles, and periodicals as "a comprehensive compilation of materials relating to the Communist, Socialist, and Anarchist movements in Brazil over a period of half a century." An introductory essay traces the development of the radical left in Brazil.

1380-81 Fundação do Desenvolvimento Administrativo. Administração pública, Brasil e América Latina: levantamento bibliográfico preliminar. Documento do trabalho, 8. São Paulo: 1986. 163 p. An unannotated bibliography of 670 entries, citing books, theses, journal articles, and other publications. The majority of entries refer to public administration in Brazil.

1382 _______. Administração tributária: levantamento bibliográfico preliminar. Documento do trabalho, no. 12. São Paulo: 1987. 97 p. A bibliography of 1112 entries, international in scope, but emphasizing Brazil. Includes monographs, periodical articles, reports, and other publications. Many entries include summaries of content. Title and subject indexes.

1383 _______. Política e atenção a saúde: bibliografia seletiva. Documento do trabalho, no. 10. São Paulo: 1986. 299 p. An unannotated bibliography with 1494 entries citing monographs, articles, conference proceedings, reports, and other publications related to health and public policy.

1384 Heimar, Franz-Wilhelm. Neure Studien zur Politik Brasiliens, 1960-1967. Freiburg: Arnold Bergstraesser Instituts für kulturwissen-schaftliche Forschung, 1968. 91 p. An unannotated bibliography citing studies of and statements on Brazilian politics written between 1960 and 1967, including books, chapters of books, journal articles, and papers. Covers both internal politics and foreign relations from the viewpoints of Brazilian and foreign writers.

1385 Lins, Maria Inês de Bessa. Diários oficias de estados brasileiros. Brasília: Câmara dos Deputados, 1975. 38 p. Information on the official gazettes of each state: address, content, format, number of pages, indexing, distribution, extant collections, and their physical conditions.

1386 Lombardi, Mary. Brazilian Serial Documents: A Selective and Annotated Guide. Bloomington: Indiana University Press, 1974. 445 p. A guide to the serial publications of Brazilian government agencies through 1971. Information includes place and dates of publication, frequency, and sometimes a history of the publication or a note about its contents. This guide is also useful for information about each agency covered, providing a brief history, with name changes, and citations for the decrees pertaining to these changes.

1387 Mendes, Evelyse Maria Freire. Bibliografia do pensamento político republicano: 1870-1980. 2. ed. revista e aumentada. Biblioteca do pensamento político republicano, vol. 19. Brasília: Câmara dos Deputados, Centro de Documentação e Informação, 1983. 205 p. The 1500 titles trace the history of more than a century of Brazilian political thought, divided into four chronological sections: "Propaganda republicana (1870-1890)"; "República Velha (1891-1930)"; "Revolução de 30 e Estado Novo (1931-1945)"; "Pós-guerra (1946-1970)." A fifth section summarizes selected works of great significance for the historical periods--often written by major figures, such as Epitácio Pessôa, Getúlio Vargas, and Roberto Simonsen. First edition, entitled Bibliografia do pensamento político republicano: 1870-1970, published 1981.

1388 Mesa, Rosa Quintero. Brazil. Latin American Serial Documents, vol. 2. Ann Arbor, MI: University Microfilms, 1968. 343 p. A bibliography of official Brazilian serial publications located in United States and Canadian libraries. Includes the executive, judicial, and legislative branches as well as universities, museums, libraries, and semi-autonomous entities organized or financed by the national government. Provides the following information when known: sponsoring agency and title, beginning date, frequency, title changes, and North American libraries with major holdings.

DICTIONARIES

1389 Furtado, Jorge Monteiro. Dicionário de assuntos fiscais tributários. Rio de Janeiro: Lia, 1969. 240 p. Defines terms as they relate to taxation and fiscal matters.

1390 Kielhorn, Ana Elizabeth. Dicionário de termos políticos. São Paulo: Agência Editora Iris, 1965. 200 p. Defines terms, abbreviations and acronyms related to politics which appeared in the press, in books, and in contemporary speeches, including many terms associated with politics in other countries, as well as those in use in Brazil shortly after the Revolution of 1964. This dictionary and the Manual de política contemporânea by Trotta (below) are complementary in coverage.

1391 Melo, Osvaldo Ferreira de. Dicionário de direito político. Rio de Janeiro: Forense, 1978. 135 p. A dictionary defining about 1000 terms associated with political science and political theory.

1392 Pimenta, E. Orsi. Dicionário brasileiro de política. Belo Horizonte: Editora Lê, 1982. 192 p. Defines political terms from "abertura" to "xenofobia," often in considerable detail. The terms selected for inclusion are both specific to Brazil and general. In addition to the etymology, definition, and history of the word, examples of its usage in newspapers or other publications are often given. An appendix provides the texts of various international declarations.

1393 Rodrigues, Edgar. Socialismo: uma visão alfabética. Rio de Janeiro: Editora Porta-Aberta, 1979. 298 p. A dictionary of persons and terms associated with socialism, universal in scope. Provides information on some Brazilian socialists.

1394 São Paulo (State). Fundação Prefeito Faria Lima. Centro de Estudos e Pesquisas de Administração Municipal. Dicionário orçamentário. São Paulo: 1983. 174 p. A dictionary defining terms used in public finance, especially budgets, intended to clarify the meaning of laws related to the subject.

1395 Soares, Oswaldo. Pequeno dicionário burguês-proletário. Rio de Janeiro: Civilização Brasileira, 1983. 371 p. Defines economic, political, social, and philosophical concepts related to the bourgeoisie and the proletariat.

1396 Trotta, Frederico. Manual de política contemporânea. Rio de Janeiro: Editora Leitura, 1967. 324 p. Defines terms associated with the theory and practice of politics, including many related to Brazilian political life.

OTHER SOURCES

1397 Anuário econômico fiscal. Brasília: Coordenação do Sistema de Informações Economico-Fiscais, 1970-. Detailed revenue statistics providing data on amounts collected, industries paying taxes, occupations of individual taxpayers (amount collected and number of taxpayers), and taxes collected by region of the country and by state. Edition examined: 1982.

1398 Anuário parlamentar brasileiro. vol. 1-, 1987-. Brasília: Semprel; São Paulo: Editora Três. Lists senators and representatives by state and political party and provides considerable biographical data about each one. The introductory information includes a few portraits and illustrations. Volumes examined: 1, 1987; 2, 1988.

1399 Autoridades brasileiras. Brasília: Empresa Brasileira de Notícias. An annual directory of public officials at the national and state levels. Issues examined: 1976, 1977, 1980, 1986.

1400 Bastos, Paulo César. Superior Tribunal Militar: 173 anos de história. Brasília: Senado Federal, Centro Gráfico, 1981. 115 p. A collection of documents and facts related to Brazil's highest court of military justice. Includes biographical data, and sometimes portraits, of officials of the Conselho Supremo Militar de Justiça, the Supremo Tribunal Militar, and the Superior Tribunal Militar, the texts of key documents and laws, and a bibliography.

1401 Brazil. Arquivo Nacional. Exercício da presidência da República, 1889-1975. Rio de Janeiro: 1975. 24 p. A chronological list of all presidents and acting presidents of Brazil through 1975. Includes portraits and brief biographical data for each individual.

1402 ———. ———. Relação dos Ministros da Justiça, 1822-1974. Rio de Janeiro: 1974. unpaged. A chronological list of Brazil's ministers of justice, which includes the dates of their terms of office.

1403 Brazil. Assembléia Nacional Constituinte (48th: 1987-1991). Endereços dos constituintes, 1987/1991: 48a. legislatura. Série Fontes de referência, no. 3. Brasília: Câmara dos Deputados, Centro de Documentação e Informação, 1987. 190 p. Lists the complete name of each member of the constitutional convention ordered alphabetically by "nome parlamentar" (the name by which he is commonly known--usually a given name or nickname), address(es), birthday (excludes year of birth), name and birthday of spouse, and state represented.

1404 Brazil. Congresso. Câmara dos Deputados. Deputados brasileiros, 1826-1976. Brasília: Senado Federal, Centro Gráfico, 1976. 240 p. A directory of deputies over a period of 150 years. Information given includes party affiliation, dates served in Congress, and the state/province represented. Arranged alphabetically by given name.

1405 ———. ———. ———. Deputados brasileiros. Brasília: 1967-1971--. An ongoing biographical directory of deputies beginning with the legislature for 1967-1971. Each entry includes a portrait and information such as political party, state represented, profession, date and place of birth, family, education, governmental posts, and publications. Arranged in alphabetical order by given name, with an index by last name. At the time of this writing there were directories covering the legislatures of 1967/1971, 1971/1975, 1975/1979, 1979/1983, and 1983/1987. A supplement to the 1971/1975 edition had also been issued.

1406 _______. _______. _______. Presidentes da Câmara dos Deputados durante o Império, 1826 a 1889: relação, com ligeiros dados biográficos dos senhores presidentes da Câmara dos Deputados durante o Império, por Carlos Tavares de Lyra. Brasília: 1978. 133 p. Provides brief biographical data about both well-known and obscure political figures, some of whom played roles at both the national and provincial levels. Includes many portraits.

1407 _______. _______. _______. Súmula de discursos. Brasília: 1951-. Brief summaries of the speeches of members of the Câmara dos Deputados, arranged by name of member, with a detailed subject index to provide additional access. Frequency of publication varies. Issues examined: vol. 24, no. 3, Aug.-Sept. 1974; vol. 24, no. 4, Oct.-Dec. 1974.

1408 Brazil. Congresso. Senado. Catálogo biográfico dos senadores brasileiros, 1826 a 1986. 4 vols. Brasília: Projeto de Biografias dos Senadores do Império e da República, 1986. Biographical sketches and portraits of senators for a period of 160 years, in alphabetical order by first name.

1409 _______. _______. _______. _______. Adendo: nomes parlamentares, títulos, nobiliárquicos, caricaturas. Brasília: 1987. 70 p. Lists names used by senators, their titles of nobility, and reproduces cartoons related to the Senate and to senators.

1410 _______. _______. _______. Dados biográficos dos ex-presidentes do Senado (1826-1979): versão preliminar. Brasília: Projeto de Biografias dos Senadores do Império e da República, 1981. 80 p. Brief biographical data and more detailed information about the political and governmental activities of the presidents of the Senate over a period of 150 years. No portraits. Includes bibliographical references.

1411 _______. _______. _______. Dados biográficos dos senadores, período 1946 a 1970: documento preliminar. Brasília: Projeto de Biografias dos Senadores do Império e da República, 1981. 271 p. Biographical data for senators who served during the time period cited in the title. Senators are listed in alphabetical order by their given names. No portraits. Includes a bibliography.

1412 _______. _______. _______. Senadores: dados biográficos, nona legislatura, 1979-1983. Brasília: Senado Federal, Subsecretaria de Arquivo, 1979? 305 p. Biographical and professional data and portraits of each member of the Senate, 1979-1983.

1413 _______. _______. _______. Senadores: dados biográficos, quadragésima sétima legislatura, 1983-1987. Brasília: Senado Federal, Subsecretaria do Arquivo, 1983. 324 p. Biographical and professional data and portraits for each senator, 1983-1987.

1414 _______. _______. _______. Senadores: dados biográficos, quadrigésima oitava legislatura, 1987-1991. Brasília: 1987. 312 p. Biographical and professional information and portraits of each member of the Senate, for the period covered.

1415 _______. _______. _______. Súmulas de discursos. Brasília: vol. 1-, Jan.-June 1975-. Summarizes the speeches of senators. Arranged by name with a subject index to facilitate access. Issue examined: vol. 1, Jan.-June 1975-.

1416 Brazil. Congresso. Senado. Subsecretaria do Arquivo. Assembléias constituintes brasileiras. Brasília: 1987. 90 p. Lists the names of representatives to the constituent assemblies of 1891, 1934, and 1946 along with their political party affiliations.

1417 Brazil. Constitution. Constituição: República Federativa do Brasil, 1988. Brasília: Centro Gráfico do Senado Federal, 1988. 292 p. Text of the current constitution of Brazil. For texts of earlier constitutions see numbers 1434 and 1435.

1418 Brazil. Direção Geral da Fazenda Nacional. 1890-1967: A receita orçamentária do Brasil. Rio de Janeiro: Ministério da Fazenda, 1968. unpaged. Statistical data related to public finance. One series shows the receipts of the Treasury Department for a period exceeding seventy-five years. Other tables record the receipts of the states for a shorter period (1925-1967).

1419 Brazil. Ministério da Fazenda. Ministros da Fazenda, 1822-1972. Rio de Janeiro: 1972. 223 p. Biographical information about each Minister of Fazenda in chronological order, with separate sections for the Empire and the administration of each president. No portraits.

1420 Brazil. Ministério da Fazenda. Setor de Documentação. O

<u>erário e seus homens públicos, 1808-1974</u>. Rio de Janeiro, 197-? 112 p. A chronological list of the Ministros da Fazenda, or heads of the Treasury from the arrival of the Portuguese royal family through the Geisel administration. Includes brief biographical data for each one and major accomplishments or events at the Ministry during each term.

1421 ______. ______. Delegacia do Ministério da Fazenda--RJ. <u>Diretrizes do governo</u>. Rio de Janeiro? 1981. 83 p. Detailed information about the objectives, organization, and legislation concerning the Ministério da Fazenda, including several organization charts depicting the units that comprise it.

1422 Brazil. Ministério do Exército. Diretoria Patrimonial do Brasil. Catálogo telefônico das organizações militares do Exército no Distrito Federal. Brasília: 1989. 99 p. A telephone directory for components of the Army and their subdivisions located in Brasília, providing a useful overview of the organization in addition to telephone numbers.

1423 Brazil. Presidência. Secretaria de Imprensa e Divulgação. <u>Recebendo e visitando estadistas</u>, 1979-. Brasília: 1983-. An annual compilation of the texts of major speeches of the president of Brazil during official trips abroad, and of foreign heads of state visiting Brazil. Also includes texts of joint communiqués and declarations. Issues examined: vol. 1-5, 1979-1983.

1424 Brazil. Presidencia. Serviço de Documentação do Gabinete Civil. <u>Governos da Républica</u>. Brasília: 1984. 430 p. A chronological listing of presidents, governors of states and territories, presidents of the houses of Congress, the Tribunal das Contas da União, and the major judicial bodies from the beginning of the Republic (1889) to the early 1980's. Includes brief biographical data and portraits of the presidents of Brazil, as well as a bibliography.

1425 Brazil. Presidente. <u>Mensagens presidenciais</u>. Brasília: Câmara dos Deputados, Centro de Documentação e Informação, Coordenação de Publicações, 1978-. Reprints of presidential messages sent to Congress at the beginning of each legislative session, thereby making an important series of government documents readily available. Volumes 1-5 are reprints of earlier compilations. Vol. 1: <u>1890-1910</u>; Vol. 2: <u>1910-1914</u>; Vol. 3: <u>1915-1918</u>; Vol. 4: <u>1919-1922</u>; Vol. 5: <u>1923-1926</u>; Vol. 6: <u>1927-1930</u>; Vol. 7: <u>1933-1937</u>.

1426 Brazil. Secretaria de Economia e Finanças. <u>Receita e despesa: União, estados e municípios, exercícios de 1965/1975</u>. Finanças do Brasil, vol. 23. Brasília: 1981. 388 p. Statistical tables summarize the tax receipts and expenditures of Brazil's major administrative divisions during the ten-year period following many revisions in tax law. Aggregate statistics are provided for the municípios of each state, except for the capitals, for which separate figures are given.

1427 Brazil. Secretaria de Modernização e Reforma Administrativa. Cadastro da administração federal. 2. ed. atualizada. 13 vols. Brasília: 1978. This organization manual of the federal government covers the presidency and the agencies providing direct support for it, as well as the fifteen ministries that administer the work of the government in all sectors of activity. For each major agency and its divisions there is an organization chart, and a detailed description of its functions. Other information provided includes the date of its creation, citations to the laws that created or modified it, and the location of its headquarters. This edition updates the work of the same title, published in 1976. Its loose-leaf format permits the addition or substitution of updated information.

1428 Brazil. Secretaria de Orçamento e Finanças. Orçamento da União. Brasília: Secretaria de Planejamento da Presidência de República, Secretaria de Orçamento e Finanças. This budget for the federal government is published annually.

1429 Brazil. Secretaria de Planejamento e Orçamento. Estrutura básica e regimentos internos do Ministério da Fazenda. Brasília: 1978. 326 p. Presents a detailed look at the functions and organization of the Ministério da Fazenda through text and organization charts.

1430 Brazil. Sistema de Informações Organizacionais da Administração Federal. Poder executivo: estrutura e atribuições. 2 vols. Brasília: 1983. Provides an overview and specific details about the structure, composition, purpose, and legislation related to each ministry or entity subordinate to the presidency, as well as other entities supervised by the ministries.

1431 ______. ______. Poder executivo: estruturas básicas e organogramas. 3. ed. Brasília: 1987. 221 p. Summarizes information about agencies of the executive branch through organization charts and brief data: date of creation, purpose, activities, and enabling legislation. First edition published in 1984; second in 1985.

1432 Brazil. Sovereigns, etc. Falas do trono desde o ano de 1823 até o ano de 1889, acompanhadas dos respectivos votos de graça da Câmara Temporária. Brasília: Instituto Nacional do Livro, 1977. 544 p. Texts of the speeches of the emperors of Brazil which opened and closed the legislative assemblies, from the Assembléia Constituinte of 1823 to the twentieth legislature at the end of the Empire in 1889. Also useful for its table listing the regular and extraordinary sessions of each legislature, along with their dates.

1433 Brazil. Tribunal das Contas da União. Ministros do TCU. Brasília: 1982. 192 p. Biographical data and portraits of each minister from the creation of the Tribunal das Contas da União in 1890 until 1982. Emphasizes professional activities, publications, and honors, although basic biographical information is also included.

1434 Constituições do Brasil. Compilação dos textos, notas, revisão e índices por Adriano Campanhole and Hilton Lobo. 4. ed. São Paulo: Editora Atlas, 1979. 718 p. Texts of the Brazilian federal constitutions and lists of their signatories from the first one (March 25, 1824) to the one of October 17, 1969, in reverse chronological order. Amendments, atos institucionais and atos complementares, as well as indexes to each constitution are located in addenda.

1435 Constituição federal e constituições estaduais. 3. ed. 4 vols. Brasília: Senado Federal, Subsecretaria de Edições Técnicas, 1984. Texts of the 1969 federal constitution and of all of the state constitutions. Earlier editions issued in 1975 and 1977. The text of the current (1988) constitution can be found in no. 1417.

1436 Degenhardt, Henry W. Political Dissent: An International Guide to Dissident, Extra Parliamentary, Guerrilla and Illegal Political Movements. Detroit: Gale Research Company, 1983. 592 p. A section on Latin America provides country-by-country coverage of dissident movements: dates founded, leaders, activities. Focus is on the period 1970-1980, although there is some earlier and later coverage. Section for Brazil includes ten movements, with both the right and the left represented.

1437 Empresa Brasileira de Turismo. Organismos e autoridades federais de turismo. Rio de Janeiro: Centro Brasileiro de Informação Turística--CEBITUR, 1983. 26 p. A directory of official agencies dealing with tourism.

1438 Estatística básica de arrecadação. Brasília: Secretaria da Receita Federal, vol. 1-, Jan. 1980-. A monthly publication summarizing tax collection statistics. Former title, 1973-1979, Estatísticas tributárias básicas.

1439 Estatísticas economicas do setor público, vol. 1-, 1980-. Rio de Janeiro: Fundação Instituto Brasileiro de Geografia e

Estatística (IBGE). 1983-. Detailed public finance and budgetary statistics for state and municipal governments published annually in multi-volume sets. Published 1979-1982 under the title, Estatísticas econômicas do governo estadual e municipal. Editions examined: vol. 1, 1980; vol. 3, 1982.

1440 Forças vivas da nação: nossos políticos. São Paulo: IPM--Comércio Promoções e Marketing. Volumes for individual states provide detailed biographical data, summaries of political activity, and portraits of political figures at state and local levels. General information about each município is also supplied. The volumes examined were for Alagoas (1980), Espírito Santo (1978), Mato Grosso do Sul (1979), Minas Gerais (1980), Paraná (1978), Rio de Janeiro (1978), Santa Catarina (1980), São Paulo (1979), and Sergipe (1980).

1441 Galvão, Miguel Archanjo. Relação dos cidadãos que tomaram parte no governo do Brasil no período de março de 1808 a 15 de novembre de 1889. 2. ed. Rio de Janeiro: Arquivo Nacional, 1969. 241 p. The first part of this useful work lists the ministers that made up each cabinet during the Empire. The second part lists all presidents and captains-general of the twenty provinces during the same period.

1442 O governo presidencial do Brasil, 1889-1930: guia administrativa da primeira República, poder executivo. Série Referências 1. Brasília: Pró-Memória, Senado Federal; Rio de Janeiro: Fundação Casa de Rui Barbosa, 1985. 348 p. Information useful for the study of the history of public administration presented in tables, chronologies, and summaries which can be easily scanned to locate specific data. Indexed. Includes a bibliography.

1443 Heyremann, Claudia B. As relações Brasil-EUA, 1974-1985: cronologia. Textos no. 7. Rio de Janeiro: Pontifícia Universidade Católica--PUC/RJ, 1988. 93 p. A chronology based on articles from major newspapers and news magazines and the Resenha de atos diplomáticos issued by the Ministério das Relações Exteriores (no. 1449).

1444 Lyra, Augusto Tavares de. Instituições políticas do Império. Brasília: Senado Federal, 1979. 349 p. Provides historical background on political institutions and biographical information on public officials of the Empire. The organization of the materials combines narrative and lists of individuals in a manner that does not facilitate use. The lack of a complete index of names is another obstacle to be overcome. In spite of these defects, this work is a valuable source for much information that is difficult to obtain elsewhere.

1445 Nogueira, Octaciano, and João Sereno Firmo. Parlamentares do Império: obra comemorativa do sesquicentenário da instituição parlementar no Brasil. 2 vols. Brasília: Centro Gráfico do Senado Federal, 1973. Information about each member of the Assembléia-Geral do Império, 1823-1889. Volume 1 provides birth and death dates, education, elective and administrative positions and published sources of information about them. Volume 2 lists the dates of the ordinary and extraordinary sessions of the twenty legislative sessions held during the period, and lists senators and deputies by the states that they represented, as well as the representatives to the Cortes Constituintes de Lisboa (1821-1822). It also lists Senate officers and the ministers of state in chronological order for the entire period.

1446 Perfil da Constituinte: anuário parlamentar brasileiro. Brasília: SEMPREL, ano 1-, 1987-. Biographical sketches of delegates to Brazil's fifth Assembléia Constituinte (constitutional convention), composed of 487 deputies and seventy-two senators. Various tables summarize the composition of the Assembléia by political party, ideological viewpoints of delegates, etc.

1447 Radiografia do poder. São Paulo: Editora Tama, 1989. 301 p. Narrative, lists, organization charts, statistical tables, and illustrations outline and summarize the growth of the Left in Brazil and its probable impact on the presidential elections of 1989 and on business.

1448 Reis, Pereira. Os presidentes do Brasil: sínteses biográficas. Rio de Janeiro: Divulbrás, 1975. 265 p. Personal and political biographies of presidents from the beginning of the Republic in 1889 through 1975. Includes portraits.

1449 Resenha de política exterior do Brasil. Brasília: Ministério das Relações Exteriores. A quarterly publication which provides texts of speeches by important officials, joint communiqués, and other documents associated with foreign affairs. A supplementary issue published in 1987 lists the contents of numbers 1-50 and summarizes each document.

1450 Rodrigues, Leôncio Martins. Quem é quem na Constituinte: uma análise sócio política dos partidos e deputados. São Paulo: Oesp-Maltese, 1987. 384 p. More than half of this work is devoted to biographical profiles of the delegates to the Constitutional Convention, arranged state-by-state, while the remainder summarizes the data contained in the profiles through text and tables.

1451 Sussekind, Arnaldo. Tratados ratificados pelo Brasil. Rio de Janeiro: Livraria Freitas Bastos, 1981. 470 p. Provides the texts of international treaties ratified by Brazil dealing with international organizations, human rights, family law, patents, copyrights, financial instruments, labor law, social security, space law, diplomatic privileges and immunities, and reciprocity between Brazil and Portugal.

1452 Titulares e endereços. Brasília: Secretaria de Modernização e Reforma Administrativa, 7. ed.-, 1987-. A directory of the federal administration, naming the heads of agencies and providing addresses. The seventh edition (1987) was the first with the above title; "Sistema de Informações Organizacionais" appears at head of title. Earlier editions were entitled Cadastro da administração federal: titulares e endereços and were published as follows: 1. ed., 1978; 2. ed., 1979 (June); 3. ed., 1979 (Aug.); 4. ed., 1980; 5. ed., 1985 (June); 6. ed., 1985 (Oct.).

STATES

Amazonas

1453 Livro de autoridades. Manaus. Lists state government agencies, their officers, addresses, and telephone numbers. Edition examined: 1988.

Bahia

1454 Autoridades. Salvador: Casa Civil, Documentação. A directory of state agencies and their officials. Issue examined: 1979.

1455 Bahia. Secretaria do Planejamento, Ciência e Tecnologia. Fundação de Pesquisas. Falas e mensagens dos presidentes da Província e governadores da Bahia, 1830-1978. Publicações CPE, Série bibliografias, 4. Salvador: 1978. 93 p. A bibliography of the 138 annual reports presented by the presidents of the province of Bahia, and later the governors of the state at the openings of the legislative sessions. Indexed by subject and by name of the chief executive.

1456 Castro, Renato Berbert de. Os vice-presidentes da Província da Bahia. Coleção Frei Vicente do Salvador, vol. 1. Salvador: Fundação Cultural do Estado da Bahia, 1978. 139 p. A detailed chronology of the presidential/vice-presidential succession in the Province of Bahia, 1823-1889, follows a text outlining the circumstances, also arranged in chronological order.

Goiás

1457 Relação das autoridades. Goiânia: Secretaria de Governo, Assessoria das Relações Públicas. Names and addresses of government leaders and heads of departments. Editions examined: 1975, 1979, 1980, 1983, 1984, 1985, 1987. Title varies: Autoridades.

Maranhão

1458 Catálogo. São Luís: Secretaria de Comunicação Social. A guide to all branches of the state government and the executive officers of each agency. Edition examined: 1984.

Minas Gerais

1459 Autoridades mineiras. Belo Horizonte: Assembléia Legislativa, Assessoria de Relações Públicas. Lists approximately 2000 names and addresses of agencies and officials of the state. Edition examined: 1984.

1460 Minas Gerais. Secretaria de Estado de Estado Civil. Assessoria do Cerimonial. Mundo oficial. Belo Horizonte: 1988. 136 p. A directory of state, federal, and consular officials in Minas Gerais, as well as those of the município of Belo Horizonte. Provides name, address, and telephone number.

Paraíba

1461 Maia, Benedito. Governadores da Paraíba (1947-1980). João Pessoa: 1980. 159 p. Information on the governors of the state for a period of more than thirty years.

Paraná

1462 Cadastro organizacional. Curitiba: Secretaria de Estado do Planejamento e Coordenação Geral, Coordenadoria de Planejamento Institucional. Outlines the basic structure of the executive branch of the government of Paraná and provides information about administrative units, including their executive officers, addresses, and telephone numbers. Includes an organization chart. Title varies: 1986, Cadastro organizacional: titulares, endereços e telefones. Editions examined: 1986, 1989.

1463 Orgãos e entidades públicas estaduais: objetivos e serviços prestados. Curitiba: Secretaria de Estado de Planejamento,

Coordenação de Modernização Administrativa. Information about the structures and activities of 120 government agencies and services. It replaces an earlier publication, Guia para utilização dos serviços públicos estaduais. Issue examined: 1986.

Pernambuco

1464 Lista de autoridades. Recife: Departamento de Ceremonial do Governo de Pernambuco. Names, addresses, telephone numbers, and chief executive officers of the agencies of state government, the federal government in Pernambuco, and universities, as well as names of the mayors of cities of the state. Also illustrates the state coat of arms and flag, and gives the lyrics of the state hymn. Edition examined: 1974.

Piauí

1465 Autoridades. Teresina: Governo do Estado do Piauí, Gabinete Civil, Cerimonial. Gives names, addresses, and some personal information about the chief executives of state agencies. Edition examined: 1988.

Rio de Janeiro

1466 Lacombe, Lourenço Luiz. Os chefes do executivo fluminense. Série monografias, 1. Petrópolis: Museu Imperial, 1973. 117 p. Biographies of the presidents of the Província do Rio de Janeiro and later governors of the state in the chronological order. No portraits.

Rio Grande do Norte

1467 Rio Grande do Norte. Assembléia Legislativa. Gabinete da Presidência. Assembléia Legislativa e autoridades norte rio-grandenses. Natal: Editora Clima, 1989. 160 p. Provides addresses and brief biographical information for state legislators and heads of state agencies and federal officials in Rio Grande do Norte, and names and addresses of prefeitos of each município and "autoridades diversas," such as presidents of organizations.

1468 Souza, Raimundo Alves de. Presidentes da Assembléia Legislativa no RN: Império e República. Natal: Clima, 1988. 196 p. Biographical and professional information about the presidents of the state legislature, 1835-1988. Includes portraits of most twentieth-century presidents.

Rio Grande do Sul

1469 Guia das repartições. Porto Alegre: Estado do Rio Grande do Sul, Secretaria da Administração. A directory covering state and municipal agencies, radio and television stations, airports, newspapers, and educational institutions, as well as other institutions of interest to the general public. Editions examined: 13th, 1983; 14th, 1984; 15th, 1986; 1989.

Santa Catarina

1470 Corrêa, Carlos Humberto. Os governantes de Santa Catarina de 1739 a 1982. Florianópolis: Editora da Universidade Federal de Santa Catarina, 1983. 356 p. "Relação de todos aqueles que, efetiva ou interinamente, exerceram o governo da Capitania, da Província e do Estado de Santa Catarina." Biographical information and pen-and-ink portraits. A mimeographed publication by the same author entitled Guia dos governantes de Santa Catarina, was issued in 1979 by the state's Secretaria de Educação e Cultura. It provided minimal information--the name of the governor and the date that he took office. In the introduction it is described as a small part of a fuller biographical study.

1471 Guia dos serviços públicos. Florianópolis: Fundação Catarinense de Trabalho. Names, addresses, telephone numbers, and hours of federal, state, and municipal government agencies functioning in Santa Catarina. Indexed by type of service. Edition examined: 1984.

1472 Santa Catarina. Casa Militar. Cerimonial. Principais autoridades do Estado de Santa Catarina. Florianópolis: 1985. 49 leaves. Contains names, addresses, telephone numbers, and principal officers of state agencies, foundations, the military, federal agencies in the state, and other groups.

São Paulo

1473 Alves, Odair Rodrigues. Os homens que governam São Paulo. São Paulo: Nobel; Editora da Universidade de São Paulo, 1986. 189 p. Biographical information and summaries of the administrations of the chief executive officers of the province and state from colonial days to 1984, arranged in chronological order. Includes a bibliography.

1474 Expo nacional dos municípios: edição para o Estado de São Paulo. São Paulo: Rede Municipalista de Divulgação e Imprensa. A directory of state and local agencies and officials, providing basic data about each município including its location in relation to the capital, and biographical information about its officials. Many portraits and other illustrations. Issues examined: 1971/1972; 1972/1973; 1975/1976.

1475 Perfil da administração pública paulista. São Paulo: Fundação do Desenvolvimento Administrativo--FUNDAP, 1978-. Outlines the composition, reporting structure, responsibilities, functions, and legislation related to the secretariats and the cabinet of the executive branch of the government of the state of São Paulo. Also provides organization charts. Editions examined: 1st, 1978; 2nd, 1980; 3rd, 1982; 4th, 1986.

1476 São Paulo (State). Fundação Sistema Estadual de Análise de Dados. Relação de nomes, cargos e endereços do Governo Estadual de São Paulo. São Paulo: SEADE. An annual publication listing all agencies of state government, their responsibilities and principal administrators, as well as agencies of the city of São Paulo and their officials, and the mayor of each município in the state. Editions examined: 5th, 1981; 7th, 1983; 11th, 1987.

PUBLISHING AND PRINTING

STYLE MANUALS

1477 Editoração de publicações oficiais. Brasília: Associação dos Bibliotecários do Distrito Federal, Comissão de Publicações Oficiais Brasileiros [e] Departamento de Imprensa Nacional, 1987. 248 p. This style manual for government publications includes the text of related legislation.

1478 Folha de S. Paulo. Manual geral da redação. 1. ed. São Paulo: 1984. This manual, prepared by the staff of a major newspaper, defines terms associated with editing, publishing, and printing.

1479 Gomes, Edegard. Manual de redação: normas gerais. Rio de Janeiro: F. Alves, 1974. 264 p. In addition to instructions on the preparation of government and business documents and communications, and examples of correct form, they are also carefully defined, making this work a useful source of information about them. There is an appendix of abbreviations and words used in official documents, business, and the stock market.

1480 Kury, Adriano da Gama. Elaboração e editoração de trabalhos de nível universitário (especialmente na area humanística). Rio de Janeiro: Fundação Casa de Rui Barbosa, 1980. 92 p. A style manual for scholarly works, emphasizing the humanities in the examples, with a section on how to do research. Useful appendixes on citing authors' names according to Brazilian practice, and on abbreviations frequently used in bibliographies.

1481 Moíses, Massaud. Guia prático de redação. 5. ed. São Paulo: Cultrix, 1973. 143 p. A guide for editing the printed word, focusing on diacritics, punctuation, and spelling.

GENERAL SOURCES

1482 Associação dos Bibliotecários do Distrito Federal. Comissão de Publicações Oficiais Brasileiras. Editoras oficiais brasileiros de publicações periódicas. Brasília: 1983. 137 p. "645 órgãos editores oficiais brasileiros, cujos nomes foram extraídos de dados que estão sendo atualizados pelo IBICT, não sendo portanto exaustivo." Gives only the name of the publishing agency; does not cite the titles published.

1483 Berger, Paulo. A tipografia no Rio de Janeiro: impressores bibliográficos, 1808-1900. Rio de Janeiro: Cia. Industrial de Papel, Pirahy, 1984. 226 p. Reproductions of examples of works of carioca presses, from the first officially approved printing press in Brazil (1808) to the end of the nineteenth century. Brief histories and biographical data about their owners is included when known. The introduction surveys the history of Brazilian printing. A good index covers names of printers and of presses.

1484 Bibliografia sobre política do livro no Brasil. São Paulo: FIESP-CIESP/DECAD/Biblioteca Roberto Simonsen, 1984. 40 leaves. The 203 entries of this unannotated bibliography cover all aspects of book publishing in Brazil. Since it was prepared for the "Seminário sobre o Livro Técnico no Brasil" (Sept. 1983), it emphasizes technical books, but publishing in general is well covered.

1485 Brazil. Congresso. Câmara dos Deputados. Coordenação de Biblioteca. Catálogo dos editores oficiais brasileiros: área federal. 2. ed. Brasília: 1977. 123 p. This useful publication serves not only as a source of information about which agencies of the Brazilian federal government publish materials, but also as a directory, giving the addresses and telephone numbers of the agencies listed.

1486 British Council. Directory of Publishing and Bookselling in Brazil. Rio de Janeiro: 1980. 179 p. A directory of the Brazilian publishing and bookselling worlds, intended to assist British publishers in entering the Brazilian market. It is a very good compilation of information combining text and statistics with lists of publishers, publishers' associations, importers and distributors of books, and prospective institutional buyers of books, such as libraries and universities.

1487 Ferreira, Maria Nazareth. Imprensa operária no Brasil. São Paulo: Editora Atica, 1988. 85 p. In addition to a historical overview of this topic from its beginning to the present, this work includes a chronological list of labor movement periodicals and newspapers from 1847 through 1986, giving their titles, publishers, and places of publication.

1488 Gandelman, Henrique. Guia básico de direitos autorais. Porto Alegre: Ed. Globo, 1982. 238 p. A guide to Brazilian copyright law for the written word, music, cinema, computer software, etc. Entries, such as "co-autoria," refer the user to applicable sections of the copyright law, which is printed in its entirety. A bibliography completes the work.

1489 Guia das editoras brasileiras 2. ed. Rio de Janeiro: Sindicato Nacional dos Editores de Livros, 1980. 104 p. Names, addresses, and telephone numbers of 481 publishers, along with their founding dates, and the subjects in which they specialize, arranged by state. Indexed by name of publisher and subject, with keys to the subjects in English, French and Portuguese.

1490 Hallewell, Laurence. Books in Brazil: A History of the Publishing Trade. Metuchen, NJ: Scarecrow Press, 1982. 485 p. An excellent history of publishing in Brazil from its beginnings in the colonial period to contemporary times. Although not in reference format, it is easy to use for reference purposes because of the topical headings within chapters which make scanning easy and its good index. Includes many useful statistical tables and interesting illustrations, including portraits. This work was published in Portuguese in an updated and revised version with an expanded index (O livro no Brasil: sua história, São Paulo: 1985).

1491 Ipanema, Marcello de, and Cybelle de Ipanema. Imprensa fluminense: ensaios e trajetos. Rio de Janeiro: Instituto de Comunicação Ipanema, 1984. 441 p. A well-indexed work consisting of narrative about the press in the state of Rio de Janeiro (past and present) and extensive bibliographic data about newspapers and periodicals published there. Includes chronological listing of periodicals published in Niterói and elsewhere (see also no. 1498).

1492 Os jornais de bairro na cidade de São Paulo. São Paulo: Secretaria Municipal de Cultura, 1985. 165 p. Summarizes the history and provides current information about neighborhood newspapers in São Paulo arranged by region of the city and then by title. Includes photographs of the first page of each newspaper.

1493 Knychala, Catarina Helena. O livro de arte brasileiro I: teoria, história, descrição, 1808-1890. Rio de Janeiro: Presença em convênio com o Instituto Nacional do Livro e Fundação Nacional Pró-Memória, 1983. 166 p. A chronological survey of the history of fine Brazilian books as artifacts, with subdivisions by city or publisher. Includes illustrations of poor quality and a useful bibliography. The second volume is described in no. 1494.

1494 _______. O livro de arte brasileiro II: bibliografia descritiva de 50 livros de arte, I. Rio de Janeiro: Presença em convênio com o Instituto Nacional do Livro, Fundação Nacional Pró-Memória, 1984. 210 p. Detailed descriptions of fifty fine examples of Brazilian books with high quality paper, book design, typography, binding, and illustrations. This work originated as a thesis, and other parts of the thesis were published in 1983 under the title O livro de arte brasileiro I (no. 1493).

1495 Leuenroth, Edgard. A organização dos jornalistas brasileiros, 1908-1951. São Paulo: COM-ARTE, 1987. 200 p. Lists organizations of journalists state-by-state and at the national level with historical and descriptive information about each one. Other sections cover state and national congresses of journalists, agreements related to journalism, and texts of basic documents in the field. This work was originally prepared by its author, a well-known journalist, for the Quarto Congresso Nacional de Jornalistas, held in 1951 in Recife.

1496 Melo, Manoel Rodrigues de. Dicionário da imprensa no Rio Grande do Norte, 1909-1987. Coleção documentos potiguares, 3. São Paulo: Cortez; Natal: Fundação José Augusto, 1987. 269 p. Historical, bibliographic, and descriptive information on newspapers and periodicals published in Rio Grande do Norte, with an appendix of the names/pseudonyms of many writers of the state. Index of serials by place of publication.

1497 Miccolis, Leila. Catálogo de imprensa alternativa. Rio de Janeiro: Secretaria Municipal de Cultura; Rio Arte, 1986. 108 p. Bibliographic information, physical description, content, and persons associated with many alternative or counter-culture periodicals available at the Centro de Imprensa Alternativa e Cultura Popular, Rio de Janeiro. Coverage through 1982.

1498 Morel, Marco. Jornalismo popular nas favelas cariocas. Rio de Janeiro: Rio Arte, 1986. 142 p. Describes, analyzes, and reproduces the front pages of eight newspapers published in the favelas of Rio de Janeiro, and lists eleven others. Includes a content analysis of the papers as a group and provides a bibliography.

1499 Museu de Arte de São Paulo. História da tipografia no Brasil. São Paulo: 1979. 277 p. Although this major exhibition catalog was not designed as a reference book, it serves that purpose well. Its introduction provides a summary of the development of printing in each Brazilian state and gives brief information about many presses. The main body of the catalog reproduces the title pages of many printed works from the earliest produced in Brazil (1747) to the early twentieth century, with emphasis on the nineteenth century. Representative works of printers from various states comprise a large part of this section. Notes accompanying the reproductions identify the authors of the works, giving brief biographical information. An index of the names of authors and printing presses greatly enhances this work.

1500 Nascimento, Luiz do. História da imprensa de Pernambuco: 1821-1954. Recife: Universidade Federal de Pernambuco, Editora Universitaria, 1966-. A chronological history of periodical literature in the state of Pernambuco from 1821 to the middle of the twentieth century. Under each year is a title-by-title listing of periodicals which began publication. Each entry includes a bibliographic and physical description of the periodical, and other available information about content, history, etc. As of 1982, eight of fourteen projected volumes had been published: Vol. I: Diário de Pernambuco (1825-1954)--a detailed history of this important newspaper; Vol. 2: Diários do Recife, 1829-1900; Vol. 3: Diários do Recife, 1901-1954; Vol. 4: Periódicos do Recife, 1821-1850; Vol. 5: Periódicos do Recife, 1851-1875; Vol. 6: Periódicos do Recife, 1876-1900; Vol. 7: Periódicos do Recife, 1901-1915; Vol. 8: Periódicos do Recife, 1916-1930. The first edition of Vol. 1 was issued by the Arquivo Público in 1962.

1501 Paula, Ademar Antônio de, and Mário Carramillo Neto. Artes gráficas no Brasil: registros 1746-1941. São Paulo: Laserprint, 1989. 168 p. An overview of printing in Brazil through text and illustrations, including many photographs. Text in English and Portuguese. Includes a brief bibliography.

1502 Pinheiro Filho, Celso. História da imprensa no Piauí. 2. ed. Teresina: Projeto Petrônio Portella; Academia Piauense de Letras, 1988. 107 p. This work, first published in 1972, surveys the history of journalism in Piauí and includes a list of periodicals published in the state, 1832-1972.

1503 Piper, Rudolf. Garotas de papel. São Paulo: Global Editora, 1976. 190 p. A history in pictures and text of the evolution of "pinup" and "cheesecake" publications, with emphasis on Brazil. The work includes a list--described as complete--of Brazilian pinup and humor magazines in chronological order of beginning date of publication, starting in 1837. In addition to title and dates of publication, information about each magazine includes publisher, place of publication, and brief descriptive comments. Includes illustrations.

1504 Ramos, José Nabantino. Jornalismo: dicionário enciclopédico.

Biblioteca dicionários e enciclopédias, vol. 10. Rio de Janeiro: IBRASA--Instituição Brasileira de Difusão Cultural, S.A. 1970. 371 p. A dictionary of terms associated with journalism in the Brazilian context. Also includes texts of related laws, a bibliography, and an index.

1505 Sant'Ana, Moacir Medeiros de. História da imprensa em Alagoas, 1831-1981. Maceió: Arquivo Público de Alagoas, 1987. 236 p. Detailed information on journalism, journalists, the official press, periodicals, and newspapers in Alagoas in a well-indexed narrative format, supplemented by lists of titles, bibliography, and illustrations, including reproductions of the mastheads or covers of serials. Well-indexed.

1506 Universidade de São Paulo. Departamento de Jornalismo e Editoração. Jornalismo e editoração na USP: produção científica e técnico-profissional do corpo docente (1967-1987). São Paulo: Instituto de Pesquisas de Comunicação Jornalística e Editorial, Departamento de Jornalismo e Editoração, Escola de Comunicações e Artes, Universidade de São Paulo, 1987. 136 p. Professional publications are listed under the name of each faculty member.

RELIGION

BIBLIOGRAPHY AND GENERAL WORKS

1507 Barbosa, Eni. Projeto Ecclesia: inventário analítico da documentação cultural-histórica do Estado do Rio Grande do Sul. Série CPHAE, Cadernos Técnicos, 2. Porto Alegre: Coordenaria do Patrimônio Histórico e Artístico do Estado, 1986. 182 p. An inventory of historical and cultural documentation related to Roman Catholic and Lutheran churches in Rio Grande do Sul. Part 1, which was the only volume examined, includes brief general information on each parish and an inventory of churches and other buildings belonging thereto.

1508 Bibliografia sobre religiosidade popular. Estudos da CNBB/ Conferência Nacional dos Bispos do Brasil, 27. São Paulo: Edições Paulinas, 1981. 104 p. An unannotated bibliography citing books and periodical articles on popular religion in general and in Brazil, including popular Catholicism, Protestantism, Afro-Brazilian and Oriental religions, spiritism, indigenous religions, and others.

1509 Landim, Leilah. Os sinais do tempo: diversidade religiosa no Brasil. Cadernos do ISER, no. 23. Rio de Janeiro: Instituto de Estudos da Religião, 1990. 274 p. Essays describing the history, beliefs, current practice, and leadership of a variety of religions in contemporary Brazil. Each essay includes a bibliography.

1510 Schiavo, José. Dicionário de personagens bíblicas: Antigo e Novo Testamento. n.p.: Ediouro, n.d. Identifies biblical characters.

1511 Schlesinger, Hugo, and Humberto Porto. Crenças, seitas, e símbolos religiosos. São Paulo: Edições Paulinas, 1983. 386 p. A dictionary of religious beliefs, sects, and symbols, worldwide in scope, including many references to religion in Brazil. Excludes biographical information.

1512 _______, and _______. Guia bibliográfico do diálogo cristão-judeo. São Paulo: Conselho de Fraternidade Cristão Judaica, 1985. 144 p. An unannotated bibliography, international in scope, on Christian-Jewish relations. Its three sections cover official government documents, books, and periodicals which regularly devote attention to the subject, and it includes many Brazilian publications. The introduction is in Portuguese, English, French, and Spanish.

1513 _______, and _______. Líderes religiosos da humanidade. 2 vols. São Paulo: Edições Paulinas, 1986. A biographical dictionary of past and present religious leaders, universal in scope. Includes many Brazilians and missionaries to Brazil.

CATHOLICISM

1514 Anuário católico do Brasil. Petrópolis: Vozes. An irregularly published directory. Covers the clergy from parish priests to cardinals, and includes information on such topics as church schools, media, religious orders, and others. There is a brief history of each diocese. Editions examined: 1965, 1970/1971, 1977, 1985, 1989.

1515 Azzi, Riolando. Presença da Igreja Católica na sociedade brasileira, 1921-1979. Caderno do ISER, no. 13. Rio de Janeiro: Instituto Superior de Estudos da Religião, 1981. 130 leaves. Most of this work (101 leaves) is comprised of a chronology, which, in addition to listing religious events, records the involvement of the Church in politics and social movements. A preliminary essay focuses on the "Restauração Católica," (1921-1960). Includes a bibliography.

1516 Azzi, Riolando, and José Oscar Deozzo. Os religiosos no Brasil: enfoques históricos. São Paulo: Edições Paulinas, 1986. 218 p. Summarizes the history of Roman Catholic religious orders and institutions in Brazil from the middle of the nineteenth century through the early decades of the twentieth century, including the phase known as the "Reforma Católica." The chronological arrangement and detailed table of contents make this work easy to consult for specific information.

1517 Botelho Megale, Nilza. Cento e sete invocações da Virgem Maria no Brasil: história, iconografia, folclore. Petrópolis:

Vozes, 1980. 372 p. A guide to liturgical and popular cults of the Virgin Mary in Brazilian religious life, including cults indigenous to Brazil and those originating elsewhere. Provides information on the history, current forms of devotion, and places in Brazil where each cult is popular. The sections on iconography are weak, usually relying on verbal descriptions instead of illustrations. A bibliography concludes the work.

1518 Brazil. Serviço de Estatística Demográfica, Moral e Política. Estatística do culto católico: províncias eclesiásticas do Brasil. Rio de Janeiro. Statistics for the Roman Catholic Church by ecclesiastical province and by município: parishes, membership, and sacraments administered. Editions covering the years 1964, 1968, and 1971 were examined (published 1967, 1974, and 1974 respectively). The 1964 edition was entitled Estatística do culto católico romano, 1964.

1519 Lipiner, Elias. Santa Inquisição: terror e linguagem. Rio de Janeiro: Editora Documentário, 1977. 147 p. Defines and explains terms and expressions used by the Inquisition in Portugal and in Brazil. Includes citations to related bibliography.

1520 Luna, Lino do Monte Carmello. Memória histórica e biográfica do clero pernambucano. 2. ed. Recife: Governo do Estado de Pernambuco, Secretaria de Educação e Cultura, 1976. 122 p. The second edition of a work originally published in 1857 which summarizes the history of the clergy in Pernambuco and provides biographical information about the lives and work of the bishops and other church officials. Includes a chronology of bishops.

1521 Membros da Conferência Nacional dos Bispos do Brasil. São Paulo: Edições Paulinas, 1984. 268 p. Biographical and career data about each member of the National Conference of Bishops. Includes portraits.

1522 Moura, Odilão. As idéias católicas no Brasil: direções do pensamento católico do Brasil no siglo XX. São Paulo: Editora Convívio, 1978. 255 p. Although this is a survey rather than a reference book in the strictest sense, its brief chapters, emphasizing factual information rather than analysis, combined with a detailed index of names, makes it useful as a reference tool. In addition to an overall survey of Brazilian Catholic thought in the twentieth century, it highlights some of the leaders, and discusses regional differences in Catholic thought and practice. Extensive notes and bibliographic footnotes enhance its value.

1523 Ramos, Alberto Gaudêncio. Cronologia eclesiástica do Pará.

Belém: Gráfica Falangola, 1985. 305 p. An ecclesiastical chronology of Pará covering the years 1608 through mid-1984, with a name index to facilitate access to the information therein.

PROTESTANTISM

1524 Brazil. Serviço de Estatística Demográfica, Moral e Política. Estatística do culto protestante do Brasil. Rio de Janeiro. State-by-state and município-by-município statistics on Protestant denominations, congregations, membership, and other aspects of religious practice. Volumes covering 1964, 1967, and 1968 were examined (published 1968, 1973 and 1973, respectively).

1525 Read, William R., and Frank A. Ineson. Brazil 1980: The Protestant Handbook. Monrovia, CA: MARC, 1973. 405 p. Report of a computer analysis of the growth of Protestantism in Brazil during the 1950's and 1960's on a município-by-município, denomination-by-denomination basis. Combines text, statistics, maps, and other graphics. Also includes directories of domestic and foreign missionary groups at work in Brazil and of Protestant theological seminaries there, as well as a glossary of acronyms and other terms, and a good bibliography.

1526 Reily, Duncan Alexander. História documental do protestantismo no Brasil. São Paulo: Associação de Seminários Teológicos Evangélicos (ASTE), 1984. 429 p. Summarizes briefly the history and development of "mainline" Protestant denominations and organizations in Brazil, and supplies the texts of basic documents associated with each one. The term "document" is broadly defined to include official decisions, confessions of faith, formal agreements, letters, excerpts from diaries, articles, and other contemporary writings. Indexes of subjects and names provide additional access to the text, which is organized in easy-to-scan outline format.

POSITIVISM

1527 Medeiros, Ana Lígia Silva and Maria Luiza de Andrade Queiroz. Igreja e apostolado positivista do Brasil: versão preliminar. Rio de Janeiro: Fundação Getúlio Vargas, Centro de Pesquisa e Documentação de História Contemporânea do Brasil, 1981. 123 p. An unannotated bibliography of materials related to positivist thought, important after 1870 in

Brazilian politics, economics, and social thought. Based on the collection of the Igreja Apostolado Positivista do Brasil, which includes many rare items.

SPIRITISM AND AFRO-BRAZILIAN RELIGIONS

1528 Anuário espírita. Araras, SP: Instituto de Difusão Espírita, 1964-. An annual compilation of events, publications, and people associated with spiritualism, as well as more general articles about it.

1529 Bastos, Abguar. Os cultos mágico-religiosos no Brasil: os aparatos, os cerimoniais, as alfaias, os feitiços. São Paulo: HUCITEC, 1979. 233 p. Cults covered are "Xangô, Candomblé, Pará, Macumba, Cambinda, Umbanda, Quimbanda, Catimbó, Linha de Mesa, Babaçuê, Tambor-de-mina, Pajelança, Toré, Cabula."

1530 Brazil. Serviço de Estatística Demográfica, Moral e Política. Estatística do culto espírita do Brasil. Rio de Janeiro. State-by-state and município-by-município statistics of the spiritist religion. Includes statistics for specific cults. The edition examined covered 1964 (published 1967).

1531 _______. _______. Estatística do culto espírita do Brasil: ramo kardecista. Rio de Janeiro. State-by-state and município-by-município statistics for the kardecista branch of spiritualism. Issues examined covered 1967 and 1968 (both published in 1973).

1532 _______. _______. Estatística do culto espírita do Brasil: ramo umbandista. Rio de Janeiro. State-by-state and município-by-município statistics for the practice of umbanda. Editions examined covered 1967 and 1968 (both published in 1973).

1533 Cacciatore, Olga Gudolle. Dicionário de cultos afro-brasileiros, com origem das palavras. Rio de Janeiro: Forense Universitária, 1977. 279 p. A carefully researched dictionary of terms (including the names of divinities) used in the practice of candomblé, macumba, quimbanda, umbanda, and other Brazilian cults of African origin. Includes a useful bibliography.

1534 Carybé. Iconografia dos deuses africanos no candomblé da Bahia: aquarelas. São Paulo: Editora Raízes Artes Gráficas, 1980. 300 p. Includes 128 watercolors that visually document the practice of candomblé in Bahia, illustrating deities, rites, costume, and artifacts. The introduction by Jorge Amado, descriptive and explanatory text by anthropologists Pierre Verger and Waldeloir Rego accompanied by a bibliography, all add to this useful work.

1535 Costa, Fernando. A prática do candomblé no Brasil. Rio de Janeiro: Editora Renes, 1974. 144 p. A brief but clear introduction to the major divinities and ceremonies of candomblé, illustrated with many photographs.

1536 Dicionário de umbanda. São Paulo: Roval Editora, 197-? 106 p. Briefly defines the vocabulary used in the practice of umbanda. Should be used as a complement to the more thorough Dicionário de cultos afro-brasileiros by Cacciatore (no. 1533).

1537 Lody, Raul. Pencas de balangandãs da Bahia: um estudo etnográfico das jóias-amuletos. Rio de Janeiro: Instituto Nacional do Folclore, 1988. 167 p. Photographs and text in tabular format illustrate and describe the amulets and other objects comprising the African and Afro-Brazilian material culture used in candomblé in contemporary Bahia.

1538 Oliveira, Jorge de. Ritual prático do candomblé e seus mistérios. Rio de Janeiro: Editora Espiritualista, 1973. 143 p. Explanations and instructions for practicing the rituals of candomblé written for the novice.

1539 Paula, João Teixeira de. Dicionário enciclopédico ilustrado: espiritismo, metapsíquica, parapsicologia. 3. ed. Porto Alegre: Bels, 1976. 293 p. Defines the terms and concepts of spiritualism, metaphysics, and parapsychology, using many examples and illustrative photographs from their practice in Brazil.

1540 Ribeiro, José. O jogo de búzios e as cerimônias esotéricas dos cultos afro-brasileiros. 4. ed. Rio de Janeiro: Polo Mágico, 1985. 140 p. Identifies and explains the significance of many ceremonies of Afro-Brazilian cults.

1541 Sangirardi, Júnior. Deuses da Africa e do Brasil: candomblé & umbanda. Rio de Janeiro: Civilização Brasileira, 1988. 206 p. A guide to the pantheon of candomblé and umbanda. Explains the significance of each god and goddess, relates them to other religions practiced in Brazil, and provides illustrations of them and the objects used in their worship. Includes a glossary of terms and a short bibliography.

1542 Santos, Gilton S. Pontos cantados e riscados. São Paulo: Tríade Editorial, 1987. 166 p. A manual providing the texts of songs and chants and illustrating the symbols used in the practice of umbanda.

1543 Souza, José Ribeiro de. Dicionário africano de umbanda: africano e português e português e africano. 2. ed. Rio de Janeiro: Editora Espiritualista, 1972. 390 p. This dictionary, which the author refers to as a "dicionário africano das línguas sudanesas," gives equivalents in several African dialects and Portuguese, and sometimes gives longer definitions and explanations. The words covered are "muito usadas e divulgadas hoje nos terreiros, tendas, centros, Xangôs e Candomblés diversos existentes de Norte a Sul, de Leste a Oeste do nosso Brasil."

1544 3000 pontos riscados e cantados na umbanda e candomblé. 11 ed. Rio de Janeiro: Editora Eco, 1974. 319 p. Provides the words of 1500 songs used to summon, praise, or dismiss the divinities of umbanda and candomblé, and 1500 sketches of the cabalistic symbols used to summon them.

1545 Varella, João Sebastião das Chagas. Manual do filho de santo. Rio de Janeiro: Editora Espiritualista, 1973. 159 p. Explanations and instructions for practicing the rituals of umbanda, written for the lay person.

SOCIAL CONDITIONS

BIBLIOGRAPHY

1546 Almeida, Maria Lêda Rodrigues de. Família e desenvolvimento, uma análise bibliográfica: relatório final. Grupo de Estudos sobre Família, Documento no. 2. n.p.: Centro Latino-Americano de Pesquisas em Ciências Sociais--CLAPCS; CNPq, 1971. 39 leaves. An essay analyzing seventy-three scholarly books and periodical articles on the Brazilian family is concluded with a bibliography of these publications. In addition to providing bibliographic data, it identifies the central theme and summarizes the content of each work and notes the research technique and methodology used.

1547 Banco Nacional de Habitação. Departamento de Pesquisas. Pesquisas realizadas pelo BNH. Ed. preliminar. Rio de Janeiro: 1980. 51 p. An annotated bibliography of research published as a result of BNH research, as well as a list of projects in progress. Research encompasses the fields of housing, construction, sanitation, urbanization, etc.

1548 Bibliografia sobre juventude na América Latina: problems sociais, psicológicos, estudantis e aspirações. Rio de Janeiro: Centro Latino-Americano de Pesquisas em Ciências Sociais; Centro Brasileiro de Pesquisas Educacionais, 1969. 22 leaves. An unannotated bibliography of 210 citations covering all of Latin America, with many citations to Brazilian publications.

1549 Brazil. Congresso. Senado. Subsecretaria de Biblioteca. Planejamento familiar, controle de natalidade, população e assuntos correlatos. Bibliografia, 2. Brasília: 1983. 15 leaves. An unannotated bibliography of 240 entries citing books and periodical articles about family planning, birth control, population, and related topics. International in scope, with emphasis on Brazil.

1550 Estácio, Ivanilze. Crianças e adolescentes, aspectos sócio-culturais: bibliografia, 1980-1990. São Paulo: RB--Research & Bibliography, 1990. 39 p. A partially annotated bibliography of 238 monographs, periodical articles, theses, and other publications related to children and adolescents, with emphasis on social and cultural aspects.

1551 Filmografia do habitat. Brasília: SEPLAN--Secretaria de Planejamento; CNPq--Conselho Nacional de Desenvolvimento Científico e Tecnológico, Coordenação Editorial, 1982. 198 p. Cites films produced in Brazil and elsewhere in the field of housing, with emphasis on urban settings, architecture, and sanitation. Provides basic information about each film, and a brief synopsis.

1552 Semenzato, Geraldo. A nova geração--desafio nacional: pesquisa bibliográfica com ênfase sobre o menor-problema social. Rio de Janeiro: 1978. 48 leaves. An unannotated bibliography of books, journal articles, laws, and projected laws related to minors, especially delinquent and abandoned children.

OTHER SOURCES

1553 Estatísticas sobre a situação do menor no Brasil: 1980. Brasília: Instituto de Planejamento Econômico e Social--IPEA; Instituto de Planejamento--IPLAN, 1985. 94 p. A series of statistical tables on the socio-economic situation of the Brazilian population under age eighteen, based on data from the 1980 census.

1554 Ferreira, Francisco de Paula. Dicionário de bem-estar social. São Paulo: Cortez, 1982. 362 p. Defines terms used in the various aspects of social welfare: teaching, research, planning, delivery of services, and administration. In addition to formal terms, it defines slang words such as "boia fria" (temporary agricultural workers residing in cities), and it identifies major Brazilian welfare institutions.

1555 Fundação Instituto Brasileiro de Geografia e Estatística. Indicadores sociais: regiões metropolitanas, aglomerações urbanas, municípios com mais de 100.000 habitantes. Rio de Janeiro: 1988. 271 p. A compilation of social indicators based on the 1980 census covering population, education, labor force, and housing.

1556 Fundo de Assistência Social do Palácio do Governo. Guia informativo de recursos comunitários. São Paulo: Imprensa

Oficial do Estado, 1978. 107 p. Covers government agencies devoted to many aspects of community development and social welfare at the national, state (São Paulo), and local (city of São Paulo) levels. Describes their functions, services, and means of access to them, and gives their addresses. Useful for an overview of the wide range of activities in these fields as well as for more specific information about individual agencies.

1557 Habitação, saneamento e desenvolvimento urbano: cadastro setorial de pesquisas, 80/83. Brasília: Sistema e Linha de Acompanhamento de Projetos, Secretaria de Planejamento, 1983-. Data on research and development projects in the fields of housing, sanitation, and urban development. Includes those completed and those in progress. Volume examined: 1.

1558 Indicadores sociais: tabelas selecionadas. Rio de Janeiro: Instituto Brasileiro de Geografia e Estatística, 1979-. Statistical tables on many aspects of Brazilian demography, the family, the labor force, income distribution, housing, education, and health. Volumes examined: 1 (1979); 2 (1984).

1559 Peres, José Augusto de Souza. Dicionário de pesquisa social. João Pessoa: Editora Universitária/UFPb, 1977. 193 p. Defines terms associated with the social sciences.

1560 Vieira, Pedro José Meirelles. Glossário de serviço social: terminologia, expressões e atividades ligadas ao serviço social e ao bem-estar social. Rio de Janeiro: 1981. 181 p. A glossary of terms related to many aspects of social service and social welfare.

STATISTICS

The census reports and statistical compilations cited here concentrate on general statistics, with emphasis on demography. These providing data related to specific subjects--education, for example--are listed under the appropriate subjects.

BIBLIOGRAPHY AND GENERAL SOURCES

1561 Goyer, Doreen S., and Eliane Domschke. The International Population Census Bibliography: Revision and Update, 1945-1977. New York: Academic Press, 1980. 711 p. A bibliography of "all known, bona fide, national, population censuses," published over three decades for all nations, including Brazil. Entries for each country also include the name of its statistical agency and the distributor of its published census materials.

1562 Graham, Ann Hartness. Subject Guide to Statistics in the Presidential Reports of the Brazilian Provinces, 1830-1889. Austin: Institute of Latin American Studies, The University of Texas at Austin, 1977. 454 p. Combines a bibliography of the annual reports (relatórios) of the provincial presidents to the legislatures, with a detailed subject index of statistical material found in them, from the earliest report located for each province to the end of the Empire (1889).

1563 Merrick, Thomas W. The Demographic History of Brazil. The Brazilian Curriculum Guide Specialized Bibliography. Albuquerque: Latin American Institute, University of New Mexico, 1985 or 1986. 17 p. An annotated bibliography on Brazilian demography follows an essay tracing the development and growth of the country's population.

1564 Rodrigues, Milton Camargo da Silva. Dicionário brasileiro de estatística, seguido de um vocabulário inglês-português. 2. ed. Rio de Janeiro: Fundação IBGE--Instituto Brasileiro de Estatística, 1970. 350 p. A dictionary defining 2480 technical terms associated with statistics, followed by an English-Portuguese statistics vocabulary with 2665 entries. The first edition, Vocabulário brasileiro de estatística, appeared in 1956 in Boletim no. 203 of the Faculdade de Filosofia, Ciências e Letras, Universidade de São Paulo.

CENSUS MATERIALS

1565 Fundação Instituto Brasileiro de Geografia e Estatística. Censo demográfico: Brasil. VIII recenseamento geral--1970. Série nacional, vol. 1. Rio de Janeiro: 1973. 267 p. A one-volume summary of the 1970 census.

1566 _______. Censo demográfico: Brasil, VIII recenseamento geral--1970. Série regional. 25 vols. in 29. Rio de Janeiro: IBGE, 1972-1973. Detailed census data for each state.

1567 _______. Censo demográfico: dados distritais. IX recenseamento geral do Brasil--1980. 23 vols. Rio de Janeiro: IBGE, 1982-1983. Census data by mesorregiões, microregiões municípios, and distritos within each state.

1568 _______. Censo demográfico: dados gerais, migração, instruição, fecundidade, mortalidade. IX recenseamento geral do Brasil--1980. 26 vols. Rio de Janeiro: IBGE, 1982. Census data for Brazil as a whole and for each state.

1569 _______. Censo demográfico: famílias e domicílios. IX recenseamento geral do Brasil--1980. 26 vols. Rio de Janeiro: IBGE, 1983. Covers housing, appliances, family composition, and income.

STATISTICAL COMPILATIONS

Most of the statistical sources cited here cover the period from 1965 through the early 1980s. However, a few compilations of retrospective statistics are also included.

1570 Anuário estatístico do Brasil, vol. 1-, 1908/1912-. Rio de Janeiro: Fundação Instituto Brasileiro de Geografia e Estatística, 1916-. Provides statistics on Brazil's physical aspects (climate, water, natural resources, etc.), demography, economy, and social, cultural, administrative, and political conditions. This compilation has been published annually by the official statistics gathering agency since 1916. Publication was suspended 1913-1935. Most recent edition examined: 1987/1988.

1571 Anuário estatístico EMBRATUR. Rio de Janeiro: vol. 1-, 1970-. Statistics on foreign tourists in Brazil, Brazilian tourists abroad, internal tourism, and the tourism infrastructure, as well as the activities of the official tourism agency, the Empresa Brasileira de Turismo (EMBRATUR). Issue examined: 1977.

1572 Atualidade estatística do Brasil. Rio de Janeiro: Fundação Instituto Brasileiro de Geografia e Estatística, 1968-1970. Basic demographic and other statistical data was summarized in the three annual volumes that were published before this publication was superseded by the Sinopse estatística do Brasil (no. 1588).

1573 Brasil: séries estatísticas retrospectivas, vol. 1-, 1959/1968-. Rio de Janeiro: Instituto Brasileiro de Geografia e Estatística, 1970-. An irregularly issued publication which supersedes O Brasil em números, the latter having been published in two volumes in 1960 and 1966. The statistical data is based on that found in the Anuário estatístico do Brasil. Retrospective data on population, economic sectors, prices, public finance, banking, the stock market, and social conditions, are presented in series that enable the user to identify trends. The years covered in each table vary according to available data. Some material is presented graphically in charts, graphs, and maps. A useful source for a quantitative overview of many important aspects of Brazilian life. Includes information on the sources for each table. Edition examined: 1977.

1574 Brazil. Secretaria de Articulação e Estudos de Planejamento. Retrato Brasil: educação, cultura, desportos. Brasília. 1985-. A statistical compilation focusing on education at all levels, culture (television, radio, cinema, theatre, museums, libraries, cultural associations, the periodical press, and publishers), and physical education and sports. The cover title bears the dates 1970-1990, but volume 1, Estatisticas básicas (published 1985), which was the only volume examined, included data through 1984.

1575 Brazil. Secretaria Nacional de Ações Básicas de Saúde. Divisão Nacional de Epidemiologia. Estatísticas de mortalidade: Brasil, 1980. Brasília: Centro de Documentação do Ministério da Saúde, 1983. 354 p. Mortality statistics by cause of death for Brazil as a whole, each state/territory, and the capital city of each state.

1576 Estatísticas do registro civil. vol. 1-, 1974-. Rio de Janeiro: Fundação Instituto Brasileiro de Geografia e Estatística, 1979-. Annual statistical records of births, marriages, and deaths for the country as a whole, by state/territory, and by município. Continues Registro civil do Brasil. Issues examined covered the years 1974-1983.

1577 Fundação Instituto Brasileiro de Geografia e Estatística. Indicadores mesorregionais: características demográficas e sócio-econômicas. Rio de Janeiro: 1979. 440 p. Demographic, social and economic statistics by areas with 600,000 or more inhabitants, intended to facilitate regional planning, but also useful for many other purposes.

1578 _______. Perfil estatístico de crianças e mães no Brasil. Rio de Janeiro: 1979. 233 p. Demographic and social statistics related to mothers, young people, and children, based on data collected in 1975 and 1976, although a few tables provide data for earlier years. The data presented are for Brazil as a whole or broken down into seven socio-economic regions. Topics covered include population, vital statistics, education, employment, health, nutrition, and housing.

1579 _______. Perfil estatístico de crianças e mães no Brasil: aspectos nutricionais, 1974-1975. Rio de Janeiro: 1982. 267 p. A detailed study of nutrition in Brazil, conducted by the Estudo Nacional de Despesa Familiar in 1974-1975. It characterizes the nutritional status of preschool children and the socio-economic status of their families in two geographic areas representing extremes of development: the state of São Paulo and the Northeast. Data is presented in tables, graphics, and text.

1580 _______. Perfil estatístico de crianças e mães no Brasil: aspectos sócio-econômicos da mortalidade infantil em áreas urbanas. Rio de Janeiro: IBGE/UNICEF, 1986. 92 p. Provides statistics and explanatory text on four topics: the evolution of urban population in Brazil; the evolution of infant mortality; the role of recent health and sanitation policies in the decline of infant mortality; and recent infant mortality in urban areas.

1581 _______. Perfil estatístico de crianças e mães no Brasil: características sócio-demográficas, 1970-1977. Rio de Janeiro: 1982. 424 p. Demographic and social statistics related to mothers, young people, and children based on data collected for the census of 1970, and the Pesquisas Nacionais por Amostra de Domicílio (PNAD) of 1977, for Brazil as a whole, the Northeast, the state of São Paulo, and the metropolitan area of the city of São Paulo. The data cover such topics as fertility, mortality, education, family structure, employment, and income.

1582 _______. Perfil estatístico de crianças e mães no Brasil: mortalidade infantil e saúde na década de 80. Rio de Janeiro: 1989. 129 p. Statistics, charts, and text depict and analyze the causes of recent infant mortality, characteristics of infant mortality in Rio de Janeiro and São Paulo; estimates of infant mortality, 1980-1987; the health of children in Ceará, and health care expenditures in the 1980s.

1583 _______. Perfil estatístico de crianças e mães no Brasil: sistema de acompanhamento da situação-econômica de crianças e adolescentes, 1981, 1983, 1986. 6 vols. Rio de Janeiro: 1989. Includes data for the 1980s reflecting the socioeconomic condition of families, education, and the participation of children and adolescents in the work force and in family income.

1584 _______. Perfil estatístico de crianças e mães no Brasil: situação de saúde, 1981. Rio de Janeiro: 1984. 264 p.

1585 _______. Series estatísticas retrospectivas. Rio de Janeiro: Fundação IBGE, 1986-. A series of retrospective statistics published in observance of the fiftieth anniversary of the IBGE. Volumes 1 and 2 are facsimile editions. Vol. 1: Repertório estatístico do Brasil: quadros retrospetivos, no. 1. Separata do Anuário estatística do Brasil, ano V, 1939/1940. Rio de Janeiro: 1941. 138 p. Vol. 2 in 3 volumes: t. 1: Introdução; indústria extrativa (1907; 555 p.); t. 2: Indústria extrativa (1908; 470 p.); t. 3: Indústria de transportes; indústria fabril (Rio de Janeiro: Centro Industrial do Brasil, 1909; 156 p.

1586 Pesquisa nacional por amostra de domicílios. Rio de Janeiro: Fundação Instituto Brasileiro de Geografia e Estatística, 1967-. Statistics related to education, the labor force, working conditions, income, housing, and family composition, based on a sample. Published quarterly 1967-1973, and annually since 1976. Edition examined: 1986.

1587 Silva, Joaquim Norberto de Souza. Investigações sobre os recenseamentos da população geral do Império e da cada provincia de per si tentados desde os tempos coloniais até hoje. Ed. facsimilada. 1870; Resumo histórico dos inquéritos censitários realizados no Brazil. São Paulo: Instituto de Pesquisas Econômicas, 1986. 251 p. These two titles, reissued together in one publication, both provide important material for the history of Brazilian censuses, including summaries of nineteenth century census data, and a survey of census-taking and publication. The first one was originally published as a memória annexed to the Relatório of the Ministério do Império in 1870. The second title was first published in Volume I, "Introdução" of the Recenseamento do Brazil taken in Sept., 1922, and published by the Directoria Geral de Estatística in Rio de Janeiro in 1922.

1588 Sinopse de dados culturais. Brasília: Ministério da Educação e Cultura, Serviço de Estatística da Educação e Cultura, 1985- . A compilation of cultural statistics covering radio, television, publishers, cinema, theatre, museums, libraries, and cultural organizations. Editions examined cover the years 1982 and 1983 and are based on the "Pesquisa de 1983."

1589 Sinopse estatística do Brasil. Rio de Janeiro: Fundação Instituto Brasileiro de Geografia e Estatística, 1971- . Summarizes data published in more detail in the Anuário estatístico do Brasil, covering many aspects of Brazilian life: population, vital statistics, the economy, social conditions, and others. It was published annually until 1973, and since then has been issued bienially. A bilingual edition (Portuguese/English) with the same title was published in 1971. Issued in English some years since 1972 under the title, Statistical Abstract of Brazil. Superseded Atualidade estatística do Brasil (no. 1572).

1590 Statistical Yearbook of Brazil, vol. 1, 1983- . Abridged English edition. Rio de Janeiro: Fundação Instituto Brasileiro de Geografia e Estatística--IBGE, 1985- . A statistical compilation covering general characteristics of the country, population, economic resources, services, transportation, communications, prices, income, public finance, monetary and financial markets, and social conditions. Volume 1 has 631 pages.

REGIONS

Central West

1591 Fundação Instituto Brasileiro de Geografia e Estatística. Sinopse estatística da Região Centro-Oeste. Rio de Janeiro: 1982. 267 p. Demographic, economic, and social statistics for the states of Mato Grosso do Sul, Mato Grosso, Goiás, and the Federal District (Brasília), with much of the data based on the census of 1980.

North

1592 Fundação Instituto Brasileiro de Geografia e Estatística. Sinopse estatística da Região Norte. Rio de Janeiro: 1981. 241 p. A compilation of demographic, social, economic, and financial statistics as well as those related to transportation, communications, and services. Includes Rondônia, Acre, Amazonas, Roraima, Pará, and Amapá.

Northeast

1593 Banco do Nordeste do Brasil, Fortaleza. Departamento de Estudos Econômicos do Nordeste. Manual de estatísticas básicas do Nordeste. 4. ed. Fortaleza: 1977. 433 p. Profiles the Northeast in terms of demography, economics, agricultural and industrial production, trade, health, education, public finance, and consumption of industrial products through tables and graphs. Also includes banking statistics of the BNB. Includes the source of the data presented in each table.

1594 Fundação Instituto Brasileiro de Geografia e Estatística. Sinopse estatística da Região Nordeste. Rio de Janeiro: 1983. 364 p. Demographic, social, economic and financial statistics, along with those related to transportation, communications, and services for Maranhão, Piauí, Ceará, Rio Grande do Norte, Paraíba, Pernambuco, Alagoas, Fernando de Noronha, Sergipe, and Bahia.

1595 Superintendência do Desenvolvimento do Nordeste. Nordeste em dados: 1960-1983. Série informações estatísticas. Recife: 1984. 197 p. Physical, demographic, economic, and social statistics for a period of more than twenty years.

1596 Superintendencia do Desenvolvimento do Nordeste. Divisão de Estudos Demográficos. Estatisticas básicas sobre população e emprego. 4 vols. Série população e emprego, 5. Recife: Ministério do Interior, Superintendência do Desenvolvimento do Nordeste, Departamento de Recursos Humanos, Divisão de Estudos Demográficos, 1977. A statistical compilation covering population, migration, the labor supply, and income in the Northeast. Includes bibliography.

South

1597 Fundação Instituto Brasileiro de Geografia e Estatística. Sinopse estatística da Região Sul. Rio de Janeiro: 1982. 248 p. Demographic, economic, and social statistics for the states of Paraná, Santa Catarina, and Rio Grande do Sul.

1598 Superintendência do Plano de Valorização Econômica da Região da Fronteira Sudoeste do País. Informe estatístico. 2 vols. Porto Alegre: 1966. Demographic and vital statistics for municípios on the southwest frontier of the country in the states of Rio Grande do Sul, Santa Catarina, Paraná, and Mato Grosso. Maps of each state locate the municípios covered.

Southeast

1599 Fundação Instituto Brasileiro de Geografia e Estatística. Sinopse estatística da Região Sudeste. Rio de Janeiro: 1984. 383 p. Demographic, economic and social statistics for the states of Espírito Santo, Minas Gerais, Rio de Janeiro, São Paulo, and the territory of Fernando de Noronha.

STATES

The Sinopses estatísticas for each state cited below are all part of the series Sinopses estatísticas estaduais, published by the Fundação Instituto Brasileiro de Geografia e Estatística. All provide summaries of physical, demographic, economic, and cultural statistics for the state covered, and therefore they are not individually annotated here. Those not actually seen by this writer are starred (*), and their pagination and series number are omitted. A few statistical yearbooks (anuários estatísticos) which were not available for examination were also cited but not annotated and they also are starred.

Acre

1600 *Anuário estatístico do Acre. Rio Branco: Departamento de Geografia e Estatística.

1601 Fundação Instituto Brasileiro de Geografia e Estatística. Sinopse estatística: Acre. Sinopses estatísticas estaduais, vol. 24. Rio de Janeiro: 1975. 174 p.

Alagoas

1602 *Fundação Instituto Brasileiro de Geografia e Estatística. Sinopse estatística: Alagoas. Rio de Janeiro: 1971.

Amapá

1603 Anuário estatístico do Amapá. Macapá: Sistema de Planejamento do Amapá, Subsistema de Informações do Amapá. Statistics related to demographic, economic, social, cultural, and political aspects of the state. Issues examined: 1987, 1988.

1604 Fundação Instituto Brasileiro de Geografia e Estatística. Sinopse estatística: Amapá, 1975. Sinopses estatísticas estaduais, vol. 23. Rio de Janeiro: 1975. 151 p.

Amazonas

1605 Anuário estatístico do Amazonas. Manaus: Governo do Estado do Amazonas, Secretaria de Estado de Planejamento e Coordenação--SEPLAN, Centro de Desenvolvimento, Pesquisa e Tecnologia do Estado do Amazonas--CODEAMA, Coordenadoria de Estatística, Difusão e Ensino. An annual compilation of demographic, economic, social, and other statistics. Title varies slightly: Anuário estatístico. Volume examined: 9, 1979/1980.

1606 Fundação Instituto Brasileiro de Geografia e Estatística. Sinopse estatística: Amazonas, 1972. Sinopses estatísticas estaduais, vol. 17. Rio de Janeiro: 1973. 113 p.

Bahia

1607 Anuário estatístico da Bahia. Salvador: Secretaria do Planejamento, Ciência e Tecnologia, Centro de Planejamento da Bahia, 1972-. Statistics related to physical aspects of the state and its economy, public finance, cultural conditions, infrastructure, and demography. Volume examined: 1978-1979.

1608 *Fundação Instituto Brasileiro de Geografia e Estatística. Sinopse estatística: Bahia. Rio de Janeiro: 1970.

Ceará

1609 *Anuário estatístico do Ceará. Fortaleza: Secretaria do Planejamento e Coordenação, Departamento de Estatística. 1973-.

1610 *Fundação Instituto Brasileiro de Geografia e Estatística. Sinopse estatística: Ceará. Rio de Janeiro: 1970.

1611 Instituto de Estatística e Informática do Estado do Ceará. Posicionamento econômico-social dos municípios cearenses para fins de alocação de recursos governamentais. Fortaleza: 1982. 420 p. Detailed statistical information at the município level on demography, agriculture, fishing, the infrastructure, commercial activities, tax receipts, education, health, and electors. Some data are presented in rank order.

Distrito Federal

1612 Anuário estatístico do Distrito Federal. Brasília: Secretaria do Governo, 1977-. Volume examined: 1988.

1613 *Fundação Instituto Brasileiro de Geografia e Estatística. Sinopse estatística: Distrito Federal. Rio de Janeiro: n.d.

Espirito Santo

1614 Anuário estatístico do Espírito Santo. Vitória: COPLAN/DEE. Demographic, economic, social, cultural and physical statistics. Issues examined: 1965, 1980/1985.

1615 Espírito Santo. Secretaria de Estado do Planejamento. Dados demográficos do Estado do Espírito Santo: resultados obtidos pela apuração dos dados do universo--Projeto Censo Escolar/ Pesquisa Sócio-Econômica, 1977. Vitória: 1978. 692 p. Detailed statistics related to demography and education by microregion and município. Includes good maps of the administrative divisions of the state, indicating population growth or decline by município.

1616 *Fundação Instituto Brasileiro de Geografia e Estatística. Sinopse estatística: Espírito Santo. Rio de Janeiro: 1970.

Goias

1617 *Fundação Instituto Brasileiro de Geografia e Estatística. Sinopse estatística: Goiás. Rio de Janeiro: 1973.

Guanabara

(See also Rio de Janeiro)

1618 Anuário estatístico da Guanabara. Rio de Janeiro: Secretaria de Planejamento e Coordenação Geral, 1971-. Demographic, economic, social, and physical statistics. Issues examined: 1971, 1972.

1619 *Fundação Instituto Brasileiro de Geografia e Estatística. Sinopse estatística: Guanabara. Rio de Janeiro: n.d.

Maranhão

1620 Anuário estatístico do Maranhão. São Luís Departamento Estadual de Estatística, 1968-. A statistical compilation related to physical characteristics, population, public administration, justice, elections, economic and social conditions, health, nutrition, and other topics. An earlier publication with the same title ceased publication in 1956. Edition examined: vol. 1, 1968.

1621 Fundação Instituto Brasileiro de Geografia e Estatística. Sinopse estatística: Maranhão. Sinopses estatísticas estaduais, vol. 20. Rio de Janeiro: 1973. 206 p.

Mato Grosso

1622 Anuario estatístico do estado de Mato Grosso. Cuiabá: Governo do Estado de Mato Grosso, Gabinete de Planejamento e Coordenação, Fundação de Pesquisas Cândido Rondon. Statistics related to physical, economic, social, cultural, and political aspects of the state, and to its infrastructure. Title varies: Anuário estatístico de Mato Grosso (1979). Editions examined: 1979, 1983, 1985, 1986, 1987-1988.

1623 Fundação Instituto Brasileiro de Geografia e Estatística. Sinopse estatística: Mato Grosso, 1971. Sinopses estatísticas estaduais, vol. 11. Rio de Janeiro: 1971. 92 p.

Mato Grosso do Sul

1624 Fundação Instituto Brasileiro de Geografia e Estatística. Mato Grosso do Sul. Rio de Janeiro: 1979. 163 p. This first statistical compilation about the state of Mato Grosso do Sul issued by the IBGE covers population, housing, animal husbandry, agriculture, industry, commerce and services.

Minas Gerais

1625 Anuário estatístico de Minas Gerais. Belo Horizonte: Secretaria de Estado do Planejamento e Coordenação Geral, Superintendência de Estatística e Informação, 1980-. Annual statistics for the state and its municípios in the areas of demography, economics, education, social conditions, agricultural and mineral production, infrastructure, public finance, and others. Resumes a series which suspended publication in 1955. Improved version of Minas Gerais: informações sócio-econômicas, 1970-1978. Editions examined: 1980, 1981, 1982, 1982/1984.

1626 *Fundação Instituto Brasileiro de Geografia e Estatística. Sinopse estatística: Minas Gerais. Rio de Janeiro: 1973.

Pará

1627 Anuário estatístico do Estado do Pará. Belém: Instituto do Desenvolvimento Ecônomico-Social do Pará, 1977-. Statistics on demography, agricultural production, extractive industries, public finance, industry, transportation, health, education, cultural activities, public safety, justice, social conditions, etc. Editions examined: 1st, 1977; 2nd, 1978; 3rd, 1979.

1628 *Fundação Instituto Brasileiro de Geografia e Estatística. Sinopse estatística: Pará. Rio de Janeiro: 1970.

Paraíba

1629 Estado da Paraíba: anuário estatístico. João Pessoa: Instituto de Planejamento de Paraiba--IPAN, Coordenaria de Estatística e Informática. A compilation of statistics on the physical characteristics, demography, health, education, culture, economy, and other aspects of Paraíba. Includes both tables and graphic representations. Edition examined: 1985.

1630 *Fundação Instituto Brasileiro de Geografia e Estatística. Sinopse estatística: Paraíba. Rio de Janeiro: 1971.

1631 Manual de dados básicos do Estado da Paraíba. João Pessoa: Companhia de Industrialização do Estado da Paraíba--CINEP, 1974-. Concentrates on economic statistics, with some attention to physical, demographic, and social aspects of the state. Editions examined: 1st, 1974; 2nd, 1976.

1632 Moura, Hélio A. Características sócio-demográficas das microrregiões da Paraíba. Recife: Fundação Joaquim Nabuco, Departamento de Estatística Aplicada, 1986. 34 p. Quantitative data about the official microregions is presented in statistical tables, charts, and maps. Topics covered are physical area, demography, education, the work force, and income.

Paraná

1633 Anuário estatístico do Paraná. Curitiba: Departamento Estadual de Estatística, 1977-. Basic statistics covering demographic, economic, and social data. Includes many maps and other graphics. Title varies: Anuário estatístico Paraná. Editions examined: vol. 2, 1978; 1983.

1634 Costa, Irací del Nero da, and Horácio Gutiérrez. Paraná:

mapas de habitantes, 1798-1830. São Paulo: Instituto de Pesquisas Econômicas, 1985. 185 p. Summarizes the early demographic development of Paraná, based on information supplied to the Portuguese Crown during the years in question. Statistical tables give the slave and free populations of several cities, and maps illustrate the development of cities over time.

1635 Fundação Instituto Brasileiro de Geografia e Estatística. Sinopse estatística: Paraná. Sinopses estatísticas estaduais, vol. 7. Rio de Janeiro: 1970. 113 p.

Pernambuco

1636 Comissão de Desenvolvimento Econômico de Pernambuco. Estatísticas básicas de Pernambuco. Recife. Physical, demographic, and economic statistics, many in series. Edition examined: 5th, 1965.

1637 *Fundação Instituto Brasileiro de Geografia e Estatística. Sinopse estatística: Pernambuco. Rio de Janeiro: n.d.

1638 Instituto de Desenvolvimento de Pernambuco. Bibliografia de dados estatísticos de Pernambuco. Recife: 1976. 101 p. Cites publications providing statistics related to demography, economics, education, agriculture, housing, sanitary engineering, public health, transportation, communications, and electrification. No annotations.

Piauí

1639 Anuário estatístico do Piauí. Teresina: Fundação Centro de Pesquisas Econômicas e Sociais do Piauí, Departamento de Estatística e Informática, 1969-. Physical, demographic, social, economic, agricultural, and industrial statistics. Volumes examined: 8, 1984/1985; 9, 1986/1987.

1640 Fundação Instituto Brasileiro de Geografia e Estatística. Sinopse estatística: Piauí, 1970. Sinopses estatísticas estaduais, vol. 10. Rio de Janeiro: 1970. 91 p.

Rio de Janeiro

(See also Guanabara)

1641 Anuário estatístico do Estado do Rio de Janeiro. Rio de Janeiro. Rio de Janeiro: Fundação Instituto de Desenvolvimento Econômico e Social do Rio de Janeiro--FIDERJ, 1978-. A compilation of physical, demographic, social, economic, health, agricultural, industrial, and other statistics. Editions examined: vol. 1, 1978; 1981.

1642 *Fundação Instituto Brasileiro de Geografia e Estatística. Sinopse estatística: Rio de Janeiro. Rio de Janeiro: 1969.

1643 Fundação Instituto de Desenvolvimento Econômico e Social do Rio de Janeiro. Sistema de Informações para o Planejamento Estadual. Sumário de dados básicos do Estado do Rio de Janeiro. Rio de Janeiro: 1976. 48 p. Statistics on the state of Rio de Janeiro during the period before it merged with the state of Guanabara (the former Distrito Federal). Covers physical characteristics, demography, social and economic conditions, agriculture, industry, and commerce.

Rio Grande do Norte

1644 Anuário estatístico: Rio Grande do Norte. Natal: Secretaria de Planejamento, Fundação Instituto de Desenvolvimento do Rio Grande do Norte--IDEC. Provides information at the state, microregion, and municipal levels on physical, demographic, social, cultural, and economic aspects of the state. Edition examined: 1986.

1645 *Fundação Instituto Brasileiro de Geografia e Estatística. Sinopse estatística: Rio Grande do Norte. Rio de Janeiro: 1971.

1646 Perfil do Estado: Rio Grande do Norte. Natal: Secretaria do Planejamento, Fundação Instituto de Desenvolvimento do Rio Grande do Norte--IDEC, vol. 1-, 1986-. A profile of the state in physical, economic, social, and administrative statistics. Cover title of vol. 1: Perfil do Estado do Rio Grande do Norte. Volume examined: 1, 1986.

Rio Grande do Sul

1647 Anuário estatístico do Rio Grande do Sul. Porto Alegre: Fundação de Economia e Estatística, 1968-. Covers general, social, and economic statistics. Volume examined: 10, 1987.

1648 Fundação de Economia e Estatística. De Província de São Pedro a Estado do Rio Grande do Sul: censos do RS, 1803-1950. Porto Alegre: 1981. 330 p. Retrospective statistics on population, agriculture, commerce, and industry and a historical summary of municípios created up to 1950. A series of maps locates existing municípios at the time of each census.

1649 _______. De Província de São Pedro a Estado do Rio Grande do Sul: censos do RS, 1960-1980. Porto Alegre: 1984. 158 p. Information on municípios created between 1951 and 1982, and statistical data on population, agriculture, commerce, and services, based on the censuses of 1960, 1970, and 1980.

1650 *Fundação Instituto Brasileiro de Geografia e Estatística. Sinopse estatística: Rio Grande do Sul. Rio de Janeiro: 1969.

Rondônia

1651 Anuário estatístico de Rondônia. Porto Velho: Governo do Estado de Rondônia, Secretaria de Estado do Planejamento e Coordenação Geral, Divisão de Estatística e Informações. A statistical compilation covering physical/geographical characteristics, demography, agriculture, industry, the infrastructure, economic, and social statistics. Volume examined: 6, 1984.

1652 Fundação Instituto Brasileiro de Geografia e Estatística. Sinopse estatística Rondônia. Sinopses estatísticas estaduais, vol. 22. Rio de Janeiro: 1975. 135 p.

Roraima

1653 Fundação Instituto Brasileiro de Geografia e Estatística. Sinopse estatística: Roraima. Sinopses estatísticas estaduais. Rio de Janeiro: 1975. 130 p.

Santa Catarina

1654 *Fundação Instituto Brasileiro de Geografia e Estatística. Sinopse estatística: Santa Catarina. Rio de Janeiro: 1971.

1655 Números de Santa Catarina. Florianópolis: Estado de Santa Catarina, Secretaria de Estado de Coordenação e Planejamento. A compilation of statistics at the município level: demography, education, sports, culture, health, sanitation, employment, social development, elections, justice, farming, forestry, fishing, construction, energy, business and services, tourism, transportation, communications, banking, prices, public finance, production. Edition examined: 1987.

1656 Santa Catarina. Gabinete de Planejamento e Coordenação Geral. Municípios catarinenses: dados básicos. 4 vols. Florianópolis: 1986. Statistical data about each of the 199 municípios of the state. Provides a brief physical description and information on demography, health, sanitation, education, culture, social development, communications, transportation, agriculture, fishing, industry, public finance, business, and services. Maps locate each município.

São Paulo

1657 Anuário estatístico do Estado de São Paulo. São Paulo: Fundação Sistema Estadual de Análise de Dados--SEADE. Statistics on physical characteristics of the state, demography, health, sanitation, employment, education, religion, justice, agriculture, industry, construction, economics, commerce, public finance, prices, and taxes. Vol. 56, 1979 resumes publication of a compilation which began in 1898 and suspended publication from time to time, most recently 1973-1978. Editions examined: 1979, 1980, 1981, 1987, 1988.

1658 Empresa Metropolitana de Planejamento de Grande São Paulo. Grande São Paulo: dados e análises dos anos 70. São Paulo: 1979? 146 p. A socio-economic picture of the ever-growing São Paulo metropolitan area, covering 1971-1975. Statistical tables are enhanced by explanatory text.

1659 ______. Grande São Paulo: indicadores básicos, 1988. São Paulo: Secretaria de Estado dos Negócios Metropolitanos, Empresa Metropolitana de Planejamento de Grande São Paulo, 1988. 91 p. A compilation of physical-geographic, political, and socio-economic statistics for the thirty-eight municípios comprising Grande São Paulo. Maps locate each município of the area.

1660 ______. Reconstituição da memória estatística da Grande São Paulo. São Paulo: EMPLASA, 1980-. Statistical series and maps trace the demographic and economic growth and development of the infrastructure of the metropolitan area from 1765 through the mid-twentieth century. Volumes examined: 1 (1980; 256 p.); 2 (1983; 208 p.)

1661 ______. Sumário de dados da Grande São Paulo. 4. ed. São Paulo: 1982? 477 p. Statistical tables on demography, the economy, public finance, urban services, social conditions, education, public health, sanitation--many of which provide series of statistics over several recent years or several decades. Excellent maps and charts clarify and enhance the statistical data.

1662 *Fundação Instituto Brasileiro de Geografia e Estatística. Sinopse estatística: São Paulo. Rio de Janeiro: n.d.

1663 Fundação Sistema Estadual de Análise de Dados. São Paulo em números: projeções demográficas. 2 vols. São Paulo: 1988. Population projections 1985-1990 for each município of the state.

1664 Hierarquia das regiões e dos municípios do estado de São Paulo. São Paulo: Sistema de Informações das Regiões do Governo, 1987. 256 p. Statistical tables ranking the 572 municípios and forty-two regions of the state by economic, social, and demographic indicators. Prepared jointly by the Secretaria de Planejamento da Presidência da República, Secretaria de Articulação com os Estados e Municípios and the Governo do Estado de São Paulo, Secretaria de Economia e Planejamento, Coordenaria de Ação Regional.

1665 Perfil municipal. vol. 1-, 1979-. Fundação Sistema Estadual de Análise de Dados. São Paulo: SEADE. A tabular profile of the municípios of the state of São Paulo providing a potpourri of statistics on such topics as population, vehicles, telephones, electrification, crime, infant mortality, creation of new jobs, value of agricultural production, and public finance. Volumes examined: 1979, 1980.

1666 Pesquisa municipal. São Paulo: Fundação Sistema Estadual de Análise de Dados--SEADE, 1981-. Provides one or two-page statistical summaries of basic data for the municípios of the state of São Paulo. Covers municipal administration, industry, construction, sanitation, health, social services, transportation, security, sports, and culture. Edition examined: 1981.

Sergipe

1667 Anuário estatístico de Sergipe. Aracajú: Secretaria de Planejamento, Instituto de Economia e Pesquisas, 1971-. Basic statistical data about many aspects of the state. Volumes examined: 1, 1971; 15, 1987.

1668 Fundação Instituto Brasileiro de Geografia e Estatística. Sinopse estatística: Sergipe. Sinopses estatísticas estaduais, vol. 15. Rio de Janeiro: 1972. 125 p.

Tocantins

1669 Fundação Instituto Brasileiro de Geografia e Estatística. Goiás Tocantins: informações básicas. Rio de Janeiro: 1989. 84 p. Basic information about the new states of Tocantins and Goiás created by the division of the former state of

Goiás in the Constitution of October, 1988. Text, statistical tables, maps, and diagrams enumerate and describe their geography, population, agriculture, industry, business, and services. Includes a list of the municípios of each state.

AUTHOR INDEX

SUBJECT INDEX

Numbers after subject terms refer to the citations in the main body of this work, not to page numbers. Subjects with twelve or more entry numbers under them are usually subdivided, although all of the numbers may not be included in the subdivisions. The subdivision "Bibliography," as in "Art--Bibliography," is the one most commonly used. The names of specific states are not used as subdivisions, but under the name of each state as a subject are subdivisions covering all of the entries for the state in question.